W9-AFB-754

THE SPRING OF CIVILIZATION

Periclean Athens

By Charles Alexander Robinson, Jr.

The Ephemerides of Alexander's Expedition

Hellenic History, with G. W. Botsford

Alexander the Great:
The Meeting of East and West in World Government and Brotherhood

An Anthology of Greek Drama

Ancient History:
From Prehistoric Times to the Death of Justinian

The History of Alexander the Great

The Spring of Civilization:
Periclean Athens

The Spring of Civilization

Periclean Athens

Edited by

Charles Alexander Robinson, Jr.

Sometime Professor of Greek Literature and Archaeology, American School of Classical Studies at Athens; Sometime Research Fellow and Visiting Lecturer, American Academy in Rome; Professor of Classics, Brown University

NEW YORK
E P Dutton and Company Inc
1954

FIRST EDITION

LIBRARY OF CONGRESS CATALOG CARD NUMBER: 53-10849

For Celia, this too

PREFACE

As the crisis in our own civilization deepens, the call for us to return to the traditional values and truths of our Christian-Judaic-Hellenic inheritance becomes more and more frequent and insistent. It is, of course, important to emphasize that our civilization is based upon that of ancient Greece, but nevertheless it is only half the story: the remarkable manifestation of the human spirit known as Hellenism, or Greek civilization, lifts our souls toward grandeur while it instructs and informs.

Like the Greeks, we are building in America a civilization based on experience and knowledge, happily free of religious and political oppression. It has been truly remarked that the typical political unit of the Greeks—the *polis* or city-state—is merely our own civilization in miniature and that their history portrays the birth, growth, and decay of a civilized society which we are able to understand. The differences between them and ourselves do not touch the abiding values of the spirit.

The ancient Greeks had many ideals—moderation and self-restraint among them—but perhaps the eagerness to know oneself explains why they were the first to create the scientific, or what we might call the modern, point of view. The true legacy of Greece consists not of art and literature as such, beautiful as they are, but of the mental attitude back of them and responsible for them. Many Greeks, at any rate, insisted on the primacy of reason.

If love of truth for its own sake and a passionate devotion to reason constitute our closest link with the Greeks, we must be quick to add that they did indeed bequeath to posterity profound and sensible thought, noble poetry, and beautiful art.

Their achievements are a timeless delight and challenge to the mind and eye and must be constantly relived, so that we may be in a better position not only to understand and correct our own civilization, but to prepare ourselves for the future as well.

The genius of the Greeks was simple. Clear of intellect and direct in their manner, they were the first people in Europe to evolve the ideal of free democracy. In time they produced the culture that civilized Rome and Europe and that provided Christianity, at the proper hour, with the vehicle for its propagation. Perhaps it is our tragedy, even more than theirs, that they succumbed politically before the imperialistic struggles of more powerful states; had not Rome intervened, the Greeks might ultimately have given the Mediterranean world not only a common culture, but also a form of government ensuring unity, freedom and permanence.

For many years I have asked myself whether it might be possible to suggest to the layman the essential meaning of Greece, and to do it in one volume. There are those who once loved ancient Greece and would like to renew their love, while others, skirting the subject, realize that a knowledge of the eternal truths of Western man is vitally important in our current many-sided struggle. Coleridge has already provided an answer for those who may wonder how an ancient civilization can help in the very practical affairs of the present: "Do not trust too much to your professional dexterity in the use of the scalping knife. Weapons of diviner mold are wielded by your adversary; and you are meeting him here on his own peculiar ground, the ground of Idea, of Thought, and of Inspiration."

It requires some temerity, of course, to imagine that the great foundations of our life can be hinted at in one volume, or that any indication can really be given of the qualities of the Greek mind and character which gave birth to the most significant achievements of human genius in Western civilization. After all, the story of ancient Greece comprises several millennia or, if we restrict ourselves to the period between Homer and Aristotle, half a millennium. Moreover, many excellent books already exist which cover ancient Greek history as a whole, or various aspects of it, such as the political institutions. There are also anthologies of its literature and of certain sections of it, such as the drama; there are volumes on its art or on special periods and types, such as sculpture; and, indeed, some books even try to suggest its entire civilization, giving snippets from its literature and so on. Many of these books and approaches are admirable. They do not, however, answer my purpose, which is to present to the general reader, and to him alone, a rounded, first-hand acquaintance in one volume with what Toynbee has called "the finest flower of the species that has ever yet come to bloom."

The first and most important condition I set myself was to keep constantly in mind that a great civilization speaks, quite literally, for itself. Moreover, I was bound to avoid excerpting, as much as feasible. The task seemed impossible, until I realized that one period, and that the greatest, might be selected and so organized as to suggest the essence of ancient Greece. This book, then, rejects as too thin or too one-sided an over-all picture of ancient Greece or a picture of one aspect of its experience, such as its literature from beginning to end. It concentrates exclusively on the chief facets—the many different angles—of Periclean Athens which, after all, is one of the few Golden Ages in the history of man.

Most persons who prepare a collection of pictures or literature for publication bemoan the limitations of space imposed upon them. For my part, I am grateful to the publishers for a generous treatment that insures a large and rounded presentation; indeed, I feel that a bigger volume might repel either by its size or cost. A reader may, of course, question my preference for this or that, but no one can say that the works included herein are not great. Six tragedies and two of Plato's Dialogues are given in their entirety; a good deal of history as well, and much art. If this induces the lay reader to go on with other books, I shall have succeeded in my main purpose.

Long professorial habit has caused me to interpose brief editorial remarks in the belief that they may provide a helpful background, but they can be readily skipped. What matters here is the message of the ancient Greeks themselves—the distinguished translations of great dramatic, philosophical and historical works no less than the photographs of masterpieces of their major and minor arts. Since these all bear on one moment in time, they do indeed complement each other and suggest to the modern reader the meaning of Periclean Athens.

I must emphasize that Periclean Athens is not equivalent to Greece in the fifth century B.C., nor is fifth-century Greece all of ancient Greece by any means. It would be difficult to assert, however, that Periclean Athens does not lie at the heart of things. Therefore I hope that readers of this book will also bring away impressions about ancient Greek civilization as a whole; reactions will doubtless vary, for concerning such important matters there can be no final judgment. Was ancient Greece a class society, and how far did the culture penetrate the masses? What did the Athenians mean by democracy anyway? Did they mean government by all the people or by a faction, or did they compromise on a mixed form? These and similar questions are raised by a perusal of the following pages, and Thucydides, among others, has an answer.

Pericles became leader of the democratic faction at Athens in 461 B.C. and died in 429 B.C. The decisive Peloponnesian War had already begun before his death, and accordingly I carry this presentation down to the end of the War and thus to the end of the century. In other words, I equate Periclean Athens chronologically—and not unreasonably—with the so-called Great Period of Classical Greece, roughly the second half of the fifth century before Christ. And I think I should say to the reader that if he comes away from these pages with the feeling that Toynbee is right—that the civilization of ancient Greece outshines every other civilization thus far known—nevertheless he will find no Utopia here. Faults and crimes are also illuminating, and it has been my earnest purpose to emphasize those of ancient Greece.

To Amy Loveman, Editor of *The Saturday Review*, I offer my

affectionate and hearty thanks for her encouragement and advice. Miss Gisela M. A. Richter, for many years the distinguished Curator of Classical Art in the Metropolitan Museum of Art, kindly discussed with me, during happy months in Rome, the subject of illustrations. Miss M. Alison Frantz, American School of Classical Studies at Athens, and Professor Saul S. Weinberg, University of Missouri, during many years of archaeological work in Greece turned themselves into expert photographers as well. They have now kindly provided me with recent photographs which I have never seen equalled for beauty and accuracy; I extend to them my warmest thanks. I am also grateful for photographs to Miss E. Louise Lucas, Librarian of the Fogg Art Museum, Harvard University; Miss Christine Alexander, Curator of Greek and Roman Art, Metropolitan Museum of Art, New York; Miss Hazel Palmer, Museum of Fine Arts, Boston. The map of Greece has been drawn by Dr. Erwin Raisz, Institute of Geographical Exploration, Harvard University; the plan of the Acropolis is based on a drawing by Gorham P. Stevens, Honorary Architect of the American School of Classical Studies at Athens. My editorial duties, as I have remarked, have led me to include comments on the general background; some of these are based, by permission of The Macmillan Company, on passages in G. W. Botsford and C. A. Robinson, Jr., *Hellenic History* (3rd ed., New York, 1950) and on passages in my *Ancient History* (New York, 1951). The Yale University Press has given me permission to reprint Clarence W. Mendell's translation of Sophocles' *Oedipus the King*, which first appeared in his *Our Seneca* (New Haven, 1941). Finally, I would mention with gratitude Henry M. Wriston, whose presidential devotion to liberal, humane education is such that the Classics are a vital part of our campus life.

C. A. Robinson, Jr.

Providence, Rhode Island
October 22, 1953

CONTENTS

ILLUSTRATIONS

MAPS

PORTRAITS

PLATES

These will be found grouped as a unit following page 424

A complete list of the seventy plates, with credits and acknowledgments, appears on pages 461, 462, 463, 464

THE SPRING OF CIVILIZATION

Periclean Athens

INTRODUCTION

Long ago, in the prehistoric days around 1400 B.C. when Crete and Mycenae and Troy dominated the Aegean Sea, the low, flat rock rising from the Attic Plain—known as the Acropolis—served as the site of the royal residence and, in time of trouble, as a refuge for the common people. A thousand years later, after the kings of Athens had disappeared and the city had outgrown its original citadel, the Acropolis became a showplace where great buildings celebrated gods and men and Athens.

It is to these buildings that you hurry when you reach Athens. Simplicity, magnificent simplicity, marks them today in their ruin as much as when they were first built. Simplicity, and its essential components—naturalness, directness, clarity—describe and explain ancient Greek civilization, but in a scene such as this it is almost impossible to meditate long on any single subject. Periclean Athens and nature—sea, mountains, plain—bear in upon you, to be sure, but so does all of history. If, for example, you should step to the northern edge of the Acropolis and take a look down into the large and busy city, you would be immediately attracted by an area, some twenty-six acres in extent, which has been cleared of its modern buildings and excavated by the American School of Classical Studies. This is the market place of classical times, but underneath it, no less than in the upper layers, are embedded the achievements and hopes and failures and crimes of 5,000 years of history.

Most fascinating of all, or so I think, are the tiny remains of Mycenaean Athens, when lordly Agamemnon set off for Troy and the most beautiful woman in the world. More instructive, certainly, and in ther way as thrilling, are the impressive monuments of the classical period and of the later days when Rome ruled the world, and young men, such as Cicero's son, came to

Reference map of
ANCIENT GREECE
Scale of Miles
0
100
ILLYRIA
MACEDONIA
LYNCESTIS
ORESTIS
MOLOSSIANS
EPIRUS
CORCYRA
THESPROTIANS
SYBOTA IS.
AMBRACIA
AMPHILOCHIANS
DOLOPIANS
THESSALY
THESSALIOTIS
HESTIAEOTIS
PELASGIOTIS
MAGNESIA
PHTHIOTIS
AENIS
MALIS
DORIS
AETOLIA
ACARNANIA
LEUCAS
ITHACA
CEPHALLENIA
ZACYNTHUS
IONIAN SEA
W. LOCRIS
E. LOCRIS
PHOCIS
BOEOTIA
EUBOEA
ATTICA
MEGARID
SALAMIS
ACHAEA
ELIS
PISATIS
ARCADIA
ARGOLIS
PELOPONNESE
MESSENIA
LACONIA
CYNURIA
CYTHERA
CHALCIDICE
THRACE
THASOS
SCYROS
CEOS
SERIPHOS
MELOS
CRETE
Epidamnus
Aegae
Pella
Methone
Pydna
Amphipolis
Eion
Olynthus
Potidaea
Torone
Dodona
Larissa
Pherae
Pagasae
Iolcus
Pharsalus
Artemisium
Histiaea
Ambracia
Ambracian Gulf
Anactorium
Thermon
Naupactus
Amphissa
Delphi
Crisa
Cirrha
Orchomenus
Chaeronea
Chalcis
Eretria
Cyme
Delium
Thebes
Thespiae
Tanagra
Oenophyta
Leuctra
Plataea
Phyle
Decelea
Aphidna
Marathon
Eleusis
Acharnae
Athens
Phaleron
Piraeus
Pegae
Megara
Corinth
Aegium
Pellene
Sicyon
Nemea
Mycenae
Argos
Epidaurus
Aegina
Saronic Gulf
Troezen
Elis
Olympia
Mantinea
Tegea
Lepreum
Megalopolis
Mt. Ithome
Messene
Sellasia
Sparta
Amyclae
Pylos
Sphacteria
Methone
Cythium
Cydonia
Mt. Leuca
Mt. Pangaeus
Mt. Athos
Mt. Olympus
Mt. Ossa
Mt. Pelion
Tempe
Strymon R.
Axius R.
Haliacmon R.
Peneus R.
Spercheius R.
Achelous R.
Alpheus R.
Eurotas R.
Thermaic Gulf
Gulf of Pagasae
Malian Gulf
Corinthian Gulf
Argolic Gulf
Messenian Gulf
Laconian Gulf
Rhithymna
20
21
22
23
24
41
40
39
38
37
36
35

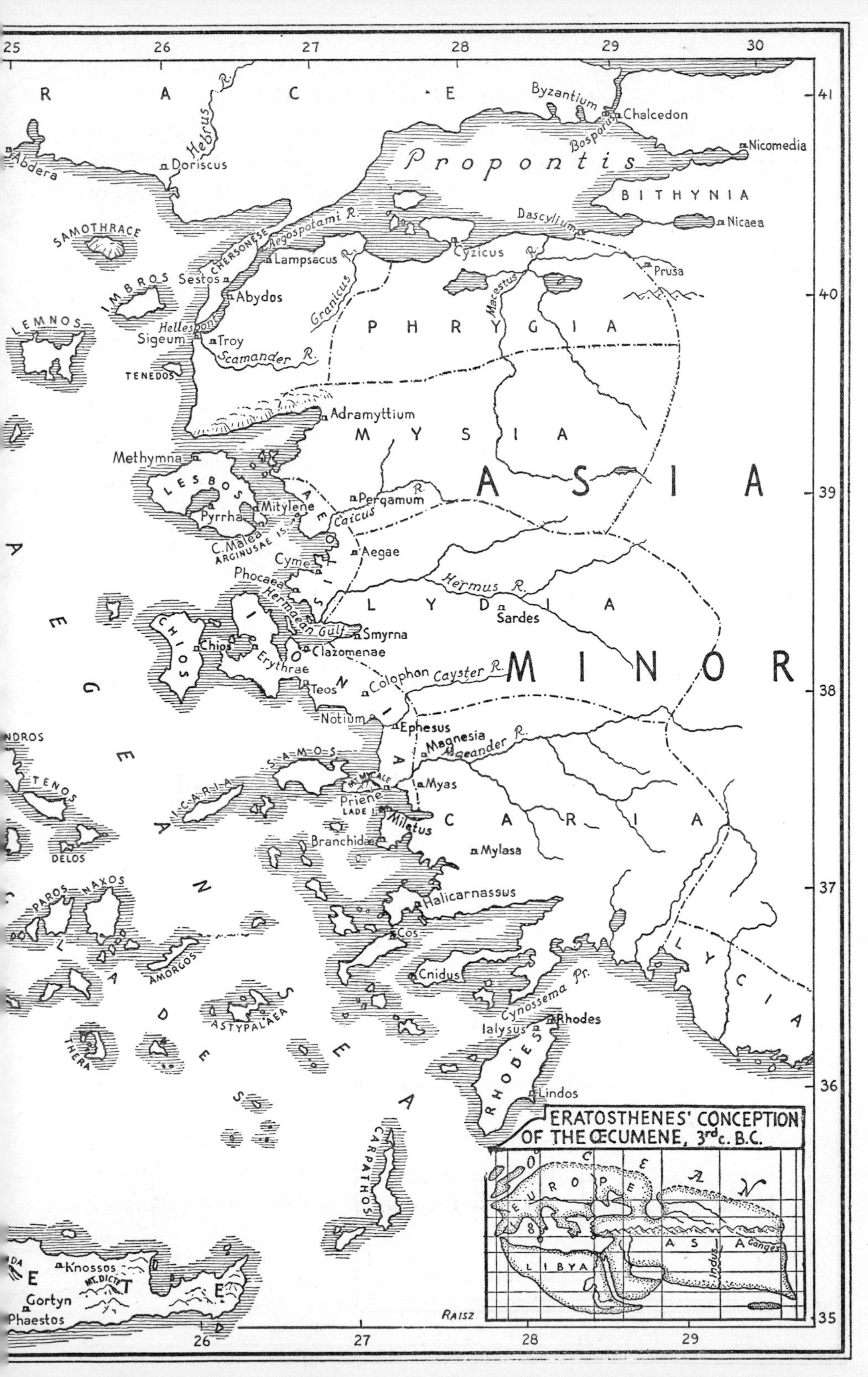

25
26
27
28
29
30
R A C E
Hebrus R.
Byzantium
Chalcedon
Bosporus
Nicomedia
Abdera
Doriscus
Propontis
BITHYNIA
SAMOTHRACE
Aegospotami R.
Dascylium
Nicaea
CHERSONESE
Cyzicus
Lampsacus
Prusa
IMBROS
Sestos
Abydos
Granicus
Macestus R.
LEMNOS
Hellespont
Sigeum
Troy
PHRYGIA
Scamander R.
TENEDOS
Adramyttium
MYSIA
Methymna
LESBOS
AEOLIS
Pergamum
ASIA
Mitylene
Pyrrha
Caicus R.
C. Malea
ARGINUSAE IS.
Aegae
Cyme
Phocaea
Hermus R.
Hermaean Gulf
LYDIA
Sardes
CHIOS
Chios
Smyrna
Erythrae
Clazomenae
IONIA
MINOR
Colophon
Cayster R.
Teos
Notium
Ephesus
Magnesia
Maeander R.
SAMOS
ICARIA
MT. MYCALE
Priene
Myas
LADE I.
Miletus
CARIA
Branchidae
Mylasa
AEGEAN SEA
NDROS
TENOS
DELOS
PAROS
NAXOS
Halicarnassus
Cos
AMORGOS
Cnidus
CYCLADES
ASTYPALAEA
Cynossema Pr.
Rhodes
Ialysus
THERA
RHODES
Lindos
CARPATHOS
LYCIA
41
40
39
38
37
36
35
Knossos
MT. DICTE
CRETE
Gortyn
Phaestos
RAISZ
ERATOSTHENES' CONCEPTION OF THE ŒCUMENE, 3rd c. B.C.
OCEAN
EUROPE
ASIA
LIBYA
Indus
Ganges

Athens for an education. To all this add the mediaeval, or Byzantine, period, the backwash of Franks from the Fourth Crusade, the centuries of Venetian and Turkish rule, the armies of the ages, the daily struggles of ordinary people, and you begin to round out your picture of the city which has fired the imagination of men through the centuries.

Sooner or later, of course, your thoughts return to the buildings you have come to see. They represent no Utopia—what has ever been done that we ought to do over again?—but they do symbolize one of the few Golden Ages that man has thus far been able to achieve. And you will want to know what was responsible for it.

That is a question to which no one has yet found the answer. In the *Persians* of Aeschylus the Persian queen asks precisely the same question, "What is this Athens, of which all men speak?" But the foreigner who has seen the play in modern Athens, and has felt the ripple of proud possession which passes over the audience at the familiar lines, will perhaps recognize that the answer was best suggested by the ancient playwright himself when he set the quality of Athens in the democratic spirit of her people, and let a Persian give his queen the incomprehensible response: "They bow to no man and are no man's slaves." There is ancient Greece's great discovery—man—not only its discovery, but the challenge, so to speak, that it has flung down to posterity. When they had placed man in the center of things, the Greeks then established the ideal of the dignity of the individual and, as a natural corollary, the institution of free democracy. That is to say, though some Greeks practised oligarchy in one form or another, others preferred to trust in the superiority of the people's collective judgment.

If we are not surprised that the most intellectual of all people in history should make this great discovery, we must nevertheless emphasize the role played by geography as well. The long mountain ranges, which everywhere hem in the little plains, made it impossible for a nation or empire to develop naturally in this land at once, but rather a smaller political unit (the *polis* or city-state), with its center in the chief town of each valley. The intimacy of life and intensity of effort nurtured by the city-states of ancient Greece helped create boundless versatility in literature, art and philosophy and, through the republican form of government which was devised in endless variety, assured to the citizens of myriad states liberty and democracy. Another advantage of the small state is that a considerable number of duties fall upon the individual, who thus receives an exceptional training in the art of civic life. This makes for versatility. It also made every Greek a politician. Intense local patriotism, responsibility, and love of liberty engendered a fearlessness which, in time of war, produced good fighters and, in time of peace, a restless inquisitive spirit willing to experiment.

Unfortunately, however, the small city-state also bred a feeling of exclusiveness that prevented the Greek from envisaging a broader citizenship. The self-sufficiency and particularism and jealousy of the city-states were the fundamental weakness of ancient Greece, and the dilemma of how to reconcile the apparent incompatibility of autonomy and federation was not resolved until the century after Athens' fall, in the days of Alexander the Great. Greek civilization had other faults, too. The suspicion which each Greek bore the other is as conspicuous as the cramping of the lives of the women and the existence of slavery. But the greatest tragedy of all—the story of how the most humane of ancient states sank into an abyss of cynicism and cruelty—must be reserved until we come to the Peloponnesian War. The Athenians, it can be said at once, opposed their narrow and exclusive interests to those of resident aliens, allies, Hellenes, and the world. Perhaps this was inevitable in an Age whose morality was essentially civic. Pericles himself asserted that the fundamental motive to right conduct is the good of the state.

It was Pericles, of course, who brought his community to a summit of civilization never before reached by the human race and who incorporated and expressed in his own personality the highest ideals of his Age. He inherited the inspiring traditions of two illustrious families, for his father, Xanthippus, had been an admiral in the Persian Wars, while his mother, Agariste, was the niece of the democratic reformer, Cleisthenes. The thrilling events of his childhood and youth attending the struggle for freedom and the founding of Empire were in Pericles transmuted into force and nobility of character directed to the political, intellectual, and moral elevation of his country.

The culture of the Periclean Age, as this time came to be known, rested on belief in the all-comprehensive perfection of the state, to whose good the citizens were to subordinate their individual interests and devote their lives alike in war and peace. The whole spirit of the Age glorified the greatness of Athens. It was Pericles' ambition that Athens should be the capital of Hellas, at once the strongest and the most beautiful city in the Greek world.

Among the many reasons for Athens' pre-eminence in the classical period of ancient Greece must be placed the fact of her Empire. It had taken imagination and confidence to create that Empire. Here was Hellas—as the world was called wherever the Hellenes, or Greeks, had settled—stretching from the Black Sea to Spain, full of proud, independent states who for centuries had been building an exuberant civilization. A very real danger eventually presented itself in the form of the predatory Persian Empire, which gradually extended its frontiers to the eastern shore of the Aegean Sea and then, early in the glorious fifth century B.C., struck against Greece proper. When the battles were over—Marathon and Thermopylae and others long since immortalized in song and story—the nimble-witted Athenians invited certain states to band together against another possible Persian invasion. Those who heeded the call were the exposed islanders and cities of the eastern and northern Aegean coasts, the very ones which would find it hardest to stand alone. The sacred island of Delos was chosen as the capital of the new defensive league.

From the very beginning the leadership of the Delian League fell to Athens, where the energizing of the political and patriotic spirit of the people was producing prodigious military, artistic, and intellectual activities. The chief architect, however, in hammering this voluntary alliance into an imperialistic Athenian Empire was Pericles. In 461 B.C. he succeeded to the leadership of the democratic faction at Athens, and until his death in 429 B.C. he was the master of the state. Though his position was challenged more than once, he continued to be elected year after year to the executive board of ten generals. His opposition lay among the conservative aristocrats, who stood for peace with both Sparta and Persia, whereas Pericles believed that Athens could steer an independent, if not hostile, course in world affairs. His followers, for their part, loved the pomp of Empire, the large fleet which provided jobs for rowers, and the imperial tribute which paid for so much at home.

Under Pericles, moreover, an undiluted democracy was achieved in theory, but in practice, at any rate, his personality and certain aristocratic checks combined to act as a brake on extremism. Thucydides, the great historian, put it exactly when he said that "under Pericles Athens was a democracy in name only, but in reality the rule of the first citizen."

In the light of all this, it is tempting to reflect on Pericles' deathbed statement. "No living Athenian," he boasted, "ever put on mourning because of me." And yet, his policies led Athens into conflict with oligarchical Sparta (431 B.C.); perhaps he was certain that Athens would win the War, as well it might have, but he died near its beginning. Leadership at Athens then fell to demagogues, until finally the excesses of the masses wrecked both the Athenian Empire and the democratic constitution (404 B.C.). Among the tragedies of the Peloponnesian War may be counted the fact that ever afterward the political and the cultural leadership of Hellas were divorced.

It was the extraordinary enthusiasm and ability of the Athenians, no less than the attraction which the city held for others, that brought Greek civilization to its highest peak. A galaxy of brilliant men lived in the violet-crowned city from 460 to 400 B.C. In the busy capital and its port, Piraeus, labored citizens, resident aliens, and slaves, while farmers, both large and small, cultivated their fields in the Attic Plain. The marble quarries of Mt. Pentelicus, the silver mines of Laurium, and the clay fields of the potter added to the natural wealth. At the same time, the tribute of the Empire made possible the construction of great buildings as well as payment for public services, thus giving the ordinary citizen enough leisure to attend actively to the affairs of state.

Although life was a serious business for the citizens of this imperialistic democracy, it was also happy. Problems of government and Empire challenged their intellects and satisfied their pride; industry, commerce, and farming provided their livelihood; the traffic at Piraeus made them aware of a large world; and, above all, a democratic constitution gave an outlet to their inventive minds.

The growth of the power of the city masses at Athens and Piraeus determined the imperialistic, no less than the democratic, character of the state. Payment for public services and for public works required a large state income, and the only way to provide this was through the imperial tribute. And since the maintenance of the Empire depended upon the navy, and the navy upon the rowers, the poorest class of citizens (who did the rowing) held decisive political power.

Sovereignty at Athens was vested in the popular Assembly, which embraced all male citizens over eighteen years of age. The Assembly held forty regular meetings a year, and thus a citizen gave a good deal of his time to affairs of state. He might also be chosen by lot—as an elderly man—to serve for a year as one of the 6,000 jurors; or, with luck (since the city's total population was about a quarter of a million), as a member of the Council of Five Hundred, which prepared measures for consideration by the Assembly. At the top of the large list of magistrates stood the board of ten generals, who were elected annually.

The generals not only commanded the army and navy, but also fulfilled most of the functions falling in a modern state to the Ministry or Cabinet. Accordingly, an Athenian who undertook to guide the policy of his state had to bear a heavier weight of responsibility than has been necessary in any less democratic form of government. The masses who constituted the Assembly —fullers, cobblers, copper-smiths, stone-masons, hucksters, farmers—could not be expected to have the same acquaintance with the details of policy, especially in foreign relations, that might be presupposed in a select body of public men, such for instance as the Roman Senate or a modern parliament. The Athenian democracy had to place greater trust in its advisers, and require of them expert knowledge. If a statesman succeeded, his glory was splendid, but if he failed, he was liable to severe punishment. The good of the state, that is to say, came first, but it was a state made up of free men who were thought to serve it best by self-discipline.

The fundamental motive to right conduct, we have quoted Pericles as saying, was the good of the state. These are his words in the Funeral Oration: "I would have you day by day fix your eyes upon the greatness of Athens till you become filled with the love of her; and when you are impressed by the spectacle of her glory, reflect that this Empire she owes to men with the fighter's daring, the wise man's understanding of his duty, and the good man's self-discipline in its performance, to men who if they failed in any ordeal disdained to deprive the city of their services, but sacrificed their lives as the best offerings in her behalf." * The patriotic devotion here required was too intense to be lasting. Nevertheless, on balance, the successes and achievements of Pericles and his city were so great that Athens quickly became "the teacher of Greece" and eventually of Rome and posterity.

* Alfred Zimmern's translation in part.

DRAMA

The culture of the Periclean Age, we have said, rested on belief in the all-comprehensive perfection of the state; it rested also on traditional belief purified by an expanding intelligence and humanism—belief in the power, wisdom, and goodness of the gods, in the superiority of the fathers, in the beneficence of the heroes of old. Into this culture, however, had been implanted the germ of individualism. Poets and sophists took the lead in questioning the problems of life and the old answers to them. During the second half of the fifth century B.C., the new progressive tendencies struggled with the old conservatism in a conflict fiercer and deadlier than was the strife of battle between Athenians and Peloponnesians.

The Athenians needed the teachings and inspiration of their great poets, for to meet the varied requirements of the citizen in this intense democracy, where life was civic duty, a man had to be well educated, not in books but in public affairs. This practical instruction was narrow, however. A broader, more idealistic education the Athenians received from the choral songs at festivals and particularly from the drama presented in the theater. More than sixty days, distributed throughout the year, were given to festivals, including dramatic exhibitions. Every year, too, from one to two thousand boys and men appeared before the public in choruses for the dramatic and other exhibitions which required them. These and other choral services rotated among the qualified citizens, thus giving all, or nearly all, a training in music and some study of literature.

Although Greek tragic drama was always associated with religion and religious ritual, nevertheless the plays themselves are concerned fundamentally with human values, with man's dignity and his individual responsibility, with problems raised by the existence of evil, by conflicts of duty and endurance under stress. The presence of gods or of some superhuman force in these dramas reminds us that man, though free, does not live unto himself alone. The plays are on the level of universal tragedy and bear out the definition, made almost a century after the Periclean Age by Aristotle in his *Poetics,* to the effect that tragedy is an "imitation" of an action that is serious, complete, and of a certain magnitude, while its function is—by rousing pity and fear—to provide a *catharsis,* or purging, of these and like emotions. The ideal tragic hero, continues Aristotle, must be a highly renowned though not a pre-eminently virtuous man whose misfortune is brought upon him by some error of judgment or frailty, rather than by vice and depravity.

And so in *Oedipus the King,* for example, the feelings of pity and fear are aroused by the tragic situation in which Oedipus finds himself, but with the completion of the play the same emotions are purified in the minds of the audience by the nobility of Oedipus' conduct under stress. Still, had Aristotle lived a century earlier and been influenced by fifth-century standards, he probably would have emphasized that the emotional function of tragedy was secondary to the intellectual one.

The majority of the dramatists who spoke to their fellow citizens in fifth-century Athens are irretrievably lost; others are known to us by name only. Those who have survived are represented by a mere fraction of their total production. In spite of the loss of so many masterpieces, three of the four greatest tragedians in history are Greeks. The earliest of these, Aeschylus (ca. 525-456 B.C.), was born near Athens at Eleusis, which was the home of the official Mysteries, a fact that doubtless made a lifelong impression upon him. Though the most creative of Athenian dramatists, Aeschylus desired above all else to be considered a loyal citizen who had fought for his country at Marathon. In his day the man of deeds was greater than the artist, and it is almost in spite of himself that we describe him as a literary man. Also in his day, of course, thought and custom at Athens gravitated irresistibly toward democracy. Aeschylus became the great representative of this tendency in literature. Though a noble, he glowed with a passion for freedom and gave his sympathy without reserve to the lowly. Against the aristocratic tradition which made the noble good and god-beloved and the poor base and vicious, Aeschylus upheld a more rational view of right and wrong and of their reward and punishment.

The gods, says Aeschylus, are merciful; with their aid a man may work out his own redemption in suffering, but for future tranquillity there is need of resignation. This tempering of justice with mercy was in keeping with a growing spirit of kindliness, which expressed itself in diverse forms. Indeed, we are surprised to discover in the martial Periclean Age so much humanity and such strong yearnings for peace. In the poets there is less of the glory of war than of its cruelty and suffering.

Not only the kindliness of the Age but also its religious spirit found their clearest expression in poets such as Aeschylus. Progressive though he was, Aeschylus held fast to the hereditary faith of his race, exalted and purified by his splendid intelligence and brilliant imagination. In touch with the best thought of the time, he could only conceive of Zeus as combining in the highest degree power, splendor, and sublimity; he gives us scenes and conceptions which, in their grandeur, are altogether too bold for representation.

Aeschylus wrote approximately ninety plays, of which seven are now extant. Of these the *Agamemnon* is probably the greatest. It is the story of Atreus' crime and the curse that fell on his sons, Agamemnon and Menelaus; of Agamemnon's wickedness at Troy and his murder on his return home—of the inevitable retribution, that is to say, that overtakes evil. An ominous gloom pervades the play, but it is broken now and then by moments of joy. Above all stands Zeus, who brings all things to pass, but the individual characters are strongly drawn and are given some opportunity for the display of personal initiative. Into their mouths Aeschylus, with deep religious conviction, puts noble sentiments couched in beautiful language and imagery.

While it is true that the poets were the teachers of Athens, they had no sense of mission. Certainly Sophocles (ca. 496-406 B.C.) did not consciously regard himself as a teacher, nor, on the other hand, was he a skeptic, like Euripides; in religious matters he simply presented the better side of the gods as normal. The real concern of Sophocles was the human fortunes of his characters. This inevitably grew out of his background, for as a man of wealth and education, who had been born in the fashionable Athenian suburb of Colonus, he served the state in various capacities and mingled with all classes of people. More than any other Athenian, perhaps, he typified the Greek ideal. For example, in the year 443 B.C. he was chief treasurer of the Athenian Empire; and three years later, having meanwhile produced the *Antigone,* he was general in the Samian War. As a poet, Sophocles was chiefly interested in the effect of life upon a man's character and soul. The old legends were his vehicle, and his plays, which combine an exceptional harmony of beauty and reason and are almost perfect from the point of view of dramatic technique, show him to be not only a great artist, but also the most human of Greek tragedians. In the words of Matthew Arnold, he is the supreme example of a tragic poet "who saw life steadily and saw it whole."

Sophocles wrote more than a hundred plays, but only seven survive entire. Three of these—*Oedipus the King, Oedipus at Colonus,* and *Antigone*—deal with the Theban saga. The House of Cadmus, founder of Thebes, is doomed to misfortune because it has offended the gods. Oedipus, heir to the power and woes of this stock, is driven unwittingly to the commission of a dreadful sin, for he fulfills the awful prophecy that he will murder his father and marry his mother. He suffers unspeakable agony of mind, and his children inherit the curse. His two sons kill each other in a civil war known as "The Seven against Thebes"; his daughter, Antigone, is buried alive; the whole family sinks into ruin. The guilt, growing from generation to generation, brings its legitimate punishment. It is natural, however, that the scientific, inquiring spirit of the Periclean Age, involving rationalism and religious doubt, should reflect itself in the troubled life of these plays. But in the end all doubts are overwhelmed by catastrophe.

An age seems to separate Sophocles from Euripides (ca. 480-406 B.C.). In the older poet beats the heart of Hellenism; his younger contemporary, who reputedly was of humble origin, is distinctly the first of the moderns. Euripides was the great exponent of the new spirit of individualism. The apostle of humanism, he issued his dramas as epistles to mankind. His message was the moral and spiritual interpretation of Protagoras: Man is the measure of all things. The keen intellect and the sensitive conscience, developed by a marvelous civilization, are presented with all the artistic allurements of dramatic genius as the standards whereby to judge truth and right on earth and in heaven. Casting off from traditional moorings, he pilots mankind over the surging seas of thought and emotion, but his ship reaches no haven. Poet of the submerged majority of mankind, Euripides descends to the level of common folk, to sympathize with beggars and cripples, with women and slaves.

Skeptic and bitter realist though he was, and understanding human nature as few have done, Euripides nevertheless wrote some magical and brilliant verse; he has not only violent invective, but tender pathos as well. The *Medea,* one of the eighteen plays that have survived from the original total of approximately ninety-two, is high tragedy, the story of a woman who is abandoned by the man she loves and for whom she has surrendered everything. *The Trojan Women,* on the other hand, is at once an indictment of aggressive war in general and of Athenian aggression in particular. It is a tremendous pageant of the horrors of war and of the inevitable doom which war brings upon both victors and vanquished.

Most of the tragedies of the Periclean Age were first produced at the Greater or City Dionysia, a spring-time festival in honor of Dionysus, the god of fertility and patron of the theater. The atmosphere surrounding their production was not only religious, however, but also keenly competitive, for the playwrights vied with each other to be selected in the first place, and at the end of the festival official verdicts were delivered. The production of the plays was in the hands of the individual dramatists. So seriously did the Athenians take their drama that a wealthy citizen—known as a *choregos**—was assigned the financial responsibility of training the chorus. This was a group of approximately fifteen amateurs. In the earlier plays the chorus had an important role, but with time it diminished. Nevertheless the chorus had the wonderful function of making the audience feel itself a part of the play, of joining with it in reflecting public opinion or perhaps in glimpsing the future. Moreover, the choral song always gave the poet the opportunity to write beautiful lyrics. A pair of choral passages is known as *strophe* and *antistrophe* —"turn" and "counterturn"—for the chorus, while singing, performed various evolutions. We have almost no information concerning the singing and dancing, beyond the fact that they were an integral part of the drama.

The actors, who were always men, were highly trained and were paid by the government. Normally there were three actors in a tragedy, though an actor might take more than one part. Because of the large size of the theater, changes in facial expression could not be recognized by the audience. To compensate for this handicap the actors wore masks, in order to set at least the general type of the character. The masks had an additional value in that they served as megaphones, even though the acoustics of the ancient theaters were excellent.

These plays were first presented in the theater of Dionysus, an open-air structure on the southern slope of the Acropolis seating about 18,000 persons. The original audiences were the most critical and outspoken in history, for they had been educated by a succession of great dramatists, and many members of the audience had at one time or another taken part in dramatic exhibitions.

* Successful *choregoi* loved to commemorate their triumphs with so-called choregic monuments.

Aeschylus. Capitoline Museum, Rome

AESCHYLUS

Agamemnon

Translated by E. D. A. MORSHEAD

First produced in 458 B.C. It won first prize; altogether Aeschylus won first prize thirteen times.

CHARACTERS IN THE PLAY

A Watchman

Chorus of Argive Elders

Agamemnon, son of Atreus and King of Argos

Clytemnestra, wife of Agamemnon

A Herald

Cassandra, a prophetess, daughter of Priam, King of Troy, and now the slave of Agamemnon

Aegisthus, son of Thyestes; cousin of Agamemnon; lover of Clytemnestra

ARGUMENT

Thyestes had seduced the wife of his brother Atreus, who in turn had killed Thyestes' children and served them to their father at a banquet. The curse that fell on Atreus was inherited by his sons, Agamemnon and Menelaus. When Helen, wife of Menelaus, fled to Troy with Paris, the Greek fleet assembled at Aulis, but was detained by unfavorable winds. At the behest of the prophet Calchas, Agamemnon, leader of the host, sacrificed his daughter, Iphigeneia, and thus won the favor of the goddess Artemis; the fleet then sailed for Troy. Ten years later, at the opening of the play, Clytemnestra is alienated from Agamemnon, her husband, and secretly in love with his enemy, Aegisthus, the surviving son of Thyestes. Unlike Lady Macbeth, with whom she is often compared, the superb and imperious Clytemnestra remains unbroken to the end of the play, a symbolic link, as it were, in the resistless chain of blood-revenge, a veritable tool of the forces that punish evil.

SCENE

In front of the palace of Agamemnon at Argos. Nearby are altars and statues of the gods. A Watchman is stationed on the roof of the palace.

AGAMEMNON

Watchman.

I pray the gods to quit me of my toils,
To close the watch I keep, this livelong year;
For as a watch-dog lying, not at rest,
Propped on one arm, upon the palace-roof
Of Atreus' race, too long, too well I know
The starry conclave of the midnight sky,
Too well, the splendours of the firmament,
The lords of light, whose kingly aspect shows—
What time they set or climb the sky in turn—
The year's divisions, bringing frost or fire.

And now, as ever, am I set to mark
When shall stream up the glow of signal-flame,
The bale-fire bright, and tell its Trojan tale—
Troy town is ta'en: such issue holds in hope
She in whose woman's breast beats heart of man.

Thus upon mine unrestful couch I lie,
Bathed with the dews of night, unvisited
By dreams—ah me!—for in the place of sleep
Stands Fear as my familiar, and repels
The soft repose that would mine eyelids seal.
And if at whiles, for the lost balm of sleep,
I medicine my soul with melody
Of trill or song—anon to tears I turn,
Wailing the woe that broods upon this home,
Not now by honour guided as of old.

But now at last fair fall the welcome hour
That sets me free, whene'er the thick night glow
With beacon-fire of hope deferred no more.
All hail!

(*A beacon-light is seen reddening the distant sky.*)

Fire of the night, that brings my spirit day,
Shedding on Argos light, and dance, and song,
Greetings to fortune, hail!

Let my loud summons ring within the ears
Of Agamemnon's queen, that she anon
Start from her couch and with a shrill voice cry
A joyous welcome to the beacon-blaze,
For Ilion's fall; such fiery message gleams
From yon high flame; and I, before the rest,
Will foot the lightsome measure of our joy;
For I can say, My master's dice fell fair—
Behold! the triple sice, the lucky flame!
Now be my lot to clasp, in loyal love,
The hand of him restored, who rules our home:
Home—but I say no more: upon my tongue
Treads hard the ox o' the adage.
                                        Had it voice,
The home itself might soothliest tell its tale;
I, of set will, speak words the wise may learn,
To others, nought remember nor discern.

(*Exit. The Chorus of Argive Elders enters, each leaning on a staff. During their song Clytemnestra appears in the background, kindling the altars.*)

Chorus.

Ten livelong years have rolled away,
Since the twin lords of sceptred sway,
By Zeus endowed with pride of place,
The doughty chiefs of Atreus' race,
  Went forth of yore,
To plead with Priam, face to face,
  Before the judgment-seat of War!

A thousand ships from Argive land
Put forth to bear the martial band,
That with a spirit stern and strong
Went out to right the kingdom's wrong—
Pealed, as they went, the battle-song,
  Wild as the vultures' cry;
When o'er the eyrie, soaring high,
In wild bereavèd agony,
Around, around, in airy rings,
They wheel with oarage of their wings,
But not the eyas-brood behold,
That called them to the nest of old;

But let Apollo from the sky,
Or Pan, or Zeus, but hear the cry,
The exile cry, the wail forlorn,
Of birds from whom their home is torn—
On those who wrought the rapine fell,
Heaven sends the vengeful fiends of hell.

Even so doth Zeus, the jealous lord
And guardian of the hearth and board,
Speed Atreus' sons, in vengeful ire,
'Gainst Paris—sends them forth on fire,
Her to buy back, in war and blood,
Whom one did wed but many woo'd!
And many, many, by his will,
The last embrace of foes shall feel,
And many a knee in dust be bowed,
And splintered spears on shields ring loud,
Of Trojan and of Greek, before
That iron bridal-feast be o'er!
But as he willed 'tis ordered all,
And woes, by heaven ordained, must fall—
Unsoothed by tears or spilth of wine
Poured forth too late, the wrath divine
Glares vengeance on the flameless shrine.

And we in gray dishonoured eld,
Feeble of frame, unfit were held
To join the warrior array
That then went forth unto the fray:
And here at home we tarry, fain
Our feeble footsteps to sustain,
Each on his staff—so strength doth wane,
And turns to childishness again.
For while the sap of youth is green,
And, yet unripened, leaps within,
The young are weakly as the old,
And each alike unmeet to hold
The vantage post of war!
And ah! when flower and fruit are o'er,
  And on life's tree the leaves are sere,
  Age wendeth propped its journey drear,

As forceless as a child, as light
And fleeting as a dream of night
Lost in the garish day!

But thou, O child of Tyndareus,
  Queen Clytemnestra, speak! and say
  What messenger of joy to-day
Hath won thine ear? what welcome news,
That thus in sacrificial wise
E'en to the city's boundaries
Thou biddest altar-fires arise?
Each god who doth our city guard,
And keeps o'er Argos watch and ward
  From heaven above, from earth below—
The mighty lords who rule the skies,
The market's lesser deities,
  To each and all the altars glow,
Piled for the sacrifice!
And here and there, anear, afar,
Streams skyward many a beacon-star,
Conjur'd and charm'd and kindled well
By pure oil's soft and guileless spell,
Hid now no more
Within the palace' secret store.

O queen, we pray thee, whatsoe'er,
  Known unto thee, were well revealed,
That thou wilt trust it to our ear,
  And bid our anxious heart be healed!
That waneth now unto despair—
Now, waxing to a presage fair,
Dawns, from the altar, Hope—to scare
From our rent hearts the vulture Care.

Strophe 1

List! for the power is mine, to chant on high
  The chiefs' emprise, the strength that omens gave!
List! on my soul breathes yet a harmony,
  From realms of ageless powers, and strong to save!

How brother kings, twin lords of one command,
  Led forth the youth of Hellas in their flower,
Urged on their way, with vengeful spear and brand,
  By warrior-birds, that watched the parting hour.

Go forth to Troy, the eagles seemed to cry—
  And the sea-kings obeyed the sky-kings' word,
When on the right they soared across the sky,
  And one was black, one bore a white tail barred.

High o'er the palace were they seen to soar,
  Then lit in sight of all, and rent and tare,
Far from the fields that she should range no more,
  Big with her unborn brood, a mother-hare.

Antistrophe 1

And one beheld, the soldier-prophet true,
  And the two chiefs, unlike of soul and will,
In the twy-coloured eagles straight he knew,
  And spake the omen forth, for good and ill.

(Ah woe and well-a-day! but be the issue fair!)

Go forth, he cried, and Priam's town shall fall.
  Yet long the time shall be; and flock and herd,
The people's wealth, that roam before the wall,
  Shall force hew down, when Fate shall give the word.

But O beware! lest wrath in Heaven abide,
  To dim the glowing battle-forge once more,
And mar the mighty curb of Trojan pride,
  The steel of vengeance, welded as for war!

For virgin Artemis bears jealous hate
  Against the royal house, the eagle-pair,
Who rend the unborn brood, insatiate—
  Yea, loathes their banquet on the quivering hare.

  (Ah woe and well-a-day! but be the issue fair!)

Epode

For well she loves—the goddess kind and mild—
  The tender new-born cubs of lions bold,
Too weak to range—and well the sucking child
  Of every beast that roams by wood and wold.

So to the Lord of Heaven she prayeth still,
  "Nay, if it must be, be the omen true!
Yet do the visioned eagles presage ill;
  The end be well, but crossed with evil too!"

Healer Apollo! be her wrath controll'd,
  Nor weave the long delay of thwarting gales,
To war against the Danaans and withhold
  From the free ocean-waves their eager sails!

She craves, alas! to see a second life
  Shed forth, a curst unhallowed sacrifice—
'Twixt wedded souls, artificer of strife,
  And hate that knows not fear, and fell device.

At home there tarries like a lurking snake,
  Biding its time, a wrath unreconciled,
A wily watcher, passionate to slake,
  In blood, resentment for a murdered child.

Such was the mighty warning, pealed of yore—
  Amid good tidings, such the word of fear,
What time the fateful eagles hovered o'er
  The kings, and Calchas read the omen clear.

(In strains like his, once more,
Sing woe and well-a-day! but be the issue fair!)

Strophe 2

Zeus—if to The Unknown
  That name of many names seem good—
Zeus, upon Thee I call.
  Thro' the mind's every road

I passed, but vain are all,
Save that which names thee Zeus, the Highest One,
Were it but mine to cast away the load,
The weary load, that weighs my spirit down.

Antistrophe 2

He that was Lord of old,
In full-blown pride of place and valour bold,
Hath fallen and is gone, even as an old tale told!
And he that next held sway,
By stronger grasp o'erthrown
Hath pass'd away!
And whoso now shall bid the triumph-chant arise
To Zeus, and Zeus alone,
He shall be found the truly wise.

Strophe 3

'Tis Zeus alone who shows the perfect way
Of knowledge: He hath ruled,
Men shall learn wisdom, by affliction schooled.

In visions of the night, like dropping rain,
Descend the many memories of pain
Before the spirit's sight: through tears and dole
Comes wisdom o'er the unwilling soul—
A boon, I wot, of all Divinity,
That holds its sacred throne in strength, above the sky!

Antistrophe 3

And then the elder chief, at whose command
The fleet of Greece was manned,
Cast on the seer no word of hate,
But veered before the sudden breath of Fate—

Ah, weary while! for ere they put forth sail,
Did every store, each minish'd vessel, fail,
While all the Achaean host
At Aulis anchored lay,
Looking across to Chalcis and the coast
Where refluent waters welter, rock, and sway;

Strophe 4

And rife with ill delay
From northern Strymon blew the thwarting blast—
Mother of famine fell,
That holds men wand'ring still
Far from the haven where they fain would be!—
And pitiless did waste
Each ship and cable, rotting on the sea,
And, doubling with delay each weary hour,
Withered with hope deferred th' Achaeans' warlike flower.

But when, for bitter storm, a deadlier relief,
And heavier with ill to either chief,
Pleading the ire of Artemis, the seer avowed,
The two Atreidae smote their sceptres on the plain,
And, striving hard, could not their tears restrain!

Antistrophe 4

And then the elder monarch spake aloud—
Ill lot were mine, to disobey!
And ill, to smite my child, my household's love
and pride!
To stain with virgin blood a father's hands, and slay
My daughter, by the altar's side!
'Twixt woe and woe I dwell—
I dare not like a recreant fly,
And leave the league of ships, and fail each true ally;
For rightfully they crave, with eager fiery mind,
The virgin's blood, shed forth to lull the adverse
wind—
God send the deed be well!

Strophe 5

Thus on his neck he took
Fate's hard compelling yoke;
Then, in the counter-gale of will abhorr'd, accursed,
To recklessness his shifting spirit veered—
Alas! that Frenzy, first of ills and worst,
With evil craft men's souls to sin hath ever stirred!

And so he steeled his heart—ah, well-a-day—
Aiding a war for one false woman's sake,
His child to slay,
And with her spilt blood make
An offering, to speed the ships upon their way!

Antistrophe 5

Lusting for war, the bloody arbiters
Closed heart and ears, and would nor hear nor heed
The girl-voice plead,
Pity me, Father! nor her prayers,
Nor tender, virgin years.

So, when the chant of sacrifice was done,
Her father bade the youthful priestly train
Raise her, like some poor kid, above the altar-stone,
From where amid her robes she lay
Sunk all in swoon away—
Bade them, as with the bit that mutely tames the steed,
Her fair lips' speech refrain,
Lest she should speak a curse on Atreus' home and seed,

Strophe 6

So, trailing on the earth her robe of saffron dye,
With one last piteous dart from her beseeching eye
Those that should smite she smote—
Fair, silent, as a pictur'd form, but fain
To plead, Is all forgot?
How oft those halls of old,
Wherein my sire high feast did hold,
Rang to the virginal soft strain,
When I, a stainless child,
Sang from pure lips and undefiled,
Sang of my sire, and all
His honoured life, and how on him should fall
Heaven's highest gift and gain!

Antistrophe 6

And then—but I beheld not, nor can tell,
  What further fate befel:
But this is sure, that Calchas' boding strain
  Can ne'er be void or vain.
This wage from Justice' hand do sufferers earn,
  The future to discern:
And yet—farewell, O secret of To-morrow!
  Fore-knowledge is fore-sorrow.
Clear with the clear beams of the morrow's sun,
  The future presseth on.
Now, let the house's tale, how dark soe'er,
  Find yet an issue fair!—
So prays the loyal, solitary band
  That guards the Apian land.

(*They turn to Clytemnestra, who leaves the altars and comes forward.*)

O queen, I come in reverence of thy sway—
For, while the ruler's kingly seat is void,
The loyal heart before his consort bends.
Now—be it sure and certain news of good
Or the fair tidings of a flatt'ring hope,
That bids thee spread the light from shrine to shrine,
I, fain to hear, yet grudge not if thou hide.

Clytemnestra.
As saith the adage, From the womb of Night
Spring forth, with promise fair, the young child Light.
Ay—fairer even than all hope my news—
By Grecian hands is Priam's city ta'en!

Chorus.
What say'st thou? doubtful heart makes treach'rous ear.

Clytemnestra.
Hear them again, and plainly—Troy is ours!

Chorus.
Thrills thro' my heart such joy as wakens tears.

Clytemnestra.
Ay, thro' those tears thine eye looks loyalty.

Chorus.

But hast thou proof, to make assurance sure?

Clytemnestra.

Go to; I have—unless the god has lied.

Chorus.

Hath some night-vision won thee to belief?

Clytemnestra.

Out on all presage of a slumb'rous soul!

Chorus.

But wert thou cheered by Rumour's wingless word?

Clytemnestra.

Peace—thou dost chide me as a credulous girl.

Chorus.

Say then, how long ago the city fell?

Clytemnestra.

Even in this night that now brings forth the dawn.

Chorus.

Yet who so swift could speed the message here?

Clytemnestra.

From Ida's top Hephaestus, lord of fire,
Sent forth his sign; and on, and ever on,
Beacon to beacon sped the courier-flame.
From Ida to the crag, that Hermes loves,
Of Lemnos; thence unto the steep sublime
Of Athos, throne of Zeus, the broad blaze flared.
Thence, raised aloft to shoot across the sea,
The moving light, rejoicing in its strength,
Sped from the pyre of pine, and urged its way,
In golden glory, like some strange new sun,
Onward, and reached Macistus' watching heights.
There, with no dull delay nor heedless sleep,
The watcher sped the tidings on in turn,
Until the guard upon Messapius' peak
Saw the far flame gleam on Euripus' tide,
And from the high-piled heap of withered furze
Lit the new sign and bade the message on.
Then the strong light, far-flown and yet undimmed,
Shot thro' the sky above Asopus' plain,

Bright as the moon, and on Cithaeron's crag
Aroused another watch of flying fire.
And there the sentinels no whit disowned,
But sent redoubled on, the hest of flame—
Swift shot the light, above Gorgopis' bay,
To Aegiplanctus' mount, and bade the peak
Fail not the onward ordinance of fire.
And like a long beard streaming in the wind,
Full-fed with fuel, roared and rose the blaze,
And onward flaring, gleamed above the cape,
Beneath which shimmers the Saronic bay,
And thence leapt light unto Arachne's peak,
The mountain watch that looks upon our town.
Thence to th' Atreides' roof—in lineage fair,
A bright posterity of Ida's fire.
So sped from stage to stage, fulfilled in turn,
Flame after flame, along the course ordained,
And lo! the last to speed upon its way
Sights the end first, and glows unto the goal.
And Troy is ta'en, and by this sign my lord
Tells me the tale, and ye have learned my word.

Chorus.

To heaven, O queen, will I upraise new song:
But, wouldst thou speak once more, I fain would hear
From first to last the marvel of the tale.

Clytemnestra.

Think you—this very morn—the Greeks in Troy,
And loud therein the voice of utter wail!
Within one cup pour vinegar and oil,
And look! unblent, unreconciled, they war.
So in the twofold issue of the strife
Mingle the victor's shout, the captives' moan.
For all the conquered whom the sword has spared
Cling weeping—some unto a brother slain,
Some childlike to a nursing father's form,
And wail the loved and lost, the while their neck
Bows down already 'neath the captive's chain.

And lo! the victors, now the fight is done,
Goaded by restless hunger, far and wide
Range all disordered thro' the town, to snatch
Such victual and such rest as chance may give
Within the captive halls that once were Troy—
Joyful to rid them of the frost and dew,
Wherein they couched upon the plain of old—
Joyful to sleep the gracious night all through,
Unsummoned of the watching sentinel.
Yet let them reverence well the city's gods,
The lords of Troy, tho' fallen, and her shrines;
So shall the spoilers not in turn be spoiled.
Yea, let no craving for forbidden gain
Bid conquerors yield before the darts of greed.
For we need yet, before the race be won,
Homewards, unharmed, to round the course once more.
For should the host wax wanton ere it come,
Then, tho' the sudden blow of fate be spared,
Yet in the sight of gods shall rise once more
The great wrong of the slain, to claim revenge.
Now, hearing from this woman's mouth of mine,
The tale and eke its warning, pray with me,
Luck sway the scale, with no uncertain poise,
For my fair hopes are changed to fairer joys.

Chorus.

A gracious word thy woman's lips have told,
Worthy a wise man's utterance, O my queen;
Now with clear trust in thy convincing tale
I set me to salute the gods with song,
Who bring us bliss to counterpoise our pain.

(*Exit Clytemnestra.*)

Zeus, Lord of heaven! and welcome night
Of victory, that hast our might
With all the glories crowned!
On towers of Ilion, free no more,
Hast flung the mighty mesh of war,

And closely girt them round,
Till neither warrior may 'scape,
Nor stripling lightly overleap
The trammels as they close, and close,
Till with the grip of doom our foes
In slavery's coil are bound!

Zeus, Lord of hospitality,
In grateful awe I bend to thee—
'Tis thou hast struck the blow!
At Alexander, long ago,
We marked thee bend thy vengeful bow,
But long and warily withhold
The eager shaft, which, uncontrolled
And loosed too soon or launched too high,
Had wandered bloodless through the sky.

Strophe 1

Zeus, the high God!—whate'er be dim in doubt,
This can our thought track out—
The blow that fells the sinner is of God,
And as he wills, the rod
Of vengeance smiteth sore. One said of old,
The gods list not to hold
A reckoning with him whose feet oppress
The grace of holiness—
An impious word! for whensoe'er the sire
Breathed forth rebellious fire—
What time his household overflowed the measure
Of bliss and health and treasure—
His children's children read the reckoning plain,
At last, in tears and pain.

On me let weal that brings no woe be sent,
And therewithal, content!
Who spurns the shrine of Right, nor wealth nor power
Shall be to him a tower,
To guard him from the gulf: there lies his lot,
Where all things are forgot.

Antistrophe 1

Lust drives him on—lust, desperate and wild,
  Fate's sin-contriving child—
And cure is none; beyond concealment clear,
  Kindles sin's baleful glare.
As an ill coin beneath the wearing touch
  Betrays by stain and smutch
Its metal false—such is the sinful wight.
  Before, on pinions light,
Fair Pleasure flits, and lures him childlike on,
  While home and kin make moan
Beneath the grinding burden of his crime;
  Till, in the end of time,
Cast down of heaven, he pours forth fruitless prayer
  To powers that will not hear.

  And such did Paris come
  Unto Atreides' home,
And thence, with sin and shame his welcome to repay,
  Ravished the wife away—

Strophe 2

And she, unto her country and her kin
Leaving the clash of shields and spears and arming
    ships,
And bearing unto Troy destruction for a dower,
  And overbold in sin,
Went fleetly thro' the gates, at midnight hour.
  Oft from the prophets' lips
Moaned out the warning and the wail—Ah woe!
Woe for the home, the home! and for the chieftains,
    woe!
  Woe for the bride-bed, warm
Yet from the lovely limbs, the impress of the form
  Of her who loved her lord, awhile ago!
    And woe! for him who stands
Shamed, silent, unreproachful, stretching hands
  That find her not, and sees, yet will not see,
      That she is far away!

And his sad fancy, yearning o'er the sea,
Shall summon and recall
Her wraith, once more to queen it in his hall.
And sad with many memories,
The fair cold beauty of each sculptured face—
And all to hatefulness is turned their grace,
Seen blankly by forlorn and hungering eyes!

Antistrophe 2

And when the night is deep,
Come visions, sweet and sad, and bearing pain
Of hopings vain—
Void, void and vain, for scarce the sleeping sight
Has seen its old delight,
When thro' the grasps of love that bid it stay
It vanishes away
On silent wings that roam adown the ways of sleep.

Such are the sights, the sorrows fell,
About our hearth—and worse, whereof I may not
tell.
But, all the wide town o'er,
Each home that sent its master far away
From Hellas' shore,
Feels the keen thrill of heart, the pang of loss,
to-day.
For, truth to say,
The touch of bitter death is manifold!
Familiar was each face, and dear as life,
That went unto the war,
But thither, whence a warrior went of old,
Doth nought return—
Only a spear and sword, and ashes in an urn!

Strophe 3

For Ares, lord of strife,
Who doth the swaying scales of battle hold,
War's money-changer, giving dust for gold,

Sends back, to hearts that held them dear,
Scant ash of warriors, wept with many a tear,
Light to the hand, but heavy to the soul;
Yea, fills the light urn full
With what survived the flame—
Death's dusty measure of a hero's frame!

Alas! one cries, and yet alas again!
Our chief is gone, the hero of the spear,
And hath not left his peer!
Ah woe! another moans—my spouse is slain,
The death of honour, rolled in dust and blood,
Slain for a woman's sin, a false wife's shame!
Such muttered words of bitter mood
Rise against those who went forth to reclaim;
Yea, jealous wrath creeps on against th' Atreides' name.

And others, far beneath the Ilian wall,
Sleep their last sleep—for goodly chiefs and tall,
Couched in the foeman's land, whereon they gave
Their breath, and lords of Troy, each in his Trojan grave.

Antistrophe 3

Therefore for each and all the city's breast
Is heavy with a wrath suppress,
As deep and deadly as a curse more loud
Flung by the common crowd:
And, brooding deeply, doth my soul await
Tidings of coming fate,
Buried as yet in darkness' womb.
For not forgetful is the high gods' doom
Against the sons of carnage: all too long
Seems the unjust to prosper and be strong,
Till the dark Furies come,
And smite with stern reversal all his home,
Down into dim obstruction—he is gone,
And help and hope, among the lost, is none!

O'er him who vaunteth an exceeding fame,
  Impends a woe condign;
The vengeful bolt upon his eyes doth flame,
  Sped from the hand divine.
This bliss be mine, ungrudged of God, to feel—
  To tread no city to the dust,
  Nor see my own life thrust
Down to a slave's estate beneath another's heel!

Epode

Behold, throughout the city wide
Have the swift feet of Rumour hied,
  Roused by the joyful flame:
But is the news they scatter, sooth?
Or haply do they give for truth
  Some cheat which heaven doth frame?
A child were he and all unwise,
  Who let his heart with joy be stirred,
To see the beacon-fires arise,
  And then, beneath some thwarting word,
  Sicken anon with hope deferred.
  The edge of woman's insight still
  Good news from true divideth ill;
Light rumours leap within the bound
That fences female credence round,
But, lightly born, as lightly dies
The tale that springs of her surmise.

Soon shall we know whereof the bale-fires tell,
The beacons, kindled with transmitted flame;
Whether, as well I deem, their tale is true,
Or whether like some dream delusive came
The welcome blaze but to befool our soul.
For lo! I see a herald from the shore
Draw hither, shadowed with the olive-wreath—
And thirsty dust, twin-brother of the clay,
Speaks plain of travel far and truthful news—
No dumb surmise, nor tongue of flame in smoke,
Fitfully kindled from the mountain pyre;
But plainlier shall his voice say, All is well,

Or—but away, forebodings adverse, now,
And on fair promise fair fulfilment come!
And whoso for the state prays otherwise,
Himself reap harvest of his ill desire!

(*Enter a Herald from Agamemnon's army.*)

Herald.

O land of Argos, fatherland of mine!
To thee at last, beneath the tenth year's sun,
My feet return; the bark of my emprise,
Tho' one by one hope's anchors broke away,
Held by the last, and now rides safely here.
Long, long my soul despaired to win, in death,
Its longed-for rest within our Argive land:
And now all hail, O earth, and hail to thee,
New-risen sun! and hail our country's God,
High-ruling Zeus, and thou, the Pythian lord,
Whose arrows smote us once—smite thou no more!
Was not thy wrath wreaked full upon our heads,
O king Apollo, by Scamander's side?
Turn thou, be turned, be saviour, healer, now!
And hail, all gods who rule the street and mart
And Hermes hail! my patron and my pride,
Herald of heaven, and lord of heralds here!
And Heroes, ye who sped us on our way—
To one and all I cry, Receive again
With grace such Argives as the spear has spared.

Ah, home of royalty, belovèd halls,
And solemn shrines, and gods that front the morn!
Benign as erst, with sun-flushed aspect greet
The king returning after many days.
For as from night flash out the beams of day,
So out of darkness dawns a light, a king,
On you, on Argos—Agamemnon comes.
Then hail and greet him well! such meed befits
Him whose right hand hewed down the towers of Troy
With the great axe of Zeus who righteth wrong—
And smote the plain, smote down to nothingness
Each altar, every shrine; and far and wide
Dies from the whole land's face its offspring fair.

Such mighty yoke of fate he set on Troy—
Our lord and monarch, Atreus' elder son,
And comes at last with blissful honour home;
Highest of all who walk on earth to-day—
Not Paris nor the city's self that paid
Sin's price with him, can boast, Whate'er befal,
The guerdon we have won outweighs it all.
But at Fate's judgment-seat the robber stands
Condemned of rapine, and his prey is torn
Forth from his hands, and by his deed is reaped
A bloody harvest of his home and land
Gone down to death, and for his guilt and lust
His father's race pays double in the dust.

Chorus.

Hail, herald of the Greeks, new-come from war.

Herald.

All hail! not death itself can fright me now.

Chorus.

Was thine heart wrung with longing for thy land?

Herald.

So that this joy doth brim mine eyes with tears.

Chorus.

On you too then this sweet distress did fall——

Herald.

How say'st thou? make me master of thy word.

Chorus.

You longed for us who pined for you again.

Herald.

Craved the land us who craved it, love for love?

Chorus.

Yea, till my brooding heart moaned out with pain.

Herald.

Whence thy despair, that mars the army's joy?

Chorus.

Sole cure of wrong is silence, saith the saw.

Herald.

Thy kings afar, couldst thou fear other men?

Chorus.

Death had been sweet, as thou didst say but now.

Herald.

'Tis true; Fate smiles at last. Throughout our toil,
These many years, some chances issued fair,
And some, I wot, were chequered with a curse.
But who, on earth, hath won the bliss of heaven,
Thro' time's whole tenor an unbroken weal?
I could a tale unfold of toiling oars,
Ill rest, scant landings on a shore rock-strewn,
All pains, all sorrows, for our daily doom.
And worse and hatefuller our woes on land;
For where we couched, close by the foeman's wall,
The river-plain was ever dank with dews,
Dropped from the sky, exuded from the earth,
A curse that clung unto our sodden garb,
And hair as horrent as a wild beast's fell.
Why tell the woes of winter, when the birds
Lay stark and stiff, so stern was Ida's snow?
Or summer's scorch, what time the stirless wave
Sank to its sleep beneath the noon-day sun?
Why mourn old woes? their pain has passed away;
And passed away, from those who fell, all care,
For evermore, to rise and live again.
Why sum the count of death, and render thanks
For life by moaning over fate malign?
Farewell, a long farewell to all our woes!
To us, the remnant of the host of Greece,
Comes weal beyond all counterpoise of woe;
Thus boast we rightfully to yonder sun,
Like him far-fleeted over sea and land.
The Argive host prevailed to conquer Troy,
And in the temples of the gods of Greece
Hung up these spoils, a shining sign to Time.
Let those who learn this legend bless aright
The city and its chieftains, and repay
The meed of gratitude to Zeus who willed
And wrought the deed. So stands the tale fulfilled.

Chorus.

Thy words o'erbear my doubt: for news of good,
The ear of age hath ever youth enow:
But those within and Clytemnestra's self
Would fain hear all; glad thou their ears and mine.

(*Re-enter Clytemnestra.*)

Clytemnestra.

Last night, when first the fiery courier came,
In sign that Troy is ta'en and razed to earth,
So wild a cry of joy my lips gave out,
That I was chidden—Hath the beacon watch
Made sure unto thy soul the sack of Troy?
A very woman thou, whose heart leaps light
At wandering rumours!—and with words like these
They showed me how I strayed, misled of hope.
Yet on each shrine I set the sacrifice,
And, in the strain they held for feminine,
Went heralds thro' the city, to and fro,
With voice of loud proclaim, announcing joy,
And in each fane they lit and quenched with wine
The spicy perfumes fading in the flame.
All is fulfilled: I spare your longer tale—
The king himself anon shall tell me all.

Remains to think what honour best may greet
My lord, the majesty of Argos, home.
What day beams fairer on a woman's eyes
Than this, whereon she flings the portal wide,
To hail her lord, heaven-shielded, home from war?
This to my husband, that he tarry not,
But turn the city's longing into joy!
Yea, let him come, and coming may he find
A wife no other than he left her, true
And faithful as a watch-dog to his home,
His foemen's foe, in all her duties leal,
Trusty to keep for ten long years unmarred
The store whereon he set his master-seal.
Be steel deep-dyed, before ye look to see
Ill joy, ill fame, from other wight, in me!

Herald.

'Tis fairly said: thus speaks a noble dame,
Nor speaks amiss, when truth informs the boast.

(*Exit Clytemnestra.*)

Chorus.

So has she spoken—be it yours to learn
By clear interpreters her specious word.
Turn to me, herald—tell me if anon
The second well-loved lord of Argos comes?
Hath Menelaus safely sped with you?

Herald.

Alas—brief boon unto my friends it were,
To flatter them, for truth, with falsehoods fair!

Chorus.

Speak joy, if truth be joy, but truth, at worst—
Too plainly, truth and joy are here divorced.

Herald.

The hero and his bark were rapt away
Far from the Grecian fleet? 'tis truth I say.

Chorus.

Whether in all men's sight from Ilion borne,
Or from the fleet by stress of weather torn?

Herald.

Full on the mark thy shaft of speech doth light,
And one short word hath told long woes aright.

Chorus.

But say, what now of him each comrade saith?
What their forebodings, of his life or death?

Herald.

Ask me no more: the truth is known to none,
Save the earth-fostering, all-surveying Sun.

Chorus.

Say, by what doom the fleet of Greece was driven?
How rose, how sank the storm, the wrath of heaven?

Herald.

Nay, ill it were to mar with sorrow's tale
The day of blissful news. The gods demand
Thanksgiving sundered from solicitude.
If one as herald came with rueful face
To say, The curse has fallen, and the host
Gone down to death; and one wide wound has reached
The city's heart, and out of many homes
Many are cast and consecrate to death,
Beneath the double scourge, that Ares loves,
The bloody pair, the fire and sword of doom—

If such sore burden weighed upon my tongue,
'Twere fit to speak such words as gladden fiends.
But—coming as he comes who bringeth news
Of safe return from toil, and issues fair,
To men rejoicing in a weal restored—
Dare I to dash good words with ill, and say
How the gods' anger smote the Greeks in storm?
For fire and sea, that erst held bitter feud,
Now swore conspiracy and pledged their faith,
Wasting the Argives worn with toil and war.
Night and great horror of the rising wave
Came o'er us, and the blasts that blow from Thrace
Clashed ship with ship, and some with plunging prow
Thro' scudding drifts of spray and raving storm
Vanished, as strays by some ill shepherd driven.
And when at length the sun rose bright, we saw
Th' Aegean sea-field flecked with flowers of death,
Corpses of Grecian men and shattered hulls.
For us indeed, some god, as well I deem,
No human power, laid hand upon our helm,
Snatched us or prayed us from the powers of air,
And brought our bark thro' all, unharmed in hull:
And saving Fortune sat and steered us fair,
So that no surge should gulf us deep in brine,
Nor grind our keel upon a rocky shore.

So 'scaped we death that lurks beneath the sea,
But, under day's white light, mistrustful all
Of fortune's smile, we sat and brooded deep,
Shepherds forlorn of thoughts that wandered wild,
O'er this new woe; for smitten was our host,
And lost as ashes scattered from the pyre.
Of whom if any draw his life-breath yet,
Be well assured, he deems of us as dead,
As we of him no other fate forebode.
But heaven save all! If Menelaus live,
He will not tarry, but will surely come:
Therefore if anywhere the high sun's ray
Descries him upon earth, preserved by Zeus,
Who wills not yet to wipe his race away,

Hope still there is that homeward he may wend.
Enough—thou hast the truth unto the end.

(*Exit Herald.*)

Strophe 1

Chorus.

Say, from whose lips the presage fell?
Who read the future all too well,
  And named her, in her natal hour,
  Helen, the bride with war for dower?
'Twas one of the Invisible,
  Guiding his tongue with prescient power.
On fleet, and host, and citadel,
  War, sprung from her, and death did lour,
When from the bride-bed's fine-spun veil
She to the Zephyr spread her sail.
Strong blew the breeze—the surge closed o'er
The cloven track of keel and oar,
  But while she fled, there drove along,
  Fast in her wake, a mighty throng—
Athirst for blood, athirst for war,
  Forward in fell pursuit they sprung,
Then leapt on Simois' bank ashore,
  The leafy coppices among—
No rangers, they, of wood and field,
But huntsmen of the sword and shield.

Antistrophe 1

Heaven's jealousy, that works its will,
Sped thus on Troy its destined ill,
  Well named, at once, the Bride and Bane;
  And loud rang out the bridal strain;
But they to whom that song befel
  Did turn anon to tears again;
Zeus tarries, but avenges still
  The husband's wrong, the household's stain!
He, the hearth's lord, brooks not to see
Its outraged hospitality.

Even now, and in far other tone,
Troy chants her dirge of mighty moan,
  Woe upon Paris, woe and hate!
  Who wooed his country's doom for mate—
This is the burthen of the groan,
  Wherewith she wails disconsolate
The blood, so many of her own
  Have poured in vain, to fend her fate;
Troy! thou hast fed and freed to roam
A lion-cub within thy home!

Strophe 2

A suckling creature, newly ta'en
From mother's teat, still fully fain
  Of nursing care; and oft caressed,
  Within the arms, upon the breast,
Even as an infant, has it lain;
  Or fawns and licks, by hunger pressed,
The hand that will assuage its pain;
  In life's young dawn, a well-loved guest,
A fondling for the children's play,
A joy unto the old and gray.

Antistrophe 2

But waxing time and growth betrays
The blood-thirst of the lion-race,
  And, for the house's fostering care,
  Unbidden all, it revels there,
And bloody recompense repays—
  Rent flesh of kine, its talons tare:
A mighty beast, that slays, and slays,
  And mars with blood the household fair,
A God-sent pest invincible,
A minister of fate and hell.

Strophe 3

Even so to Ilion's city came by stealth
  A spirit as of windless seas and skies,
A gentle phantom-form of joy and wealth,
  With love's soft arrows speeding from its eyes—
Love's rose, whose thorn doth pierce the soul in subtle wise.

Ah, well-a-day! the bitter bridal-bed,
When the fair mischief lay by Paris' side!
What curse on palace and on people sped
With her, the Fury sent on Priam's pride,
By angered Zeus! what tears of many a widowed bride!

Antistrophe 3

Long, long ago to mortals this was told,
How sweet security and blissful state
Have curses for their children—so men hold—
And for the man of all-too prosperous fate
Springs from a bitter seed some woe insatiate.

Alone, alone, I deem far otherwise;
Not bliss nor wealth it is, but impious deed,
From which that after-growth of ill doth rise!
Woe springs from wrong, the plant is like the seed—
While Right, in honour's house, doth its own likeness
breed.

Strophe 4

Some past impiety, some gray old crime,
Breeds the young curse, that wantons in our ill,
Early or late, when haps th' appointed time—
And out of light brings power of darkness still,
A master-fiend, a foe, unseen, invincible;

A pride accursed, that broods upon the race
And home in which dark Atè holds her sway—
Sin's child and Woe's, that wears its parents' face;

Antistrophe 4

While Right in smoky cribs shines clear as day,
And decks with weal his life, who walks the righteous way.

From gilded halls, that hands polluted raise,
Right turns away with proud averted eyes,
And of the wealth, men stamp amiss with praise,
Heedless, to poorer, holier temples hies,
And to Fate's goal guides all, in its appointed wise.

(*Enter Agamemnon in a chariot, accompanied by another which carries Cassandra and other spoils of war.*)

Hail to thee, chief of Atreus' race,
Returning proud from Troy subdued!
How shall I greet thy conquering face?
How nor a fulsome praise obtrude,
Nor stint the meed of gratitude?
For mortal men who fall to ill
Take little heed of open truth,
But seek unto its semblance still:
The show of weeping and of ruth
To the forlorn will all men pay,
But, of the grief their eyes display,
Nought to the heart doth pierce its way.
And, with the joyous, they beguile
Their lips unto a feignèd smile,
And force a joy, unfelt the while;
But he who as a shepherd wise
Doth know his flock, can ne'er misread
Truth in the falsehood of his eyes,
Who veils beneath a kindly guise
A lukewarm love in deed.
And thou, our leader—when of yore
Thou badest Greece go forth to war
For Helen's sake—I dare avow
That then I held thee not as now;
That to my vision thou didst seem
Dyed in the hues of disesteem.
I held thee for a pilot ill,
And reckless, of thy proper will,
Endowing others doomed to die
With vain and forced audacity!
Now from my heart, ungrudgingly,
To those that wrought, this word be said—
Well fall the labour ye have sped—
Let time and search, O king, declare
What men within thy city's bound
Were loyal to the kingdom's care,
And who were faithless found.

Agamemnon.

First, as is meet, a king's All-hail be said
To Argos, and the gods that guard the land—
Gods who with me availed to speed us home,
With me availed to wring from Priam's town
The due of justice. In the court of heaven
The gods in conclave sat and judged the cause,
Not from a pleader's tongue, and at the close,
Unanimous into the urn of doom
This sentence gave, On Ilion and her men,
Death: and where hope drew nigh to pardon's urn
No hand there was to cast a vote therein.
And still the smoke of fallen Ilion
Rises in sight of all men, and the flame
Of Atè's hecatomb is living yet,
And where the towers in dusty ashes sink,
Rise the rich fumes of pomp and wealth consumed.
For this must all men pay unto the gods
The meed of mindful hearts and gratitude:
For by our hands the meshes of revenge
Closed on the prey, and for one woman's sake
Troy trodden by the Argive monster lies—
The foal, the shielded band that leapt the wall,
What time with autumn sank the Pleiades.
Yea, o'er the fencing wall a lion sprang
Ravening, and lapped his fill of blood of kings.

Such prelude spoken to the gods in full,
To you I turn, and to the hidden thing
Whereof ye spake but now: and in that thought
I am as you, and what ye say, say I.
For few are they who have such inborn grace,
As to look up with love, and envy not,
When stands another on the height of weal.

Deep in his heart, whom jealousy hath seized,
Her poison lurking doth enhance his load;
For now beneath his proper woes he chafes,
And sighs withal to see another's weal.

I speak not idly, but from knowledge sure—
There be who vaunt an utter loyalty,
That is but as the ghost of friendship dead,
A shadow in a glass, of faith gone by.
One only—he who went reluctant forth
Across the seas with me—Odysseus—he
Was loyal unto me with strength and will,
A trusty trace-horse bound unto my car.
Thus—be he yet beneath the light of day,
Or dead, as well I fear—I speak his praise.

Lastly, whate'er be due to men or gods,
With joint debate, in public council held,
We will decide, and warily contrive
That all which now is well may so abide:
For that which haply needs the healer's art,
That will we medicine, discerning well
If cautery or knife befit the time.

Now, to my palace and the shrines of home,
I will pass in, and greet you first and fair,
Ye gods, who bade me forth, and home again—
And long may Victory tarry in my train!

(*Enter Clytemnestra, followed by maidens bearing purple robes.*)

Clytemnestra.

Old men of Argos, lieges of our realm,
Shame shall not bid me shrink lest ye should see
The love I bear my lord. Such blushing fear
Dies at the last from hearts of human kind.
From mine own soul and from no alien lips,
I know and will reveal the life I bore,
Reluctant, through the lingering livelong years,
The while my lord beleaguered Ilion's wall.

First, that a wife sat sundered from her lord,
In widowed solitude, was utter woe—
And woe, to hear how rumour's many tongues
All boded evil—woe, when he who came
And he who followed spake of ill on ill,
Keening Lost, lost, all lost! thro' hall and bower.

Had this my husband met so many wounds,
As by a thousand channels rumour told,
No network e'er was full of holes as he.
Had he been slain, as oft as tidings came
That he was dead, he well might boast him now
A second Geryon of triple frame,
With triple robe of earth above him laid—
For that below, no matter—triply dead,
Dead by one death for every form he bore.
And thus distraught by news of wrath and woe,
Oft for self-slaughter had I slung the noose,
But others wrenched it from my neck away.
Hence haps it that Orestes, thine and mine,
The pledge and symbol of our wedded troth,
Stands not beside us now, as he should stand.
Nor marvel thou at this: he dwells with one
Who guards him loyally; 'tis Phocis' king,
Strophius, who warned me erst, Bethink thee, queen,
What woes of doubtful issue well may fall!
Thy lord in daily jeopardy at Troy,
While here a populace uncurbed may cry
"Down with the council, down!" bethink thee too.
'Tis the world's way to set a harder heel
On fallen power.
For thy child's absence then
Such mine excuse, no wily afterthought.
For me, long since the gushing fount of tears
Is wept away; no drop is left to shed.
Dim are the eyes that ever watched till dawn,
Weeping, the bale-fires, piled for thy return,
Night after night unkindled. If I slept,
Each sound—the tiny humming of a gnat,
Roused me again, again, from fitful dreams
Wherein I felt thee smitten, saw thee slain,
Thrice for each moment of mine hour of sleep.

All this I bore, and now, released from woe,
I hail my lord as watch-dog of a fold,
As saving stay-rope of a storm-tossed ship,
As column stout that holds the roof aloft,
As only child unto a sire bereaved,
As land beheld, past hope, by crews forlorn,

As sunshine fair when tempest's wrath is past,
As gushing spring to thirsty wayfarer.
So sweet it is to 'scape the press of pain.
With such salute I bid my husband hail!
Nor heaven be wroth therewith! for long and hard
I bore that ire of old.
                    Sweet lord, step forth,
Step from thy car, I pray—nay, not on earth
Plant the proud foot, O king, that trod down Troy!
Women! why tarry ye, whose task it is
To spread your monarch's path with tapestry?
Swift, swift, with purple strew his passage fair,
That justice lead him to a home, at last,
He scarcely looked to see.
                         For what remains,
Zeal unsubdued by sleep shall nerve my hand
To work as right and as the gods command.

Agamemnon.

Daughter of Leda, watcher o'er my home,
Thy greeting well befits mine absence long,
For late and hardly has it reached its end.
Know, that the praise which honour bids us crave,
Must come from others' lips, not from our own:
See too that not in fashion feminine
Thou make a warrior's pathway delicate;
Not unto me, as to some Eastern lord,
Bowing thyself to earth, make homage loud.
Strew not this purple that shall make each step
An arrogance; such pomp beseems the gods,
Not me. A mortal man to set his foot
On these rich dyes? I hold such pride in fear,
And bid thee honour me as man, not god.
Fear not—such footcloths and all gauds apart,
Loud from the trump of Fame my name is blown
Best gift of heaven it is, in glory's hour,
To think thereon with soberness: and thou—
Bethink thee of the adage, Call none blest
Till peaceful death have crowned a life of weal.
'Tis said: I fain would fare unvexed by fear.

Clytemnestra.

Nay, but unsay it—thwart not thou my will!

Agamemnon.

Know, I have said, and will not mar my word.

Clytemnestra.

Was it fear made this meekness to the gods?

Agamemnon.

If cause be cause, 'tis mine for this resolve.

Clytemnestra.

What, think'st thou, in thy place had Priam done?

Agamemnon.

He surely would have walked on broidered robes.

Clytemnestra.

Then fear not thou the voice of human blame.

Agamemnon.

Yet mighty is the murmur of a crowd.

Clytemnestra.

Shrink not from envy, appanage of bliss.

Agamemnon.

War is not woman's part, nor war of words.

Clytemnestra.

Yet happy victors well may yield therein.

Agamemnon.

Dost crave for triumph in this petty strife?

Clytemnestra.

Yield; of thy grace permit me to prevail!

Agamemnon.

Then, if thou wilt, let some one stoop to loose
Swiftly these sandals, slaves beneath my foot:
And stepping thus upon the sea's rich dye,
I pray, Let none among the gods look down
With jealous eye on me—reluctant all,
To trample thus and mar a thing of price,
Wasting the wealth of garments silver-worth.

Enough hereof: and, for the stranger maid,
Lead her within, but gently: God on high
Looks graciously on him whom triumph's hour
Has made not pitiless. None willingly
Wear the slave's yoke—and she, the prize and flower
Of all we won, comes hither in my train,
Gift of the army to its chief and lord.
—Now, since in this my will bows down to thine,
I will pass in on purples to my home.

Clytemnestra.

A Sea there is—and who shall stay its springs?
And deep within its breast, a mighty store,
Precious as silver, of the purple dye,
Whereby the dipped robe doth its tint renew.
Enough of such, O king, within thy halls
There lies, a store that cannot fail; but I—
I would have gladly vowed unto the gods
Cost of a thousand garments trodden thus,
(Had once the oracle such gift required)
Contriving ransom for thy life preserved.
For while the stock is firm the foliage climbs,
Spreading a shade, what time the dog-star glows;
And thou, returning to thine hearth and home,
Art as a genial warmth in winter hours,
Or as a coolness, when the lord of heaven
Mellows the juice within the bitter grape.
Such boons and more doth bring into a home
The present footstep of its proper lord.
Zeus, Zeus, Fulfilment's lord! my vows fulfil,
And whatsoe'er it be, work forth thy will!

(*Exeunt Agamemnon and Clytemnestra into the palace.*)

Strophe 1

Chorus.

Wherefore for ever on the wings of fear
  Hovers a vision drear
Before my boding heart? a strain,
Unbidden and unwelcome, thrills mine ear,
  Oracular of pain.

Not as of old upon my bosom's throne
Sits Confidence, to spurn
Such fears, like dreams we know not to discern.
Old, old and gray long since the time has grown,
Which saw the linkèd cables moor
The fleet, when erst it came to Ilion's sandy shore;

Antistrophe 1

And now mine eyes and not another's see
Their safe return.

Yet none the less in me
The inner spirit sings a boding song,
Self-prompted, sings the Furies' strain—
And seeks, and seeks in vain,
To hope and to be strong!

Ah! to some end of Fate, unseen, unguessed,
Are these wild throbbings of my heart and breast—
Yea, of some doom they tell—
Each pulse, a knell.
Lief, lief I were, that all
To unfulfilment's hidden realm might fall.

Strophe 2

Too far, too far our mortal spirits strive,
Grasping at utter weal, unsatisfied—
Till the fell curse, that dwelleth hard beside,
Thrust down the sundering wall. Too fair they blow,
The gales that waft our bark on Fortune's tide!
Swiftly we sail, the sooner all to drive
Upon the hidden rock, the reef of woe.

Then if the hand of caution warily
Sling forth into the sea
Part of the freight, lest all should sink below,
From the deep death it saves the bark: even so,
Doom-laden though it be, once more may rise
His household, who is timely wise.

How oft the famine-stricken field
Is saved by God's large gift, the new year's yield!

Antistrophe 2

But blood of man once spilled,
Once at his feet shed forth, and darkening the plain,—
Nor chant nor charm can call it back again.

So Zeus hath willed:
Else had he spared the leech Asclepius, skilled
To bring man from the dead: the hand divine
Did smite himself with death—a warning and a sign.

Ah me! if Fate, ordained of old,
Held not the will of gods constrained, controlled,
Helpless to us-ward, and apart—
Swifter than speech my heart
Had poured its presage out!
Now, fretting, chafing in the dark of doubt,
'Tis hopeless to unfold
Truth, from fear's tangled skein; and, yearning to proclaim
Its thought, my soul is prophecy and flame.

(*Re-enter Clytemnestra.*)

Clytemnestra.

Get thee within thou too, Cassandra, go!
For Zeus to thee in gracious mercy grants
To share the sprinklings of the lustral bowl,
Beside the altar of his guardianship,
Slave among many slaves. What, haughty still?
Step from the car; Alcmena's son, 'tis said,
Was sold perforce and bore the yoke of old.
Ay, hard it is, but, if such fate befall,
'Tis a fair chance to serve within a home
Of ancient wealth and power. An upstart lord,
To whom wealth's harvest came beyond his hope,
Is as a lion to his slaves, in all
Exceeding fierce, immoderate in sway.
Pass in: thou hearest what our ways will be.

Chorus.

Clear unto thee, O maid, is her command,
But thou—within the toils of Fate thou art—
If such thy will, I urge thee to obey;
Yet I misdoubt thou dost nor hear nor heed.

Clytemnestra.

I wot—unless like swallows she doth use
Some strange barbarian tongue from oversea—
My words must speak persuasion to her soul.

Chorus.

Obey: there is no gentler way than this.
Step from the car's high seat and follow her.

Clytemnestra.

Truce to this bootless waiting here without!
I will not stay: beside the central shrine
The victims stand, prepared for knife and fire—
Offerings from hearts beyond all hope made glad.
Thou—if thou reckest aught of my command,
'Twere well done soon: but if thy sense be shut
From these my words, let thy barbarian hand
Fulfil by gesture the default of speech.

Chorus.

No native is she, thus to read thy words
Unaided: like some wild thing of the wood,
New-trapped, behold! she shrinks and glares on thee.

Clytemnestra.

'Tis madness and the rule of mind distraught,
Since she beheld her city sink in fire,
And hither comes, nor brooks the bit, until
In foam and blood her wrath be champed away.
See ye to her; unqueenly 'tis for me,
Unheeded thus to cast away my words.

(*Exit Clytemnestra.*)

Chorus.

But with me pity sits in anger's place.
Poor maiden, come thou from the car; no way
There is but this—take up thy servitude.

Cassandra.

Woe, woe, alas! Earth, Mother Earth! and thou
Apollo, Apollo!

Chorus.

Peace! shriek not to the bright prophetic god,
Who will not brook the suppliance of woe.

Cassandra.

Woe, woe, alas! Earth, Mother Earth! and thou
Apollo, Apollo!

Chorus.

Hark, with wild curse she calls anew on him,
Who stands far off and loathes the voice of wail.

Cassandra.

Apollo, Apollo!
God of all ways, but only Death's to me,
Once and again, O thou, Destroyer named,
Thou hast destroyed me, thou, my love of old!

Chorus.

She grows presageful of her woes to come,
Slave tho' she be, instinct with prophecy.

Cassandra.

Apollo, Apollo!
God of all ways, but only Death's to me,
O thou Apollo, thou Destroyer named!
What way hast led me, to what evil home?

Chorus.

Know'st thou it not? The home of Atreus' race:
Take these my words for sooth and ask no more.

Cassandra.

Home cursed of God! Bear witness unto me,
Ye visioned woes within—
The blood-stained hands of them that smite their kin—
The strangling noose, and, spattered o'er
With human blood, the reeking floor!

Chorus.

How like a sleuth-hound questing on the track,
Keen-scented unto blood and death she hies!

Cassandra.

Ah! can the ghostly guidance fail,
Whereby my prophet-soul is onwards led?
Look! for their flesh the spectre-children wail,
Their sodden limbs on which their father fed!

Chorus.

Long since we knew of thy prophetic fame,—
But for those deeds we seek no prophet's tongue.

Cassandra.

God! 'tis another crime—
Worse than the storied woe of olden time,
Cureless, abhorred, that one is plotting here—
A shaming death, for those that should be dear!
Alas! and far away, in foreign land,
He that should help doth stand!

Chorus.

I knew th' old tales, the city rings withal—
But now thy speech is dark, beyond my ken.

Cassandra.

O wretch, O purpose fell!
Thou for thy wedded lord
The cleansing wave hast poured —
A treacherous welcome!
How the sequel tell?
Too soon 'twill come, too soon, for now, even now,
She smites him, blow on blow!

Chorus.

Riddles beyond my rede—I peer in vain
Thro' the dim films that screen the prophecy.

Cassandra.

God! a new sight! a net, a snare of hell,
Set by her hand—herself a snare more fell!
A wedded wife, she slays her lord,
Helped by another hand!
Ye powers, whose hate
Of Atreus' home no blood can satiate,
Raise the wild cry above the sacrifice abhorred!

Chorus.

Why biddest thou some fiend, I know not whom,
Shriek o'er the house? Thine is no cheering word.
Back to my heart in frozen fear I feel
My waning life-blood run—
The blood that round the wounding steel
Ebbs slow, as sinks life's parting sun—
Swift, swift and sure, some woe comes pressing on!

Cassandra.

Away, away—keep him away—
The monarch of the herd, the pasture's pride,
Far from his mate! In treach'rous wrath,
Muffling his swarthy horns, with secret scathe
She gores his fenceless side!
Hark! in the brimming bath,
The heavy plash—the dying cry—
Hark—in the laver—hark, he falls by treachery!

Chorus.

I read amiss dark sayings such as thine,
Yet something warns me that they tell of ill.
O dark prophetic speech,
Ill tidings dost thou teach
Ever, to mortals here below!
Ever some tale of awe and woe
Thro' all thy windings manifold
Do we unriddle and unfold!

Cassandra.

Ah well-a-day! the cup of agony,
Whereof I chant, foams with a draught for me.
Ah lord, ah leader, thou hast led me here—
Was't but to die with thee whose doom is near?

Chorus.

Distraught thou art, divinely stirred,
And wailest for thyself a tuneless lay,
As piteous as the ceaseless tale
Wherewith the brown melodious bird
Doth ever Itys! Itys! wail,
Deep-bowered in sorrow, all its little life-time's day!

Cassandra.

Ah for thy fate, O shrill-voiced nightingale!
Some solace for thy woes did Heaven afford,
Clothed thee with soft brown plumes, and life apart
from wail—
But for my death is edged the double-biting sword!

Chorus.

What pangs are these, what fruitless pain,
Sent on thee from on high?
Thou chantest terror's frantic strain,
Yet in shrill measured melody.
How thus unerring canst thou sweep along
The prophet's path of boding song?

Cassandra.

Woe, Paris, woe on thee; thy bridal joy
Was death and fire upon thy race and Troy!
And woe for thee, Scamander's flood!
Beside thy banks, O river fair,
I grew in tender nursing care
From childhood unto maidenhood!
Now not by thine, but by Cocytus' stream
And Acheron's banks shall ring my boding scream.

Chorus.

Too plain is all, too plain!
A child might read aright thy fateful strain.
Deep in my heart their piercing fang
Terror and sorrow set, the while I heard
That piteous, low, tender word,
Yet to mine ear and heart a crushing pang.

Cassandra.

Woe for my city, woe for Ilion's fall!
Father, how oft with sanguine stain
Streamed on thine altar-stone the blood of cattle, slain
That heaven might guard our wall!
But all was shed in vain.
Low lie the shattered towers whereas they fell,
And I—ah burning heart!—shall soon lie low as well.

Chorus.

Of sorrow is thy song, of sorrow still!
Alas, what power of ill
Sits heavy on thy heart and bids thee tell
In tears of perfect moan thy deadly tale?
Some woe—I know not what—must close thy piteous wail.

Cassandra.

List! for no more the presage of my soul,
Bride-like, shall peer from its secluding veil;
But as the morning wind blows clear the east,
More bright shall blow the wind of prophecy,
And as against the low bright line of dawn
Heaves high and higher yet the rolling wave,
So in the clearing skies of prescience
Dawns on my soul a further, deadlier woe,
And I will speak, but in dark speech no more.
Bear witness, ye, and follow at my side—
I scent the trail of blood, shed long ago.

Within this house a choir abidingly
Chants in harsh unison the chant of ill;
Yea, and they drink, for more enhardened joy,
Man's blood for wine, and revel in the halls,
Departing never, Furies of the home.
They sit within, they chant the primal curse,
Each spitting hatred on that crime of old,
The brother's couch, the love incestuous
That brought forth hatred to the ravisher.
Say, is my speech or wild and erring now,
Or doth its arrow cleave the mark indeed?
They called me once, The prophetess of lies,
The wandering hag, the pest of every door—
Attest ye now, She knows in very sooth
The house's curse, the storied infamy.

Chorus.

Yet how should oath—how loyally soe'er
I swear it—aught avail thee? In good sooth,
My wonder meets thy claim: I stand amazed
That thou, a maiden born beyond the seas,
Dost as a native know and tell aright
Tales of a city of an alien tongue.

Cassandra.

This is my power—a boon Apollo gave.

Chorus.

God though he were, yearning for mortal maid?

Cassandra.

Ay! what seemed shame of old is shame no more.

Chorus.

Such finer sense suits not with slavery.

Cassandra.

He strove to win me, panting for my love.

Chorus.

Came ye by compact unto bridal joys?

Cassandra.

Nay—for I plighted troth, then foiled the god.

Chorus.

Wert thou already dowered with prescience?

Cassandra.

Yea—prophetess to Troy of all her doom.

Chorus.

How left thee then Apollo's wrath unscathed?

Cassandra.

I, false to him, seemed prophet false to all.

Chorus.

Not so—to us at least thy words seem sooth.

Cassandra.

Woe for me, woe! Again the agony—
Dread pain that sees the future all too well
With ghastly preludes whirls and racks my soul.
Behold ye—yonder on the palace roof
The spectre-children sitting—look, such things
As dreams are made on, phantoms as of babes,
Horrible shadows, that a kinsman's hand
Hath marked with murder, and their arms are full—
A rueful burden—see, they hold them up,
The entrails upon which their father fed!

For this, for this, I say there plots revenge
A coward lion, couching in the lair—
Guarding the gate against my master's foot—
My master—mine—I bear the slave's yoke now.
And he, the lord of ships, who trod down Troy,
Knows not the fawning treachery of tongue
Of this thing false and dog-like—how her speech
Glozes and sleeks her purpose, till she win
By ill fate's favour the desirèd chance,
Moving like Atè to a secret end.
O aweless soul! the woman slays her lord—
Woman? what loathsome monster of the earth
Were fit comparison? The double snake—
Or Scylla, where she dwells, the seaman's bane,
Girt round about with rocks? some hag of hell,
Raving a truceless curse upon her kin?
Hark—even now she cries exultingly
The vengeful cry that tells of battle turned—
How fain, forsooth, to greet her chief restored!
Nay then, believe me not: what skills belief
Or disbelief? Fate works its will—and thou
Wilt see and say in ruth, Her tale was true.

Chorus.

Ah—'tis Thyestes' feast on kindred flesh—
I guess her meaning and with horror thrill,
Hearing no shadow'd hint of th' o'er-true tale,
But its full hatefulness: yet, for the rest,
Far from the track I roam, and know no more.

Cassandra.

'Tis Agamemnon's doom thou shalt behold.

Chorus.

Peace, hapless woman, to thy boding words!

Cassandra.

Far from my speech stands he who sains and saves.

Chorus.

Ay—were such doom at hand—which God forbid!

Cassandra.

Thou prayest idly—these move swift to slay.

Chorus.

What man prepares a deed of such despite?

Cassandra.

Fool! thus to read amiss mine oracles.

Chorus.

Deviser and device are dark to me.

Cassandra.

Dark! all too well I speak the Grecian tongue.

Chorus.

Ay—but in thine, as in Apollo's strains,
Familiar is the tongue, but dark the thought.

Cassandra.

Ah ah the fire! it waxes, nears me now—
Woe, woe for me, Apollo of the dawn!

Lo, how the woman-thing, the lioness
Couched with the wolf—her noble mate afar—
Will slay me, slave forlorn! Yea, like some witch,
She drugs the cup of wrath, that slays her lord,
With double death—his recompense for me!
Ay, 'tis for me, the prey he bore from Troy,
That she hath sworn his death, and edged the steel!
Ye wands, ye wreaths that cling around my neck,
Ye showed me prophetess yet scorned of all—
I stamp you into death, or e'er I die—

Down, to destruction!
Thus I stand revenged—
Go, crown some other with a prophet's woe.
Look! it is he, it is Apollo's self
Rending from me the prophet-robe he gave.
God! while I wore it yet, thou saw'st me mocked
There at my home by each malicious mouth—
To all and each, an undivided scorn.
The name alike and fate of witch and cheat—
Woe, poverty, and famine—all I bore;
And at this last the god hath brought me here
Into death's toils, and what his love had made,
His hate unmakes me now: and I shall stand
Not now before the altar of my home,
But me a slaughter-house and block of blood
Shall see hewn down, a reeking sacrifice.
Yet shall the gods have heed of me who die,
For by their will shall one requite my doom.
He, to avenge his father's blood outpoured,
Shall smite and slay with matricidal hand.
Ay, he shall come—tho' far away he roam,
A banished wanderer in a stranger's land—
To crown his kindred's edifice of ill,
Called home to vengeance by his father's fall:
Thus have the high gods sworn, and shall fulfil.
And now why mourn I, tarrying on earth,
Since first mine Ilion has found its fate
And I beheld, and those who won the wall
Pass to such issue as the gods ordain?
I too will pass and like them dare to die!

(*She turns and looks upon the palace door.*)

Portal of Hades, thus I bid thee hail!
Grant me one boon—a swift and mortal stroke,
That all unwrung by pain, with ebbing blood
Shed forth in quiet death, I close mine eyes.

Chorus.

Maid of mysterious woes, mysterious lore,
Long was thy prophecy: but if aright
Thou readest all thy fate, how, thus unscared,
Dost thou approach the altar of thy doom,
As fronts the knife some victim, heaven-controlled?

Cassandra.

Friends, there is no avoidance in delay.

Chorus.

Yet who delays the longest, his the gain.

Cassandra.

The day is come—flight were small gain to me!

Chorus.

O brave endurance of a soul resolved!

Cassandra.

That were ill praise, for those of happier doom.

Chorus.

All fame is happy, even famous death.

Cassandra.

Ah sire, ah brethren, famous once were ye!

(*She moves to enter the house, then starts back.*)

Chorus.

What fear is this that scares thee from the house?

Cassandra.

Pah!

Chorus.

What is this cry? some dark despair of soul?

Cassandra.

Pah! the house fumes with stench and spilth of blood.

Chorus.

How? 'tis the smell of household offerings.

Cassandra.

'Tis rank as charnel-scent from open graves.

Chorus.

Thou canst not mean this scented Syrian nard?

Cassandra.

Nay, let me pass within to cry aloud
The monarch's fate and mine—enough of life.
Ah friends!
Bear to me witness, since I fall in death,
That not as birds that shun the bush and scream
I moan in idle terror. This attest
When for my death's revenge another dies,
A woman for a woman, and a man
Falls, for a man ill-wedded to his curse.
Grant me this boon—the last before I die.

Chorus.

Brave to the last! I mourn thy doom foreseen.

Cassandra.

Once more one utterance, but not of wail,
Though for my death—and then I speak no more.

Sun! thou whose beam I shall not see again,
To thee I cry, Let those whom vengeance calls
To slay their kindred's slayers, quit withal
The death of me, the slave, the fenceless prey.

Ah state of mortal man! in time of weal,
A line, a shadow! and if ill fate fall,
One wet sponge-sweep wipes all our trace away—
And this I deem less piteous, of the twain.

(*Exit into the palace.*)

Chorus.

Too true it is! our mortal state
With bliss is never satiate,
And none, before the palace high
And stately of prosperity,
Cries to us with a voice of fear,
Away! 'tis ill to enter here!

Lo! this our lord hath trodden down,
By grace of heaven, old Priam's town,
And praised as god he stands once more
On Argos' shore!
Yet now—if blood shed long ago
Cries out that other blood shall flow—
His life-blood, his, to pay again
The stern requital of the slain—
Peace to that braggart's vaunting vain,
Who, having heard the chieftain's tale,
Yet boasts of bliss untouched by bale!

(*A loud cry from within.*)

Voice of Agamemnon.

O I am sped—a deep, a mortal blow.

Chorus.

Listen, listen! who is screaming as in mortal agony?

Voice of Agamemnon.

O! O! again, another, another blow!

Chorus.

The bloody act is over—I have heard the monarch's cry—
Let us swiftly take some counsel, lest we too be doomed to die.

One of the Chorus.

'Tis best, I judge, aloud for aid to call,
"Ho! loyal Argives! to the palace, all!"

Another.

Better, I deem, ourselves to bear the aid,
And drag the deed to light, while drips the blade.

Another.

Such will is mine, and what thou say'st I say:
Swiftly to act! the time brooks no delay.

Another.

Ay, for 'tis plain, this prelude of their song
Foretells its close in tyranny and wrong.

Another.

Behold, we tarry—but thy name, Delay,
They spurn, and press with sleepless hand to slay.

Another.

I know not what 'twere well to counsel now—
Who wills to act, 'tis his to counsel how.

Another.

Thy doubt is mine: for when a man is slain,
I have no words to bring his life again.

Another.

What? e'en for life's sake, bow us to obey
These house-defilers and their tyrant sway?

Another.

Unmanly doom! 'twere better far to die—
Death is a gentler lord than tyranny.

Another.

Think well—must cry or sign of woe or pain
Fix our conclusion that the chief is slain?

Another.

Such talk befits us when the deed we see—
Conjecture dwells afar from certainty.

Leader of the Chorus.

I read one will from many a diverse word,
To know aright, how stands it with our lord!

(*The palace doors open, disclosing Clytemnestra, who comes forward. The body of Agamemnon lies, muffled in a long robe, within a silver-sided laver; the corpse of Cassandra is laid beside him.*)

Clytemnestra.

Ho, ye who heard me speak so long and oft
The glozing word that led me to my will—
Hear how I shrink not to unsay it all!
How else should one who willeth to requite
Evil for evil to an enemy
Disguised as friend, weave the mesh straitly round him,
Not to be overleaped, a net of doom?
This is the sum and issue of old strife,
Of me deep-pondered and at length fulfilled.
All is avowed, and as I smote I stand
With foot set firm upon a finished thing!
I turn not to denial: thus I wrought
So that he could nor flee nor ward his doom.
Even as the trammel hems the scaly shoal,
I trapped him with inextricable toils,
The ill abundance of a baffling robe;
Then smote him, once, again—and at each wound
He cried aloud, then as in death relaxed
Each limb and sank to earth; and as he lay,
Once more I smote him, with the last third blow,
Sacred to Hades, saviour of the dead.
And thus he fell, and as he passed away,
Spirit with body chafed; each dying breath
Flung from his breast swift bubbling jets of gore,
And the dark sprinklings of the rain of blood
Fell upon me; and I was fain to feel
That dew—not sweeter is the rain of heaven
To cornland, when the green sheath teems with grain.

Elders of Argos—since the thing stands so,
I bid you to rejoice, if such your will:
Rejoice or not, I vaunt and praise the deed,
And well I ween, if seemly it could be,

'Twere not ill done to pour libations here,
Justly—ay, more than justly—on his corpse
Who filled his home with curses as with wine,
And thus returned to drain the cup he filled.

Chorus.

I marvel at thy tongue's audacity,
To vaunt thus loudly o'er a husband slain.

Clytemnestra.

Ye hold me as a woman, weak of will,
And strive to sway me: but my heart is stout,
Nor fears to speak its uttermost to you,
Albeit ye know its message. Praise or blame,
Even as ye list,—I reck not of your words.
Lo! at my feet lies Agamemnon slain,
My husband once—and him this hand of mine,
A right contriver, fashioned for his death.
Behold the deed!

Strophe 1

Chorus.

Woman, what deadly birth,
What venomed essence of the earth
Or dark distilment of the wave,
To thee such passion gave,
Nerving thine hand
To set upon thy brow this burning crown,
The curses of thy land?
Our king by thee cut off, hewn down!
Go forth—they cry—accursèd and forlorn,
To hate and scorn!

Clytemnestra.

O ye just men, who speak my sentence now,
The city's hate, the ban of all my realm!
Ye had no voice of old to launch such doom
On him, my husband, when he held as light
My daughter's life as that of sheep or goat,
One victim from the thronging fleecy fold!
Yea, slew in sacrifice his child and mine,
The well-loved issue of my travail-pangs,
To lull and lay the gales that blew from Thrace.
That deed of his, I say, that stain and shame,
Had rightly been atoned by banishment;

But ye, who then were dumb, are stern to judge
This deed of mine that doth affront your ears.
Storm out your threats, yet knowing this for sooth,
That I am ready, if your hand prevail
As mine now doth, to bow beneath your sway:
If God say nay, it shall be yours to learn
By chastisement a late humility.

Antistrophe 1

Chorus.

Bold is thy craft, and proud
Thy confidence, thy vaunting loud;
Thy soul, that chose a murd'ress' fate,
Is all with blood elate —
Maddened to know
The blood not yet avenged, the damnèd spot
Crimson upon thy brow.
But Fate prepares for thee thy lot—
Smitten as thou didst smite, without a friend,
To meet thine end!

Clytemnestra.

Hear then the sanction of the oath I swear—
By the great vengeance for my murdered child,
By Atè, by the Fury unto whom
This man lies sacrificed by hand of mine,
I do not look to tread the hall of Fear,
While in this hearth and home of mine there burns
The light of love—Aegisthus—as of old
Loyal, a stalwart shield of confidence—
As true to me as this slain man was false,
Wronging his wife with paramours at Troy,
Fresh from the kiss of each Chryseis there!
Behold him dead—behold his captive prize,
Seeress and harlot—comfort of his bed,
True prophetess, true paramour—I wot
The sea-bench was not closer to the flesh,
Full oft, of every rower, than was she.
See, ill they did, and ill requites them now.
His death ye know: she as a dying swan
Sang her last dirge, and lies, as erst she lay,
Close to his side, and to my couch has left
A sweet new taste of joys that know no fear.

Strophe 2

Chorus.

Ah woe and well-a-day! I would that Fate—
Not bearing agony too great,
Nor stretching me too long on couch of pain—
Would bid mine eyelids keep
The morningless and unawakening sleep!
For life is weary, now my lord is slain,
The gracious among kings!
Hard fate of old he bore and many grievous things,
And for a woman's sake, on Ilian land—
Now is his life hewn down, and by a woman's hand.

O Helen, O infatuate soul,
Who bad'st the tides of battle roll,
O'erwhelming thousands, life on life,
'Neath Ilion's wall!
And now lies dead the lord of all.
The blossom of thy storied sin
Bears blood's inexpiable stain,
O thou that erst, these halls within,
Wert unto all a rock of strife,
A husband's bane!

Clytemnestra.

Peace! pray not thou for death as though
Thine heart was whelmed beneath this woe,
Nor turn thy wrath aside to ban
The name of Helen, nor recall
How she, one bane of many a man,
Sent down to death the Danaan lords,
To sleep at Troy the sleep of swords,
And wrought the woe that shattered all.

Antistrophe 2

Chorus.

Fiend of the race! that swoopest fell
Upon the double stock of Tantalus,
Lording it o'er me by a woman's will,
Stern, manful, and imperious—
A bitter sway to me!
Thy very form I see,
Like some grim raven, perched upon the slain,
Exulting o'er the crime, aloud, in tuneless strain!

Clytemnestra.

Right was that word—thou namest well
The brooding race-fiend, triply fell!
From him it is that murder's thirst,
Blood-lapping, inwardly is nursed—
Ere time the ancient scar can sain,
New blood comes welling forth again.

Strophe 3

Chorus.

Grim is his wrath and heavy on our home,
  That fiend of whom thy voice has cried,
Alas, an omened cry of woe unsatisfied,
  An all-devouring doom!

Ah woe, ah Zeus! from Zeus all things befall—
  Zeus the high cause and finisher of all!—
Lord of our mortal state, by him are willed
  All things, by him fulfilled!

Yet ah my king, my king no more!
What words to say, what tears to pour
  Can tell my love for thee?
The spider-web of treachery
She wove and wound, thy life around,
  And lo! I see thee lie,
And thro' a coward, impious wound
  Pant forth thy life and die!
A death of shame—ah woe on woe!
A treach'rous hand, a cleaving blow!

Clytemnestra.

My guilt thou harpest, o'er and o'er!
I bid thee reckon me no more
  As Agamemnon's spouse.
The old Avenger, stern of mood
For Atreus and his feast of blood,
  Hath struck the lord of Atreus' house,
And in the semblance of his wife
  The king hath slain.—
Yea, for the murdered children's life,
  A chieftain's in requital ta'en.

Antistrophe 3

Chorus.

Thou guiltless of this murder, thou!
Who dares such thought avow?
Yet it may be, wroth for the parent's deed,
The fiend hath holpen thee to slay the son.
Dark Ares, god of death, is pressing on
Thro' streams of blood by kindred shed,
Exacting the accompt for children dead,
For clotted blood, for flesh on which their sire did feed.

Yet ah my king, my king no more!
What words to say, what tears to pour
Can tell my love for thee?
The spider-web of treachery
She wove and wound, thy life around,
And lo! I see thee lie,
And thro' a coward, impious wound
Pant forth thy life and die!
A death of shame—ah woe on woe!
A treach'rous hand, a cleaving blow!

Clytemnestra.

I deem not that the death he died
Had overmuch of shame:
For this was he who did provide
Foul wrong unto his house and name:
His daughter, blossom of my womb,
He gave unto a deadly doom,
Iphigeneia, child of tears!
And as he wrought, even so he fares.
Nor be his vaunt too loud in hell;
For by the sword his sin he wrought,
And by the sword himself is brought
Among the dead to dwell.

Strophe 4

Chorus.

Ah whither shall I fly?
For all in ruin sinks the kingly hall;
Nor swift device nor shift of thought have I,
To 'scape its fall.

A little while the gentler rain-drops fail;
I stand distraught—a ghastly interval,
Till on the roof-tree rings the bursting hail
Of blood and doom. Even now fate whets the steel
On whetstones new and deadlier than of old,
The steel that smites, in Justice' hold,
Another death to deal.
O Earth! that I had lain at rest
And lapped for ever in thy breast,
Ere I had seen my chieftain fall
Within the laver's silver wall,
Low-lying on dishonoured bier!
And who shall give him sepulchre,
And who the wail of sorrow pour?
Woman, 'tis thine no more!
A graceless gift unto his shade
Such tribute, by his murd'ress paid!
Strive not thus wrongly to atone
The impious deed thy hand hath done.
Ah who above the god-like chief
Shall weep the tears of loyal grief?
Who speak above his lowly grave
The last sad praises of the brave?

Clytemnestra.

Peace! for such task is none of thine.
By me he fell, by me he died,
And now his burial rites be mine!
Yet from these halls no mourners' train
Shall celebrate his obsequies;
Only by Acheron's rolling tide
His child shall spring unto his side,
And in a daughter's loving wise
Shall clasp and kiss him once again!

Antistrophe 4

Chorus.

Lo! sin by sin and sorrow dogg'd by sorrow—
And who the end can know?
The slayer of to-day shall die to-morrow—
The wage of wrong is woe.
While Time shall be, while Zeus in heaven is lord,
His law is fixed and stern;

On him that wrought shall vengeance be outpoured—
The tides of doom return.
The children of the curse abide within
These halls of high estate—
And none can wrench from off the home of sin
The clinging grasp of fate.

Clytemnestra.

Now walks thy word aright, to tell
This ancient truth of oracle;
But I with vows of sooth will pray
To him, the power that holdeth sway
O'er all the race of Pleisthenes—
Tho' dark the deed and deep the guilt,
With this last blood, my hands have spilt,
I pray thee let thine anger cease!
I pray thee pass from us away
To some new race in other lands,
There, if thou wilt, to wrong and slay
The lives of men by kindred hands.

For me 'tis all sufficient meed,
Tho' little wealth or power were won,
So I can say, 'Tis past and done.
The bloody lust and murderous,
The inborn frenzy of our house,
Is ended, by my deed!

(*Enter Aegisthus with a bodyguard.*)

Aegisthus.

Dawn of the day of rightful vengeance, hail!
I dare at length aver that gods above
Have care of men and heed of earthly wrongs.
I, I who stand and thus exult to see
This man lie wound in robes the Furies wove,
Slain in requital of his father's craft.
Take ye the truth, that Atreus, this man's sire,
The lord and monarch of this land of old,
Held with my sire Thyestes deep dispute,
Brother with brother, for the prize of sway,
And drave him from his home to banishment.
Thereafter, the lorn exile homeward stole
And clung a suppliant to the hearth divine,

And for himself won this immunity—
Not with his own blood to defile the land
That gave him birth. But Atreus, godless sire
Of him who here lies dead, this welcome planned—
With zeal that was not love he feigned to hold
In loyal joy a day of festal cheer,
And bade my father to his board, and set
Before him flesh that was his children once.
First, sitting at the upper board alone,
He hid the fingers and the feet, but gave
The rest—and readily Thyestes took
What to his ignorance no semblance wore
Of human flesh, and ate: behold what curse
That eating brought upon our race and name!
For when he knew what all unhallowed thing
He thus had wrought, with horror's bitter cry
Back-starting, spewing forth the fragments foul,
On Pelops' house a deadly curse he spake—
As darkly as I spurn this damnèd food,
So perish all the race of Pleisthenes!
Thus by that curse fell he whom here ye see,
And I—who else?—this murder wove and planned;
For me, an infant yet in swaddling bands,
Of the three children youngest, Atreus sent
To banishment by my sad father's side:
But Justice brought me home once more, grown now
To manhood's years; and stranger tho' I was,
My right hand reached unto the chieftain's life,
Plotting and planning all that malice bade.
And death itself were honour now to me,
Beholding him in Justice' ambush ta'en.

Chorus.

Aegisthus, for this insolence of thine
That vaunts itself in evil, take my scorn.
Of thine own will, thou sayest, thou hast slain
The chieftain, by thine own unaided plot
Devised the piteous death: I rede thee well,
Think not thy head shall 'scape, when right prevails,
The people's ban, the stones of death and doom.

Aegisthus.

This word from thee, this word from one who rows
Low at the oars beneath, what time we rule,
We of the upper tier? Thou'lt know anon,
'Tis bitter to be taught again in age,
By one so young, submission at the word.
But iron of the chain and hunger's throes
Can minister unto an o'erswoln pride
Marvellous well, ay, even in the old.
Hast eyes, and seest not this? Peace—kick not thus
Against the pricks, unto thy proper pain!

Chorus.

Thou womanish man, waiting till war did cease,
Home-watcher and defiler of the couch,
And arch-deviser of the chieftain's doom!

Aegisthus.

Bold words again! but they shall end in tears.
The very converse, thine, of Orpheus' tongue:
He roused and led in ecstasy of joy
All things that heard his voice melodious;
But thou as with the futile cry of curs
Wilt draw men wrathfully upon thee. Peace!
Or strong subjection soon shall tame thy tongue.

Chorus.

Ay, thou art one to hold an Argive down—
Thou, skilled to plan the murder of the king,
But not with thine own hand to smite the blow!

Aegisthus.

That fraudful force was woman's very part,
Not mine, whom deep suspicion from of old
Would have debarred. Now by his treasure's aid
My purpose holds to rule the citizens.
But whoso will not bear my guiding hand,
Him for his corn-fed mettle I will drive
Not as a trace-horse, light-caparisoned,
But to the shafts with heaviest harness bound.
Famine, the grim mate of the dungeon dark,
Shall look on him and shall behold him tame.

Chorus.

Thou losel soul, was then thy strength too slight
To deal in murder, while a woman's hand,
Staining and shaming Argos and its gods,
Availed to slay him? Ho, if anywhere
The light of life smite on Orestes' eyes,
Let him, returning by some guardian fate,
Hew down with force her paramour and her!

Aegisthus.

How thy word and act shall issue, thou shalt shortly understand.

Chorus.

Up to action, O my comrades! for the fight is hard at hand.
Swift, your right hands to the sword hilt! bare the weapon as for strife—

Aegisthus.

Lo! I too am standing ready, hand on hilt for death or life.

Chorus.

'Twas thy word and we accept it: onward to the chance of war!

Clytemnestra.

Nay, enough, enough, my champion! we will smite and slay no more.
Already have we reaped enough the harvest-field of guilt:
Enough of wrong and murder, let no other blood be spilt.
Peace, old men! and pass away unto the homes by Fate decreed,
Lest ill valour meet our vengeance—'twas a necessary deed.
But enough of toils and troubles—be the end, if ever, now,
Ere thy talon, O Avenger, deal another deadly blow.
'Tis a woman's word of warning, and let who will list thereto.

Aegisthus.

But that these should loose and lavish reckless blossoms of the tongue,
And in hazard of their fortune cast upon me words of wrong,
And forget the law of subjects, and revile their ruler's word—

Chorus.

Ruler? but 'tis not for Argives, thus to own a dastard lord!

Aegisthus.

I will follow to chastise thee in my coming days of sway.

Chorus.

Not if Fortune guide Orestes safely on his homeward way.

Aegisthus.

Ah, well I know how exiles feed on hopes of their return.

Chorus.

Fare and batten on pollution of the right, while 'tis thy turn.

Aegisthus.

Thou shalt pay, be well assurèd, heavy quittance for thy pride.

Chorus.

Crow and strut, with her to watch thee, like a cock, his mate beside!

Clytemnestra.

Heed not thou too highly of them—let the cur-pack growl and yell:
I and thou will rule the palace and will order all things well.

Sophocles.
Lateran Museum,
Rome

SOPHOCLES

Oedipus the King

Translated by Clarence W. Mendell

First produced soon after 430 B.C. It won second prize; Sophocles won first prize more than twenty times.

CHARACTERS IN THE PLAY

Oedipus, King of Thebes

Priest of Zeus

Jocasta, Queen of Thebes; widow of Laius, the late King, and now wife of Oedipus

Creon, brother of Jocasta

Teiresias, a blind prophet

A Messenger, from Corinth

A Herdsman, formerly in the service of Laius

Second Messenger

Chorus of Theban Elders

A crowd of Suppliants, men, women, and children

ARGUMENT

Laius and Jocasta, King and Queen of Thebes, had received an oracle that a son born to them would kill his father and marry his mother. When the son was born, he was brought to Mt. Cithaeron, rescued, and reared as the son of Polybus and Merope, King and Queen of Corinth. Some years later, when a strange monster, known as the Sphinx, began to kill the people of Thebes, Laius went to Delphi to seek the oracle's aid. On the way, he was slain. Not long afterward, Oedipus came to Thebes. He guessed the Sphinx's riddle and slew it. The grateful Thebans offered him the throne and the hand of Jocasta. Several years pass, and two sons and two daughters are born to Oedipus and Jocasta. The play opens at a point when a pestilence has fallen on Thebes. Though Oedipus offers no plea of ignorance as he learns the horrible truth about himself, but accepts the responsibility for his acts, are we not overwhelmed nevertheless by the tragedy of man powerless in the face of forces greater than himself?

SCENE

Before the palace of Oedipus at Thebes. Nearby is an altar, beside which stand a priest and suppliants of all ages. Oedipus enters.

OEDIPUS THE KING

Oedipus.

My children, ancient Cadmus' newest brood,
What is this embassy that waits impatient
Bedecked with suppliant branches? All our town
Is filled with sound of holy sacrifice
And paeans too and wailing misery.
These things, my children, I have deemed it wrong
To learn from others: I went forth myself,
I, famed on the lips of all men, Oedipus.
But tell me, sire—for thou art fit to speak
For these—in what mood stand ye there? In fear
Or loyalty? Stony of heart the man
Who finds no pity for such embassy.

Priest.

O Oedipus, that rulest o'er my land,
Thou seest us, how of every age we sit
Before thy altars, some not yet endowed
With strength for distant flight, and some
Heavy with age who serve as priests (myself
The priest of Zeus) and other some elect
From all the tribes. Within the market-place
Sits the whole populace in suppliant garb
By Pallas' twofold shrine revered, or where
Ismenus' sacred soil speaks prophecy.
For, as thou seest too, our commonwealth
Labors full sore nor yet avails to lift
Its head above the billowing surge of death,
Wasting alike in the rich crops of earth
And in her grazing herds, while women suffer
The pangs of barren childbirth. Through her midst
The fire-bearing god, mad pestilence,
Hurling his shafts, scourges relentlessly
Our city till, beneath his hand, the home
Of Cadmus is made void and Hades black
With groans and lamentations is enriched.
Not with the gods do I now make thee one
Nor these thy children seated at thy gate,
But first of all mankind we reckon thee
In ways of men and in perplexities
Haling from heaven above. 'Twas thou that camest

Loosing our Cadmeian city from the toll
We paid the singer of harsh harmonies,
Learning no clue from us: no other man
Instructed thee but by the lore of god,
Men say, believing, thou didst right our life.
Now too, o Oedipus, that rulest all,
Turning to thee we all petition thee:
Discover straight some remedy for us.
It may be thou shalt hearken to the voice
Of god or of some man, thou knowest whose.
For yesterday's experience methinks
Best validetes the counsel of today.
Up then, and save thy city, thou who art
Best of mankind; up, gird thyself, for thee
This country calls its savior, honoring
Thy past devotion. Never let memory
Recall thy rule, how once erect we stood
Upraised only to fall. Nay save the state.
A happy rescue from the cursed Sphinx
Thou gavest us long since: be now the same.
And thou wouldst rule this city as thou dost,
Better to rule o'er men than emptiness.
Fortress and ship alike become as naught
Bereft of humankind to dwell therein.

Oedipus.

My children pitiable, not strange to me,
Familiar rather are the things ye ask.
Full well I know your anguish—yet, howe'er
Ye suffer all, there is no one of you
Whose suffering equals mine. Your several griefs
Touch each one man, no other than yourselves:
My spirit groans for all the city—ay,
For me and you alike. Ye rouse me not
From sleep, for, be assured, I have shed tears
Uncounted; many a path my mind has traced,
And that which I have found—one only means
To remedy our lot—that have I followed,
Sending Menoeceus' son, my brother Creon,
Unto Apollo's Pythian shrine to learn
What word or act of mine might save the state.
Already with the loitering length of days
Time tortures me in wonder how he fares.

For well beyond what old experience
Bids us expect he still is absent. When
He comes, I shall not then be derelict
In my fulfilment of god's whole behest.

Priest.

Timely thy word, O King, for these but now
Point me to where already Creon comes.

Oedipus.

O Lord Apollo, may he come endued
With bright good fortune, as his eye is bright.

Priest.

'Tis safe to hazard that his news is good:
Else not with fruited laurel were he decked.

Oedipus.

Soon shall we know for he can hear us now.
My lord and kinsman, son of Menoeceus,
What message dost thou bring us from the god?

(*Enter Creon.*)

Creon.

Good news, for I declare that even ills,
If they but end aright, may all be well.

Oedipus.

What news is this? For neither bold of heart
Nor fearful am I at thy present word.

Creon.

If thou wouldst hear in presence of these men
I am prepared to speak—or else within.

Oedipus.

Speak to them all. Heavier the grief I bear
For them than for my own heart's suffering.

Creon.

Speak then I will my message from the god.
Lord Phoebus bade us all outspokenly
Drive forth the pestilence that's bred within
Our land nor fatten it beyond control.

Oedipus.

And with what exorcism? What is the means?

Creon.

Exile or death, repaying ancient death.
For blood it is that overwhelms our state.

Oedipus.

Upon what man does god decree this chance?

Creon.

Laius, my lord, was one time sovereign here
Over our land, ere ever thou didst come.

Oedipus.

I know by hearsay, for I saw him not.

Creon.

And he being dead, comes clear god's high command
Forthwith to punish those his murderers.

Oedipus.

And they are where? Where shall be found the clue
Hard to unravel of such ancient crime?

Creon.

Within this land he said. That which is sought
Is found; the unconsidered vanishes.

Oedipus.

At home or in the country or abroad
Did Laius happen on his bloody fate?

Creon.

Faring upon a mission, as he said,
Laius returned no more from his emprise.

Oedipus.

No comrade of the road, no messenger
Beheld the deed that one might learn from him?

Creon.

Dead are they all save one who terrified
Fled with one word alone of all he saw.

Oedipus.

And what was that? One thing may lead to much
If we but gain some slight foothold of hope.

Creon.

Robbers he said encountered on the way,
Not one but many, killed him ruthlessly.

Oedipus.

How could a robber save by gold suborned
From Thebes, attain to such bold arrogance?

Creon.

Suspicion spake as much but, Laius dead,
No champion was there in our misery.

Oedipus.

What dread disaster could restrain the state
From learning all, its master so destroyed?

Creon.

The riddling Sphinx compelled us to resign
Mystery remote for questions close at hand.

Oedipus.

From the beginning then I'll prove it clear.
For just is Phoebus, rightly too thyself
Hast laid on me this duty to the dead.
So shalt thou find me rightly an ally
Unto this land obedient to the god.
For not alone as boon to distant friends
But for myself I'll scotch this pestilence.
Seeing that whoso slew him, he likewise
Fearing my venging hand, might slay me too.
Hence if I fail him not I benefit
Myself. Up then, my people, speedily
Stand from these altars, raise your suppliant staves.
Let someone gather here the citizens
Of Thebes, assured that I shall compass all
And we shall stand revealed all fortunate
Under god's guiding help—or fallen quite.

Priest.

My children, let us rise. It was for this
Which now he tells us that we gathered here
And so may Phoebus with his oracle
Be savior too and end the pestilence.

(*Exeunt. Enter Chorus of Theban Elders.*)

Strophe 1

Chorus.

O thou Word, sweet spoken, of Zeus
How shall I name thee?
Forth from the Pythian shrine
Gleaming with gold art come
Unto glorious Thebes.
And my quivering heart is taut and I shudder with fear,
Thou Delian God,
As low on my knees I pray.

Comes there a fate unknown
Or again with the circling years
Recurring woe?
Tell me, thou child of golden Hope, Word ever living.

Antistrophe 1

First to thee, o daughter of Zeus,
Deathless Athena,
Make I my suppliant prayer;
Artemis too I call
She who ranges the hills
And she sits on the throne high raised in the gathering place;
And Phoebus who shoots
Afar over earth his darts:
Threefold defenders, come
As of old at our city's need
Ye came to save,
Banishing far the flame of woe: come now to save us.

Strophe 2

Woe, woe is me, countless the pains I bear;
All that is mine is doomed:
No shaft of wit
Brings me deliverance;
No generations new
To cherish my fatherland
No more do the mothers of Thebes, bearing their sons
Suffer the pain and live,
But soul on soul, like birds, ye may see them fly
Swifter than fire
On to the distant strand, home of the western god.

Antistrophe 2

Beyond our ken, countless the city's dead;
Foul on the plain they lie
In cruel ranks;
Mothers bereft, gray haired,
In supplication bent
And wives by the altar side,
They groan for the ills that are ours: sorrows untold:
Paeans of woe that burst
From aged lips that moan for a city doomed.

Wherefore for these
Send us some bulwark fair, golden daughter of Zeus.

Strophe 3

Ares too, god of the raging death:
Helmet nor shield are his
But the flame and the shouting.
Back, turn him back, far from our fatherland,
Back on a favoring breeze
To Amphitrite's couch
Or the harbor welcomeless of the Thracian surge.
For now if the night leave aught
Day comes apace to consume.
O, father above, on him,
Lord of the lightning flash,
Hurl now thy thunderbolt.

Antistrophe 3

Lord of light, god of the golden bow
Scatter thy shafts untamed
To defend us, we pray thee.
Aye and the fire gleaming of Artemis
Which on the Lycian hills,
She flashes peak by peak;
And the golden mitered god of our native land
Whose face with the wine is red,
Bacchus, I call, with thy rout
Of maenads attended, come.
Come with the flaming torch,
Smite thou the god disowned.

(*Enter Oedipus.*)

Oedipus.

Ye pray, and what ye pray for—if straightway
Ye hearken to my words and give me aid
Against the pestilence—ye may attain:
Deliverance and surcease from your woes—
Words of a stranger to this history,
A stranger to the deed. Not far alone
Could I without a hint pursue the quest.

Wherefore, your latest citizen, do I
Make proclamation to the Cadmeian land:
Whoso of you knows by whose hand assailed
Laius the son of Labdacus was slain
I bid him tell me all. But if he fear
For his own self, then let him none the less
Denounce himself, for he shall suffer naught
Save banishment. So too if any man
Knows that the culprit came from other lands
Let him not hold his tongue, for whoso speaks
Reward is his and gratitude beside.
But if ye will not speak, if dumb with fear
Ye seek to shield or friend or self from harm
Then hearken to the purpose that is mine.
No man soever from this sovereign realm
Whose rule is mine, by shelter or by word
Shall aid the murderer, or e'er admit
His presence at the litany or shrine
Of sacrifice or at the lustral fire,
But thrust him from his home, knowing full well
He is the accursed thing as now the god
By Pythian oracle hath made us know.
So do I purpose to ally myself
With god and with the dead. Here I invoke
This curse upon the guilty one or all
Wretched to plumb the depths of misery.
Likewise upon myself if knowingly
I harbor in my house the murderer
I imprecate the curses I have named.
So upon each of you I lay a charge
To heed these words—for my sake and the god's
And for our city in its barrenness
Abandoned of the gods and perishing.
For even if it were not sent from heaven,
This plague upon us, yet, 'twere unthinkable
To leave still unavenged the death
Of one so noble and your king withal
Nor track it down. Now since I hold the power
That once was his, and am the heir as well
Of his own marriage couch, possess the wife
That lay with him and would have borne to us
A common offspring had not fate ill timed,

Striking him down, forbidden, I pronounce
Myself his champion, even as his son,
And I shall leave no single thing untried
To find and seize that man who put to death
The son of Labdacus, heir to the line
Of Polydorus and of Cadmus too,
Ancient Agenor's latest progeny.
Meantime for such as see not eye to eye
With this my purpose, I invoke the gods
To grant them harvest neither in their fields
Nor in their homes, but with this pestilence
Or some more terrible, to end their line.
But citizens of this Cadmeian realm
That hearken to my words, on them I pray
May Justice smile forever and the gods.

Chorus.

O King, upon my oath as thou dost ask
I speak: I did not kill the man, nor know
The murderer. To say who did the deed
Was Phoebus' task who laid on us the quest.

Oedipus.

Right is thy judgment, but to force the gods
Unwilling, that may no man undertake.

Chorus.

Fain would I say what seemeth second best.

Oedipus.

If there be yet a third best, speak it out.

Chorus.

After lord Phoebus he who seeth most
In harmony, our lord Teiresias,
Might best reward our present questioning.

Oedipus.

Nor has this thought escaped me. I have sent
At Creon's bidding twice to summon him,
Nor understand why he came not long since.

Chorus.

All other hints were vague and ancient tales.

Oedipus.

What hints then are there? I would know each word.

Chorus.

'Twas said some travelers had murdered him.

Oedipus.

So have I heard, but none saw him who saw.

Chorus.

Nor if he knows what fear is will he stay
When he has heard thy curses now invoked.

Oedipus.

Words may not frighten him who fears no deed.

Chorus.

But lo he comes who shall convict the man.
For these are bringing now the godlike seer
In whom alone of men is born the truth.

(*Enter Teiresias, led by a boy.*)

Oedipus.

Teiresias, whose mind doth ponder all
Things known and things unspeakable on earth
And in the heavens above, though seeing naught
Thou knowest in what plight our city stands
Wherefrom, my lord, we find in thee alone
Our sole deliverer. For Phoebus' word
(Perchance thou hast not heard from messengers)
Comes back in answer to our questionings
Telling of one release from pestilence
And only one, if we by searching out
Should find and slay forthwith the murderers
Of Laius or should drive them from our land.
Wherefore begrudge us not thy counseling
Whether from augury or from the lore
Of other ways prophetic thou knowest aught.
But save alike thyself, the city, me,
And fend from all the taint of murder done.
For we are in thy hands: man's noblest toil
Is helping others to the uttermost.

Teiresias.

Alas, alas, how frightful to be wise
Where wisdom brings no gain. I knew this well
But had forgotten. Else had I never come.

Oedipus.

What sayest thou? How downcast art arrived.

Teiresias.

Release me to my home. Most easily
Shall we two bear our fates, if thou consent.

Oedipus.

Strange are thy words nor friendly to the state
That gives thee sustenance, if thou speak not.

Teiresias.

Not so: for thine own words as I perceive
Come not in season. Be not mine the same.

Oedipus.

By all the gods I beg thee, leave us not,
If thou knowest aught, me and these suppliants.

Teiresias.

Aye for ye all are ignorant. Mine own
Misfortunes shall I hide, to speak not thine.

Oedipus.

What is this word? Thou knowest and wilt not speak
But wouldst betray thy city unto death?

Teiresias.

Neither myself nor thee shall I distress.
Why ask in vain? Thou shalt not learn from me

Oedipus.

Basest of all base men, that wouldst enrage
The hardest rock, wilt never speak, but still
Present thyself unmoved in stubborness?

Teiresias.

My wrath thou blamest but thine own so near
Thou seest not, and yet upbraidest me.

Oedipus.

Who would not rage to hear such words as thine
Wherewith even now thou dost outrage the state?

Teiresias.

'Twill come though by my silence hidden deep.

Oedipus.

Then what will come thou too must speak to me.

Teiresias.

I'll speak no further; wherefore if thou wilt,
Vent to the full thy wildest storm of rage.

Oedipus.

Truly I'll leave unsaid no single word
Of all I think. Such is my rage. Know then
What I believe: that thou didst plot this deed.

Performed it too save only that thy hands
Wrought not the act. And hadst thou now thy sight
I'd say the murder too was all thine own.

Teiresias.

Is't true? I charge thee then from thy decree
Swerve not, nor from this day forevermore
Speak unto these or me: thou art the man
That bringest on this land the curse of guilt.

Oedipus.

Thus shameless wouldst thou speak and still expect
Somewhere to find a refuge from thy fate?

Teiresias.

Safety is mine. I speak the all powerful truth.

Oedipus.

Who taught thee then? 'Twas not thy priestly art.

Teiresias.

I learned of thee, that forced my unwilling speech.

Oedipus.

What speech? Lest I should err, speak it once more.

Teiresias.

Hast thou not known or wouldst thou spread a net?

Oedipus.

Unknowable it seems—speak it again.

Teiresias.

I say thou art the slayer that thou wouldst find.

Oedipus.

Not to thy joy hast spoken twice such words.

Teiresias.

Shall I say more then that shall irk thee more?

Oedipus.

Say what thou wilt, for thou shalt say in vain.

Teiresias.

I say that thou hast lived most shamefully
Unwitting with thy kin, nor knowest thy plight.

Oedipus.

Does think unharmed still to repeat such things?

Teiresias.

Aye, if there be in truth protecting strength.

Oedipus.

There is, for all save thee—but not for thee
For thou art blind in ear and mind and eye.

Teiresias.

These jeerings prove thee wretched for e'er long
Each man of these shall hurl them back at thee.

Oedipus.

Thou dwellest in continuous night, nor canst
Hurt me or any man that sees the day.

Teiresias.

'Tis not thy fate to fall by hand of mine.
Apollo shall suffice, the charge is his.

Oedipus.

Was't Creon's thought or thine this treachery?

Teiresias.

Creon ne'er did thee harm but thou thyself.

Oedipus.

O Wealth and Power and Craft outreaching craft
Throughout our jealous life. What envious thrust
Can we be safe from if for this throne's sake
Whereof by gift I ne'er solicited
Thebes made me master, if for this my lord
Creon the faithful, friend since first I came,
Secretly plotting seeks to thrust me forth,
Suborning for his end this muddling priest
That knows the wiles of wealth, sees faultlessly
Where gain is for the getting, yet straightway
Sought for his priestcraft stumbles and is blind.
For tell me when hast thou shown prophecy?
Why when the riddling bitch bedeviled us
Didst thou not speak some safety to the state?
'Twas hardly for a chance arrival then
To spell that riddle, prophecy forsooth
Was needed then. Yet from thy twittering birds
Thou spakest naught, nor knewest aught from god.
'Twas I who came, I, Oedipus, that had
No knowledge of it all, and yet prevailed
By simple wisdom with no lore of birds.
Whom thou wouldst exile in the expectancy
Of high position close to Creon's throne.
Sorrow shall be the harvest—thine and his—
Of this prophetic sowing. Wert not old
Such thought as thine should bring thee violence.

Chorus.

Oedipus, both his words and thine appear
Spoken in anger, so at least I judge.
Such words we need not: be it our concern
How best we may fulfill god's oracle.

Teiresias.

Tyrant thou art—yet cannot so refuse
The right to answer. That much lies within
My power. No slave am I to thee or any man
Beside—only to Loxias. Wherefore
Write me not down to Creon's patronage.
Thou chidest me with blindness. Hear me say
That eyes thou hast but seest not thy plight,
Not even where thou livest nor with whom.
Dost know from whom thou'rt born? Nay, ignorant,
Thou hast made thyself the foe of thine own kin
That dwell with Hades or yet tread the earth.
Thee shall thy mother's curse, thy father's too,
Swift footed, two edged, drive from out this land
With eyes that see now, seeing then no more.
What refuge there that shall not echo back
Thy piteous cry—what haunt of desolate
Cithaeron—when thou seest the anchorage
Whither on favoring breeze, into this home
Thou hast sailed in to shipwreck. Other ills
Countless (thou seest them not) shall level thee
With thine own self and thy begotten seed.
Revile thou as thou wilt the word I speak
And Creon too, for in the whole wide world
No man shall be so smitten as thyself.

Oedipus.

Can such things then be borne from such as he?
Begone to thy perdition—get thee gone—
Out of this house—begone I say, begone.

Teiresias.

I had not come hadst thou not summoned me.

Oedipus.

I knew thee not, that thou wouldst speak the fool
Or I had never brought thee to my house.

Teiresias.

I am but as I am—to thee a fool,
Yet wise indeed to those that gave thee birth.

Oedipus.

Who? Stay. Canst say who 'twas that gave me birth?

Teiresias.

This day shall give thee birth and give thee death.

Oedipus.

Forever riddles, riddles, dost thou speak.

Teiresias.

And art not thou the best to answer these?

Oedipus.

Chide me with that. Thou'lt find me fortunate.

Teiresias.

That was the fortune that hath ruined thee.

Oedipus.

I care not if the city so be saved.

Teiresias.

Then do I go—come boy and lead me home.

Oedipus.

Aye, let him lead thee, lingering here thou art
A nuisance, 'twere relief to have thee gone.

Teiresias.

I go for I have spoken that for which
I came, nor feared thy face; thou hast no power
Over my lips. But hark to what I say.
He whom thou seekest issuing thy threats
And heralding the death of Laius—he
Dwells here within—an alien visitor—
So is the tale—but shall appear at last
Native born Theban—yet no joy be his
At that discovery. For blind where once
He saw, a rich man beggared, he shall go
Forth to a foreign land feeling his way
With helpless staff, proving at last to be
Brother and sire to his own progeny.
And unto her that bore him in the womb
Both son and husband, to his aged sire
Betrayer first and then his murderer.
Go thou within and on these prophecies
Think well—if in one single circumstance
Thou find me false, denounce my prophet's role.

(*Exeunt Teiresias and Oedipus separately.*)

Strophe 1

Chorus.

Voice, god-sent from Delphi's rock,
Whose was the deed
Ill-wrought with blood-stained hands
Unspeakable? To lands
Afar with the speed wind-swift of the winged steed
Now must he take his flight nor longer mock
The embattled son of Zeus that leaps
Swift following
With the brandished flame that never sleeps
And Fate insatiate unpitying.

Antistrophe 1

Flashing from Parnassus' peaks
Gleaming with snow
Behest imperative
To find the fugitive
That far through the trackless wood and the caves below
Wanders alone distraught and ever seeks
To avert the doom whose heartless Fate
Relentlessly
From Apollo's shrine immaculate
Pursuing shapes unmoved his destiny.

Strophe 2

Dread is the word, dread is the augury
And the truth who knows?
Words have I none: fluttering hopes I see
And anon fear in their place. For the morrow shows
Darkness deep as today.
What old grief can I say
Breeding hate of our royal line
Now might sully the fame long won
By Polybus' son
Or fasten on him the doom of the word divine.

Antistrophe 2

Zeus knoweth all, Zeus and the Delphian lord
With all-seeing eye.
Yea, but of man, priests with prophetic word
Why unto them yield we credulity?
Though in wisdom of mind
Man may humble mankind,
Never shall I till the truth be clear
Grant his guilt who released our state
From ruinous Fate
Outwitted the riddling monster and banished fear.

(*Enter Creon.*)

Creon.

My fellow citizens, I am informed
That Oedipus the King hath uttered here
Grave charges against me. And so I come
Resentful, seeing that in our present plight
If he believe that aught in word or deed
From me hath injured him, I have no will
Under suspicion to prolong my life.
Not simple is the harm that such a charge
Does me but manifold if I am thought
False to my city and to you, my friends.

Chorus.

Such was the charge he made perchance
Not in cool wisdom but in bitter wrath.

Creon.

And said he also that by my advice
The seer put forth his lying prophecies?

Chorus.

So spake he but with what intent, who knows?

Creon.

But with a mind unclouded and clear eye
Brought he this charge against me? Tell me that.

Chorus.

I know not. For I am not wont to see
What kings perform. But look, he comes himself.

(*Enter Oedipus.*)

Oedipus.

Thou? Thou? How art thou come? Such brazen front
Of daring hast thou as to approach my house,
The murderer proven of this man and now
Usurper manifest of this my throne?
Come tell me by the gods, was't cowardice
Or folly seen in me that tempted thee
To such a plotting or didst think the act
Would not betray thy stealthy treachery
Or even perchance that I might wittingly
Ignore it? Is it not a fool's attempt
With neither force nor friends to seek a throne
That only numbers and great wealth can win?

Creon.

Knowest then what must be? Hearken thou shalt
To answering words: and so with knowledge judge.

Oedipus.

Trickster with words I know thee—yet am I
Not quickly taught, knowing thy deadly hate.

Creon.

First hear from me one word that I shall speak.

Oedipus.

So be thou'lt not assert thou art not base.

Creon.

And thou conceive some gain in stubbornness
Unyoked with wisdom, then thou art not wise.

Oedipus.

And thou conceive escape from punishment,
Doing a kinsman ill, thou art not wise.

Creon.

Therein thou speakest true, I grant it thee;
Yet show what wrong from me thou hast endured.

Oedipus.

Didst thou advise or not that I must send
To fetch forthwith this prophesying priest?

Creon.

Aye and now too approve such policy.

Oedipus.

How long ago was it that Laius hence—

Creon.

Did what? I follow not thy questioning.

Oedipus.
Was spirited by fatal violence?

Creon.
Long span of years must fill that reckoning.

Oedipus.
And was this priest a priest in those days too?

Creon.
As wise as now and honored equally.

Oedipus.
Made he then any mention of my name?

Creon.
He did not—or at least when I was nigh.

Oedipus.
And of the murdered king—made ye no search?

Creon.
Assuredly we searched but learned no clue.

Oedipus.
Why then did not this wise man speak these things?

Creon.
I know not; knowing not I hold my tongue.

Oedipus.
This much thou knowest and wouldst be wise to speak.

Creon.
What thing? For if I know it, I'll not deny.

Oedipus.
That had Teiresias not conferred with thee
He had not named me Laius' murderer.

Creon.
If he says so, thou knowest. I too have right
To question thee as thou hast questioned me.

Oedipus.
Ask what thou wilt: thou shalt not prove my guilt.

Creon.
How then, hast thou my sister for thy wife?

Oedipus.
That question surely may not be denied.

Creon.
And dost thou rule on equal terms with her?

Oedipus.
All that her heart desires she has from me.

Creon.
And am I not a third with equal power?

Oedipus.

Thou art in truth and so art proven base.

Creon.

Nay, if thou usest reason with thyself
Consider first: would any choose to rule
Encompassed round with terror if the same
Authority might rest in perfect peace?
For I at any rate have never sought
To be a king rather than have the right
Of kingly powers—nor any man of sense.
And now from thee with naught to terrify
I have all favor; ruled I here alone
Much must I do perforce against my will.
How then should any crown appear to me
Sweeter than royal privilege secure?
Not yet am I so foolish as to seek
For other goal than honor linked with gain.
Now all men greet me, all men wish me well
And those that would reach thee, bespeak my ear
Since there alone lies prospect of success.
Why then should I abandoning the sure
Advantage that is mine, seek other where?
No mind that harbors wisdom can be false.
And I have neither loved folly myself
Nor could I join another in such act.
Wherefore send now to Pytho for the proof
Of these my words: find out the oracle:
Ask if I told it true. And furthermore
If thou canst prove that with Teiresias
I ever have connived, then not with one
But with a twofold vote, thine own and mine,
Take me and slay me. Only charge me not
In secret with dark counsels. Justice ne'er
Lightly deems bad men good or good men bad.
To cast away a faithful friend I deem
No wiser than to fling aside one's life.
This truth in time thou'lt learn, since time alone
Reveals the just. A single passing day
Amply suffices to disclose the base.

Chorus.

Wise words, my lord, for one that would not slip;
The swift in counsel rarely counsel best.

Oedipus.

When he who plots in secret moves apace
I too must counsel swiftly. Else my ends,
The while I linger sleeping foolishly,
Are lost forever, his forever gained.

Creon.

What wilt thou then? Wouldst drive me from the land?

Oedipus.

That least of all: my will is death not flight,
Proclaiming to the world base envy's power.

Creon.

These are the words of stubborn unbelief.

Oedipus.

Thou hast not acted to inspire belief.

Creon.

Thou seemst not sane.

Oedipus.

Yet am in my affairs.

Creon.

Thou shouldst be so in mine.

Oedipus.

But thou art base.

Creon.

What if thou knowest naught?

Oedipus.

Yet must I rule.

Creon.

Not if thy rule be wrong.

Oedipus.

O city mine!

Creon.

Not thine alone—for Thebes is mine as well.

Chorus.

Desist, my lords. Most happily for you
I see Jocasta coming from the house.
Her help should end this present quarreling.

(*Enter Jocasta.*)

Jocasta.

What foolish strife of words, all ill-advised,
Is this ye raise? Are ye not then ashamed,
Your country perishing, to air abroad

Your private wrongs? Nay, rather come within
Nor magnify your petty difference.

Creon.

Nay sister, for thy husband Oedipus
Makes twofold threat against me—either death
By violence or exile from this land.

Oedipus.

'Tis so for, woman, with base treachery
I caught him plotting ill against my life.

Creon.

Never may joy be mine but death accursed
If I am guilty of thy lightest charge.

Jocasta.

Now by the gods believe him, Oedipus,
For his oath's sake that he has sworn and for
My sake as well and these that stand by thee.

Chorus.

Yield thee, my King, hearken I pray.

Oedipus.

What is thy will?

Chorus.

Grant him belief, wise hitherto, pledging his oath.

Oedipus.

Knowest thou what thou wilt?

Chorus.

Aye.

Oedipus.

Then declare it me.

Chorus.

Never should friend by friend, sworn under oath,
Lightly be thrust aside.

Oedipus.

Know then assuredly asking of me this boon
Exile for me or death
Follows thy prayer.

Chorus.

Nay by the god of light
By Helios' self, first of the gods above,
May I in misery
Friendless of god and man
Wretchedly die,
If in my inmost breast lurks such desire.

Yearns now my sorrowing heart
Torn by my country's plight
Mocked by thy strife.

Oedipus.

Let him then go, even though it mean my death
Or if dishonored into banishment
I must depart. Thy words, not his, prevail.
For him where'er he be my hate pursues.

Creon.

Grudging is thy surrender, arrogant
Thy wrath. Natures like thine by Fate's decree
Are ever to themselves hardest to bear.

Oedipus.

Wilt thou not leave me and begone?

Creon.

I go.
Thou canst not comprehend—these know me just.

(*Exit Creon.*)

Chorus.

Why, o my Queen, why dost delay?
Lead him within.

Jocasta.

First I must know what hath entailed strife such as this.

Chorus.

Groundless suspicion here: rankling injustice there.

Jocasta.

Nurtured by both?

Chorus.

Aye.

Jocasta.

And the cause?

Chorus.

More than enough to me
Seems now the harm that's done, while yet my country bleeds.

Oedipus.

Seest thou then thy zeal
Whither it leads?

Chorus.

Not only once, my King—
I say again, fool should I be and worse
Witless and reft of sense
Should I be false to thee
Thou that didst come
Bringing new life to me, saving the state
Tossed on a raging sea
Aye and again to be
Savior and guide.

Jocasta.

Tell me, my lord, I charge thee by the gods,
Whence came to thee this wrath unquenchable?

Oedipus.

Thee will I tell—I love thee more than these—
'Twas Creon and his plots against my life.

Jocasta.

Speak plainly if indeed thou hast plain cause.

Oedipus.

He plainly names me Laius' murderer.

Jocasta.

Speaking his own words or some other man's?

Oedipus.

Making a bastard priest spokesman for him
To keep unsoiled his own lips, craftily.

Jocasta.

Then think no more of it—hearken to me
And know that never yet hath mortal man
Shared in prophetic art. I'll show to thee
Sure proof of these my words. There came of old
A prophecy to Laius, I say not
From Phoebus' self but from his ministers,
How death should come to him by his son's hand
That should be born to Laius and to me.
Yet—so the rumor hath it—Laius died
Murdered by robbers—strangers—where forsooth
The triple crossroads meet. That child of ours
Not three days old, its ankles bound with thongs,
By others' hands, Laius had left exposed
Far on the trackless hillside. So, I ween,

Apollo did not make of that poor child
His father's murderer nor did fulfill
The fears of Laius that his fate should come
At his child's hand. So did the words of priests
Foretell. Give them no heed. For what god needs
He can himself most easily disclose.

Oedipus.

What restless thoughts of terror, o my wife
Hast thou engendered in my troubled mind?

Jocasta.

What hath disturbed thee that thou speakest so?

Oedipus.

Methought I heard thee say that Laius' death
O'ertook him where the triple crossroads meet.

Jocasta.

So ran the story and hath never ceased.

Oedipus.

Where is the spot that saw the murder done?

Jocasta.

Phocis the land is called—a branching road
Leads there from Delphi and from Daulia.

Oedipus.

How long the time from that event till now?

Jocasta.

'Twas just before thy coming that the word
Was brought to us—ere thou wast King of Thebes.

Oedipus.

O Zeus, what is thy will to do with me?

Jocasta.

Why, Oedipus, should this so trouble thee?

Oedipus.

Ask me not yet—but tell me this instead.
Laius, what was his form, what years were his?

Jocasta.

His stature tall, silver just streaked his hair,
And in appearance not unlike to thee.

Oedipus.

Woe, woe, is me: it seems that I have hurled,
Unwitting, dreadful curses on myself.

Jocasta.

How sayest; my lord, I tremble at thy word.

Oedipus.

I fear in truth Teiresias still hath sight.
But thou mayst show. Tell me this one thing more.

Jocasta.

I tremble, yet I'll answer and thou wilt.

Oedipus.

Did Laius go alone, or like a king,
Surrounded by his spearmen royally?

Jocasta.

Five men in all, a herald one, the King
Rode in his chariot, the rest afoot.

Oedipus.

Alas, 'tis all too clear. Who was the man
That here returning made report to thee?

Jocasta.

A servant that escaped, alone of all.

Oedipus.

And now perchance is in the palace here?

Jocasta.

Not so, for when he came to Thebes and found
Thee on the throne, with Laius dead, he pled,
Seizing my hand, to be dispatched far hence
Into the fields, the pastures of our flocks,
That so he might not see the city more.
And I consented. Faithful service given
Deserved such favor, aye and greater too.

Oedipus.

Might someone bring him here without delay?

Jocasta.

'Tis possible. Why dost thou wish it so?

Oedipus.

I fear that I have spoken overmuch.
And for this reason I would see the man.

Jocasta.

The man shall come anon, yet o my lord,
I too deserve to know what troubles thee.

Oedipus.

Nor shalt thou be denied when such dread fear
Possesses me. For whither should I turn
If not to thee, fast in misfortune's clutch?
My father was King Polybus, the lord
Of Corinth, and my mother Merope.

Dorian she. And I was held the first
Of all the citizens, till there befell
A chance surprising yet not meriting
My great concern thereat. A banqueter
Befuddled with much wine, hurled in my face
The taunt that I was not my father's son.
Much angered, for that day I held my peace
Though hardly: on the next I questioned straight
My parents both who flamed with instant wrath
At him who spake the insult. From their scorn
I took some comfort, but anon the taunt
Rankled unceasing, while the rumor spread.
Wherefore without their knowledge I betook
Myself to Pytho. Whence, touching the quest
That brought me thither, Phoebus caring naught
Sent me away unanswered, yet himself
Vouchsafing other knowledge, bade me know
Dread horror past believing: 'twas my fate
By wedlock with my mother to beget
Offspring abhorrent in the eyes of all
Mankind and be besides the murderer
Of mine own father. When I heard these words
Guided by heaven's stars I fled apace
Corinth and all her land that so I might
Escape fulfilment of the oracle.
Making my way I came unto the spot
Where thou dost say this King of thine was slain.
The truth I'll tell thee, for thou art my wife:
Nearing this triple crossways as I went,
A herald met me and a traveler
Drawn in a carriage, as thou saidst, by colts.
Straightway the herald and the old man too
Were both for pushing me aside. I struck
In righteous anger at the charioteer
Who jostled me; the old man when he saw,
Watching the moment when I passed him close,
Reached from the car and with his two-pronged goad
Smote me upon the head. Unequally
He paid that debt, for with quick reckoning
Struck by the staff in this my hand, he plunged
Headlong from out the chariot. All the rest
I killed, forthwith. Now if there chanced to be

Twixt Laius and this stranger any bond
Of kinship who in all this wretched world
More wretched than myself? What man more cursed:
Whom not a soul may welcome in the home,
Stranger nor friend, nor speak a word to me
But all must thrust me out. No other man
Invoked this curse but I myself decreed
Such things against myself. The dead man's couch
I have polluted with the self-same hands
That slew him. Am I cursed in very truth?
Am I not all unholy? I must flee
And fleeing may not look upon my own
Nor tread the pathways of my fatherland,
Fearing that Fate foretold, that I should wed
My mother and become the murderer
Of Polybus my father who begat
And reared me. Surely one may well believe
'Tis from some cruel god that on my head
Such fate hath fallen. Never, o gods above
August and holy, never may I see
That day. Rather from sight of all mankind
May I be hidden far, nor e'er behold
The stain of such a doom clinging to me.

Chorus.

Dreadful to me, my lord, these things, yet till
Thou hearest from that witness, nurse thy hope.

Oedipus.

So much of hope is all that's left me now:
To await the herdsman and to hear his tale.

Jocasta.

And when he comes, what wouldst thou hear from him?

Oedipus.

I'll tell thee: if his story still remain
Consistent with thine own, then I am cleared.

Jocasta.

What word of mine hath so impressed thee then?

Oedipus.

By thine account he said in telling thee
Robbers killed Laius. If he still persist
Nor change the number, then I killed him not.

For one and many tally not; but if
He now maintain 'twas but a single man
Surely the deed can only be mine own.

Jocasta.

Nay but he told it so, be well assured,
Nor can deny it now, the city heard,
Not I alone. And if he now deny
Or change his story, he can never prove
That Laius' murder came as prophesied.
Since Loxias said that by his own son's hand
Laius must die. And surely 'twas not he,
That wretched child, that slew him. Nay, himself
Did perish long before. Wherefore henceforth
I'll look not here nor there for oracles.

Oedipus.

Just is thy reasoning. Yet do not fail
To give thine orders that the peasant come.

Jocasta.

I'll send in haste, but let us go within—
Naught would I do that fits not with thy will.

(*Exeunt Oedipus and Jocasta.*)

Strophe 1

Chorus.

Come whensoe'er it will may Fate o'ertake me still
Guarding each word and act with reverent awe
For swift are the laws of Fate
That have fared from heaven's gate
And god on Olympus' height hath made each law.
No mortal brought them forth, no lethal breath
Awaits them: hall-marked with divinity they know not death.

Antistrophe 1

But arrogance breeds force, swift on its course
When glutted full, proud arrogance climbs high,
Snatches the cornice—then, clutching foothold in vain
Plunges, far down on heartless crags to lie.
But the strife that leads to good I shall ever ask,
And to god who rules on high perform my task.

Strophe 2

Whosoe'er in word or deed
Acts with arrogance
Whoso will not justice heed,
Godward looks askance,
Him may justice overtake
Him may Fate unhappy shake
If he get not gain with praise
If he keep not all his ways
Pure from stain of guilt.
Else why this offering here of love,
This worship of dance to the gods above?

Antistrophe 2

Never again to Delphi's shrine
Shall I go with heart's desire,
Never again to Abbae's pine
Nor Olympus' altar fire,
If there be not here
Such music clear
As proveth divinity.
But o thou god if thou hearest aught,
Thou Zeus that rulest on high,
May our impious acts with evil wrought
Scape not thy watchful eye.
For the prophet's word
By our dead King heard,
With holy horror fraught,
Has vanished like air
And Apollo's care,
Is held as naught.

(*Enter Jocasta, bearing garlands.*)

Jocasta.

Lords of this land, my purpose is resolved
To visit now the temples of the gods
Bearing this wreath and gifts for sacrifice.
For Oedipus' emotions run too high
Beneath his sufferings. Not like a man
Of wisdom doth he judge these new events
By what is old, yielding to each new voice

So be it speak of terrors. Therefore, since
My counseling is vain, to thee I come,
Lycian lord Apollo, suppliant,
(For thou art nearest) to petition thee:
Grant us release without defilement: now
Terror possesses us as who behold
Smitten with fear the captain of their ship.

(*Enter a Messenger.*)

Messenger.

Strangers I fain would learn from you where dwells
King Oedipus—or better, where is he?

Chorus.

Here stands his palace and himself within.
This is his wife, the mother of his brood.

Messenger.

Happy be she forever, may she dwell
Always in happiness, being his Queen.

Jocasta.

Blessed be thy lot too whoe'er thou art
For so thy words deserve. But speak: wherefore
Dost thou now come: what news wouldst thou impart?

Messenger.

Good news unto this house and to the King.

Jocasta.

What is it and from whom thine embassy?

Messenger.

From Corinth, and the word that I shall speak
Shall bring thee happiness, and grief as well.

Jocasta.

What word is that that hath such twofold power?

Messenger.

The dwellers of the Isthmian land will make
Him King of Corinth, so the rumor ran.

Jocasta.

How so? Is not old Polybus their king?

Messenger.

Nay, for Death holds him fast within the tomb.

Jocasta.

How sayest thou? Is Polybus then dead?

Messenger.

If I speak not the truth then let me die.

Jocasta.

Maiden, run swift and tell thy master this.
Where are ye then, ye oracles of god?
This was the man that, long since, Oedipus
Feared and avoided lest he be constrained
To murder him, and now the self-same King
Lies dead, outdone by Fate and not by him.

(*Enter Oedipus.*)

Oedipus.

O dearest wife, Jocasta, why, I pray
Hast thou now summoned me from out the house?

Jocasta.

Hearken to this man's word, then judge thyself
The outcome of the dreaded oracles.

Oedipus.

Who is the man? What would he say to me?

Jocasta.

Coming from Corinth he brings messages
Of Polybus thy father, and his death.

Oedipus.

How sayest thou stranger, speak now for thyself.

Messenger.

If this must be my first report then know
That he has gone indeed the way of Death.

Oedipus.

By violence, or died he by disease?

Messenger.

Slight matters turn the scale when one is old.

Oedipus.

Illness it was then that brought him low.

Messenger.

Aye, and the long long tale of passing years.

Oedipus.

Alas, alas, why therefore O my wife
Should one look ever to the Pythian shrine
Or hearken to the cry of birds? 'Twas they
That would have made me murderer of him
My father, yet it seems he now is dead
While here I stand unarmed and innocent—

Unless he died of longing for his son:
So only could one blame me. And in truth
Polybus lies in Hades and hath swept
With him the oracles and proved them naught.

Jocasta.

And said I not long since it would be so?

Oedipus.

Thou didst, and yet by fear I was misled.

Jocasta.

Now therefore give them not a single thought.

Oedipus.

Surely I still must fear my mother's couch.

Jocasta.

What fear should be for mortal man whose life
Fate rules supreme, nor can he aught foresee?
Better to live by chance as best ye may.
Nor shouldst thou fear this wedlock horrible
With thine own mother: many men there be
That in their dreams have done this act. He best
Supports his life who counts these things as naught.

Oedipus.

Well spoken were thy words save that she lives
Who bore me: since she lives she still compels
Terror in me, fair though thy counselings.

Jocasta.

And yet thy father's death should give thee pause.

Oedipus.

'Tis true I grant thee, but my mother lives.

Messenger.

What woman is it whom thou fearest so?

Oedipus.

Merope, who was wife to Polybus.

Messenger.

And what the fear that she inspires in thee?

Oedipus.

An oracle that came, stranger, from god.

Messenger.

Mayst tell it, or must others know it not?

Oedipus.

Truly I may. Loxias spoke of old
How I must marry with my mother, then
Shed with these hands of mine, my father's blood.

Corinth and I have therefore been long since
Strangers and happily too save that it's sweet
To look on those who brought us to the light.

Messenger.

Such was the fear that wrought thy banishment?

Oedipus.

Aye, that I might not work my father's death.

Messenger.

How then have I not freed thee from thy fear
Coming, my lord, with welcome messages?

Oedipus.

And truly thou shalt have thy just reward.

Messenger.

I will confess that was my secret hope
That I might profit by thy coming home.

Oedipus.

Home will I never come while she yet lives.

Messenger.

My son, 'tis clear thou knowest not what thou dost.

Oedipus.

How so, old man? Tell me now by the gods.

Messenger.

If for this cause thou wilt not now return.

Oedipus.

'Tis cause enough, lest Phoebus prove his word.

Messenger.

And from thy parents thou incur some guilt?

Oedipus.

Just so, for that shall always be my fear.

Messenger.

Dost know, then, that thy fears are all for naught?

Oedipus.

How can that be and I a child of theirs?

Messenger.

For Polybus was never kin of thine.

Oedipus.

What sayest thou? Polybus not my sire?

Messenger.

No more than I myself, as much, no more.

Oedipus.

Why match thyself with him who caused my birth?

Messenger.
Nay, he begat thee not, nor he nor I.

Oedipus.
Wherefore if this be so, called he me son?

Messenger.
Delivered by these hands, a gift thou wert.

Oedipus.
And could he love me so when gotten thus?

Messenger.
He could by virtue of long childlessness.

Oedipus.
Thou, hadst thou bought me or didst find this gift?

Messenger.
I found thee in Cithaeron's wooded glades.

Oedipus.
Purposing what didst wander to this land?

Messenger.
In charge of flocks that ranged these mountainsides.

Oedipus.
Thou wert a shepherd and a hireling then?

Messenger.
My son, I was thy savior in those days.

Oedipus.
How so, what suffering didst thou save me from?

Messenger.
Whereof thine ankles give thee evidence.

Oedipus.
Alas, why call to mind that ancient woe?

Messenger.
I loosed thine ankles fastened with a thong.

Oedipus.
An outrage from my days in swaddling clothes.

Messenger.
And from that outrage thou hast still thy name.

Oedipus.
Speak, by the gods; was that a parent's deed?

Messenger.
I know not, he knows best that gave thee me.

Oedipus.
Thou didst not find me? I was given thee?

Messenger.

Another shepherd placed thee in my hands.

Oedipus.

What man is that? Dost know? Canst point him out?

Messenger.

'Twas one of Laius' shepherds, so 'twas said.

Oedipus.

His who was King in Thebes in days gone by?

Messenger.

Aye his indeed, a herdsman of that King.

Oedipus.

Lives the man still that I might look on him?

Messenger.

Ye men of Thebes should know that best of all.

Oedipus.

Knows any man of you of whom he speaks
Or have ye seen this shepherd in the town
Or on the upland pastures? Let such speak.
The time is come that these things be revealed.

Chorus.

Methinks it is no other than the man
Thou hast desired to see. Jocasta now
Surely might best reveal to thee the truth.

Oedipus.

O wife and Queen, knowest thou whom but now
We summoned hither? Speaks he of the same?

Jocasta.

What matters whom he mentioned? Give no thought
To what he said, for all such thoughts are vain.

Oedipus.

It may not be. With such proofs in my grasp
I must discover now my lineage.

Jocasta.

No by the gods, if thou hast any care
For thine own life, ask not. My woe's enough.

Oedipus.

Fear not, for though from triple servitude
I find my line thou shalt not so be base.

Jocasta.

Believe me none the less: touch not this thing.

Oedipus.

I may not so believe thee, I must learn.

Jocasta.

For thine own sake I speak and counsel well.

Oedipus.

These counselings have long since vexed my soul.

Jocasta.

O hapless man, god grant thee ignorance.

Oedipus.

Let someone bring this shepherd to me straight:
This woman, let her boast her royal line.

Jocasta.

Alas, most wretched man; for this one word
I speak thee now, none else forevermore.

(*Exit Jocasta.*)

Chorus.

Why has she gone, thy Queen, o Oedipus,
In frenzied grief? I fear that from this deep
Silence of hers misfortune shall break forth.

Oedipus.

Let come what will. Low though my lineage
Be proven, yet I'll know it. She perchance
Womanlike in her pride may fear in shame
To face mine origin. I hold myself
Own child of Fortune; she beneficent
Shall never cause me shame. Her child am I
Brother of all the months whose passing course
Made me now small now great and being such
In parentage pray god I never prove
False to that mother Fortune nor desert
The search that shall yet prove my lineage.

Strophe

Chorus.

Now by Olympus high
If aught of prophecy
Or wisdom lie
Within this breast
Tomorrow's moon shall see
Our Oedipus stand confessed
Thy countryman, Cithaeron, and thy son,
This dance a duty done
In loyalty.
Lord god, Apollo, let these our deeds be blessed.

Antistrophe

Whose was the goddess' womb
That unto Pan bore thee
    Through wooded coomb
    And grass grown run
Pursued relentlessly?
    Or art thou Apollo's son?
For dear to him is every upland way.
    Or Hermes'—who shall say?
        Or was it he
Great Bacchus loved of the nymphs on Helicon?

(*Enter a Herdsman.*)

Oedipus.

Sir, if I too who never met the man,
May yet venture a guess, yonder, methinks
I see the herdsman whom we seek. In years
He matches well this stranger and besides
Servants they are of mine conducting him.
Yet better is thy knowledge than mine own
Since thou hast seen the fellow ere today.

Chorus.

I know him, have no doubt, of Laius' men
Shepherd of all most faithful to the King.

Oedipus.

Thee first I question; didst thou mean this man,
Stranger from Corinth?

Messenger.

Aye, the man thou seest.

Oedipus.

Thou too old man, look hither, answer me
My question: wast thou ever Laius' man?

Herdsman.

I was, a house born slave, no market prize.

Oedipus.

What task was thine? How didst thou spend thy life?

Herdsman.

The larger part in following the herds.

Oedipus.

What were the regions thou didst most frequent?

Herdsman.

Cithaeron mostly and its neighborhood.

Oedipus.

This fellow here, hast ever seen him there?

Herdsman.

What doing, sir, and what man dost thou mean?

Oedipus.

Who stands before thee: hast met him before?

Herdsman.

Not so that I might say at once from memory.

Messenger.

Nor any wonder. Yet, my lord, I can
Clearly recall what now he has forgot.
I doubt not he remembers well the time
When for three summers clear from spring until
Arcturus' rising we together roamed
These stretches of Cithaeron, he with two
Herds while I tended one. When winter came
I drove my flocks to Corinth home, he his
To Laius' folds. Is this the truth I speak
Or do I tell of things that never were?

Herdsman.

The truth indeed, and yet 'twas long ago.

Messenger.

Come tell me then, canst thou recall how once
Thou gavest me a child to rear as mine?

Herdsman.

How now? Why dost thou question me of that?

Messenger.

For this is he who was a baby then.

Herdsman.

Destruction take thee, wilt thou hold thy tongue?

Oedipus.

Old man, revile him not, thy words not his
Seem most to need amendment, chide him not.

Herdsman.

And what, good master, have I done amiss?

Oedipus.

Refusing thus to answer what he asks.

Herdsman.

He asks in ignorance, and all in vain.

Oedipus.

Thou speak not freely, thou shalt speak in pain.

Herdsman.

By all the gods, force not an aged man.

Oedipus.

Will someone quickly bind the fellow's hands?

Herdsman.

Ah wretched me, for what, what wouldst thou know?

Oedipus.

The child, didst give it to him as he says?

Herdsman.

I did, and would to god I had died then.

Oedipus.

Thou shalt die now and thou speak not the truth.

Herdsman.

And if I do, more surely shall I die.

Oedipus.

The fellow seems determined to delay.

Herdsman.

Not I, I told you that I gave the child.

Oedipus.

Whence had thou it, was't thine or someone's else?

Herdsman.

'Twas not mine own, I had it from a man.

Oedipus.

A Theban? One of these? And from what home?

Herdsman.

No, by the gods, my lord, ask me no more.

Oedipus.

Thou art a dead man if I ask again.

Herdsman.

Well then it was a child of Laius' house.

Oedipus.

A slave, or one free born of his own race?

Herdsman.

Alas I tremble on the brink of speech.

Oedipus.

And I of hearing, yet perforce, I must.

Herdsman.

His own the child was called. The Queen within
Thy wife may best confirm to thee the fact.

Oedipus.

Was it she gave the child?

Herdsman.

'Twas she, my lord.

Oedipus.

What was her purpose?

Herdsman.

I should kill the child.

Oedipus.

Unnatural mother.

Herdsman.

Oracles she feared.

Oedipus.

What?

Herdsman.

He should kill his parent, so 'twas said.

Oedipus.

How then didst thou bestow him on this man?

Herdsman.

In pity, sire, thinking that he would take
The child to his own country, yet it seems
He saved him to misfortune. If thou art
The man he says, then dreadful is thy doom.

Oedipus.

Alas, alas. It must then all be true.
O light of day, may I ne'er look on thee
Again, who now am found cursed at my birth,
Wedded in incest, steeped in mine own blood.

(*Exeunt.*)

Strophe 1

Chorus.

Alas, alas for the years of mortality:
I count ye as naught.
Who is he that hath ever found
More than a vision of empty sound
By fancy wrought?
And ever the vision ends in calamity.

For now, my King, soul wracked and sore distressed,
Thy fate do I behold
Woes manifold
And I count no mortal blessed.

Antistrophe 1

Beyond man's skill did he speed his unerring shaft
And won to his goal
Fortune's prize of prosperity
Slaying the Sphinx with her mystery
And stopped the toll
Of that death she levied: foully she wrought and laughed
Till thou didst come, champion and tower of might.
Henceforth all conquering
Art hailed as king
In this land of god's delight.

Strophe 2

And now on the lips of all
Whose fate so black?
While the Furies of madness in hungry pack
Cry for thy fall.
For into a harbor strange thou hast sailed
Where the deathless laws of the gods have failed,
Where the same unhallowed love prevailed
On sire and son in the self-same hall.
What god bestowed
This poisonous boon, this fatal goad
To sow where his father sowed?

Antistrophe 2

But time that is never blind
Hath now disclosed
What the dwellers of earth, to the light exposed,
Shudder to find.
Seed of begetter and him begot
In the self-same furrow that sensed them not
And I would to god thy thrice-cursed lot
Were hidden darkly from all mankind.
I mourn thy plight
That unto me brought sudden light
To end in eternal night.

(*Enter a Second Messenger.*)

Second Messenger.
Ye ever-honored most in Thebes what deeds
Shall smite your ears, what sights shall ye behold
What grief is yours if to tradition true
Ye still revere the house of Labdacus.
Waters of Ister, streams of Phasis ne'er
Can cleanse this dwelling, such the dreadful deed,
It hides but shall disclose, no deed of chance
But wittingly contrived. Always those griefs
Hurt most whose choice the world shall mark our own.

Chorus.
Already we have witnessed here such deeds
As might call forth such cry; what hast thou more?

Second Messenger.
To take the shortest course for him who speaks
And him who hears: the Queen Jocasta is dead.

Chorus.
O lady of ill fortune, by what means?

Second Messenger.
By her own hand. The part most horrible,
The sight of it, is spared thee. What remains
Of all her woe within my memory
Straight shalt thou hear. Frantic with mad despair
She came within the ante chamber. Then
Rushed to the wedding couch, with both her hands
Tearing her hair, dashed shut the doors behind
Invoking Laius, dead these many years,
And called to mind that son that he begot
So long ago by whom he died and left
Her that had borne him wretched to produce
Offspring to share with his. She cried against
That marriage which to her misfortune raised
A double brood, husband by husband got
And children by her child. How after that
She perished I know not, for Oedipus
Burst in with shouting who allowed us not
Further to look upon her misery
Since on his frenzy rested all our eyes.

Madly he raged, asking of us a sword
And calling for the wife that was no wife
The mother's womb that bore alike himself
And his own children. In his madness some
Divinity did guide him for 'twas none
Of us poor mortals who were standing by.
Then with a dreadful shout, as beckoned on
He hurled himself upon the double doors—
Back from their sockets bent the yielding bolts—
And rushed within. There we beheld his wife
Hanged by a twisted cord still swaying there.
And when he saw her, with a mighty cry
He loosed the rope that held her. As she lay
Stretched on the ground, followed a gruesome sight.
For from her dress he tore the golden brooch
That held it. Raising it aloft he smote
Full on his eyeballs shouting as he struck
That they should nevermore behold what he
Had suffered nor the evil he had wrought.
Darkened forever they might never look
Again on what they had no right to see,
Failing to recognize what most they ought.
And with such imprecations 'twas not once
But many times he beat upon his eyes.
The bloody eyeballs burst upon his beard
Not in slow drops of blood but in one black
Down-rushing stream of blood, like shower of hail.
Such are the woes that issue from these twain,
Husband and wife commingled. What was once
Their happy lot, and happiness in truth,
This day is turned to wailing, madness, death
And all the woes that are, are theirs today.

Chorus.

Hath now the wretched man some rest from pain?

Second Messenger.

He shouts aloud that some one draw the bolts
And show to all in Thebes the murderer
Of his own father and his mother too.
With blasphemies that I may not repeat
He swears to hurl himself forth from this land
Nor still remain a curse unto the house,

Under the curse he spoke. Yet someone's strength
And guidance too he needs, his agony
Is more than human strength can bear. Thou too
Shalt see, for now the unbolted palace gates
Open to show a sight that can but win
Thy fierce abhorrence but thy pity too.

(*Enter the blinded Oedipus.*)

Chorus.

O agony too sore for sight
Beyond the utmost range
Of human agony.
What madness, hapless man, assailed thy soul?
What angered god
O'erleaping space
Struck down thine ill-starred Fortune?
Woe is me,
Much as I fain would learn,
Frozen with horror, impotent,
I dare not ask nor look but overwhelmed
Shudder and hold my peace.

Oedipus.

Woe, woe is mine.
Where in mine agony
Shall I be borne?
Fluttering words are naught.
Where, god, the end?

Chorus.

Where there is no relief for ear or eye.

Oedipus.

O cloud of the nether night,
Abhorrent, unspeakable,
Wafted on following breezes fraught with death
Alas the goad of memory strikes
Piercing my heart
Cruelly joined in one with the stabs
Of the golden brooch.

Chorus.

No wonder in thy plight there comes to thee
A double grief, a twofold pain to bear.

Oedipus.

O friend that art steadfast still
Thou only art left to me.
Pity for suffering blindness makes thee kind.
Alas thy presence speaks to me
Blind though I am.
Darkness like death is mine, yet I know
Thou hast left me not.

Chorus.

O doer of dread deeds, how couldst thou dare
Destroy thine eyes? What god compelled that act?

Oedipus.

Lord of the Delphian shrine,
Apollo, god of the taut strong bow,
Wrought for me woe on woe:
His was the curse
But the hand that struck was mine;
Mine was the blow.
God! Would I see again
Whose opened eyes
Could naught behold that held not memory's curse?

Chorus.

True is that word of thine.

Oedipus.

What should I see? Shall I ever know
Love or a welcoming word?
Banish me ere ye too
Fall neath the blight that clings
Round me accursed
Hated of god, damned through eternity.

Chorus.

Twofold thy misery: for, being damned,
Thou still canst feel. Would god I knew thee not.

Oedipus.

Cursed forever be
The hand that loosed from my feet the thong
Striking the shackles off
Giving me life
When I lay a helpless babe.
Graceless the deed;
Better were death for me
Than live a curse
To mine own self and all that touches me.

Chorus.

Better were death indeed.

Oedipus.

Then had I not with the curse of god
Drenched in my father's blood
Mounted the couch of her,
Mother and queen to me.
Outlaw from earth
Outlaw from heaven, woe beyond woe is mine.

Chorus.

I cannot say thy counsel was the best
For death would be to thee a very boon.

Oedipus.

Instruct me not that all is evilly
Contrived. I cannot bear more counseling
For had I now my sight could I endure
To face my father in the halls of hell,
To look upon my mother? I have wrought
Such wrongs against those two as would make death
By hanging seem as nothing. Can ye think
Beside that sight of mine own progeny
Begotten as they were could give me joy?
Not in mine eyes at least. Not Thebes herself,
Not all her parapets, her sculptured gods
Seeing that I of all her citizens
Fairest of promise, now accursed, have won
The doom of seeing these no more, myself
The spokesman of the curse bidding men thrust
Forth from the city the unholy one,
Disclosed by god of Laius' royal line.
Could I with such a brand upon me look
Upon my fellow citizens? Not I,
And were there means to dam the fountain head
Of hearing, I had not withheld to close
This wretched body fast that neither sight
Nor sound should penetrate. Our thoughts should dwell
Beyond the reach of evil, o Cithaeron, why
Didst thou accept my life? Why didst thou not
Slay me at once? So had I never shown
Myself unto the world and whence I sprang.
O Polybus and Corinth and that home
Once called mine own, how fair the object seemed

Of thy kind nurture, and how foul beneath
Proven at last both base and basely born.
O triple crossroads and that hidden glade
Narrowing through the oak trees where those three
Roads met that drank mine own blood by my hand
Drawn from my father's veins, do ye then still
Remember me, the deed I showed you there
And coming hither wrought again? O rites
Of wedlock, ye that brought me forth and gave
Harvest to me sown in the self-same field
Confounding name of father, brother, son,
Of mother, bride, and wife to consummate
All that is held most shameful of mankind.
Yet what is foul to do is foul to speak.
Wherefore by all the gods with utmost speed
Hide me in some far hiding place or slay
Outright or cast me in the sea where none
May e'er behold me more. Come, scruple not
To touch this wretched man. Ye need not fear.
No mortal but myself may bear this guilt.

(*Enter Creon.*)

Chorus.

Lo at thy words comes Creon who may best
Grant thy request or counsel thee for he
Alone is left our guardian in thy place.

Oedipus.

Alas what word is left for me to speak
To him? What truth shall he behold in me
Who proved myself to him in all things false?

Creon.

I am not come to mock thee, Oedipus,
Nor speak reproaches for thy evil past.
But if ye here respect no more the race
Of man at least show reverence to the flame
All nourishing of Helios nor expose
Pollution such as this which neither light
Of day, nor earth, nor rains of heaven may bear.
With all your speed lead him within. The woes
Of kindred they alone should see and hear
To whom the bonds of kinship give the right.

Oedipus.

Nay, by the gods, since thou hast quelled my fear
Coming thus nobly to a man so base
Grant me one boon. For thine own sake I'll speak.

Creon.

What favor dost thou ask so eagerly?

Oedipus.

Cast me forth swiftly from this land, where I
May share no more in human intercourse.

Creon.

That had I done, be well assured, save that
I would be taught of god what's best to do.

Oedipus.

God hath already spoken bidding us
Destroy the unholy man that slew his sire.

Creon.

Such was his word yet seeing where we stand
'Tis best to learn anew our proper course.

Oedipus.

Wilt ask advice about one so accursed?

Creon.

Aye for thyself wilt now believe god's word.

Oedipus.

One charge I lay on thee, one last request.
To her that lies within give burial
As seemeth best to thee. So shalt thou give
Last rites unto thine own. But never doom
This city of my fathers to receive
Me as a citizen to dwell therein.
Nay send me forth to live where rises steep
Cithaeron, called mine own, the living tomb
My father and my mother gave to me:
Thus at their hands who willed it I may die.
Yet this I know. Never shall dread disease
Nor human ill destroy me. I was snatched
From death, to serve some stranger will of god.
For me let Fate lead where it will. And more
I ask no favor, Creon, for my sons.
They are now men and wheresoe'er they are
Shall win their livelihood. I crave thy care
For my two daughters. Piteous is their lot
Who know no table but mine own, have shared

All things with me. Grant too, most noble lord,
That I may touch them once again and mourn
With them this evil plight. Could I but place
My hands on them methinks I could believe
That they were mine as when I saw them here.

(*Enter Antigone and Ismene, Oedipus' daughters.*)

O god what shall I say? Do I not hear
Their weeping voices? Hast thou pitied me
And brought my daughters, Creon? Is it so?

Creon.

'Tis so. 'Twas I that brought them, knowing well
From thy past joy what comfort they might give.

Oedipus.

God give thee blessing and a happier fate
Than mine for this good act. Where are ye there,
My children? Hither, hither come and take
These hands that are in truth a brother's hands.
Hands which wrought havoc with your father's eyes
That saw so clearly once. Yet seeing naught
Nor gaining wisdom's light, he gave you life
By his own mother. 'Tis for you I weep
Whom now I may not see. But I perceive
What bitterness of life amongst mankind
Henceforth is yours. What friendly gatherings
Will you attend, what feasts whose end for you
Shall not be weeping in the place of joy?
And when you reach the years of womanhood
With thoughts of marriage, who will then assume
Reproaches that must ever fall alike
On my descendants and on yours? What woe
Exists that is not ours? Your father slew
His sire, quickened the womb that gave him life
To bring you forth. Such is your heritage.
Who then shall wed you? There is none that lives.
Unwedden, barren, 'tis your doom to die.
But o Menoeceus' son, since thou alone
Art left to father these—for she and I

That brought them to the light are lost indeed—
Suffer them not—thy kin—to wander lone
Beggared and husbandless nor make them one
With this my misery. Nay pity them
Seeing their youth deprived of everything
Save what may come from thee. Take thou this hand
And grant my wish. To you my children much
I should bequeath of counsel were thy minds
Mature. Now let this be your constant prayer
That wheresoe'er chance place your lot, ye live
With happier fate than was your father's share.

Creon.

All sufficient now thy mourning. Thou must go within the house.

Oedipus.

Yield I must, though yield I would not.

Creon.

Aye, for all things have their time.

Oedipus.

Knowest how I might go freely?

Creon.

If thou sayest I shall know.

Oedipus.

If thou wouldst but grant me exile.

Creon.

That lies on the knees of god.

Oedipus.

Yet to god am I most hateful.

Creon.

Hence may win thy wish perchance.

Oedipus.

Thou dost will it?

Creon.

Nay, 'tis never mine to speak what I mean not.

Oedipus.

Send me then within the palace.

Creon.

Go, but leave thy children here.

Oedipus.

Rob me not of them I pray thee.

Creon.

Seek not to prevail in all.
For the power thou once hast wielded has not followed to the end.

Chorus.

Ye that dwell in Thebes behold him. Oedipus thy King is this,
He who solved the far-famed riddle, mightiest in all Thebes was he.
On his fortune who that dwelt here gazed not once with envious eye?
Now behold what surge of evil hath encompassed him about.
So the while we wait the outcome of the fateful final day
We may call no mortal happy till his course of life is done
And he reach the goal of darkness, find his heaven free from pain.

SOPHOCLES

Oedipus at Colonus

Translated by Lewis Campbell

Written by Sophocles when he was almost ninety, it was first produced posthumously in 401 B.C. and won first prize. The ode in praise of Colonus, Sophocles' birthplace—"Gleaming Colonus, where the nightingale in cool green covert warbleth ever clear"—is the most famous lyric in Greek literature.

CHARACTERS IN THE PLAY

Oedipus, old and blind

Antigone } his daughters
Ismene }

An Athenian

Theseus, King of Athens

Creon, of Thebes

Polyneices, the elder son of Oedipus

A Messenger

Chorus of Elders of Colonus

ARGUMENT

Oedipus had continued to live at Thebes for many years after the conclusion of the events described in *Oedipus the King.* Then Creon banished him, with the consent of Oedipus' sons, Eteocles and Polyneices. Eventually Creon ceased to be king, and the two brothers quarreled over the succession. Polyneices fled to Argos, married the daughter of King Adrastus, and has now levied an army to support his pretensions to the Theban throne. Recently an oracle has proclaimed that if Oedipus dies in Attica, Athens will prosper and Thebes suffer: actually, from the religious point of view, the death of the aged and innocent Oedipus, who pleads the venial nature of an offense committed in ignorance although long since purified by his suffering, represents the highest achievement of paganism. As we listen to the Messenger's description of Oedipus' last moments, our souls are in truth lifted toward grandeur.

SCENE

At Colonus in Attica, a suburb of Athens. In the background is the sacred grove of the Eumenides, or Gentle Powers, a euphemistic title for the Erinyes or Furies. The blind Oedipus, led by his daughter Antigone, enters.

OEDIPUS AT COLONUS

Oedipus.

Antigone, child of the old blind sire,
What land is here, what people? Who to-day
Shall dole to Oedipus, the wandering exile,
Their meagre gifts? Little I ask, and less
Receive without a murmur, since my woes,
And the long years ripening the noble mind,
Have schooled me to content.—But, O my child
If thou espiest where we may sit, though near
Some holy precinct, stay me and set me there,
Till we may learn where we are come. 'Tis ours
To hear the will of strangers and obey.

Antigone.

Woe-wearied father, yonder city's wall
That shields her, looks far distant; but this ground
Is surely sacred, thickly planted over
With olive, bay and vine, within whose bowers
Thick-fluttering song-birds make sweet melody.
Here then repose thee on this unhewn stone.
Thou hast travelled far to-day for one so old.

Oedipus.

Seat me, my child, and be the blind man's guard.

Antigone.

Long time hath well instructed me in that.

Oedipus.

Now, canst thou tell me where we have set our feet?

Antigone.

Athens I know, but not the nearer ground.

Oedipus.

Ay, every man that met us in the way
Named Athens.

Antigone.

Shall I go, then, and find out
The name of the spot?

Oedipus.

Yes, if 'tis habitable.

Antigone.

It is inhabited. Yet I need not go.
I see a man even now approaching here.

Oedipus.

How? Makes he toward us? Is he drawing nigh?

Antigone.

He is close beside us. Whatsoe'er thou findest
Good to be spoken, say it. The man is here.

(*Enter an Athenian.*)

Oedipus.

O stranger, learning from this maid, who sees
Both for herself and me, that thou art come
With timely light to clear our troubled thought—

Athenian.

Ere thou ask more, come forth from where thou sittest!
Ye trench on ground forbidden human tread.

Oedipus.

What ground? And to what Power thus consecrate?

Athenian.

None may go near, nor dwell there. 'Tis possessed
By the dread sisters, children of Earth and Night.

Oedipus.

What holy name will please them, if I pray?

Athenian.

"All-seeing Gentle Powers" the dwellers here
Would call them. But each land hath its own rule.

Oedipus.

And gently may they look on him who now
Implores them, and will never leave this grove!

Athenian.

What saying is this?

Oedipus.

The watchword of my doom.

Athenian.

Yet dare I not remove thee, till the town
Have heard my purpose and confirm the deed.

Oedipus.

By Heaven I pray thee, stranger, scorn me not,
Poor wanderer that I am, but answer me.

Athenian.

Make clear thy drift. Thou'lt get no scorn from me.

Oedipus.

Then, pray thee, tell me how ye name the place
Where now I sit.

Athenian.

The region all around
Is sacred. For 'tis guarded and possessed
By dread Poseidon, and the Titan mind
That brought us fire—Prometheus. But that floor
Whereon thy feet are resting, hath been called
The brazen threshold of our land, the stay
Of glorious Athens, and the neighbouring fields
Are fain to honour for their patron-god
Thee, O Colonus, first of Knights, whose name

(*Pointing to a statue.*)

They bear in brotherhood and own for theirs.
Such, friend, believe me, is this place, not praised
In story, but of many a heart beloved.

Oedipus.

Then is the land inhabited of men?

Athenian.

By men, who name them from Colonus there.

Oedipus.

Have they a lord, or sways the people's voice?

Athenian.

Lord Theseus, child of Aegeus, our late king.

Oedipus.

Will some one of your people bring him hither?

Athenian.

Wherefore? What urgent cause requires his presence?

Oedipus.

He shall gain mightily by granting little.

Athenian.

Who can gain profit from the blind?

Oedipus.

The words
These lips will utter, shall be full of sight.

Athenian.

Well, thou look'st nobly, but for thy hard fate.
This course is safe. Thus do. Stay where I found thee,
Till I go tell the neighbour townsmen here
Not of the city, but Colonus. They
Shall judge for thee to abide or to depart.

(*Exit.*)

Oedipus.

Tell me, my daughter, is the man away?

Antigone.

He is gone, father. I alone am near.
Speak what thou wilt in peace and quietness.

Oedipus.

Dread Forms of holy Fear, since in this land
Your sanctuary first gave my limbs repose,
Be not obdurate to my prayer, nor spurn
The voice of Phoebus, who that fateful day,
When he proclaimed my host of ills to come,
Told me of rest after a weary time,
Where else but here? "When I should reach my bourne,
And find repose and refuge with the Powers
Of reverend name, my troubled life should end
With blessing to the men who sheltered me,
And curses on their race who banished me
And sent me wandering forth." Whereof he vouched me
Sure token, or by earthquake, or by fire
From heaven, or thundrous voices. And I know
Some aery message from your shrine hath drawn me
With wingèd whisper to this grove. Not else
Had ye first met me coming, nor had I
Sate on your dread unchiselled seat of stone,
With dry cold lips greeting your sober shrine.
Then give Apollo's word due course, and give
Completion to my life, if in your sight
These toils and sorrows past the human bound
Seem not too little. Kindly, gentle powers,
Offspring of primal darkness, hear my prayer!
Hear it, Athens, of all cities queen,
Great Pallas' foster-city! Look with ruth
On this poor shadow of great Oedipus,
This fading semblance of his kingly form.

Antigone.

Be silent now. There comes an aged band
With jealous looks to know thine errand here.

Oedipus.

I will be silent, and thine arm shall guide
My footstep under covert of the grove
Out of the path, till I make sure what words

These men will utter. Warily to observe
Is the prime secret of the prudent mind.

(*Exeunt into the grove. Enter Chorus of Elders of Colonus.*)

Strophe

Chorus.

Look out! Who can it be?
Where is he? Vanished! Gone! Oh where?
Most uncontrolled of men!
Look well, inquire him out,
Search keenly in every nook!
—Some wanderer is the aged wight,
A wanderer surely, not a native here.
Else never had he gone within
The untrodden grove
Of these unmarried, unapproachable in might,
Whose names we dare not breathe,
But pass their shrine
Without a look, without a word,
Uttering the unheard voice of reverential thought.
But now, one comes, they tell, devoid of awe,
Whom, peering all around this grove
I find not, where he abideth.

Oedipus (*behind*).

Behold me! For I "see by sound,"
As mortals say,

Chorus.

Oh, Oh!
With horror I see him, with horror hear him speak.

Oedipus.

Pray you, regard me not as a transgressor!

Chorus.

Defend us, Zeus! Who is that aged wight?

Oedipus.

Not one of happiest fate,
Or enviable, O guardians of this land!
'Tis manifest; else had I not come hither
Led by another's eyes, not moored my bark
On such a slender stay.

Antistrophe

Chorus.

Alas! And are thine eyes
Sightless? O full of misery,
As thou look'st full of years!
But not, if I prevent,
Shalt thou bring down this curse.
Thou art trespassing. Yet keep thy foot
From stumbling in that verdant, voiceless dell,
Where running water as it fills
The hallowed bowl,
Mingles with draughts of honey. Stranger, hapless one!
Avoid that with all care.
Away! Remove!
Distance impedes the sound. Dost hear,
Woe-burdened wanderer? If aught thou carest to bring
Before our council, leave forbidden ground,
And there, where all have liberty,
Speak,—but till then, avaunt thee!

Oedipus.

Daughter, what must I think, or do?

Antigone.

My sire!
We must conform us to the people's will,
Yielding ere they compel.

Oedipus.

Give me thy hand.

Antigone.

Thou hast it.

Oedipus.

—Strangers, let me not
Be wronged, when I have trusted you
And come from where I stood!

Chorus.

Assure thee, from this seat
No man shall drag thee off against thy will.

Oedipus.

Farther?

Chorus.

Advance thy foot.

Oedipus.

Yet more?

Chorus.

Assist him onward,
Maiden; thou hast thy sight.

Antigone.

Come, follow, this way follow with thy darkened steps,
Father, the way I am leading thee.

Chorus.

Content thee, sojourning in a strange land,
O man of woe!
To eschew whate'er the city holds in hate,
And honour what she loves!

Oedipus.

Then do thou lead me, child,
Where with our feet secure from sin
We may be suffered both to speak and hear.
Let us not war against necessity.

Chorus.

There! From that bench of rock
Go not again astray.

Oedipus.

Even here?

Chorus.

Enough, I tell thee.

Oedipus.

May I sit?

Chorus.

Ay, crouch thee low adown
Crooking thy limbs, upon the stone.

Antigone.

Father, this task is mine.—
Sink gently down into thy resting-place,

Oedipus.

Woe is me!

Antigone.

Supporting on this loving hand
Thy reverend aged form.

Oedipus.

Woe, for my cruel fate!

(*Oedipus is seated.*)

Chorus.

Now thou unbendest from thy stubborn ways,
O man of woe!
Declare, what mortal wight thou art,
That, marked by troublous fortune, here art led.
What native country, shall we learn, is thine?

Oedipus.

O strangers, I have none!
But do not—

Chorus.

What dost thou forbid, old sir?

Oedipus.

Do not, oh, do not ask me who I am,
Nor probe me with more question.

Chorus.

What dost thou mean?

Oedipus.

My birth is dreadful.

Chorus.

Tell it forth.

Oedipus.

What should I utter, O my child? Woe is me!

Chorus.

Thy seed, thy father's name, stranger, pronounce!

Oedipus.

Alas! What must I do? My child!

Antigone.

Since no resource avails thee, speak!

Oedipus.

I will. I cannot hide it further.

Chorus.

Ye are long about it. Haste thee!

Oedipus.

Know ye of one
Begotten of Laius?

Chorus.

Horror! Horror! Oh!

Oedipus.

Derived from Labdacus?

Chorus.

O Heaven!

Oedipus.

Fate-wearied Oedipus?

Chorus.

Art thou he?

Oedipus.

Fear not my words.

Chorus.

Oh! Oh!

Oedipus.

Unhappy me!

Chorus.

Oh!

Oedipus.

Daughter, what is coming?

Chorus.

Away! Go forth. Leave ye the land. Begone!

Oedipus.

And where, then, is the promise thou hast given?

Chorus.

No doom retributive attends the deed
That wreaks precedent wrong.
Deceit, matched with deceit, makes recompense
Of evil, not of kindness. Get thee forth!
Desert that seat again, and from this land
Unmooring speed thee away, lest on our state
Thou bring some further bale!

Antigone.

O strangers, full of reverent care!
Since ye cannot endure my father here,
Aged and blind,
Because ye have heard a rumour of the deeds
He did unknowingly,—yet, we entreat you,
Strangers, have pity on me, the hapless girl,
Who pray for mine own sire and for none else,
—Pray, looking in your eyes with eyes not blind,
As if a daughter had appeared to you,
Pleading for mercy to the unfortunate.
We are in your hands as in the hand of God,
Helpless. O then accord the unhoped-for boon!
By what is dear to thee, thy veriest own,
I pray thee,—chattel or child, or holier name!

Search through the world, thou wilt not find the man
Who could resist the leading of a God.

Chorus.

Daughter of Oedipus, be well assured
We view with pity both thy case and his,
But fear of Heavenly wrath confines our speech
To that we have already said to thee.

Oedipus.

What profit lives in fame and fair renown
By unsubstantial rumour idly spread?
When Athens is extolled with peerless praise
For reverence, and for mercy!—She alone
The sufferer's shield, the exile's comforter!
What have I reaped hereof? Ye have raised me up
From yonder seat, and now would drive me forth
Fearing a name! For there is nought in me
Or deeds of mine to make you fear. My life
Hath more of wrong endured than of wrong done,
Were it but lawful to disclose to you
Wherefore ye dread me,—not my sin but theirs,
My mother's and my sire's. I know your thought.
Yet never can ye fasten guilt on me,
Who, though I had acted with the clear'st intent,
Were guiltless, for my deed requited wrong.
But as it was, all blindly I went forth
On that dire road, while they who planned my death
Planned it with perfect knowledge. Therefore, sirs,
By Heaven I pray you, as ye have bid me rise,
Protect your suppliant without fail; and do not
In jealous reverence for the blessed Gods
Rob them of truest reverence, but know this:—
God looks upon the righteousness of man
And his unrighteousness, nor ever yet
Hath one escaped who wrought iniquity.
Take part, then, with the Gods, nor overcloud
The golden fame of Athens with dark deeds;
But as ye have pledged your faith to shelter me,
Defend me and rescue, not rejecting me
Through mere abhorrence of my ruined face.
For on a holy mission am I come,

Sent with rich blessings for your neighbours here.
And when the head and sovereign of your race
Is present, ye shall learn the truth at full.
Till then, be gracious to me, and not perverse.

Chorus.

Thy meaning needs must strike our hearts with awe,
Old wanderer! so weighty are the words
That body it forth. Therefore we are content
The Lord of Athens shall decide this case.

Oedipus.

And where is he who rules this country, sirs?

Chorus.

He keeps his father's citadel. But one
Is gone to fetch him, he who brought us hither.

Oedipus.

Think you he will consider the blind man,
And come in person here to visit him?

Chorus.

Be sure he will,—when he hath heard thy name.

Oedipus.

And who will carry that?

Chorus.

'Tis a long road;
But rumour from the lips of wayfarers
Flies far and wide, so that he needs must hear;
And hearing, never doubt but he will come.
So noised in every land hath been thy name,
Old sovereign,—were he sunk in drowsiness,
That sound would bring him swiftly to thy side.

Oedipus.

Well, may he come to bless his city and me!
When hath not goodness blessed the giver of good?

Antigone.

O Heavens! What shall I say, what think, my father?

Oedipus.

Daughter Antigone, what is it?

Antigone.

I see
A woman coming towards us, mounted well
On a fair Sicilian palfrey, and her face
With brow-defending hood of Thessaly

Is shadowed from the sun. What must I think?
Is it she or no? Can the eye so far deceive?
It is. 'Tis not. Unhappy that I am,
I know not.—Yes, 'tis she. For drawing near
She greets me with bright glances, and declares
Beyond a doubt, Ismene's self is here.

Oedipus.

What say'st thou, daughter?

Antigone.

That I see thy child,
My sister. Soon her voice will make thee sure.

(*Enter Ismene.*)

Ismene.

Father and sister—names how sweet to me!
Hard hath it been to find you, yea, and hard
I feel it now to look on you for grief.

Oedipus.

Child, art thou here?

Ismene.

Father! O sight of pain!

Oedipus.

Offspring and sister!

Ismene.

Woe for thy dark fate!

Oedipus.

Hast thou come, daughter?

Ismene.

On a troublous way.

Oedipus.

Touch me, my child!

Ismene.

I give a hand to both.

Oedipus.

To her and me?

Ismene.

Three linked in one sad knot.

Oedipus.

Child, wherefore art thou come?

Ismene.

In care for thee.

Oedipus.

Because you missed me?

Ismene.

Ay, and to bring thee news,
With the only slave whom I could trust.

Oedipus.

And they,
Thy brethren, what of them? Were they not there
To take this journey for their father's good?

Ismene.

Ask not of them. Dire deeds are theirs to-day.

Oedipus.

How in all points their life obeys the law
Of Egypt, where the men keep house and weave
Sitting within-doors, while the wives abroad
Provide with ceaseless toil the means of life.
So in your case, my daughters, they who should
Have ta'en this burden on them, bide at home
Like maidens, while ye take their place, and lighten
My miseries by your toil. Antigone,
E'er since her childhood ended, and her frame
Was firmly knit, with ceaseless ministry
Still tends upon the old man's wandering,
Oft in the forest ranging up and down
Fasting and barefoot through the burning heat
Or pelting rain, nor thinks, unhappy maid,
Of home or comfort, so her father's need
Be satisfied. And thou, that camest before,
Eluding the Cadmeians, and didst tell me
What words Apollo had pronounced on me,
And when they banished me, stood'st firm to shield me,
What news, Ismene, bring'st thou to thy sire
To-day? What mission sped thee forth? I know
Thou com'st not idly, but with fears for me.

Ismene.

Father, I will not say what I endured
In searching out the place that sheltered thee.
To tell it o'er would but renew the pain.
But of the danger now encompassing
Thine ill-starred sons,—of that I came to speak.

At first they strove with Creon and declared
The throne should be left vacant and the town
Freed from pollution,—paying deep regard
In their debate to the dark heritage
Of ruin that o'ershadowed all thy race.
Far different is the strife which holds them now,
Since some great Power, joined to their sinful mind,
Incites them both to seize on sovereign sway.
Eteocles, in pride of younger years,
Robbed elder Polyneices of his right,
Dethroned and banished him. To Argos then
Goes exiled Polyneices, and obtains
Through intermarriage a strong favouring league,
Whose word is, "Either Argos vanquishes
The seed of Cadmus or exalts their fame."
This, father, is no tissue of empty talk,
But dreadful truth, nor can I tell where Heaven
Is to reveal his mercy to thy woe.

Oedipus.

And hadst thou ever hoped the Gods would care
For mine affliction, and restore my life?

Ismene.

I hope it now since this last oracle.

Oedipus.

What oracle hath been declared, my child?

Ismene.

That they shall seek thee forth, alive or dead,
To bring salvation to the Theban race.

Oedipus.

Who can win safety through such help as mine?

Ismene.

'Tis said their victory depends on thee.

Oedipus.

When shrunk to nothing, am I indeed a man?

Ismene.

Yea, for the Gods uphold thee, who then destroyed.

Oedipus.

Poor work, to uphold in age who falls when young!

Ismene.

Know howsoe'er that Creon will be here
For this same end, ere many an hour be spent.

Oedipus.

For what end, daughter? Tell me in plain speech.

Ismene.

To set thee near their land, that thou may'st be
Beyond their borders, but within their power.

Oedipus.

What good am I, thus lying at their gate?

Ismene.

Thine inauspicious burial brings them woe.

Oedipus.

There needs no oracle to tell one that.

Ismene.

And therefore they would place thee near their land,
Where thou may'st have no power upon thyself.

Oedipus.

Say then, shall Theban dust o'ershadow me?

Ismene.

The blood of kindred cleaving to thy hand,
Father, forbids thee.

Oedipus.

Never, then, henceforth,
Shall they lay hold on me!

Ismene.

If that be true,
The brood of Cadmus shall have bale.

Oedipus.

What cause
Having appeared, will bring this doom to pass?

Ismene.

Thy wrath, when they are marshalled at thy tomb.

Oedipus.

From whom hast thou heard this?

Ismene.

Sworn messengers
Brought such report from Delphi's holy shrine.

Oedipus.

Hath Phoebus so pronounced my destiny?

Ismene.

So they declare who brought the answer back.

Oedipus.

Did my sons hear?

Ismene.

They know it, both of them.

Oedipus.

Villains, who, being informed of such a word,
Turned not their thoughts toward me, but rather chose
Ambition and a throne!

Ismene.

It wounds mine ear
To hear it spoken, but the news I bring
Is to that stern effect.

Oedipus.

Then I pray Heaven
The fury of their fate-appointed strife
May ne'er be quenched, but that the end may come
According to my wish upon them twain
To this contention and arbitrament
Of battle which they now assay and lift
The threatening spear! So neither he who wields
The sceptred power should keep possession still,
Nor should his brother out of banishment
Ever return:—who, when their sire—when I
Was shamefully thrust from my native land,
Checked not my fall nor saved me, but, for them,
I was driven homeless and proclaimed an exile.
Ye will tell me 'twas in reason that the State
Granted this boon to my express desire.
Nay; for in those first hours of agony,
When my heart boiled, and it seemed sweetest to me
To die the death, and to be stoned with stones,
No help appeared to yield me that relief.
But after lapse of days, when all my pain
Was softened, and I felt that my hot spirit
Had run to fierce excess of bitterness
In wreaking mine offence—then, then the State
Drove me for ever from the land, and they,
Their father's sons, who might have saved their father,
Cared not to help him, but betrayed by them,
For lack of one light word, I wandered forth
To homeless banishment and beggary.
But these weak maidens to their nature's power
Have striven to furnish me with means to live

And dwell securely, girded round with love.
My sons have chosen before their father's life
A lordly throne and sceptred sovereignty.
But never shall they win me to their aid,
Nor shall the Theban throne for which they strive
Bring them desired content. That well I know,
Comparing with my daughter's prophecies
Those ancient oracles which Phoebus once
Spake in mine ear. Then let them send to seek me
Creon, or who is strongest in their State.
For if ye, strangers, will but add your might
To the protection of these awful Powers,
The guardians of your deme, to shelter me,
Ye shall acquire for this your State a saviour
Mighty to save, and ye shall vex my foes.

Chorus.

Thou art worthy of all compassion, Oedipus,
Thyself and these thy daughters. Now, moreover,
Since thou proclaim'st thyself our country's saviour,
I would advise thee for the best.

Oedipus.

Kind sir,
Be my good guide. I will do all thou biddest.

Chorus.

Propitiate then these holy powers, whose grove
Received thee when first treading this our ground.

Oedipus.

What are the appointed forms? Advise me, sirs.

Chorus.

First see to it that from some perennial fount
Clean hands provide a pure drink-offering.

Oedipus.

And when I have gotten this unpolluted draught?

Chorus.

You will find bowls, formed by a skilful hand,
Whose brims and jutting handles you must crown.

Oedipus.

With leaves or flocks of wool, or in what way?

Chorus.

With tender wool ta'en from a young ewe-lamb.

Oedipus.

Well, and what follows to complete the rite?

Chorus.

Next, make libation toward the earliest dawn.

Oedipus.

Mean'st thou from those same urns whereof thou speakest?

Chorus.

From those three vessels pour three several streams,
Filling the last to the brim.

Oedipus.

With what contents
Must this be filled? Instruct me.

Chorus.

Not with wine,
But water and the treasure of the bee.

Oedipus.

And when leaf-shadowed Earth has drunk of this,
What follows?

Chorus.

Thou shalt lay upon her then
From both thy hands a row of olive-twigs—
Counting thrice nine in all—and add this prayer—

Oedipus.

That is the chief thing,—that I long to hear.

Chorus.

As we have named them Gentle, so may they
From gentle hearts accord their suppliant aid;—
Be this thy prayer, or whoso prays for thee,
Spoken not aloud, but so that none may hear;
And in departing, turn not. This being done,
I can stand by thee without dread. But else,
I needs must fear concerning thee.

Oedipus.

My daughters,
Have ye both heard our friends who inhabit here?

Antigone.

Yea, father; and we wait for thy command.

Oedipus.

I cannot go. Two losses hinder me,
Two evils, want of strength and want of sight.
Let one of you go and perform this service.
One soul, methinks, in paying such a debt

May quit a million, if the heart be pure.
Haste, then, to do it. Only leave me not
Untended. For I cannot move alone
Nor without some one to support me and guide.

Ismene.

I will be ministrant. But let me know
Where I must find the place of offering.

Chorus.

Beyond this grove. And, stranger maid, if aught
Seem wanting, there is one at hand to show it.

Ismene.

Then to my task. Meantime, Antigone,
Watch by our sire. We must not make account
Of labour that supplies a parent's need.

(*Exit.*)

Strophe 1

Chorus.

Thy long since slumbering woe I would not wake
again,
But yet I long to learn.

Oedipus.

What hidden lore?

Chorus.

The pain
That sprang against thy life with spirit-mastering force.

Oedipus.

Ah, sirs, as ye are kind, re-open not that source
Of unavoided shame.

Chorus.

Friend, we would hear the tale
Told truly, whose loud breath doth hourly more prevail.

Oedipus.

Misery!

Chorus.

Be not loth!

Oedipus.

O bitterness!

Chorus.

Consent.
For all thou didst require we gave to thy content.

Antistrophe 1

Oedipus.

Oh, strangers, I have borne an all-too-willing brand,
Yet not of mine own choice.

Chorus.

Whence? We would understand.

Oedipus.

Nought knowing of the curse she fastened on my head
Thebè in evil bands bound me.

Chorus.

Thy mother's bed,
Say, didst thou fill? mine ear still echoes to the noise.

Oedipus.

'Tis death to me to hear, but, these, mine only joys,
Friends, are my curse.

Chorus.

O Heaven!

Oedipus.

The travail of one womb
Hath gendered all you see, one mother, one dark doom.

Strophe 2

Chorus.

How? Are they both thy race, and–

Oedipus.

Sister branches too,
Nursed at the self-same place with him from whom they grew.

Chorus.

O horror!

Oedipus.

Aye, not one, ten thousand charged me then!

Chorus.

O sorrow!

Oedipus.

Never done, an ever-sounding strain.

Chorus.

O crime!

Oedipus.

By me ne'er wrought.

Chorus.

But how?

Oedipus.

The guerdon fell.
Would I had earned it not from those I served too well.

Antistrophe 2

Chorus.

But, hapless, didst thou slay—

Oedipus.

What seek ye more to know?

Chorus.

Thy father?

Oedipus.

O dismay! Ye wound me, blow on blow.

Chorus.

Thy hand destroyed him.

Oedipus.

Yes. Yet lacks there not herein
A plea for my redress.

Chorus.

How canst thou clear that sin?

Oedipus.

I'll tell thee. For the deed, 'twas proved mine,—
Oh 'tis true!
Yet by Heaven's Law I am freed:—I wist not whom I slew.

Chorus.

Enough. For lo! where Aegeus' princely son,
Theseus, comes hither, summoned at thy word.

(*Enter Theseus.*)

Theseus.

From many voices in the former time
Telling thy cruel tale of sight destroyed
I have known thee, son of Laius, and to-day
I know thee anew, in learning thou art here.
Thy raiment, and the sad change in thy face,
Proclaim thee who thou art, and pitying thee,
Dark-fated Oedipus, I fain would hear
What prayer or supplication thou preferrest
To me and to my city, thou and this
Poor maid who moves beside thee. Full of dread
Must be that fortune thou canst name, which I
Would shrink from, since I know of mine own youth,

How in strange lands a stranger as thou art
I bore the brunt of perilous circumstance
Beyond all others; nor shall any man,
Like thee an alien from his native home,
Find that I turn away from succouring him.
I am a man and know it. To-morrow's good
Is no more mine than thine or any man's.

Oedipus.

Thy noble spirit, Theseus, in few words
Hath made my task of utterance brief indeed.
Thou hast told aright my name and parentage
And native city. Nought remains for me
But to make known mine errand, and our talk
Is ended.

Theseus.

Tell me plainly thy desire.

Oedipus.

I come to offer thee this woe-worn frame,
As a free boon,—not goodly in outward view.
A better gift than beauty is that I bring.

Theseus.

What boon dost thou profess to have brought
with thee?

Oedipus.

Thou shalt know by-and-by,—not yet awhile.

Theseus.

When comes the revelation of thine aid?

Oedipus.

When I am dead, and thou hast buried me.

Theseus.

Thou cravest the last kindness. What's between
Thou dost forget or else neglect.

Oedipus.

Herein
One word conveys the assurance of the whole.

Theseus.

You sum up your petition in brief form.

Oedipus.

Look to it. Great issues hang upon this hour.

Theseus.

Mean'st thou in this the fortune of thy sons
Or mine?

Oedipus.

I mean the force of their behest
Compelling my removal hence to Thebes.

Theseus.

So thy consent were sought, 'twere fair to yield.

Oedipus.

Once I was ready enough. They would not then.

Theseus.

Wrath is not wisdom in misfortune, man!

Oedipus.

Nay, chide not till thou knowest.

Theseus.

Inform me, then!
I must not speak without just grounds.

Oedipus.

O Theseus,
I am cruelly harassed with wrong heaped on wrong.

Theseus.

Mean'st thou that prime misfortune of thy birth?

Oedipus.

No. That hath long been rumoured through the world.

Theseus.

What, then, can be thy grief? If more than that,
'Tis more than human.

Oedipus.

Here is my distress:—
I am made an outcast from my native land
By mine own offspring. And return is barred
For ever to the man who slew his sire.

Theseus.

How then should they require thee to go near,
And yet dwell separate?

Oedipus.

The voice of Heaven
Will drive them to it.

Theseus.

As fearing what reverse
Prophetically told?

Oedipus.

Destined defeat
By Athens in the Athenian land.

Theseus.

What source
Of bitterness 'twixt us and Thebes can rise?

Oedipus.

Dear son of Aegeus, to the Gods alone
Comes never Age nor Death. All else i' the world
Time, the all-subduer, merges in oblivion.
Earth and men's bodies weaken, fail, and perish:
Faith withers, breach of faith springs up and grows,
And neither men nor cities that are friends
Breathe the same spirit with continuing breath.
Love shall be turned to hate, and hate to love
With many hereafter, as with some to-day.
And though, this hour, between great Thebes and thee
No cloud be in the heaven, yet moving Time
Enfolds a countless brood of days to come,
Wherein for a light cause they shall destroy
Your now harmonious league with severing war,
Even where my slumbering form, buried in death,
Coldly shall drink the life-blood of my foes,
If Zeus be Zeus, and his son Phoebus true.
I would not speak aloud of mysteries.
Then let me leave where I began. Preserve
Thine own good faith, and thou shalt never say,
Unless the Gods shall fail me, that for nought
Athens took Oedipus to dwell with her.

Chorus.

My lord, long since the stranger hath professed
Like promises of blessing to our land.

Theseus.

And who would dare reject his proffered good?
Whose bond with us of warrior amity
Hath ne'er been sundered,—and to-day he comes
A God-sent suppliant, whose sacred hand
Is rich with gifts for Athens and for me.
In reverent heed whereof I ne'er will scorn
The boon he brings, but plant him in our land.
And if it please our friend to linger here,
Ye shall protect him:—if to go with me
Best likes thee, Oedipus,—ponder, and use
Thy preference. For my course shall join with thine.

Oedipus.

Ye Heavens, reward such excellence!

Theseus.

How, then?
Is it thy choice now to go home with me?

Oedipus.

Yea, were it lawful. But in this same spot—

Theseus.

What wouldst thou do? I'll not withstand thy will.

Oedipus.

I must have victory o'er my banishers.

Theseus.

Thy dwelling with us, then, is our great gain?

Oedipus.

Yes, if thou fail me not, but keep thy word.

Theseus.

Nay, fear not me! I will aye be true to thee.

Oedipus.

I will not bind thee, like a knave, with oaths.

Theseus.

Oaths were no stronger than my simple word.

Oedipus.

What will ye do, then?

Theseus.

What is that thou fearest?

Oedipus.

They will come hither.

Theseus.

Thy guards will see to that.

Oedipus.

Beware, lest, if you leave me—

Theseus.

Tell not me,
I know my part.

Oedipus.

Terror will have me speak.

Theseus.

Terror and I are strangers.

Oedipus.

But their threats!
Thou canst not know—

Theseus.

I know that none shall force
Thee from this ground against thy will. Full oft
Have threatening words in wrath been voluble,
Yet, when the mind regained her place again,
The threatened evil vanished. So to-day
Bold words of boastful meaning have proclaimed
Thy forcible abduction by thy kin.
Yet shall they find (I know it) the voyage from Thebes,
On such a quest, long and scarce navigable.
Whate'er my thought, if Phoebus sent thee forth,
I would bid thee have no fear. And howsoe'er,
My name will shield thee from all injury.

(*Exit.*)

Strophe 1

Chorus.

Friend! in our land of conquering steeds thou art come
To this Heaven-fostered haunt, Earth's fairest home,
Gleaming Colonus, where the nightingale
In cool green covert warbleth ever clear,
True to the clustering ivy and the dear
Divine, impenetrable shade,
From wildered boughs and myriad fruitage made,
Sunless at noon, stormless in every gale.
Wood-roving Bacchus there, with mazy round,
And his nymph nurses range the unoffended ground.

Antistrophe 1

And nourished day by day with heavenly dew
Bright flowers their never-failing bloom renew,
From eldest time Deo and Cora's crown
Full-flowered narcissus, and the golden beam
Of crocus, while Cephisus' gentle stream
In runnels fed by sleepless springs
Over the land's broad bosom daily brings
His pregnant waters, never dwindling down.
The quiring Muses love to seek the spot
And Aphrodite's golden car forsakes it not.

Strophe 2

Here too a plant, nobler than e'er was known
On Asian soil, grander than yet hath grown
In Pelops' mighty Dorian isle, unsown,
Free, self-create, the conquering foeman's fear,
The kind oil-olive, silvery-green,
Chief nourisher of childish life, is seen
To burgeon best in this our mother-land.
No warrior, young, nor aged in command,
Shall ravage this, or scathe it with the spear;
For guardian Zeus' unslumbering eye
Beholds it everlastingly,
And Athens' grey-eyed Queen, dwelling for ever near.

Antistrophe 2

Yet one more praise mightier than all I tell
O'er this my home, that Ocean loves her well,
And coursers love her, children of the wave.
To grace these roadways Prince Poseidon first
Framed for the horse, that else had burst
From man's control, the spirit-taming bit.
And the trim bark, rowed by strong arms, doth flit
O'er briny seas with glancing motion brave.
—Poseidon! Lord of waters, thine the gift!
Thou hast established our fair town
For ever in this proud renown—
The Sea-nymphs' plashing throng glide not more smoothly swift.

Antigone.

O land exalted thus in blessing and praise,
Now is thy time to prove these brave words true.

Oedipus.

What hath befallen, my daughter?

Antigone.

Here at hand,
Not unaccompanied, is Creon, father.

Oedipus.

Dear aged friends, be it yours now to provide
My safety and the goal of my desire!

Chorus.

It shall be so. Fear nought. I am old and weak,
But Athens in her might is ever young.

(*Enter Creon.*)

Creon.

Noble indwellers of this Attic ground,
I see as 'twere conceived within your eyes
At mine approach some new-engendered fear.
Nay, shrink not back, nor utter one harsh word.
I bring no danger with me, for my age
Is feeble, and the state whereto I come
Is mighty,—none in Hellas mightier,—
That know I well. But I am sent to bring
By fair persuasion to our Theban plain
The reverend form of him now present here.
Nor came this mission from one single will,
But the commands of all my citizens
Are on me, seeing it falls to me by birth
To mourn his sorrows most of all the state.
Thou, then, poor sufferer, lend thine ear to me
And come. All Cadmus' people rightfully
Invite thee with one voice unto thy home,
I before all,—since I were worst of men,
Were I not pained at thy misfortunes, sir,
—To see thee wandering in the stranger's land
Aged and miserable, unhoused, unfed,
Singly attended by this girl, whose fall
To such a depth of undeservèd woe
I could not have imagined! Hapless maid!
Evermore caring for thy poor blind head,
Roving in beggary, so young, with no man
To marry her,—exposed to all mischance.
O misery, what deep reproach I have laid
On thee and me and all our ill-starred race!
But who can hide evil that courts the day?
Thou, therefore, Oedipus, without constraint,
(By all the Gods of Cadmus' race I pray thee)
Withdraw this horror from the sight of men
By coming to the ancestral city and home
Of thy great sires, bidding a kind farewell
To worthiest Athens, as is meet. But Thebes,
Thy native land, yet more deserves thy love.

Oedipus.

Thou unabashed in knavery, who canst frame
For every cause the semblance of a plea
Pranked up with righteous seeming, why again
Would'st thou contrive my ruin, and attempt
To catch me where I most were grieved being caught?
Beforetime, when the trouble of my soul
Was plaguing me, and I would fain have rushed
To instant banishment, thou wouldst not then
Grant this indulgence to my strong desire.
But when I had fed my passion to the full,
And all my pleasure was to live at home,
Then 'twas thy choice to chase and banish me,
Nor was this name of kindred then so dear.
And now once more, when thou behold'st this city
And people joined in friendly bands with me,
Now thou art bent to drag me off again,
Hiding hard policy with courtly show.
Strange kindness, to love men against their will!
Suppose, when thou wert eager in some suit,
No grace were granted thee, but all denied,
And when thy soul was sated, then the boon
Were offered, when such grace were graceless now;
—Poor satisfaction then were thine, I ween!
Even such a gift thou profferest me to-day,
Kind in pretence, but really full of evil.
These men shall hear me tell thy wickedness.
Thou comest to take me, not unto my home,
But to dwell outlawed at your gate, that so
Your Thebè may come off untouched of harm
From her encounter with Athenian men.
Ye shall not have me thus. But you shall have
My vengeful spirit ever in your land
Abiding for destruction,—and my sons
Shall have this portion in their father's ground,
To die thereon. Know I not things in Thebes
Better than thou? Yea, for 'tis mine to hear
Safer intelligencers,—Zeus himself,
And Phoebus, high interpreter of Heaven.
Thou bring'st a tongue suborned with false pretence,
Sharpened with insolence;—but in shrewd speech
Thou shalt find less of profit than of bane.

This thou wilt ne'er believe. Therefore begone!
Let me live here. For even such life as mine
Were not amiss, might I but have my will.

Creon.

Which of us twain, believ'st thou, in this talk
Hath more profoundly sinned against thy peace?

Oedipus.

If thou prevail'st with these men present here
Even as with me, I shall be well content.

Creon.

Unhappy man, will not even Time bring forth
One spark of wisdom to redeem thine age?

Oedipus.

Thou art a clever talker. But I know
No just man who in every cause abounds
With eloquent speech.

Creon.

'Tis not to abound in speech,
When one speaks fitting words in season.

Oedipus.

Oh!
As if thy words were few and seasonable!

Creon.

Not in the dotard's judgment.

Oedipus.

Get thee gone!
I speak their mind as well—and dog not me
Beleaguering mine appointed dwelling-place!

Creon.

These men shall witness—for thy word is naught;
And for thy spiteful answer to thy friends,
If once I seize thee—

Oedipus.

Who shall seize on me
Without the will of my protectors here?

Creon.

Well, short of that, thou shalt have pain, I trow.

Oedipus.

What hast thou done, that thou canst threaten thus?

Creon.

One of thy daughters I have sent in charge.
This other, I myself will quickly take.

Oedipus.

Oh, cruel!

Creon.

Soon thou'lt have more cause to cry.

Oedipus.

Hast thou my child?

Creon.

I will have both ere long.

Oedipus.

Dear friends, what will ye do? Will ye forsake me?
Will you not drive the offender from your land?

Chorus.

Stranger, depart at once! Thou hast done wrong,
And wrong art doing.

Creon (*to attendants*).

Now then, lead her away
By force, if she refuse to go with you.

Antigone.

Ah me! unhappy! Whither shall I flee?
What aid of God or mortal can I find?

Chorus.

What dost thou, stranger?

Creon.

I will lay no hand
On him, but on my kinswoman.

Oedipus.

Alas!
Lords of Colonus, will ye suffer it?

Chorus.

Thou art transgressing, stranger.

Creon.

Nay, I stand
Within my right.

Chorus.

How so?

Creon.

I take mine own.

Oedipus.

Athens to aid!

Chorus.

Stranger, forbear! What dost thou?
Let go, or thou shalt try thy strength with us.

Creon.

Unhand me!

Chorus.

Not while this intent is thine.

Creon.

If you harm me, you will have war with Thebes.

Oedipus.

Did I not tell you this would come?

Chorus.

Release
The maid with speed.

Creon.

Command where you have power.

Chorus.

Leave hold, I say!

Creon.

Away with her, say I!

Chorus.

Come hither, neighbours, come!
My city suffers violence. Wrongful men
Are hurting her with force. Come hither to me!

Antigone.

Unhappy, I am dragged away,—O strangers!

Oedipus.

Where art thou, O my child?

Antigone.

I go away
Against my will.

Oedipus.

Reach forth thy hands, my daughter!

Antigone.

I cannot.

Creon.

Off with her!

Antigone.

Alas, undone!

(*Exit, guarded.*)

Creon.

Thou shalt not have these staves henceforth to prop
Thy roaming to and fro. Take thine own way!
Since thou hast chosen to thwart thy nearest kin,—
Beneath whose orders, though a royal man,
I act herein,—and thine own native land.
The time will surely come when thou shalt find
That in this deed and all that thou hast done
In opposition to their friendly will,
Thou hast counselled foolishly against thy peace,
Yielding to anger, thy perpetual bane.

(*Going.*)

Chorus.

Stranger, stand where thou art!

Creon.

Hands off, I say!

Chorus.

Thou shalt not go, till thou restore the maids.

Creon.

Soon, then, my city shall retain from you
A weightier cause of war. I will lay hands
Not on the maidens only.

Chorus.

What wilt thou do?

Creon.

Oedipus I will seize and bear away.

Chorus.

Great Heaven forfend!

Creon.

It shall be done forthwith,
Unless the ruler of this land prevent me.

Oedipus.

O shameless utterance! Wilt thou lay thy hold
On me?

Creon.

Be silent! Speak no more!

Oedipus.

No more?
May these dread Goddesses not close my lips
To this one prayer of evil against thee,
Thou villain, who, when I have lost mine eyes,

Bereavest me of all that I had left
To make my darkness light! Therefore I pray,
For this thy wrongful act, may He in heaven
Whose eye sees all things, Helios, give to thee
Slowly to wither in an age like mine!

Creon.

Men of this land, bear witness to his rage!

Oedipus.

They see us both, and are aware that I
Repay thee but with words for deeds of wrong.

Creon.

No longer will I curb my wrath. Though lonely
And hindered by mine age, I will bear off
This man!

Oedipus.

Me miserable!

Chorus.

How bold thou art,
If standing here thou think'st to do this thing!

Creon.

I do.

Chorus.

Then Athens is to me no city.

Creon.

Slight men prevail o'er strength in a just cause.

Oedipus.

Hear ye his words?

Chorus.

He shall not make them good.
Be witness, Zeus!

Creon.

Zeus knows more things than thou.

Oedipus.

Is not this violence?

Creon.

Violence you must bear.

Chorus.

Come, chieftain of our land!
Come hither with all speed. They pass the bound.

(*Enter Theseus.*)

Theseus.

Wherefore that shouting? Daunted by what fear
Stayed ye me sacrificing to the God
Who guards this deme Colonus? Let me know
What cause so hastened my reluctant foot.

Oedipus.

Dear friend (I know thy voice addressing us),
One here hath lately done me cruel wrong.

Theseus.

Who is the wrong-doer, say, and what the deed?

Oedipus.

This Creon, whom thou seest, hath torn away
The loving pair of girls that were mine all.

Theseus.

Can this be possible?

Oedipus.

Thou hear'st the truth.

Theseus.

Then one of you run to the altar-foot
Hard by, and haste the people from the rite,
Horsemen and footmen at the height of speed
To race unto the parting of the roads
Where travellers from both gorges wont to meet.
Lest there the maidens pass beyond our reach
And I be worsted by this stranger's might
And let him laugh at me. Be swift! Away!
—For him, were I as wroth as he deserves,
He should not go unpunished from my hand.
But now he shall be ruled by the same law
He thought to enforce. Thou goest not from this land
Till thou hast set these maids in presence here;
Since by thine act thou hast disgraced both me
And thine own lineage and thy native land,
Who with unlicensed inroad hast assailed
An ancient city, that hath still observed
Justice and equity, and apart from law
Ratifies nothing; and, being here, hast cast
Authority to the winds, and made thine own
Whate'er thou wouldst, bearing it off perforce,—
Deeming of me forsooth as nothing worth,
And of my city as one enslaved to foes

Or void of manhood. Not of Thebè's will
Come such wild courses. It is not her way
To foster men in sin, nor would she praise
Thy conduct, if she knew that thou hast robbed
Me and the gods, dragging poor suppliant wights
From their last refuge at thy will.—I would not,
Had I perchance set foot within thy land,
Even were my cause most righteous, have presumed,
Without consent of him who bore chief sway,
To seize on any man, but would have known
How to behave myself on foreign ground.
Thou bring'st disgrace on thine own mother-state
All undeservedly, and the weight of years
Hath made thee aged, but not wise.—Again
I bid those maids now to be brought with speed,
Unless thou would'st be made a sojourner
In Athens by compulsion. This I speak
Not with my lips alone, but from my will.

Chorus.

Stranger, dost thou perceive? Thy parentage
Is owned as noble, but thine evil deeds
Are blazoned visibly.

Creon.

Great Aegeus' son!
Not as misprising this thy city's strength
In arms, or wisdom in debate, I dared
This capture, but in simple confidence
Thy citizens would not so envy me
My blood-relations, as to harbour them
Against my will,—nor welcome to their hearths
A man incestuous and a parricide,
The proved defiler of his mother's bed.
Such was the mount of Ares that I knew,
Seat of high wisdom, planted in their soil,
That suffers no such lawless vagabond
To dwell within the borders of your realm.
Relying on that I laid my hands upon
This quarry; nor had done so, were it not
For the deep curse he laid on me and mine.
That moved me to requital, since even Age
Still bears resentment, till the power of death
Frees men from anger, as from all annoy.

Being sovereign here thou wilt do thy pleasure. I,
Though I have justice on my side, am weak
Through being alone. Yet if you meddle with me,
Old as I am, you'll find me dangerous.

Oedipus.

O boldness void of shame! Whom dost thou think
Thy obloquy most harms, this agèd head
Or thine, who hast thus let pass thy lips the crimes
I have borne unwittingly. So Heaven was pleased
To wreak some old offence upon our race.
Since in myself you will find no stain of sin
For which such ruinous error 'gainst myself
And mine own house might be the recompense.
Tell me, I pray thee, if a word from Heaven
Came to my father through the oracle
That he should die by his son's hand,—how then
Can this be justly a reproach to me,
The child not yet begotten of my sire,
An unborn nothing, unconceived? Or if,
Born as I was to misery, I met
And killed my father in an angry fray,
Nought knowing of what I did or whom I slew,
What reason is't to blame the unwitting deed?
And, oh, thou wretch! art not ashamed to force me
To speak that of my mother, thine own sister,
Which I will speak, for I will not keep silence,
Since thou hast been thus impious with thy tongue.
She was my mother, oh, the bitter word!
Though neither knew it, and having borne me, she
Became the mother of children to her son,
An infamous birth! Yet this I know, thy crime
Of speech against us both is voluntary.
But all involuntary was my deed
In marriage and is this mine utterance now.
No,—that shall not be called a bosom-sin,
Nor shall my name be sullied with the deed,
Thy tongue would brand on me, against my sire.
For answer me one question. If today,
Here, now, one struck at thee a murderous stroke,—
At thee, the righteous person,—wouldst thou ask
If such assailant were thy sire, or strike
Forthwith? Methinks, as you loved life, your hand

Would strike before you questioned of the right,
Or reasoned of his kindred whom you slew.
Such was the net that snared me: such the woes
Heaven drave me to fulfil. My father's spirit,
Came he to life, would not gainsay my word.
But thou, the seeming just man, to whose mouth
No matter is too dreadful or too deep
For words, so rail'st on me, in such a presence.
Well thou dost flatter the great name of Theseus,
And Athens in her glory stablished here,
But midst thy fulsome praises thou forgettest
How of all lands that yield the immortal Gods
Just homage of true piety, this land
Is foremost. Yet from hence thou would'st beguile
Me, the aged suppliant. Nay, from hence thou would'st drag
Myself with violence, and hast reft away
My children. Wherefore I conjure these powers,
With solemn invocation and appeal,
To come and take my part, that thou may'st know
What men they are who guard this hallowed realm.

Chorus.

My lord, the stranger deserves well. His fate
Is grievous, but the more demands our aid.

Theseus.

Enough of words. The captors and their prey
Are hasting;—we, they have wronged, are standing still.

Creon.

I am powerless here. What dost thou bid me do?

Theseus.

Lead us the way they are gone. I too must be
Thine escort, that if hereabout thou hast
Our maidens, thou mayest show them to my sight.
But if men flee and bear them, we may spare
Superfluous labour. Others hotly urge
That business, whom those robbers shall not boast
Before their Gods to have 'scaped out of this land.
Come, be our guide! Thou hast and hast not. Fortune
Hath seized thee seizing on thy prey. So quickly
Passes the gain that's got by wrongful guile.
Nay, thou shalt have no helper. Well I wot
Thou flew'st not to this pitch of truculent pride

Alone, or unsupported by intrigue;
But thy bold act hath some confederate here.
This I must look into, nor let great Athens
Prove herself weaker than one single man.
Hast caught my drift? Or is my voice as vain
Now, as you thought it when you planned this thing?

Creon.

I will gainsay nought of what thou utterest here.
But once in Thebes, I too shall know my course.

Theseus.

Threaten, but go! Thou, Oedipus, remain
In quietness and perfect trust that I,
If death do not prevent me, will not rest
Till I restore thy children to thy hand.

(*Exeunt Theseus and Creon.*)

Strophe 1

Chorus.

Soon shall the wheeling foes
Clash with the din of brazen-throated War.
Would I were there to see them close,
Be the onset near or far!
Whether at Daphne's gorge to Phoebus dear,
Or by the torch-lit shore
Where kind maternal powers for evermore
Guard golden mysteries of holy fear
To nourish mortal souls
Whose voice the seal of silent awe controls
Imprinted by the Eumolpid minister.
There, on that sacred way,
Shall the divinest head
Of royal Theseus, rouser of the fray,
And those free maids, in their two squadrons led,
Meet in the valorous fight
That conquers for the right.

Antistrophe 1

Else, by the snow-capped rock,
Passing to westward, they are drawing nigh
The tract beyond the pasture high
Where Oea feeds her flock.
The riders ride, the rattling chariots flee

At racing speed.—'Tis done!
He shall be vanquished. Our land's chivalry
Are valiant, valiant every warrior son
Of Theseus.—On they run!
Frontlet and bridle glancing to the light,
Forward each steed is straining to the fight,
Forward each eye and hand
Of all that mounted band,
Athena's knighthood, champions of her name
And his who doth the mighty waters tame,
Rhea's son that from of old
Doth the Earth with seas enfold.

Strophe 2

Strive they? Or is the battle still to be?
An eager thought in me
Is pleading, "Soon must they restore
The enduring maid, whose kinsmen vex her sore!"
To-day shall Zeus perform his will.
The noble cause wins my prophetic skill.
Oh! had I wings, and like a storm-swift dove
Poised on some aery cloud might there descry
The conflict from above,
Scouring the region with mine eye!

Antistrophe 2

Sovran of Heaven, all-seeing Zeus, afford
Unto this nation's lord
Puissance to crown the fair emprise,
Thou, and all-knowing Pallas, thy dread child!
Apollo, huntsman of the wild,
—Thou and thy sister, who doth still pursue
Swift many-spotted stags,—arise, arise,
With love we pray you, be our champions true!
Yea, both together come
To aid our people and our home!

(*Enter Antigone, Ismene, and Theseus.*)

Ah! wanderer friend, thou wilt not have to accuse
Thy seer of falsehood. I behold the maids
This way once more in safe protection brought.

Oedipus.

Where? Is it true? How say you?

Antigone.

Father, father
Oh that some God would give thee once to see
The man whose royal virtue brings us hither!

Oedipus.

My daughters, are ye there?

Antigone.

Saved by the arm
Of Theseus and his most dear ministers.

Oedipus.

Come near me, child, and let your father feel
The treasure he had feared for ever gone.

Antigone.

Not hard the boon which the heart longs to give.

Oedipus.

Where are ye, where?

Antigone.

Together we draw near.

Oedipus.

Loved saplings of a solitary tree!

Antigone.

A father's heart hides all.

Oedipus.

Staves of mine age!

Antigone.

Forlorn supporters of an ill-starred life!

Oedipus.

I have all I love; nor would the stroke of death
Be wholly bitter, with you standing by.
Press close to either side of me, my children;
Grow to your sire, and ye shall give me rest
From mine else lonely, hapless, wandering life.
And tell your tale as briefly as ye may,
Since at your age short speaking is enough.

Antigone.

Here is our saviour. He shall tell thee all,
And shorten labour both for us and thee.

Oedipus.

Think it not strange, dear friend, that I prolong
The unhoped-for greeting with my children here.

Full well I know, the joy I find in them
Springs from thee only, and from none beside.
Thou, thou alone hast saved them. May the Gods
Fulfil my prayer for thee and for thy land!
Since only in Athens, only here i' the world,
Have I found pious thought and righteous care,
And truth in word and deed. From a full heart
And thankful mind I thus requite thy love,
Knowing all I have is due to none but thee.
Extend to me, I pray thee, thy right hand,
O King, that I may feel thee, and may kiss,
If that be lawful, thy dear head! And yet
What am I asking? How can one like me
Desire of thee to touch an outlawed man,
On whose dark life all stains of sin and woe
Are fixed indelibly? I will not dare—
No, nor allow thee!—None but only they
Who have experience of such woes as mine
May share their wretchedness. Thou, where thou art
Receive my salutation, and henceforth
Continue in thy promised care of me
As true as to this moment thou hast proved.

Theseus.

I marvel not at all if mere delight
In these thy daughters lengthened thy discourse,
Or led thee to address them before me.
That gives me not the shadow of annoy.
Nor am I careful to adorn my life
With words of praise, but with the light of deeds.
And thou hast proof of this. For I have failed
In nought of all I promised, aged King!
Here stand I with thy children in full life
Unharmed in aught the foe had threatened them.
And now why vaunt the deeds that won the day,
When these dear maids will tell them in thine ear?
But let me crave thy counsel on a thing
That crossed me as I came. Small though it seem
When told, 'tis worthy of some wonder, too.
Be it small or great, men should not let things pass.

Oedipus.

What is it, O son of Aegeus? Let me hear,
I am wholly ignorant herein.

Theseus.

We are told
One, not thy townsman, but of kin to thee,
Hath come in unawares, and now is found
Kneeling at great Poseidon's altar, where
I sacrificed, what time ye summoned me.

Oedipus.

What countryman, and wherefore suppliant there?

Theseus.

One thing alone I know. He craves of thee
Some speech, they say, that will not hold thee long.

Oedipus.

His kneeling there imports no trivial suit.

Theseus.

All he desires, they tell me, is to come,
Have speech with thee, and go unharmed away.

Oedipus.

Who can he be that kneels for such a boon?

Theseus.

Think, if at Argos thou a kinsman hast
Who might desire to obtain so much of thee.

Oedipus.

Dear friend! Hold there! No more!

Theseus.

What ails thee, man?

Oedipus.

Ask it not of me!

Theseus.

What? Speak plainly forth.

Oedipus.

Thy words have shown me who the stranger is.

Theseus.

And who is he that I should say him nay?

Oedipus.

My son, O King,—hateful to me, whose tongue
Least of the world I could endure to hear.

Theseus.

What pain is there in hearing? Canst thou not
Hear, and refuse to do what thou dislikest?

Oedipus.

My Lord, I have come to loathe his very voice.
I pray thee, urge me not to yield in this.

Theseus.

Think that the God must be considered too;
The right of suppliants may compel thy care.

Antigone.

Father, give ear, though I be young that speak.
Yield to the scruple of the King, who claims
This reverence for his people's God;—and yield
To us who beg our brother may come near.
Take heart! He will not force thee from thy will.
What harm can come of hearkening? Wisdom's ways
Reveal themselves through words. He is thy son:
Whence, were his heartless conduct against thee
Beyond redemption impious, O my sire,
Thy vengeance still would be unnatural.
Oh let him!—Others have had evil sons
And passionate anger, but the warning voice
Of friends hath charmed their mood. Then do not thou
Look narrowly upon thy present griefs,
But on those ancient wrongs thou didst endure
From father and from mother. Thence thou wilt learn
That evil passion ever ends in woe.
Thy sightless eyes are no light argument
To warn thee through the feeling of thy loss.
Relent and hear us! 'Tis a mere disgrace
To beg so long for a just boon. The King
Is kind to thee. Be generous in return.

Oedipus.

Child, your dear pleading to your hard request
Hath won me. Let this be as ye desire.
Only, my lord, if he is to come near,
Let no man's power molest my liberty.

Theseus.

I need no repetition, aged friend,
Of that request. Vaunt will I not; but, thou,
Be sure, if Heaven protect me, thou art free.

(*Exit.*)

Strophe

Chorus.

Who, loving life, hath sought
To outlive the appointed span,
Shall be arraigned before my thought
For an infatuate man.
Since the added years entail
Much that is bitter;—joy
Flies out of ken, desire doth fail,
The wished-for moments cloy.
But when the troublous life,
Be it less or more, is past,
With power to end the strife
Comes rescuing Death at last.
Lo! the dark bridegroom waits! No festal choir
Shall grace his destined hour, no dance, no lyre!

Antistrophe

Far best were ne'er to be;
But, having seen the day,
Next best by far for each to flee
As swiftly as each may,
Yonder from whence he came;
For once let Youth be there
With her light fooleries, who shall name
The unnumbered brood of Care?
No trial spared, no fall!
Feuds, battles, murders, rage,
Envy, and last of all,
Despised, dim, friendless age!
Ay, there all evils, crowded in one room,
Each at his worst of ill, augment the gloom.

Epode

Such lot is mine, and round this man of woe,
—As some grey headland of a northward shore
Bears buffets of all wintry winds that blow,—
New storms of Fate are bursting evermore
In thundrous billows, borne
Some from the waning light,
Some through mid-noon, some from the rising morn,
Some from the realm of Night.

Antigone.

Ah! Who comes here? Sure 'tis the Argive man
Approaching hitherward, weeping amain.
And, father, it is he!

Oedipus.

Whom dost thou mean?

Antigone.

The same our thoughts have dwelt on all this while,
Polyneices. He is here.

(*Enter Polyneices.*)

Polyneices.

What shall I do?
I stand in doubt which first I should lament,
My own misfortune or my father's woe,
Whom here I find an outcast in his age
With you, my sisters, in the stranger land,
Clothed in such raiment, whose inveterate filth
Horridly clings, wasting his reverend form,
While the grey locks over the eye-reft brow
Wave all unkempt upon the ruffling breeze.
And likewise miserable appears the store
He bears to nourish that time-wasted frame.
Wretch that I am! Too late I learn the truth,
And here give witness to mine own disgrace,
Which is as deep as thy distress. Myself
Declare it. Ask not others of my guilt.
But seeing that Zeus on his almighty throne
Keeps Mercy in all he doth to counsel him,
Thou, too, my father, let her plead with thee!
The evil that is done may yet be healed;
It cannot be augmented. Art thou silent?
O turn not from me, father! Speak but once!
Wilt thou not answer, but with shame dismiss me
Voiceless, nor make known wherefore thou art wroth?
O ye his daughters, one with me in blood,
Say, will not ye endeavour to unlock
The stern lips of our unrelenting sire?
Let him not thus reject in silent scorn
Without response the suppliant of Heaven!

Antigone.

Thyself, unhappy one, say why thou camest.
Speech ofttimes, as it flows, touching some root
Of pity or joy, or even of hate, hath stirred
The dumb to utterance.

Polyneices.

I will tell my need:—
First claiming for protector the dread God
From whose high altar he who rules this land
Hath brought me under safe-guard of his power,
Scatheless to speak and hear and go my way.
His word, I am well assured, will be made good,
Strangers, by you, and by my sisters twain,
And by our sire.—Now let me name mine errand.
I am banished, father, from my fatherland,
Because, being elder-born, I claimed to sit
Upon thy sovereign throne. For this offence
Eteocles, thy younger son, exiled me,
Not having won the advantage in debate
Or trial of manhood, but through guileful art
Gaining the people's will. Whereof my heart
Declares thy Fury the author; and thereto
Prophetic voices also testify.
For when I had come to Dorian Argolis,
I raised, through marriage with Adrastus' child,
An army bound in friendly league with me,
Headed by those who in the Apian land
Hold first pre-eminence and honour in war,
With whose aid levying all that mighty host
Of seven battalions, I have deeply sworn
Either to die, or drive from Theban ground
The men who thus have wrought. So far, so well.
But why come hither? Father, to crave thine aid
With earnest supplication for myself
And for my firm allies, who at this hour,
Seven leaders of seven bands embattled there,
Encompass Thebè's plain. Amphiaraus,
Foremost in augury, foremost in war,
First wields his warlike spear. Next, Oeneus' son,
Aetolian Tydeus; then Eteoclus
Of Argive lineage; fourth, Hippomedon,
Sent by his father Talaus, and the fifth

Is Capaneus, who brags he will destroy
Thebè with desolating fire. The sixth,
Parthenopaeus, from the Arcadian glen
Comes bravely down, swift Atalanta's child,
Named from his mother's lingering maidenhood
Ere she conceived him. And the seventh am I,
Thy son, or if not thine, but the dire birth
Of evil Destiny, yet named thy son,
Who lead this dauntless host from Argolis
Against the Theban land. Now one and all
We pray thee on our knees, conjuring thee
As thou dost love these maids and thine own life,
My father, to forgive me, ere I go
To be revenged upon my brother there
Who drave me forth and robbed me of my throne.
If aught in prophecy deserves belief,
'Tis certain, whom thou favourest, those shall win.
Now by the wells whereof our fathers drank
And by the Gods they worshipped, hear our prayer,
Grant this petition: since alike in woe,
Alike in poverty and banishment,
Partakers of one destiny, thou and I
Cringe to the stranger for a dwelling-place.
Whilst he at home, the tyrant, woe is me,
Laughs at us both in soft luxurious pride.
Whose might, so thou wilt favour my design,
I will lightly scatter in one little hour;
And plant thee in thy Theban palace-home
Near to myself, hurling the usurper forth.
All this with thy consent I shall achieve,
But without thee, I forfeit life and all.

Chorus.

For his sake who hath brought him, Oedipus,
Say what is meet, and let him go in peace.

Oedipus.

Ay, were it not the lord of all this land
Theseus, that brought him to me and desired
He might hear words from me,—never again
Had these tones fallen upon his ear. But now
That boon is granted him: he shall obtain,
Ere he depart, such utterance of my tongue,
As ne'er shall give him joy;—ne'er comfort thee,

Villain, who when possessed of the chief power
Which now thy brother holds o'er Theban land,
Didst banish me, thy father, who stand here,
To live in exile, clothed with such attire,
That moves thy tears now that thine own estate
Is fallen into like depth of struggling woe.
But tears are bootless. Howsoe'er I live,
I must endure, and hold thee still my murderer.
'Tis thou hast girt me round with misery,
'Tis thou didst drive me forth, and driven by thee
I beg my bread, a wandering sojourner.
Yea, had these daughters not been born to me
To tend me, I were dead, for all thou hast done.
They have rescued, they have nursed me. They are men,
Not women, in the strength of ministry.
Ye are another's, not my sons.—For this
The eye of Destiny pursues thee still
Eager to light on thee with instant doom
If once that army move toward the town
Of ancient Thebes,—the town; no dearer name,
"City" or "Country" shall beseem thy lip
Till ye both fall, stained with fraternal gore.
Long since I launched that curse against you twain
Which here again I summon to mine aid,
That ye may learn what duty children owe
To a parent, nor account it a light thing
That ye were cruel sons to your blind sire.
These maidens did not so. Wherefore my curse
Prevails against thy prayer for Thebè's throne,
If ancient Zeus, the eternal lawgiver,
Have primal Justice for his counsellor.
Begone, renounced and fatherless for me,
And take with thee, vilest of villainous men,
My imprecation:—Vain be thine attempt
In levying war against thy father's race,
Frustrate be thy return to Argos' vale:
Die foully by a fratricidal hand,
And foully slay him who hath banished thee!
Further, I bid the horror-breathing gloom
Tartarean, of the vault that holds my sire,
To banish thee from that last home: I invoke
The Spirits who haunt this ground, and the fierce God

Who hath filled you both with this unnatural hate.—
Go now with all this in thine ears, and tell
The people of Cadmus and thy firm allies
In whom thou trustest, what inheritance
Oedipus hath divided to his sons.

Chorus.

'Tis pity for thee, prince, to have come at all:
And now we bid thee go the way thou camest.

Polyneices.

Alas! Vain enterprise, and hope undone!
Oh, my poor comrades! To what fatal end
I led you forth from Argos, woe is me!
I may not tell it you,—no, nor return.
In silence I must go to meet my doom.
Daughters of this inexorable sire,
Since now ye have heard his cruel curse on me,
Ah! in Heaven's name, my sisters, do not you
Treat me despitefully, but if, one day,
Our father's execration is fulfilled
And ye shall be restored to Theban ground,
Provide me funeral honours and a grave!
So shall this ample praise which ye receive
For filial ministration, in that day
Be more than doubled through your care for me.

Antigone.

Brother, I beg thee, listen to my voice!

Polyneices.

Dearest Antigone, speak what thou wilt.

Antigone.

Turn back thy host to Argos with all speed,
And ruin not thyself and Thebè too.

Polyneices.

Impossible. If once I shrink for fear,
No longer may I lead them to the war.

Antigone.

But why renew thy rage? What benefit
Comes to thee from o'erturning thine own land?

Polyneices.

'Tis shameful to remain in banishment,
And let my brother mock my right of birth.

Antigone.

Then seest thou not how true unto their aim
Our father's prophecies of mutual death
Against you both are sped?

Polyneices.

He speaks his wish.
'Tis not for me to yield.

Antigone.

O me, unhappy!
But who that hears the deep oracular sound
Of his dark words, will dare to follow thee?

Polyneices.

They will not hear of danger from my mouth.
Wise generals tell of vantage, not of bale.

Antigone.

Art thou then so resolved, O brother mine?

Polyneices.

I am. Retard me not! I must attend
To my dark enterprise, blasted and foiled
Beforehand by my father's angry curse.
But as for you, Heaven prosper all your way,
If ye will show this kindness in my death,
For nevermore in life shall ye befriend me!
Nay, cling to me no longer. Fare ye well.
Ye will behold my living form no more.

Antigone.

O misery!

Polyneices.

Bewail me not.

Antigone.

And who
That saw thee hurrying forth to certain death
Would not bewail thee, brother?

Polyneices.

If Fate wills,
Why, I must die.

Antigone.

Nay, but be ruled by me.

Polyneices.

Give me not craven counsel.

Antigone.

Woe is me,
To lose thee!

Polyneices.

Heaven hath power to guide the event
Or thus or otherwise. Howe'er it prove,
I pray that ye may ne'er encounter ill.
All men may know, ye merit nought but good.

(*Exit. The sky is overcast—a storm is threatened.*)

Strophe 1

Chorus.

New trouble, strange trouble, deep-laden with doom,
From the sight-bereft stranger seems dimly to loom!
Or peers Fate through the gloom?
She will move toward her mark or through shining or shade;
Since no purpose of Gods ever idly was made.
Time sees the fulfilment, who lifteth to-day
What was lowly, and trampleth the lofty to clay.
Thunder! Heavens! what a sound!

Oedipus.

My children! Would but some one in the place
Haste hither Theseus, noblest among men!

Antigone.

Wherefore, my father? What is thy desire?

Oedipus.

These winged thunders of the highest will soon
Bear me away to the Unseen. Send quickly!

Antistrophe 1

Chorus.

Again, yonder crash through the fire-startled air
Wing'd from Zeus, rushes down, till my thin locks of hair,
Stiff with fear, upward stare.
My soul shrinks and cowers, for yon gleam from on high
Darts again! Ne'er in vain hath it leapt from the sky,
But flies forth amain to what task Zeus hath given.
I fear the unknown fatal edict of Heaven!
Lightning glares all around!

Oedipus.

My daughters, the divinely promised end
Here unavoidably descends on me.

Antigone.

How dost thou know it? By what certain sign?

Oedipus.

I know it perfectly. Let some one go
With speed to bring the lord of Athens hither.

Strophe 2

Chorus.

Great Heaven, how above me, beside me, around,
Peals redoubled the soul-thrilling sound!
O our God, to this land, to our mother, if aught
Thou wouldst send with some darkness of destiny fraught,
Smile gently once more! With the good let me bear
What of fortune soe'er,—
Taste no cup, touch no food, the doomed sinner may share.
Zeus, to thee, Lord, I cry!

Oedipus.

Is the King coming? Will he find me alive,
My daughters, and with reason undisturbed?

Antigone.

Say wherefore dost thou crave with such desire
The clearness of an undistracted mind?

Oedipus.

I would fully render from a grateful soul
The boon I promised, when I gained my suit.

Antistrophe 2

Chorus.

Come, my chief! come with speed! Or, if haply at hand,
On the height where the curved altars stand,
Thou art hallowing with oxen in sacrifice slain
Yonder shrine of Poseidon, dread lord of the main,
Speed hither! Be swift! The blind stranger intends
To thee, to thy friends,
To thy city, for burdens imposed, just amends.
Haste thee, King! Hear our cry!

(*Enter Theseus.*)

Theseus.

Why sounds again from hence your joint appeal,
Wherein the stranger's voice is loudly heard?
Is it some lightning-bolt new-fallen from Zeus,
Or cloud-born hail that is come rattling down?
From Heavens so black with storm nought can surprise.

Oedipus.

Prince, thou art come to my desire. Some God
Hath happily directed this thy way.

Theseus.

What is befallen? Son of Laius, tell!

Oedipus.

My path slopes downward, and before my death
I would confirm to Athens and to thee
My promised boon.

Theseus.

What sign dost thou perceive
That proves thine end so near?

Oedipus.

The Gods themselves
With herald voices are proclaiming it,
Nought failing of the fore-appointed signs.

Theseus.

What are these tokens, aged monarch, say?

Oedipus.

The loud continual thunder, and the darts
That flash in volleys from the almighty hand.

Theseus.

I may not doubt thee; for thy speech, I feel,
Hath ample witness of prophetic power.
What must I do?

Oedipus.

I will instruct thee now,
Aegeus' great son! in rites that shall remain
An ageless treasure to thy countrymen.
I will presently, with no man guiding me,
Myself point out the spot, where I must die.
This is thy secret, not to be revealed
To any one of men, or where 'tis hid
Or whereabout it lies. So through all time
This neighbouring mound shall yield thee mightier aid,

Than many a shield and help of alien spears.
More shalt thou learn, too sacred to divulge,
When yonder thou art come thyself alone.
Since to none other of these citizens
Nor even unto the children of my love
May I disclose it. 'Tis for thee to keep
Inviolate while thou livest, and when thy days
Have end, then breathe it to the foremost man
Alone, and he in turn unto the next
Successively. So shalt thou ever hold
Athens unravaged by the dragon brood.
Cities are numberless, and any one
May lightly insult even those who dwell secure.
For the eye of Heaven though late yet surely sees
When, casting off respect, men turn to crime.
Erechtheus' heir! let that be far from thee!
A warning needless to a man so wise!
Now go we—for this leading of the God
Is urgent—to the place, nor loiter more.
This way, my children! follow me! For I
Am now your guide, as ye were mine. Come on!
Nay, touch me not, but leave me of myself
To find the holy sepulchre, wherein
This form must rest beneath Athenian soil.
Come this way! Come! This way are leading me
Guide Hermes and the Queen of realms below.
O Light, all dark to me! In former time
Bright seemed thy shining! Now thy latest ray
Sheds vital influence o'er this frame. I go
To hide the close of my disastrous life
With Hades. Kind Athenian friend, farewell!
May'st thou, thy followers, and this glorious land,
Be happy, and in your endless happiness
Remember him who blessed you in his death.

(*Exeunt Oedipus, his daughters, and Theseus.*)

Strophe

Chorus.

Prince of the Powers Unseen,
  Durst we with prayers adore
Thee and thy viewless Queen,

Your aid, Aidoneus, would our lips implore!
By no harsh-sounding doom
Let him we love descend,
With calm and cloudless end,
In deep Plutonian dwelling evermore
To abide among the people of the tomb!
Long worn with many an undeservèd woe,
Just Gods will give thee glory there below.

Antistrophe

Dread Forms, who haunt this floor,
And thou, the Unconquered Beast,
That hugely liest at rest
By the dim shining adamantine door,
—Still from thy cavernous lair
Gnarling, so legends tell,
A tameless guard of Hell,—
Mayest thou this once thy vigilance forbear,
And leave large room for him now entering there.
Hear us, great Son of Darkness and the Deep;
On thee we call, God of the dreamless sleep!

(*Enter a Messenger.*)

Messenger.

Athenian citizens, my briefest tale
Were to say singly, Oedipus is gone;
But to describe the scene enacted yonder
Craves no brief speech, nor was the action brief.

Chorus.

Then he is gone! Poor man!

Messenger.

Know it once for all,
He hath left eternally the light of day.

Chorus.

Poor soul! What? Ended he with peace divine?

Messenger.

Ay, there is the main marvel. How he moved
From hence, thou knowest, for thou too wert here,
And saw'st that of his friends none guided him,
But he they loved was leader to them all.
Now, when he came to the steep pavement, rooted
With adamant foundation deep in Earth,

On one of many paths he took his stand
Near the stone basin, where Peirithous
And Theseus graved their everlasting league.
There, opposite the mass of Laurian ore,
Turned from the hollow pear-tree and the tomb
Of marble, he sate down, and straight undid
His travel-soiled attire, then called aloud
On both his children, and bade some one fetch
Pure water from a running stream. And they,
Hasting together to the neighbouring hill
Of green Demeter, goddess of the Spring,
Brought back their sire's commission speedily,
And bathed, and clothed him with the sacred robe.
When he was satisfied, and nothing now
Remained undone of all he bade them do,
The God of darkness thundered, and the maids
Stood horror-stricken on hearing; then together
Fell at their father's knees and wept and wailed
Loudly and long with beating of the breast.
He, when that sound of sorrow pierced his ear,
Caressed them in his arms and said:—"My daughters,
From this day forth you have no father more.
All that was mine is ended, and no longer
Shall ye continue your hard ministry
Of labour for my life.—And yet, though hard,
Not unendurable, since all the toil
Was rendered light through love, which ye can never
Receive on earth so richly, as from him
Bereaved of whom ye now shall live forlorn."
Such was the talk, mingled with sobs and crying,
As each clung fast to each. But when they came
To an end of weeping and those sounds were stilled,
First all was silent; then a sudden voice
Hurried him onward, making each man's hair
Bristle on end with force of instant fear.
Now here, now there, not once but oftentimes,
A God called loudly, "Oedipus, Oedipus!
Why thus delay our going? This long while
We are stayed for and thou tarriest. Come away!"
He, when he knew the summons of the God,
Gave word for royal Theseus to go near;

And when he came, said: "Friend for ever kind,
Reach thy right hand, I pray thee (that first pledge)
To these my children:—daughters, yours to him!—
And give thy sacred word that thou wilt never
Betray these willingly: but still perform
All that thou mayest with true thought for their good."
He, with grand calmness like his noble self,
Promised on oath to keep this friendly bond.
And when he had done so, Oedipus forthwith
Stroking his children with his helpless hands
Spake thus:—"My daughters, you must steel your hearts
To noble firmness, and depart from hence,
Nor ask to see or hear forbidden things.
Go, go at once! Theseus alone must stay
Sole rightful witness of these mysteries."
Those accents were the last we all o'erheard.
Then, following the two maids, with checkless tears
And groans we took our way. But by-and-by,
At distance looking round, we saw,—not him,
Who was not there,—but Theseus all alone
Holding his hand before his eyes, as if
Some apparition unendurable
Had scared his vision. In a little while,
We marked him making reverence in one prayer
To the Earth, and to the home of Gods on high.
But by what fate He perished, mortal man,
Save Theseus, none can say. No lightning-flash
From heaven, no tempest rising from the deep,
Caused his departure in that hour, but either
Some messenger from heaven, or, from beneath,
The lower part of Earth, where comes no pain,
Opening kindly to receive him in.
Not to be mourned, nor with a tearful end
Of sickness was he taken from the Earth,
But wondrously, beyond recorded fate.
If any deem my words unwise, I care not
In that man's judgment to be counted wise.

Chorus. Where are those maidens and their escort? Say.

Messenger.
They are not far off, but here. The voice of weeping
Betokens all too plainly their approach.

(*Enter Antigone and Ismene.*)

Antigone.

Alas!
How manifold the inheritance of woe
Drawn from the troubled fountain of our birth!
Indelible, ineradicable grief!
For him erewhile
We had labour infinite and unrelieved,
And now in his last hour we have to tell
Of sights and sorrows beyond thought.

Chorus.

How then?

Antigone.

Friends, ye might understand.

Chorus.

Speak. Is he gone?

Antigone.

Gone! Even as heart could wish, had wishes power.
How else, when neither war, nor the wide sea
Encountered him, but viewless realms enwrapt him,
Wafted away to some mysterious doom?
Whence on our hearts a horror of night is fallen.
Woe's me! For whither wandering shall we find
Hard livelihood, by land or over sea?

Ismene.

I know not. Let dark Hades take me off
To lie in death with my age-honoured sire!
Death were far better than my life to be.

Chorus.

Noblest of maidens, ye must learn to bear
Meekly the sending of the Gods. Be not
On fire with grief. Your state is well assured.

Antigone.

If to be thus is well, then may one long
For evil to return. Things nowise dear
Were dear to me, whiles I had him to embrace.
O father! loved one! that art wearing now
The eternal robe of darkness underground,
Old as thou wert, think not this maid and I
Will cease from loving thee!

Chorus.

He met his doom.

Antigone.

He met the doom he longed for.

Chorus.

How was that?

Antigone.

In the strange land where he desired to die
He died. He rests in shadow undisturbed;
Nor hath he left a tearless funeral.
For these mine eyes, father, unceasingly
Mourn thee with weeping, nor can I subdue
This ever-mounting sorrow for thy loss.
Ah me! Would thou hadst not desired to die
Here among strangers, but alone with thee
There, in the desert, I had seen thee die!

Ismene.

Unhappy me! What destiny, dear girl,
Awaits us both, bereaved and fatherless?

Chorus.

His end was fortunate. He rests in peace.
Dear maidens then desist from your complaint.
Sorrow is swift to overtake us all.

Antigone.

Thither again, dear girl, let us go speedily!

Ismene.

Say, for what end?

Antigone.

Desire possesses me—

Ismene.

Whereof?

Antigone.

To see the darksome dwelling-place—

Ismene.

Of whom?

Antigone.

Woe is me! Of him, our sire!

Ismene.

But how
Can this be lawful? Seest thou not?

Antigone.

How say'st thou?

Why this remonstrance?

Ismene.

Seest thou not, again,
He hath no grave and no man buried him.

Antigone.

Take me but where he lies. Then slay me there.

Ismene.

Ah! woe is me, doubly unfortunate,
Forlorn and destitute, whither henceforth
For wretched comfort must we go?

Chorus.

Fear nought,
Dear maidens!

Ismene.

Where shall we find refuge?

Chorus.

Here,
Long since, your refuge is secure.

Antigone.

How so?

Chorus.

No harm shall touch you.

Antigone.

I know that.

Chorus.

What then
Further engrosseth thee?

Antigone.

How to get home
I know not.

Chorus.

Seek not for it.

Antigone.

Weariness
O'erweighs me.

Chorus.

Hath it not before oppressed thee?

Antigone.

Before, it vexed me; now it overwhelms.

Chorus.

A mighty sea of misery is your lot.

Antigone.

Woe is me! O Zeus! And whither must we go?
Unto what doom doth my Fate drive me now?

Chorus.

Children, lament no longer. 'Tis not well
To mourn for him within whose sepulchre
Is stored the kindness of the Power below.

(*Enter Theseus.*)

Antigone.

Theseus, behold us falling at thy feet.

Theseus.

What boon, my children, are ye bent to obtain?

Antigone.

Our eyes would see our father's burial-place.

Theseus.

'Tis not permitted to go near that spot.

Antigone.

O Athens' sovereign lord, what hast thou said?

Theseus.

Dear children, 'twas your father's spoken will
That no man should approach his resting-place,
Nor human voice should ever violate
The mystery of the tomb wherein he lies.
He promised, if I truly kept this word,
My land would evermore be free from harm.
The power which no man may transgress and live,
The oath of Zeus, bore witness to our troth.

Antigone.

His wishes are enough. Then, pray thee, send
An escort to convey us to our home,
Primeval Thebes, if so we may prevent
The death that menaces our brethren there.

Theseus.

That will I; and in all that I may do
To prosper you and solace him beneath,—
Who even now passes to eternity,—
I must not falter. Come, lament no more.
His destiny hath found a perfect end.

SOPHOCLES

Antigone

Translated by Robert Whitelaw

Though it deals with the latest events of the legend, it was the earliest of the Theban saga to be written. It was first produced probably in 442 B.C. and won first prize.

CHARACTERS IN THE PLAY

Antigone } daughters of Oedipus
Ismene }

Creon, King of Thebes

A Sentinel

Haemon, son of Creon

Teiresias, a blind prophet

A Messenger

Eurydice, the wife of Creon

Second Messenger

Chorus of Theban Elders

ARGUMENT

Eteocles, the son of Oedipus and King of Thebes, had exiled his brother, Polyneices. Polyneices raised an army at Argos and led it against his native city. In the battle that followed, the two brothers fell each by the other's hand. Thus was fulfilled the curse which Oedipus, at Colonus, had pronounced upon his sons. The play opens on the day after the battle. Creon, who has become king, raises unwittingly the question of the relation between man's law and God's by decreeing that the body of Eteocles, who had died defending his city, may be buried, while that of Polyneices shall be left a prey to birds and dogs. Logicality, we learn, is wrong; instinct and tradition are right.

SCENE

An open space before the palace at Thebes. Antigone and Ismene enter.

ANTIGONE

Antigone.

O Sister-Life, Ismene's, twin with mine,
Knowest thou of the burden of our race
Aught that from us yet living Zeus holds back?
Nay, for nought grievous and nought ruinous,
No shame and no dishonour, have I not seen
Poured on our hapless heads, both thine and mine.
And even now what edict hath the prince
Uttered, men say, to all this Theban folk?
Thou knowest it and hast heard? or 'scapes thy sense,
Aimed at thy friends, the mischief of thy foes?

Ismene.

To me of friends, Antigone, no word
Hath come, or sweet or bitter, since that we
Two sisters of two brothers were bereaved,
Both on a day slain by a twofold blow:
And, now that vanished is the Argive host
Ev'n with the night fled hence, I know no more,
If that I fare the better or the worse.

Antigone.

I knew full well, and therefore from the gates
O' the court I led thee hither, alone to hear.

Ismene.

There's trouble in thy looks: thy tidings tell.

Antigone.

Yea, hath not Creon, of our two brothers slain,
Honoured with burial one, disdained the other?
For Eteocles, they say, he in the earth
With all fair rites and ceremony hath laid,
Nor lacks he honour in the world below;
But the poor dust of Polyneices dead
Through Thebes, 'tis said, the edict has gone forth
That none may bury, none make moan for him,
But leave unwept, untombed, a dainty prize
For ravening birds that gloat upon their prey.
So hath our good lord Creon to thee and me
Published, men say, his pleasure—ay, to *me*—
And hither comes, to all who know it not
Its purport to make plain, nor deems the thing

Of slight account, but, whoso does this deed,
A public death by stoning is his doom.
Thou hast it now; and quickly shall be proved
If thou art noble, or base from noble strain.

Ismene.

O rash of heart, if this indeed be so,
What help in me, to loosen or to bind?

Antigone.

Consider, toil and pain if thou wilt share.

Ismene.

On what adventure bound? What wouldst thou do?

Antigone.

To lift his body, wilt thou join with me?

Ismene.

Wouldst thou indeed rebel, and bury him?

Antigone.

My brother I will bury, and thine no less,
Whether thou wilt or no: no traitress I.

Ismene.

O all too bold—when Creon hath forbid?

Antigone.

My rights to hinder is no right of his.

Ismene.

Ah, sister, yet think how our father died,
Wrapt in what cloud of hate and ignominy
By his own sins, self-proved, and both his eyes
With suicidal hand himself he stabbed:
Then too his mother-wife, two names in one,
Fordid with twisted noose her woful life:
Last, our two brothers in one fatal day
Drew sword, O miserable, and each to each
Dealt mutual slaughter with unnatural hands:
And now shall we twain, who alone are left,
Fall like the rest, and worse—in spite of law,
And scorning kings, their edicts and their power?
Oh rather let us think, 'tis not for us,
Who are but women, to contend with men:
And the king's word is mighty, and to this,
And harsher words than this, we needs must bow.
Therefore will I, imploring of the dead
Forgiveness, that I yield but as I must,

Obey the king's commandment: for with things
Beyond our reach 'twere foolishness to meddle.

Antigone.

I'll neither urge thee, nor, if now thou'dst help
My doing, should I thank thee for thine aid.
Do thou after thy kind: thy choice is made:
I'll bury him; doing this, so let me die.
So with my loved one loved shall I abide,
My crime a deed most holy: for the dead
Longer have I to please than these on earth.
There I shall dwell for ever: be it thine
To have scorned what gods have hallowed, if thou wilt.

Ismene.

Nay, nothing do I scorn: but, how to break
My country's law—I am witless of the way.

Antigone.

Be this thy better part: I go to heap
The earth upon my brother, whom I love.

Ismene.

Alas, unhappy, how I fear for thee!

Antigone.

Fear not for me: guide thine own fate aright.

Ismene.

Yet breathe this purpose to no ear but mine:
Keep thou thy counsel well—and so will I.

Antigone.

Oh speak: for much more hatred thou wilt get,
Concealing, than proclaiming it to all.

Ismene.

This fever at thy heart by frost is fed.

Antigone.

But, whom I most should please, they most are pleased.

Ismene.

So wouldst thou: but thou canst not as thou wouldst.

Antigone.

Why, then, when strength shall fail me, I will cease.

Ismene.

Not to attempt the impossible is best.

Antigone.

Hated by me, and hated by the dead—
To him a hateful presence evermore—

Thou shouldst be, and thou shalt be, speaking thus.
But leave me, and the folly that is mine,
This worst to suffer—not the worst—since still
A worse remains, no noble death to die.

Ismene.

Go if thou wilt: but going know thyself
Senseless, yet to thy friends a friend indeed.

(*Exeunt. Enter Chorus of Theban Elders.*)

Strophe 1

Chorus.

Lo, the sun upspringing!
Fairest light we hail thee
Of all dawns that on Thebes the seven-gated
Ever broke! Eye of golden day!
Over Dirce's fount appearing,
Hence the Argive host white-shielded,
That in complete arms came hither,
Headlong homeward thou didst urge
Faster still with shaken rein.
At call of Polyneices, stirred
By bitter heat of wrangling claims,
Against our land they gathered, and they swooped
Down on us—like an eagle, screaming hoarse,
White-clad, with wings of snow—
With shields a many and with waving crests.

Antistrophe 1

But above our dwellings,
With his spears that thirsted
For our blood, at each gate's mouth of the seven
Gaping round, paused the foe—and went,
Ere his jaws with blood were sated,
Or our circling towers the torch-flame
Caught and kindled: so behind him
Raged intense the battle-din—
While for life the Serpent fought.
For Zeus the tongue of vaunting pride

Hates with exceeding hate; he marked
That torrent army's onward flood, superb
With clank of gold, and with his brandished fire
Smote down who foremost climbed
To shout his triumph on our ramparts' heights.

Strophe 2

Hurled from that height with swift reverse,
The unpitying earth received him as he fell,
And quenched the brand he fain had flung,
And quelled the mad endeavour,
The frantic storm-gusts of his windy hate.
So fared it then with him;
Nor less elsewhere great Ares dealt
Against the foemen thunderous blows—
Our trace-horse on the right.
For seven chieftains at our seven gates
Met each his equal foe: and Zeus,
Who foiled their onset, claims from all his due,
The brazen arms, which on the field they left:
Save that infuriate pair,
Who, from one father and one mother sprung,
Against each other laid in rest
Their spears, victorious both,
And each by other share one equal death.

Antistrophe 2

But now of Victory be glad:
She meets our gladness with an answering smile,
And Thebes, the many-charioted,
Hears far resound her praises:
Now then with war have done, and strife forget!
All temples of the gods
Fill we with song and night-long dance;
And, Theban Bacchus, this our mirth
Lead thou, and shake the earth!
But lo the ruler of this Theban land,
Son of Menoeceus, Creon comes,
Crowned by these new and strange events, he comes—
By will of heav'n our new-created king,
What counsel pondering?

Who by his sovereign will hath now convoked,
In solemn conference to meet,
The elders of the state;
Obedient to whose summons, we are here.

(*Enter Creon.*)

Creon.

Sirs, it hath pleased the gods to right again
Our Theban fortunes, by sore tempest tossed:
And by my messenger I summoned hither
You out of all the state; first, as I knew you
To the might o' the throne of Laius loyal ever:
Also, when Oedipus upheld the state,
And when he perished, to their children still
Ye with a constant mind were faithful found:
Now they are gone: both on one fatal field
An equal guilt atoned with equal doom,
Slayers of each other, by each other slain:
And I am left, the nearest to their blood,
To wield alone the sceptre and the realm.
There is no way to know of any man
The spirit and the wisdom and the will,
Till he stands proved, ruler and lawgiver.
For who, with a whole city to direct,
Yet cleaves not to those counsels that are best,
But locks his lips in silence, being afraid,
I held and hold him ever of men most base:
And whoso greater than his country's cause
Esteems a friend, I count him nothing worth.
For, Zeus who seeth all be witness now,
Nor for the safety's sake would I keep silence,
And see the ruin on my country fall,
Nor would I deem an enemy to the state
Friend to myself; remembering still that she,
She only brings us safe; her deck we pace,
Unfoundered 'mid the storm, our friends and we.
So for the good of Thebes her laws I'll frame:
And such the proclamation I set forth,
Touching the sons of Oedipus, ev'n now—
Eteocles, who fighting for this land
In battle has fall'n, more valiant none than he,

To bury, and no funeral rite omit,
To brave men paid--their solace in the grave:
Not so his brother, Polyneices: he,
From exile back returning, utterly
With fire his country and his fathers' gods
Would fain have burnt, fain would with kinsmen's blood
Have slaked his thirst, or dragged us captive hence:
Therefore to all this city it is proclaimed
That none may bury, none make moan for him,
But leave him lying all ghastly where he fell,
Till fowls o' the air and dogs have picked his bones.
So am I purposed: not at least by me
Shall traitors be preferred to honest men:
But, whoso loves this city, him indeed
I shall not cease to honour, alive or dead.

Chorus.

Creon, son of Menoeceus, 'tis thy pleasure
The friend and foe of Thebes so to requite:
And, whatso pleases thee, that same is law,
Both for our Theban dead and us who live.

Creon.

Look to it, then, my bidding is performed.

Chorus.

Upon some younger man impose this burden.

Creon.

To watch the body, sentinels are set.

Chorus.

What service more then wouldst thou lay on us?

Creon.

That ye resist whoever disobeys.

Chorus.

Who is so senseless that desires to die?

Creon.

The penalty is death: yet hopes deceive,
And men wax foolish oft through greed of gain.

(*Enter a Sentinel.*)

Sentinel.

That I come hither, king, nimble of foot,
And breathless with my haste, I'll not profess:
For many a doubtful halt upon the way,

And many a wheel to the right-about, I had,
Oft as my prating heart gave counsel, "Fool,
What ails thee going into the lion's mouth?"
Then, "Blockhead, wilt thou tarry? if Creon learns
This from another man, shalt thou not smart?"
So doubtfully I fared—much haste, scant speed—
And, if the way was short, 'twas long to me.
But to come hither to thee prevailed at last,
And, though the speech be nought, yet I will speak.
For I have come fast clutching at the hope
That nought's to suffer but what fate decrees.

Creon.

What is it that hath troubled thus thy mind?

Sentinel.

First for myself this let me say: the deed
I neither did, nor saw who was the doer,
And 'twere not just that I should suffer harm.

Creon.

Wisely, thyself in covert, at the mark
Thou aimest: some shrewd news, methinks, thou'lt tell.

Sentinel.

Danger to face, well may a man be cautious.

Creon.

Speak then, and go thy way, and make an end.

Sentinel.

Now I will speak. Some one ev'n now hath buried
The body and is gone; with thirsty dust
Sprinkling it o'er, and paying observance due.

Creon.

How? By what man was dared a deed so rash?

Sentinel.

I cannot tell. No mattock's stroke indeed,
Nor spade's upcast was there: hard was the ground,
Baked dry, unbroken: track of chariot-wheels
Was none, nor any sign who did this thing.
But he who kept the watch at earliest dawn
Showed to us all—a mystery, hard to clear.
Not buried was the dead man, but concealed,
With dust besprinkled, as for fear of sin:
And neither of dog, nor any beast of prey,
That came, that tore the body, found we trace.

Then bitter words we bandied to and fro,
Denouncing each the other; and soon to blows
Our strife had grown—was none would keep the peace—
For every one was guilty of the deed,
And none confessed, but all denied they knew.
And we were fain to handle red-hot iron,
Or walk through fire barefoot, or swear by heaven,
That neither had we done it, nor had shared
His secret with who planned it or who wrought.
So all in vain we questioned: and at last
One spake, and all who heard him, bowed by fear,
Bent to the earth their faces, knowing not
How to gainsay, nor doing what he said
How we might 'scape mischance. This deed to thee
He urged that we should show, and hide it not.
And his advice prevailed; and by the lot
To luckless me this privilege befell.
Unwilling and unwelcome is my errand,
A bearer of ill news, whom no man loves.

Chorus.

O king, my thought hath counselled me long since,
Haply this deed is ordered by the gods.

Creon.

Cease, ere my wrath is kindled at thy speech,
Lest thou be found an old man and a fool.
Intolerably thou pratest of the gods,
That they to yonder dead man have respect.
Yea, for what service with exceeding honour
Sought they his burial, who came here to burn
Their pillared shrines and temple-offerings,
And of their land and of their laws make havoc?
Or seest thou that the gods allow the wicked?
Not so: but some impatient of my will
Among my people made a murmuring,
Shaking their heads in secret, to the yoke
With stubborn necks unbent, and hearts disloyal.
Full certainly I know that they with bribes
Have on these men prevailed to do this deed.
Of all the evils current in this world
Most mischievous is gold. This hath laid waste
Fair cities, and unpeopled homes of men:

Many an honest heart hath the false lure
Of gold seduced to walk in ways of shame;
And hence mankind are versed in villainies,
And of all godless acts have learnt the lore.
But, who took hire to execute this work,
Wrought to their own undoing at the last.
Since, if the dread of Zeus I still revere,
Be well assured—and what I speak I swear—
Unless the author of this burial
Ye find, and in my sight produce him here,
For you mere death shall not suffice, until
Gibbeted alive this outrage ye disclose,
That ye may know what gains are worth the winning,
And henceforth clutch the wiselier, having learnt
That to seek gain in all things is not well.
For from ill-gotten pelf the lives of men
Ruined than saved more often shall ye see.

Sentinel.

May I speak a word, or thus am I dismissed?

Creon.

Know'st thou not that ev'n now thy voice offends?

Sentinel.

Do I afflict thy hearing or thy heart?

Creon.

Where I am pained, it skills not to define.

Sentinel.

The doer grieves thy mind, but I thine ears.

Creon.

That thou wast born to chatter, 'tis too plain.

Sentinel.

And therefore not the doer of this deed.

Creon.

At thy life's cost thou didst it, bought with gold.

Sentinel.

Alas!
'Tis pity, men should judge, yet judge amiss.

Creon.

Talk you of "judging" glibly as you may—
Who did this deed, I'll know, or ye shall own
That all your wondrous winnings end in loss.

Sentinel.

With all my heart I wish he may be found:
But found or no—for that's as fortune will—
I shall not show my face to you again.
Great cause I have to thank the gracious gods,
Saved past all hope and reckoning even now.

(*Exeunt Creon and the Sentinel.*)

Strophe 1

Chorus.

Many are the wonders of the world,
And none so wonderful as Man.
Over the waters wan
His storm-vext bark he steers,
While the fierce billows break
Round his path, and o'er his head:
And the Earth-mother, first of gods,
The ageless, the indomitable,
With his ploughing to and fro
He wearieth, year by year:
In the deep furrow toil the patient mules.

Antistrophe 1

The birds o' the air he snares and takes,
All the light-hearted fluttering race:
And tribes of savage beasts,
And creatures of the deep,
Meshed in his woven toils,
Own the master-mind of man.
Free lives of upland and of wild
By human arts are curbed and tamed:
See the horse's shaggy neck
Submissive to the yoke—
And strength untired of mountain-roaming bulls.

Strophe 2

Language withal he learnt,
And Thought that as the wind is free,
And aptitudes of civic life:
Ill-lodged no more he lies,
His roof the sky, the earth his bed,

Screened now from piercing frost and pelting rain;
All-fertile in resource, resourceless never
Meets he the morrow; only death
He wants the skill to shun:
But many a fell disease the healer's art hath foiled.

Antistrophe 2

So soaring far past hope,
The wise inventiveness of man
Finds diverse issues, good and ill:
If from their course he wrests
The firm foundations of the state,
Laws, and the justice he is sworn to keep,
High in the city, citiless I deem him,
Dealing with baseness: overbold,
May he my hearth avoid,
Nor let my thoughts with his, who does such deeds, agree!

(*Enter the Sentinel with Antigone.*)

What strange portentous sight is this,
I doubt my eyes, beholding? This—
How shall I gainsay what I know?—
This maiden *is*—Antigone!
Daughter of Oedipus,
Hapless child of a hapless sire,
What hast thou done? It cannot be
That thou hast transgressed the king's command—
That, taken in folly, *thee* they bring!

Sentinel.

This same is she that did the burial:
We caught her in the act. But where's the king?

Chorus.

Back from the palace in good time he comes.

(*Enter Creon.*)

Creon.

What chance is this, to which my steps are timed?

Sentinel.

Nothing, sir king, should men swear not to do;
For second thoughts to first thoughts give the lie.
Hither, I made full sure, I scarce should come
Back, by your threats beruffled as I was.

Yet here, surprised by most unlooked-for joy,
That trifles all delights that e'er I knew,
I bring you—though my coming breaks my oath—
This maiden, whom, busied about the corpse,
We captured. This time were no lots to throw:
My own good fortune this, and none but mine.
Now therefore, king, take her yourself and try her,
And question as you will: but I have earned
Full clearance and acquittal of this coil.

Creon.

Where, on what manner, was your captive taken?

Sentinel.

Burying the man, we took her: all is told.

Creon.

Art thou advised of this? Is it the truth?

Sentinel.

I say I saw her burying the body,
That you forbade. Is that distinct and clear?

Creon.

How was she seen, and taken in the act?

Sentinel.

So it fell out. When I had gone from hence,
With thy loud threats yet sounding in my ears,
We swept off all the dust that hid the limbs,
And to the light stripped bare the clammy corpse,
And on the hill's brow sat, and faced the wind,
Choosing a spot clear of the body's stench.
Roundly we chid each other to the work;
"No sleeping at your post there" was our word.
So did we keep the watch, till in mid-heaven
The sun's bright-burning orb above us hung,
With fierce noon-heat: and now a sudden blast
Swept, and a storm of dust, that vexed the sky
And choked the plain, and all the leaves o' the trees
O' the plain were marred, and the wide heaven it filled:
We with shut eyes the heaven-sent plague endured.
And, when after long time its force was spent,
We saw this maiden, and a bitter cry
She poured, as of a wailing bird that sees
Her empty nest dismantled of its brood:
So she, when she espied the body bare,
Cried out and wept, and many a grievous curse

Upon their heads invoked by whom 'twas done.
And thirsty dust she sprinkled with her hands,
And lifted up an urn, fair-wrought of brass,
And with thrice-poured libations crowned the dead.
We saw it and we hasted, and at once,
All undismayed, our captive, hemmed her round,
And with the two offences charged her there,
Both first and last. Nothing did she deny,
But made me glad and sorry, owning all.
For to have slipped one's own neck from the noose
Is sweet, yet no one likes to get his friends
In trouble: but my nature is to make
All else of small account, so I am safe.

Creon.

Speak thou, who bendest on the earth thy gaze,
Are these things, which are witnessed, true or false?

Antigone.

Not false, but true: that which he saw, he speaks.

Creon.

So, sirrah, thou art free; go where thou wilt,
Loosed from the burden of this heavy charge.

(*Exit the Sentinel.*)

But tell me thou—and let thy speech be brief—
The edict hadst thou heard, which this forbade?

Antigone.

I could not choose but hear what all men heard.

Creon.

And didst thou dare to disobey the law?

Antigone.

Nowise from Zeus, methought, this edict came,
Nor Justice, that abides among the gods
In Hades, who ordained these laws for men.
Nor did I deem *thine* edicts of such force
That they, a mortal's bidding, should o'erride
Unwritten laws, eternal in the heavens.
Not of to-day or yesterday are these,
But live from everlasting, and from whence
They sprang, none knoweth. I would not, for the breach
Of these, through fear of any human pride,
To heaven atone. I knew that I must die:

How else? Without thine edict, that were so.
And if before my time, why, this were gain.
Compassed about with ills, who lives, as I,
Death, to such life as his, must needs be gain.
So is it to me to undergo this doom
No grief at all: but had I left my brother,
My mother's child, unburied where he lay,
Then I had grieved; but now this grieves me not.
Senseless I seem to thee, so doing? Belike
A senseless judgment finds me void of sense.

Chorus.

How in the child the sternness of the sire
Shows stern, before the storm untaught to bend!

Creon.

Yet know full well that such o'er-stubborn wills
Are broken most of all, as sturdiest steel,
Of an untempered hardness, fresh from forge,
Most surely snapped and shivered should ye see.
Lo how a little curb has strength enough
To tame the restive horse: for to a slave
His masters give no license to be proud.
Insult on insult heaped! Was't not enough
My promulgated laws to have transgressed,
But, having done it, face to face with me
She boasts of this and glories in the deed?
I surely am the woman, she the man,
If she defies my power, and I submit.
Be she my sister's child, or sprung from one
More near of blood than all my house to me,
Not so shall they escape my direst doom—
She and her sister: for I count her too
Guilty no less of having planned this work.
Go, call her hither: in the house I saw her
Raving ev'n now, nor mistress of her thoughts.
So oft the mind, revolving secret crime,
Makes premature disclosure of its guilt.
But this is hateful, when the guilty one,
Detected, thinks to glorify his fault.

Antigone.

To kill me—wouldst thou more with me than this?

Creon.

This is enough: I do desire no more.

Antigone.

Why dost thou then delay? I have no pleasure
To hear thee speak—have not and would not have:
Nor less distasteful is my speech to thee.
Yet how could I have won myself a praise
More honourable than this, of burying
My brother? This from every voice should win
Approval, might but fear men's lips unseal.
But kings are fortunate—not least in this,
That they may do and speak what things they will.

Creon.

All Thebes sees this with other eyes than thine.

Antigone.

They see as I, but bate their breath to thee.

Creon.

And art thou not ashamed, from them to differ?

Antigone.

To reverence a brother is not shameful.

Creon.

And was not he who died for Thebes thy brother?

Antigone.

One mother bore us, and one sire begat.

Creon.

Yet, honouring both, thou dost dishonour him.

Antigone.

He in the grave will not subscribe to this.

Creon.

How, if no less thou dost revere the guilty?

Antigone.

'Twas not his slave that perished, but his brother.

Creon.

The enemy of this land: its champion, he.

Antigone.

Yet Death of due observance must not fail.

Creon.

Just and unjust urge not an equal claim.

Antigone.

Perchance in Hades 'tis a holy deed.

Creon.

Hatred, not ev'n in death, converts to love.

Antigone.

Not in your hates, but in your loves, I'd share.

Creon.

Go to the shades, and, if thou'lt love, love there:
No woman, while I live, shall master me.

(*Enter Ismene.*)

Chorus.

See, from the palace comes Ismene—
Sisterly drops from her eyes down-shedding:
Clouded her brows droop, heavy with sorrow;
And the blood-red tinge of a burning blush
Covers her beautiful downcast face.

Creon.

Thou, who hast crept, a serpent in my home,
Draining my blood, unseen; and I knew not
Rearing two pests, to overset my throne;
Speak—wilt thou too confess that in this work
Thou hadst a hand, or swear thou didst not know?

Ismene.

I'll say the deed was mine, if she consents:
My share of the blame I bear, and do not shrink.

Antigone.

Justice forbids thy claim; neither didst thou
Agree, nor I admit thee to my counsels.

Ismene.

I am not ashamed, in thine extremity,
To make myself companion of thy fate.

Antigone.

Whose was the deed, know Hades and the dead:
I love not friends, who talk of friendliness.

Ismene.

Sister, disdain me not, but let me pour
My blood with thine, an offering to the dead.

Antigone.

Leave me to die alone, nor claim the work
Thou wouldst not help. My death will be enough.

Ismene.

What joy have I to live, when thou art gone?

Antigone.

Ask Creon that: thou art of kin to him.

Ismene.

Why wilt thou grieve me with thy needless taunts?

Antigone.
If I mock thee, 'tis with a heavy heart.

Ismene.
What may I do to serve thee even now?

Antigone.
Look to thyself: I grudge thee not thy safety.

Ismene.
And may I not, unhappy, share thy death?

Antigone.
Thou didst make choice to live, but I to die.

Ismene.
Might I unsay my words, this were not so.

Antigone.
Wise seemed we—thou to these, and I to those.

Ismene.
But now our fault is equal, thine and mine.

Antigone.
Take heart to live: for so thou dost: but I—
Dead is my life long since—to help the dead.

Creon.
One of these two, methinks, proves foolish now;
The other's folly with her life began.

Ismene.
Nay, for, O king, misfortunes of the wise
To madness turn the wisdom that they have.

Creon.
'Tis so with thee, choosing to share her guilt.

Ismene.
How should I live alone, without my sister?

Creon.
Call her not thine: thou hast no sister now.

Ismene.
But wilt thou tear her from thy son's embrace?

Creon.
Are there no women in the world but she?

Ismene.
Not as their faith was plighted, each to each.

Creon.
An evil wife I like not for my son.

Antigone.
Haemon! beloved! hear not thy father's scorn.

Creon.

Thou and thy love to me are wearisome.

Chorus.

Wilt thou indeed snatch from thy son his bride?

Creon.

'Tis death that will unloose their marriage-bond.

Chorus.

It seems thou art resolved that she must die?

Creon.

Of that we are agreed. Delay no more:
Ye, servants, lead them in. For from this time
Women they needs must be, and range no more:
Since ev'n the bold may play the runaway,
When death he sees close-creeping on his life.

(*Exeunt Antigone and Ismene.*)

Strophe 1

Chorus.

Happy indeed is the life of the man who tastes not of trouble!
For when from the gods a house is shaken,
Fails nevermore the curse,
On most and on least of the race descending:
Like to a rolling wave,
By furious blasts from the Thraceward driven—
Out of the nethermost deeps, out of the fathomless gloom,
Casting up mire and blackness and storm-vext wrack of the sea—
And back, with a moan like thunder, from the cliffs the surf is hurled.

Antistrophe 1

So from of old to the Labdacid race comes sorrow on sorrow:
And, ev'n as the dead, so fare the living:
Respite from ills is none,
Nor one generation redeems another—
All will some god bring low.
Now o'er the last root of the house, fate-stricken,
Woe for the light that had shined, woe for the lingering hope!

Smooth over all is lying the blood-stained dust they have spread—
Rash speech, and a frantic purpose, and the gods who reign below.

Strophe 2

What human trespass, Zeus,
May circumscribe thy power,
Which neither sleep o'ercomes,
That saps the strength of all things else,
Nor months that run their tireless course,
But thou for ever with an ageless sway
The dazzling splendour dost possess
Of thine Olympian home?
'Tis now as it hath ever been,
And still in years to come
The old order will not change:
Never from human life departs
The universal scourge of man,
His own presumptuous pride.

Antistrophe 2

Hope wings her daring flight,
By strong winds borne afar—
And some are blessed; and some
Are cheated of their vain desires,
That learn their folly all too late,
When in the fire they tread with scorchèd feet.
'Twas said of old—and time approves
The wisdom of the saw—
That, when in foolish ways, that end
In ruin, gods would lead
A mortal's mind astray,
Evil that man miscalls his good:
A brief while then he holds his course
By fatuous pride unscathed.
See, thy son Haemon comes hither, of all
Thy children the last. Comes he lamenting
The doom of the maiden, his bride Antigone—
And the frustrated hope of his marriage?

(*Enter Haemon.*)

Creon.

Soon we shall know, better than seers could say.
My son, in anger art thou come to me,
Hearing the sentence, not to be reversed,
Which on thy destined bride I have pronounced?
Or am I still thy friend, do what I may?

Haemon.

Father, I am in thy hand: with thy wise counsels
Thou dost direct me; these I shall obey.
Not rightly should I deem of more account
The winning of a wife than thy good guidance.

Creon.

Be this thy dearest wish and next thy heart,
In all things to uphold thy father's will.
For to this end men crave to see grow up
Obedient children round them in their homes,
Both to requite their enemies with hate,
And render equal honour to their friends.
Whoso begets unprofitable children,
What shall be said of him, but that he gets
Grief for himself, loud laughter for his foes?
Never, my son, let for a woman's sake
Reason give way to sense, but know full well
Cold is the pleasure that he clasps, who woos
An evil woman to his board and bed.
What wounds so deeply as an evil friend?
Count then this maiden as thine enemy,
Loathe her, and give her leave, in that dark world
To which she goes, to marry with another.
For out of all the city since I found
Her only, and her openly, rebellious,
I shall not to the city break my word,
But she shall die. Let her appeal to Zeus,
And sing the sanctity of kindred blood—
What then? If in my own house I shall nurse
Rebellion, how shall strangers not rebel?
He who to his own kith and kin does right,
Will in the state deal righteously with all.
Of such a man I shall not fear to boast,
Well he can rule, and well he would obey,

And in the storm of battle at his post
Firm he would stand, a comrade staunch and true.
But praise from me that man shall never have,
Who either boldly thrusts aside the law
Or takes upon him to instruct his rulers,
Whom, by the state empowered, he should obey,
In little and in much, in right and wrong.
The worst of evils is to disobey.
Cities by this are ruined, homes of men
Made desolate by this; this in the battle
Breaks into headlong rout the wavering line;
The steadfast ranks, the many lives unhurt,
Are to obedience due. We must defend
The government and order of the state,
And not be governed by a wilful girl.
We'll yield our place up, if we must, to men;
To women that we stooped, shall not be said.

Chorus.

Unless an old man's judgment is at fault,
These words of thine, we deem, are words of wisdom.

Haemon.

Reason, my father, in the mind of man,
Noblest of all their gifts, the gods implant,
And how to find thy reasoning at fault,
I know not, and to learn I should be loth;
Yet for another it might not be amiss.
But I for thee am vigilant to mark
All that men say, or do, or find to blame.
Thy presence awes the simple citizen
From speaking words that shall not please thine ear,
But I hear what they whisper in the dark,
And how the city for this maid laments,
That of all women she the least deserving
Dies for most glorious deeds a death most cruel,
Who her own brother, fall'n among the slain,
Left not unburied there, to be devoured
By ravening dogs or any bird o' the air:—
"Should not her deed be blazoned all in gold?"
Upon the darkness still such whisper grows.
But I of all possessions that I have
Prize most, my father, thy prosperity.
Welldoing and fair fame of sire to son,

Of son to sire, is noblest ornament.
Cleave not, I pray thee, to this constant mind,
That what thou sayest, and nought beside, is truth.
For men who think that only they are wise,
None eloquent, right-minded none, but they,
Often, when searched, prove empty. 'Tis no shame,
Ev'n if a man be wise, that he should yet
Learn many things, and not hold out too stiffly.
Beside the torrent's course, of trees that bend
Each bough, thou seest, and every twig is safe;
Those that resist are by the roots uptorn.
And ships, that brace with stubborn hardihood
Their mainsheet to the gale, pursue their voyage
Keel-uppermost, their sailors' thwarts reversed.
Cease from thy wrath; be not inexorable:
For if despite my youth I too may think
My thought, I'll say that best it is by far
That men should be all-knowing if they may,
But if—as oft the scale inclines not so—
Why then, by good advice 'tis good to learn.

Chorus.

What in thy son's speech, king, is seasonable
'Tis fit thou shouldst receive: and thou in his:
For there is reason in the words of both.

Creon.

Shall I, grown grey with age, be taught indeed—
And by this boy—to think what he thinks right?

Haemon.

Nothing that is not right: though I am young,
Consider not my years, but how I act.

Creon.

Is this thine act—to honour the unruly?

Haemon.

Wrongdoers, dishonour—outrage, if thou wilt!

Creon.

Hath not this maiden caught this malady?

Haemon.

The general voice of Thebes says no to that.

Creon.

Shall Thebes prescribe to me how I must govern?

Haemon.

How all too young art thou in speaking thus!

Creon.

Whose business is't but mine how Thebes is governed?

Haemon.

A city is none, that to one man belongs.

Creon.

Is it not held, the city is the king's?

Haemon.

Finely thou'dst rule, alone, a land dispeopled!

Creon.

It seems this boy will plead the woman's cause.

Haemon.

Woman art thou? my care is all for thee.

Creon.

Shameless—is't right to wrangle with thy father?

Haemon.

I see that wrong for right thou dost mistake.

Creon.

Do I mistake, to reverence my office?

Haemon.

What reverence, heaven's honours to contemn?

Creon.

O hateful spirit, ruled by a woman's will!

Haemon.

To no base service shalt thou prove me bound.

Creon.

Art thou not pleading all the time for her?

Haemon.

For thee and me, and for the gods below.

Creon.

Thou shalt not marry her, this side the grave.

Haemon.

If she must die, she shall: but not alone.

Creon.

Art grown so bold, thou dost fly out in threats?

Haemon.

What threats, to argue with a foolish purpose?

Creon.

Thou'lt rue—unwise—thy wisdom spent on me.

Haemon.

Thou art my father; or wise I scarce had called thee.

Creon.

Slave—to thy mistress babble, not to me.

Haemon.

Wouldst thou have all the talking for thine own?

Creon.

Is't come to this? But, by Olympus yonder,
Know well, thou shalt be sorry for these taunts,
Wherewith thou dost upbraid me. Slaves, what ho!
Bring that abhorence hither, that she may die,
Now, in her bridegroom's sight, whilst here he stands.

Haemon.

Neither in my sight—imagine no such thing—
Shall she be slain; nor shalt thou from this hour
Look with thine eyes upon my face again:
To friends who love thy madness I commit thee.

(*Exit Haemon.*)

Chorus.

Suddenly, sire, in anger he is gone:
Young minds grow desperate, by grief distemper'd.

Creon.

More than a man let him conceive and do;
He shall not save these maidens from their doom.

Chorus.

Both sisters art thou purposed to destroy?

Creon.

Not her whose hands sinned not; thou askest well.

Chorus.

What of the other? how shall she be slain?

Creon.

By paths untrodden of men I will conduct her,
And shut her, living in a vault, rock-hewn,
And there, with food, no more than shall suffice
To avert the guilt of murder from the city,
To Hades, the one god whom she reveres,
She, praying not to die, either shall have
Her asking, or shall learn, albeit too late,
That to revere the dead is fruitless toil.

(*Exit Creon.*)

Strophe

Chorus.

O Love, our conqueror, matchless in might,
Thou prevailest, O Love, thou dividest the prey:

In damask cheeks of a maiden
Thy watch through the night is set.
Thou roamest over the sea;
On the hills, in the shepherds' huts, thou art;
Nor of deathless gods, nor of short-lived men,
From thy madness any escapeth.

Antistrophe

Unjust, through thee, are the thoughts of the just,
Thou dost bend them, O Love, to thy will, to thy spite.
Unkindly strife thou hast kindled,
This wrangling of son with sire.
For great laws, throned in the heart,
To the sway of a rival power give place,
To the love-light flashed from a fair bride's eyes:
In her triumph laughs Aphrodite.
Me, even now, me also,
Seeing these things, a sudden pity
Beyond all governance transports:
The fountains of my tears
I can refrain no more,
Seeing Antigone here to the bridal chamber
Come, to the all-receiving chamber of Death.

(*Antigone is led out of the palace by guards.*)

Antigone.

Friends and my countrymen, ye see me
Upon the last of all my ways
Set forth, the Sun-god's latest light
Beholding, now and never more:
But Death, who giveth sleep to all,
Yet living leads me hence
To the Acherontian shore,
Of marriage rites amerced,
And me no bridal song hath ever sung,
But Acheron will make of me his bride.

Chorus.

Therefore renowned, with praise of men,
To yonder vault o' the dead thou goest,
By no slow-wasting sickness stricken,
Nor doomed to fall with those who win
The wages of the swords they drew,

But, being to thyself a law,
Alone of mortals the dark road
To deathward, living, thou shalt tread.

Antigone.

I heard of one, most piteous in her ending,
That stranger, child of Phrygian Tantalus,
On heights of Sipylus enclasped,
And ivy-like enchained,
By clinging tendrils of the branching rock,
Who day and night unceasingly
'Mid drizzle of rain and drift of snow
Slow-wasting in her place
Stands, as the tale is told,
Her lids surcharged with weeping, and her neck
And bosom drenched with falling of her tears:—
A fate most like to hers
Seals up with sleep these eyes of mine.

Chorus.

She was a goddess, sprung from gods:
Mortals, of mortal birth, are we.
But for one dead to win with those
Who rank no lower than the gods—
In life and afterwards in death—
An equal lot, were much to hear.

Antigone.

Ah, I am mocked! Nay, by our fathers' gods,
Withhold thy taunts till I am gone—
Gone and evanished from thy sight.
O Thebes, my city!
O wealthy men of Thebes!
But *ye* will witness—yes, to you I turn—
O fount Dircaean, and this sacred grove
Of Thebè the fair-charioted,
By what stern law, and how of friends unwept,
To that strange grave I go,
The massy dungeon for my burial heaped.
O luckless wight,
Exiled from earth nor housed below,
Both by the living and the dead disowned!

Chorus.

To furthest brink of boldness thou didst stray,
And stumbling there, at foot of Justice' throne,

Full heavily, my daughter, hast thou fallen:
Yet of thy father's fault belike
This suffering pays the price.

Antigone.

Thou hast touched, ev'n there, my bitterest pang of all,
A thrice-told tale, my father's grief—
And all our grievous doom that clung
About the famed Labdacidae.
O that incestuous bed
Of horror, and my father's sin—
The hapless mother who bore him to the light,
By him enclasped—wherefrom I luckless sprang:
With whom, accurst, unwedded,
I must go hence to dwell.
O brother, a bride ill-starred
Who to thy couch didst win,
How, being dead, me living thou hast slain!

Chorus.

Religion prompts the reverent deed:
But power, to whomso power belongs,
Must nowise be transgressed; and thee
A self-willed temper hath o'erthrown.

Antigone.

Unwept and unfriended,
Cheered by no song Hymenaeal—
Lo, I am led, heavy-hearted,
This road that awaits me.
The sacred light-giving eye in heaven
Now no more must I see, unhappy:
But for my fate not a tear falls,
Not a friend makes moan.

(*Enter Creon.*)

Creon.

Know ye not, songs and weepings before death
That none would pretermit, were he allowed?
Hence with her, hence, and tarry not, but deep
In her tomb-prison, even as I have said,
Leave her alone, forsaken: to die, or else
Live, in that vault entombed, if so she will:
Since of this maiden's blood our hands are clean,
Only we ban her sojourn in the light.

Antigone.

O tomb! O nuptial chamber! O house deep-delved
In earth, safe-guarded ever! To thee I come,
And to my kin in thee, who many an one
Are with Persephone, dead among the dead:
And last of all, most miserably by far,
I thither am going, ere my life's term be done.
But a good hope I cherish, that, come there,
My father's love will greet me, yea and thine,
My mother—and thy welcome, brother dear:
Since, when ye died, I with mine own hands laved
And dressed your limbs, and poured upon your graves
Libations; and like service done to thee
Hath brought me, Polyneices, now to this.
Yet well I honoured thee, the wise will say:
Since not for children's sake would I, their mother,
Nor for my husband, slain, and mouldering there,
Have travailed thus, doing despite to Thebes.
According to what law, do I speak this?
One husband slain, another might have been,
And children from another, losing these;
But, father and mother buried out of sight,
There can be born no brother any more.
Such was the law whereby I held thee first
In honour; but to Creon all mistaken,
O dear my brother, I seemed, and overbold—
And now, made captive thus, he leads me hence
No wife, no bride for ever—of marriage-joy
And nursery of children quite bereft:
So by my friends forsaken I depart,
Living, unhappy, to dim vaults of death.
Yet I transgressed—what ordinance of heaven?
Why to the gods, ill-fated, any more
Should I look up—whom call to succour—since
Impiety my piety is named?
But, if these things are pleasing to the gods,
I'll freely own I suffered for my fault;
If theirs the fault, who doomed me, may to them
No worse befall than they unjustly do!

Chorus.

Stormily still o'er the soul of the maiden
The selfsame gusts of passion sweep.

Creon.

Therefore, I warn them, ruth for their lingering,
To those who lead her, this shall cause.

Antigone.

Short shrift, swift death—ah! woe is me—
This speech portends.

Creon.

Lay to thy soul no flattering hope,
That unfulfilled this doom may be.

Antigone.

O country of Thebes and my father's city,
And gods my progenitors,
Lo, how they lead me—now, and delay not.
O all ye princes of Thebes, behold me—
Of the race of your kings, me, sole surviving—
What things at the hands of what men I suffer,
For the fear of the gods I feared.

(*Exit Antigone.*)

Strophe 1

Chorus.

Out of the sunlight so,
In brass-bound prison-courts,
Were pent the limbs of Danaë,
And in a living tomb sealed up from sight;
Albeit, O daughter, she as thou
Came of a noble line,
And that life-quickening treasure of his golden rain
She had in charge from Zeus to keep.
O dread mysterious power of fate,
That neither wealth nor war can quell,
Nor walls shut out, nor ships escape,
Dark-fleeing o'er the foam!

Antistrophe 1

And that Edonian king
Was bound, the choleric son
Of Dryas, splenetive and hot,
Fast in the rock by Dionysus chained.
Such fierce and fevered issue streams
From madness at the height.

With splenetive rash speech what madness had assailed
The vengeful god, too late he learned.
To women-worshippers inspired
Their torchlit revels he forbade,
And flutings that the Muses loved
Had silenced with his scorn.

Strophe 2

From the dark rock-portals of the divided sea
Here go the cliffs of Bosporus, and there
The savage Thracian coast
Of Salmydessus, where the neighbour-worshipped God
Of Battle saw the blinding blow accurst,
Dealt by that fierce stepdame,
Darkling descend on both the sons
Of Phineus—on their sightless orbs
That plead for vengeance, stricken through and stabbed
By the sharp shuttle in her murderous hands.

Antistrophe 2

Wasted with their sorrow, their mother's hapless fate
They hapless wept, and in their mother's shame
Had part, as those base-born:
Yet she from the old Erechtheid blood her birth derived,
And in deep caverns of the hills was nursed,
Amid her father's storms,
Child of the North-wind—up the steep
Hillsides no bounding foal so fleet,
A daughter of the gods: but her, O child,
Fate's everlasting hands availed to reach.

(*Enter Teiresias, led by a boy.*)

Teiresias.

Prince of Thebes, we come—one sight for both
Our common road descrying, as behoves
Blind men to find their way by help of others.

Creon.

What tidings, old Teiresias, dost thou bring?

Teiresias.

Hear then the prophet, and attend his speech.

Creon.

Have I aforetime from thy wisdom swerved?

Teiresias.

So, clear of shoals, thou pilotest the state.

Creon.

The service thou hast rendered I attest.

Teiresias.

Once more on razor's edge thy fortunes stand.

Creon.

Hearing thy speech, I shudder: tell me more.

Teiresias.

My art's prognostications hear and judge.
For in my ancient seat, to watch the birds
In that their general gathering-place, I sat,
And heard an unintelligible noise,
A cry and clangour of birds, confused with rage;
And what fierce fray they waged with murderous claws,
I guessed too surely by the whirr of wings.
Scared by that sound, burnt-offerings I then
Essayed on blazing altars: but no flame
Leapt from the sacrifice: a clammy ooze
Reeked from the thighs, and 'mid the ashes dripped,
Smoking and sputtering; the gall disparted,
And on the air was spent; and the thigh-bones
Of the enfolding fat fell stripped and bare.
This from this boy I heard, whose eyes beheld
The failing signs of sacrifice obscure:
Others by me are guided, I by him.
And by thy will we are afflicted thus.
For now our hearths and altars every one
Have ravening dogs and birds fouled with the flesh
Of this poor fallen son of Oedipus;
And so no flame of victims burnt may move
Gods any more to hearken to our prayers,
And birds obscene flap forth a bodeful cry,
With fat of human carrion newly gorged.
Slight not, my son, such warning. For all men,
Both great and small, are liable to err:
But he who errs no more unfortunate
Or all unwise shall be, if having tripped
He rights the wrong nor stubbornly persists.
He who persists in folly is the fool.
Give death his due: stab not the fallen foe:
What valour is in this, to slay the slain?

Wisely I speak and well; and sweet it is
To hear good counsel, when it counsels gain.

Creon.

Old man, ye all, as bowmen at a mark,
Shoot at this man, and with your prophecies
Ye practise on me too, and mine own kin
Mere merchandise and salework make of me.
Go to, get gain, and barter, if ye will,
Amber ye buy from Sardis, and fine gold
Of Ind: but him, I say, ye shall not bury:
No, not if eagles, ministers of Zeus,
Should bear him piecemeal to their Master's throne,
Will I, for fear of such pollution, grant
Leave for his burial; knowing well that men
Soil not the stainless majesty of heaven.
But, aged seer, the wisest of mankind
Dishonourably may fall, who fairly speak
Dishonourable words, and all for gain.

Teiresias.

Alas!
Who knows, or who considers, in this world—

Creon.

What wilt thou say? What commonplace is this?

Teiresias.

How prudence is the best of all our wealth?

Creon.

As folly, I suppose, our deadliest hurt.

Teiresias.

Yet with this malady art thou possest.

Creon.

Reproaches I'll not bandy with the prophet.

Teiresias.

Saying that I falsely prophesy, thou dost.

Creon.

So are all prophets; 'tis a covetous race.

Teiresias.

Greed of base gain marks still the tyrant-sort.

Creon.

Knowest thou that of thy rulers this is said?

Teiresias.

I know; for thou through me didst save the state.

Creon.

Wise in thy craft art thou, but false at heart.

Teiresias.

Secrets, fast-locked, thou'lt move me to disclose.

Creon.

Unlock them, only speaking not for gain.

Teiresias.

So, for thy part indeed, methinks I shall.

Creon.

Think not that in my purpose thou shalt trade.

Teiresias.

But surely know that thou not many more
Revolving courses of the sun shalt pass,
Ere of thine own blood one, to make amends,
Dead for the dead, thou shalt have rendered up,
For that a living soul thou hast sent below,
And with dishonour in the grave hast lodged,
And that one dead thou holdest here cut off
From presence of the gods who reign below,
All rites of death, all obsequies denied —
With whom thou shouldst not meddle, nor the gods
In heaven, but of their due thou robb'st the dead.
Therefore of Hades and the gods for thee
The Avengers wait, and ruin slow yet sure,
To take thee in the pit which thou hast dug.
Do I speak this for gold? Thyself shalt judge:
For, yet a little while, and wailings loud
Of men and women in thy house shall show.
Think, of each city too what gathering rage,
That sees its mangled dead entombed in maws
Of dogs and all fierce beasts, or borne by kites
With stench unhallowed to its hearth-crowned heights.
So like a bowman have I launched at thee
In wrath, for thou provok'st me, shafts indeed
To pierce thy heart, and fail not, from whose smart
Thou'lt not escape. But now, boy, lead me home,
That he may vent his spleen on younger men,
And learn to keep a tongue more temperate,
And in his breast a better mind than now.

(*Exit Teiresias.*)

Chorus.

The man has prophesied dread things, O king,
And gone: and never have I known—not since
These temples changed their raven locks to snow—
That aught of false this city heard from him.

Creon.

Yea, this I know, and much am I perplexed:
For hard it is to yield, but standing firm
I fear to pluck swift ruin on my pride.

Chorus.

Son of Menoeceus, be advised in time.

Creon.

Say then, what must I do? and I'll obey.

Chorus.

Go, from her prison in the rock release
The maiden, and the unburied corpse inter.

Creon.

Dost thou think this, and wouldst thou have me yield?

Chorus.

Yea, king, and quickly; for the gods cut short
With sudden scathe the foolishness of men.

Creon.

Hardly indeed, but yet with forced consent
I'll do it, stooping to necessity.

Chorus.

Do it, and go; leave not this task to others.

Creon.

Even as I am, I'll go; and, servants, haste,
That hear and hear me not: axes in hand,
All to yon spot, far-seen, make good your speed.
But I, since this way now my mind is bent,
Whom I myself have bound, myself will loose.
For now my heart misgives me, he lives best,
Whose feet depart not from the ancient ways.

(*Exit Creon.*)

Strophe 1

Chorus.

Worshipped by many names—
Glory of Theban Semele,
Child of loud-thundering Zeus—
Haunting the famed Italian fields,

Whom as a prince the hospitable vale
Of the Eleusinian Dame reveres—
Bacchus, that hast thy home
In Thebes, the home of Bacchanals,
Beside Ismenus' fertile stream,
Where the fell dragon's teeth of old were sown:

Antistrophe 1

O'er the two-crested peak,
With nymphs Corycian in thy train,
By springs of Castaly,
The streaming levin lights thy path:
And from steep Nysa's hills, with ivy clad,
And that green slope, with clustering grapes
Empurpled to the sea,
When thou wouldst visit Theban streets,
A jocund company divine
With acclamation loud conducts thee forth.

Strophe 2

Thebes of all cities most thou honourest,
Thou with thy mother, whom the lightning slew:
And now, when Thebes is sick,
And all her people the sore plague hath stricken,
Hear us and come with healing feet
O'er the Parnassian hill,
Or the resounding strait:

Antistrophe 2

Come, whom fire-breathing stars in dance obey,
The master of the voices of the night,
Of Zeus the puissant son—
Come at our call, girt with thy Thyiad troop,
That follow, with thy frenzy filled,
Dancing the livelong night,
Iacchus, thee their lord.

(*Enter a Messenger.*)

Messenger.

Neighbours of Cadmus, and the royal house
Of old Amphion, no man's life would I,
How high or low soever, praise or blame,

Since, who to-day has fortune, good or ill,
To-morrow's fortune lifts or lays him low;
No seer a constant lot foresees for men.
For Creon before was happy, as I deemed,
Who saved this land of Cadmus from its foes,
And the sole sovereignty of Thebes receiving
Prospered therein, with noble children blest.
Now all is lost. For, when the joys of life
Men have relinquished, no more life indeed
I count their living, but a living death.
For in thy house heap riches, if thou wilt;
Keep kingly state; yet, if no joy withal
Thou hast, for all things else, compared with pleasure,
I would not change the shadow of a smoke.

Chorus.

Of what grief now of princes wilt thou tell?

Messenger.

That one lies dead, whom those who live have slain.

Chorus.

Say, who is slain? And what man is the slayer?

Messenger.

Haemon is dead: his death no stranger's act.

Chorus.

Slain by himself, or by his father's hand?

Messenger.

Wroth with his pitiless sire, he slew himself.

Chorus.

O prophet, how thy prophecy comes true!

Messenger.

These things being so, consider of the rest.

Chorus.

Lo, hard at hand the miserable queen,
Eurydice: who from the house comes forth
Either by chance, or hearing of her son.

(*Enter Eurydice.*)

Eurydice.

Good townsmen all, your conference I heard,
As to the doors I came, intending now
Of Pallas to entreat her heavenly aid.
Even as I loosed the fastenings of the gate,
That opened wide, there smote my ears a word

Of sorrow all my own: backward I swooned,
Surprised by terror, in my maidens' arms:
But tell me now your tidings once again—
For, not unlearned in sorrow, I shall hear.

Messenger.

Dear mistress, I will tell thee what I saw,
And not leave out one word of all the truth.
Why should I flatter thee with glozing words,
Too soon found false? Plain truth is ever best.
Thy husband hence I followed at the heels
To that high plain, where torn by dogs the body
Of Polyneices lay, unpitied still.
A prayer we said to Hecate in the way
And Pluto, their displeasure to refrain,
Then, sprinkling with pure water, in new-stript boughs
Wrapped round and burned the fragments that remained.
A lofty funeral-mound of native earth
We heaped for him; then sought the maiden's bed,
Her bridal bed with Hades in the rock.
And from afar a voice of shrill lament
About the unhallowed chamber some one heard,
And came to Creon, and told it to his lord.
And in his ears, approaching, the wild cry
Rang doubtfully, till now there brake from him
A word of sharp despair, "O wretched man,
What fear is at my heart? and am I going
The wofullest road that ever I have gone?
It is my son's voice greets me. Good servants, go,
Go nearer quickly; and standing by the tomb,
Even to the throat of the vault peer through and look,
Where the wrenched stonework gapes, if Haemon's voice
I recognise indeed, or by the gods
Am cheated!" Crazed with his fear, he spake; and we
Looked, as he bade; and in the last of the tomb
We saw the maiden—hanged: about her neck
Some shred of linen had served her for a noose:
And fallen upon her, clasping her, he lay,
Wailing his wasted passion in the grave,
His fatal father, and his luckless bride.
His father saw, and crying a bitter cry
Went in, and with a lamentable voice
Called him, "O rash, what is it that thou hast done?

What wouldst thou? On what madness hast thou rushed?
My son, come forth: I pray thee—I implore."
But with fierce eyes the boy glared at his sire
And looks of loathing, and for answer plucked
Forth a two-hilted sword, and would have struck,
But missed him, as he fled: and in that minute,
Wroth with himself, in his own side amain
Thrust deep the steel, unhappy; and conscious still
Folded the maiden in his fainting arms;
Then, gasping out his life in one sharp breath,
Pelted her pale cheek with the crimson shower.
Dead with the dead he lies, such nuptial rites
In halls of Hades, luckless, having won;
Teaching the world, that of all human ills
With human folly is none that may compare.

(*Exit Eurydice.*)

Chorus.

How should one deem of this? The queen, without
A word, of good or evil, has gone hence.

Messenger.

Indeed, 'tis strange: but yet I feed on hope
That to lament in public for her son
She will not deign; but, as for private sorrow,
Will charge her women in the house to weep.
She is well tried in prudence, not to fail.

Chorus.

I know not; but to me the too-much silence,
No less than clamorous grief, seems perilous.

Messenger.

I will go hence to the house, and know, if aught
Of secret purpose in her raging heart
She hath kept locked from us. Thou sayest well:
The too-much silence may bode mischief too.

(*Exit the Messenger.*)

Chorus.

Lo, the king comes hither himself, in his hands
The record, not doubtful its purport, bearing;
No grief (I dare to say) wrought by another,
But the weight of his own misdoing.

(*Enter Creon with the body of Haemon.*)

Strophe

Creon.

Alas, my purblind wisdom's fatal fault,
Stubborn, and fraught with death!
Ye see us, sire and son,
The slayer and the slain.
O counsels all unblest!
Alas for thee, my son,
So young a life and so untimely quenched–
Gone from me, past recall–
Not by thy folly, but my own!

Chorus.

Ah, how too late thou dost discern the truth!

Creon.

Yea, to my cost I know: but then, methinks,
Oh then, some god with crushing weight
Leapt on me, drave me into frantic ways,
Trampling, alas for me,
In the base dust my ruined joy.
O toil and trouble of mortals–trouble and toil!

(*Enter a Second Messenger.*)

Second Messenger.

Trouble, O king, thine own and none but thine,
Thou comest, methinks, part bearing in thy hands;
Part–in the house thou hast, and soon shalt see.

Creon.

What more, what worse than evil, yet remains?

Second Messenger.

Thy wife is dead, with desperate hand ev'n now
Self-slain, for this dead son for whom she lived.

Antistrophe

Creon.

O harbour of Hades, never to be appeased,
Why art thou merciless?
What heavy news is this?
Harsh news to me of grief,

That slays me, slain before!
A woful word indeed,
Telling of slaughter upon slaughter heaped,
To me, the twice-bereaved,
At one fell swoop, of son and wife!

Chorus.

Behold and see: for now the doors stand wide.

Creon.

This second grief, ah me, my eyes behold.
What fate, ah what, remains behind?
My son I hold already in my arms:
And now, ah woe is me,
This other in my sight lies dead:
Mother and child—most piteous both to see!

Second Messenger.

Heartstricken at the altar as she fell,
Her swooning eyes she opened, and made moan
For Megareus, her son, who nobly died
Before, and for this other, and with her last
Breath cursed, the slayer of her children, thee.

Creon.

Ah me, will no one aim
Against my heart, made wild with fear,
With two-edged sword a deadly thrust?
O wretched that I am,
Fulfilled with sorrow, and made one with grief!

Second Messenger.

She did reproach thee, truly, ere she died,
And laid on thee the blame of both their deaths.

Creon.

What was the manner of her violent end?

Second Messenger.

Pierced to the heart, by her own hand, she died,
Hearing her son's most lamentable fate.

Creon.

All, all on me this guilt must ever rest,
And on no head but mine.
O my poor son, I slew thee, even I:
Let no one doubt, but that the deed was mine.
O servants, lead me quickly, lead me hence;
And let me be as one who is no more.

Chorus.

'Tis counselled well, if well with ill can be:
For bad is best, when soonest out of sight.

Creon.

I care not, let it come:
Let come the best of all my fate,
The best, the last, that ends my days:
What care I? come what will—
That I no more may see another day.

Chorus.

Let be the future: mind the present need,
And leave the rest to whom the rest concerns.

Creon.

No other wish have I; that prayer is all.

Chorus.

Pray not at all: all is as fate appoints:
'Tis not in mortals to avert their doom.

Creon.

Oh lead me hence, unprofitable; who thee
Unwittingly have slain,
Child, and my wife, unhappy; and know not now
Which way to look to either: for all things
Are crooked that I handle, and a fate
Intolerable upon my life hath leapt.

(*Creon is led away.*)

Chorus.

First of all happiness far is wisdom,
And to the gods that one fail not of piety.
But great words of the overweening
Lay great stripes to the backs of the boasters·
Taught by adversity,
Old age learns, too late, to be wise.

Euripides,
with papyrus roll
and tragic mask.
Vatican Museum,
Rome

EURIPIDES

Medea

Translated by Arthur S. Way

First produced in 431 B.C. It won third prize; Euripides was disliked for his advanced views and won first prize only four times, although after his death he was the most popular of the three dramatists.

CHARACTERS IN THE PLAY

Nurse of Medea

Medea

Jason

Creon, King of Corinth

Aegeus, King of Athens

Two sons of Jason and Medea

Attendant of the children

A Messenger

Chorus of Corinthian Women

ARGUMENT

At the command of his wicked uncle Pelias, who had usurped the throne of Iolcos in Thessaly, Jason built the first ship, known as the Argo, and sailed to distant Colchis to secure the Golden Fleece. The sorceress Medea, daughter of King Aeetes, slew the sleepless dragon, which guarded the Golden Fleece, killed her brother to delay pursuit, and escaped with Jason. Back in Thessaly, Pelias still refused to surrender the throne to Jason, whereupon Medea murdered him. Jason and Medea, with their two sons, then fled to Corinth. Some years later, at the opening of the play, Jason, with the smug egotism of a scoundrel who knew that no legal union was possible between Greek and non-Greek, has abandoned Medea, despite all that she has done for him, and married the daughter of Creon, King of Corinth. Medea is heartbroken, as anyone is when tragedy falls—but does not civilization impose restraints even on those who have great power?

SCENE

In front of Medea's house in Corinth, near the palace of Creon. The Nurse enters alone.

MEDEA

Nurse.

Would God that Argo's hull had never flown
Through those blue Clashing Rocks to Colchis-land,
Nor that in Pelion's glens had fallen ever
The axe-hewn pine, nor filled with oars the hands
Of hero-princes, who at Pelias' hest
Quested the Golden Fleece! My mistress then,
Medea, to Iolcos' towers had sailed not
With love for Jason thrilled through all her soul,
Nor had on Pelias' daughters wrought to slay
Their sire, nor now in this Corinthian land
Dwelt with her lord and children, gladdening
By this her exile them whose land received her,
Yea, and in all things serving Jason's weal,
Which is the chief salvation of the home,
When wife stands not at variance with her lord.
Now all is hatred: love is sickness-stricken.
For Jason, traitor to his babes and her,
My mistress, weddeth with a child of kings,
Daughter of Creon ruler of the land.
And, slighted thus, Medea, hapless wife,
Cries on the oaths, invokes that mightiest pledge
Of the right hand, and calls the Gods to witness
From Jason what requital she receives.
Foodless she lies, her frame to griefs resigned,
Wasting in tears all those long weary hours
Since first she knew her outraged by her lord,
Never uplifting eye, nor turning ever
From earth her face; but like a rock or sea-wave
So hearkens she to friends that counsel her;
Saving at whiles, when, turning her white neck,
All to herself she wails her sire beloved,
Her land, her home, forsaking which she came
Hither with him who holds her now dishonoured.
Now knows she, hapless, by affliction's teaching,
How good is fatherland unforfeited.
She loathes her babes, joys not beholding them.
I fear her, lest some mischief she devise.
Grim is her spirit, one that will not brook

Mishandling: yea, I know her, and I dread
Lest through her heart she thrust the whetted knife,
Through the halls stealing silent to her bed,
Or slay the king and him that weds his child,
And get herself therefrom some worse misfortune:
For dangerous is she: who begins a feud
With her, not soon shall sing the triumph-song.
But lo, her boys, their racing-sport put by,
Draw near, unwitting of their mother's ills,
For the young heart loves not to brood in grief.

(*Enter the Attendant with Medea's Children.*)

Attendant.

O ancient chattel of my mistress' home,
Why at the gates thus lonely standest thou,
Thyself unto thyself discoursing ills?
How wills Medea to be left of thee?

Nurse.

O grey attendant of the sons of Jason,
The hearts of faithful servants still are touched
By ill-betiding fortunes of their lords.
For I have come to such a pass of grief,
That yearning took me hitherward to come
And tell to earth and heaven my lady's fortunes.

Attendant.

Ceaseth not yet the hapless one from moan?

Nurse.

Cease!—her pain scarce begun, the midst far off!

Attendant.

Ah fool!—if one may say it of his lords—
Little she knoweth of the latest blow.

Nurse.

What is it, ancient? Grudge not thou to tell me.

Attendant.

Nought: I repent me of the word that 'scaped me.

Nurse.

Nay, by thy beard, from fellow-thrall hide not—
Silence, if need be, will I keep thereof.

Attendant.

I heard one saying—feigning not to hear,
As I drew near the marble thrones, where sit
The ancients round Peirene's hallowed fount,—

That Creon, this land's lord, will shortly drive
These boys from soil Corinthian with their mother?
Howbeit, if the tale I heard be true
I know not: fain were I it were not so.

Nurse.

Will Jason brook his children suffering this,
What though he be estrangèd from their mother?

Attendant.

The old ties in the race lag far behind
The new:—no friend is *he* unto this house.

Nurse.

We are undone then, if we add fresh ill
To old, ere lightened be our ship of this.

Attendant.

But thou—for 'tis not season that thy lady
Should know—keep silence, and speak not the tale.

Nurse.

Hear, babes, what father this is unto you!
I curse him—not: he is my master still:
But to his friends he stands convict of baseness.

Attendant.

What man is not?—Hast learnt this only now,
That each man loves self better than his neighbour,
For just cause some, and some for greed of gain?
So, for a bride's sake, these their father loves not.

Nurse.

Pass in, dear children, for it shall be well.
But thou, keep these apart to the uttermost:
Bring them not nigh their mother angry-souled.
For late I saw her glare, as glares a bull
On these, as 'twere for mischief; nor her wrath,
I know, shall cease, until its lightning strike.
To foes may she work ill, and not to friends!

Medea (*within*).

O hapless I!—O miseries heaped on mine head!
Ah me! ah me! would God I were dead!

Nurse.

Lo, darlings, the thing that I told you!
Lo the heart of your mother astir!
And astir is her anger: withhold you
From her sight, come not nigh unto her.

Haste, get you within: O beware ye
Of the thoughts as a wild-beast brood,
Of the nature too ruthless to spare ye
In its desperate mood.

Pass ye within now, departing
With all speed. It is plain to discern
How a cloud of lamenting, upstarting
From its viewless beginnings, shall burn
In lightnings of fury yet fiercer.
What deeds shall be dared of that soul,
So haughty, when wrong's goads pierce her,
So hard to control?

(*Exeunt Children and Attendant.*)

Medea (*within*).

Woe! I have suffered, have suffered, foul wrongs that may waken, may waken,
Mighty lamentings full well! O ye children accursed from the womb,
Hence to destruction, ye brood of a loathed one forsaken, forsaken!
Hence with your father, and perish our home in the blackness of doom!

Nurse.

Ah me, in the father's offences
What part have the babes, that thine hate
Should blast them?—forlorn innocences,
How sorely I fear for your fate!
Ah princes—how fearful their moods are! —
Long ruling, unschooled to obey,—
Unforgiving, unsleeping their feuds are.
Better life's level way.

Be it mine, if in greatness I may not,
In quiet and peace to grow old.
Sweeter name than "The Mean" shall ye say not;
But to taste it is sweetness untold.

But to men never weal above measure
Availed: on its perilous height
The Gods in their hour of displeasure
The heavier smite.

(*Enter Chorus of Corinthian Women.*)

Chorus.

I have hearkened the voice of the daughter of Colchis, the sound of the crying
Of the misery-stricken; nor yet is she stilled. Now the tale of her tell,
Grey woman; for moaned through the porch from her chamber the wail of her sighing;
And I cannot, I cannot be glad while the home in affliction is lying,
The house I have loved so well.

Nurse.

Home?—home there is none: it hath vanished away:
For my lord to a bride of the princes is thrall;
And my lady is pining the livelong day
In her bower, and for nought that her friends' lips say
On her heart may the dews of comfort fall.

Medea (*within*).

Would God that the flame of the lightning from heaven descending, descending,
Might burn through mine head!—for in living wherein any more is my gain?
Alas and alas! Would God I might bring to an ending, an ending,
The life that I loathe, and behind me might cast all its burden of pain!

Strophe

Chorus.

O Zeus, Earth, Light, did ye hear her,
How waileth the woe-laden breath
Of the bride in unhappiest plight?
What yearning for vanished delight,
O passion-distraught, should have might
To cause thee to wish death nearer—
The ending of all things, death?

Make thou not for this supplication!
If thine husband hath turned and adored
New love, that estrangèd he is,
O harrow thy soul not for this.
It is Zeus that shall right thee, I wis.
Ah, pine not in over-vexation
Of spirit, bewailing thy lord!

Medea (*within*).

O Lady of Justice, O Artemis' Majesty, see it, O see it—
Look on the wrongs that I suffer, by oaths everlasting who tied
The soul of mine husband, that ne'er from the curse he might free it, nor free it
From your vengeance!—O may I behold him at last, even him and his bride,
Them, and these halls therewithal, all shattered in ruin, in ruin!—
Wretches, who dare unprovoked to do to Medea despite!
O father, O city, whom erst I forsook, for undoing, undoing
And for shame, when the blood of my brother I spilt on the path of my flight!

Nurse.

Do ye hear what she saith, and uplifteth her cry
Unto Themis and Zeus, to the Suppliant's King,
Oath-steward of men that be born but to die?
O my lady will lay not her anger by
Soon, making her vengeance a little thing.

Antistrophe

Chorus.

If she would but come forth where we wait her,
If she would but give ear to the sound
Of our speech, that her spirit would learn
From its fierceness of anger to turn,
And her lust for revenge not burn!
O ne'er may my love prove traitor,
Never false to my friends be it found!

But go thou, and forth of the dwelling
Thy mistress hitherward lead.
Say to her that friends be we all.
O hasten, ere mischief befall
The lords of the palace-hall.
For her grief, like a tempest upswelling,
Resistless shall ruin-ward speed.

Nurse.

I will do it: but almost my spirit despaireth
To win her; yet labour of love shall it be.
But my queen on her thralls as a mad bull glareth,
Or a lioness couched mid her whelps, whoso dareth
With speech to draw near her, so tameless is she.

He should err not, who named the old singers in singing
Not cunning, but left-handed bards, for their lays
Did they frame for the mirth-tide, the festal in-bringing
Of the wine, and the feast, when the harp strings are ringing
To sweeten with melody life's sweet days:

But the dread doom of mortals, the anguish heart-rending—
Never minstrel by music hath breathed on them peace,
Nor by song with his harp-notes in harmony blending;
Albeit of these cometh death's dark ending
Unto many a home that is wrecked of these.

And yet were it surely a boon to bring healing
Of sorrow to mortals with song: but in vain
Mid the fulness of feasting ring voices clear-pealing,
And the banquet itself hath a glamour, concealing
From mortals their doom, flinging spells over pain.

(*Exit Nurse.*)

Chorus.

I have heard it, the sigh-laden cry of the daughter
Of Colchis, the woe-shrilling anguish of wailing
For the traitor to love who with false vows caught her,
Who in strength of her wrongs chideth Heaven, assailing
The Oath-queen of Zeus, who with cords all-prevailing
Forth haled her, and brought her o'er star-litten water,
Where the brine-mists hover o'er Pontus' Key,
Unto Hellas far over the boundless sea.

(*Enter Medea.*)

Medea.

Corinthian dames, I have come forth my doors
Lest ye should blame me. Many folk I know
Accounted haughty, some, for proud staid mien,
Some, stranger-shy: and some, that softly go,
Have gotten ill repute of indolence.
For justice sits not in the eyes of man,
Who, ere he hath discerned his neighbour's heart,
Hates him at sight, albeit nowise wronged.
The sojourner must learn the city's wont;
Nor praise I citizens-born, law to themselves,
Mannerless churls, which flout their fellow-folk.
But me—unlooked-for fell this blow on me,
And brake mine heart. Undone I am; have lost
All grace of life, and long to die, my friends.
For he that was mine all,—thou know'st it well,—
My lord, of all men basest hath become.
Surely, of creatures that have life and wit,
We women are of all things wretchedest,
Who, first, must needs, as buys the highest bidder,
Thus buy a husband, and our body's master
So win—for deeper depth of ill is this.
Nay, risk is dire herein,—or shall we gain
An evil lord or good? For change is shame
To woman, nor may she renounce her spouse.
And, coming to new customs, habits new,
Seer need she be, to know the thing unlearnt,
What manner of man her couch's mate shall be.
But if we learn our lesson, if our lord
Dwell with us, plunging not against the yoke,
Happy our lot: if not—no help but death.
For the man, when at home they fret his soul,
Goes forth, and stays his loathing heart's disgust,
Unto a friend or age-mate turning him.
We have but one, one heart to seek for comfort.
But we, say they, live an unperilled life
At home, while they do battle with the spear.
Falsely they deem: twice would I under shield
Stand, rather than bear childbirth peril once.
Yet thee and me the selfsame reasons touch not.

Thine is this city, thine a father's home;
Hast bliss of life and fellowship of friends.
But I, lone, cityless, and outraged thus
Of him who kidnapped me from foreign shores,
Mother nor brother have I, kinsman none,
For port of refuge from calamity.
Wherefore I fain would win of thee this boon:—
If any path be found me, or device,
Whereby to avenge these wrongs upon mine husband,
On her who weds, on him who gives the bride,
Keep silence. Woman quails at every peril,
Faint-heart to face the fray and look on steel;
But when in wedlock-rights she suffers wrong,
No spirit more bloodthirsty shall be found.

Chorus.

This will I; for 'tis just that thou, Medea,
Requite thy lord: no marvel thou dost grieve.
But I see Creon, ruler of this land,
Advancing, herald of some new decree.

(*Enter Creon.*)

Creon.

Thee the black-lowering, wroth against thy lord,
Medea, bid I forth this land to fare
An exile, taking thy two sons with thee,
And make no tarrying: daysman of this cause
Am I, and homeward go I not again
Ere from the land's bounds I have cast thee forth.

Medea.

Ah me! undone am I in utter ruin!
My foes crowd sail pursuing: landing-place
Is none from surges of calamity.
Yet, howso wronged, one question will I ask—
For what cause, Creon, dost thou banish me?

Creon.

I fear thee—need is none to cloak my words—
Lest on my child thou wreak some ill past cure.
And to this dread do many things conspire.
Wise art thou, cunning in much evil lore;
Chafed art thou, of thine husband's couch bereft:
I hear thou threatenest, so they bring me word,
To wreak on sire, on bridegroom, and on bride

Mischief. I guard mine head ere falls the blow.
Better be hated, woman, now of thee,
Than once relent, and sorely groan too late.

Medea.

Not now first, Creon,—many a time ere now
Rumour hath wronged and wrought me grievous harm.
Ne'er should the man whose heart is sound of wit
Let teach his sons more wisdom than the herd.
They are burdened with unprofitable lore,
And spite and envy of other folk they earn.
For, if thou bring strange wisdom unto dullards,
Useless shalt thou be counted, and not wise:
And, grant thy name o'ertop the self-extolled
Wits, in the city odious shalt thou be.
Myself too in this fortune am partaker.
Of some my wisdom wins me jealousy,
Some count me idle; some, o'erbusy; some
Unsocial:—yet not over-wise am I.
And thou, thou fear'st me, lest I mar thy music.
Not such am I—O Creon, dread not me—
That against princes I should dare transgress.
How hast thou wronged me? Thou hast given thy child
To whomso pleased thee. But—I hate mine husband:
And, doubtless, this in prudence hast thou done?
Nay, but I grudge not thy prosperity.
Wed ye, and prosper. But in this your land
Still let me dwell: for I, how wronged soe'er,
Will hold my peace, o'ermastered by the strong.

Creon.

Soft words to hear: but lurks mine heart within
Dread lest thou plottest mischief all the while;
And all the less I trust thee than before.
The vehement-hearted woman—yea, or man—
Is easier watched-for than the silent-cunning.
But forth with all speed: plead me pleadings none.
For this is stablished: no device hast thou
To bide with us, who art a foe to me.

Medea.

Nay,—by thy knees, and by the bride, thy child!

Creon.

Thou wastest words; thou never shalt prevail.

Medea.

Wilt drive me forth, respecting nought my prayers?

Creon.

Ay: more I love not thee than mine own house.

Medea.

O, how I call thee now to mind, my country!

Creon.

Ay, dear to me is Corinth, next my children.

Medea.

Alas! to mortals what a curse is love!

Creon.

Blessing or curse, I throw, as fortune falls.

Medea.

Zeus, may the cause of this 'scape not thy ken!

Creon.

Hence, passionate fool, and rid me of my trouble.

Medea.

Troubled am I, nor need I troubles new.

Creon.

Soon shalt thou be by servants' hands thrust out.

Medea.

Nay—nay—not this, O Creon, I beseech thee!

Creon.

A coil thou wilt make, woman, as it seems.

Medea.

I will flee forth:—not this the boon I crave.

Creon.

Why restive then?—why rid not Corinth of thee?

Medea.

Suffer me yet to tarry this one day,
And somewhat for our exile to take thought,
And find my babes a refuge, since their sire
Cares nought to make provision for his sons.
Compassionate these: a father too art thou
Of children: meet it is thou show these grace.
Not for myself I fret, if I be banished:
For them in their calamity I mourn.

Creon.

My spirit least of all is tyrannous.
Many a plan have my relentings marred:
And, woman, now I know I err herein,
Yet shalt thou win this boon. But I forewarn thee,

If thee the approaching Sun-god's torch behold
Within this country's confines with thy sons,
Thou diest:—the word is said that shall not lie.
Now, if remain thou must, remain one day—
Too short for thee to do the deeds I dread.

(*Exit Creon.*)

Chorus.

O hapless thou!
Woe's me for thy misery, woe for the trouble and anguish that meet thee!
Whitherward wilt thou turn thee?—what welcoming hand mid the strangers shall greet thee?
What home or what land to receive thee, deliverance from evils to give thee,
Wilt thou find for thee now?
How mid surge of despair to o'erwhelm thee in ruin God's hand on thine helm
Hath steered, O Medea, thy prow!

Medea.

'Tis ill done every way; who shall gainsay?
Yet nowise ill in this: deem not so yet.
Bridegroom and bride grim conflicts yet await;
Nor troubles light abide these marriage-makers.
Think'st thou that I had cringed to yon man ever,
Except to gain some gain, or work some wile?
Nor word nor touch of hand had I vouchsafed him.
But to such height of folly hath he come,
That, when he might forestall mine every plot
By banishment, this day of grace he grants me
To stay, wherein three foes will I lay dead,
The father, and the daughter, and mine husband.
And, having for them many paths of death,
Which first to take in hand I know not, friends;
Whether to set the bridal bower aflame,
Or through the heart to thrust the whetted knife,
Through yon halls stealing silent to their couch.
Yet one thing bars the way—if I be found
Crossing the threshold of the house and plotting,
Die shall I, and make mirth unto my foes.
Best the straight path, wherein my nature's cunning
Excels, by poisons to destroy them:—yea.

Now, grant them dead: what city will receive me,
What host vouchsafe a land of refuge, home
Secure, and from the avenger shield my life?
There is none. Tarrying then a little space,
If any tower of safety shall appear,
These deaths by guile and silence will I compass;
But if misfortune drive me desperate forth,
Myself will grip the sword,—yea, though I die,—
And slay, and dare the strong hand's reckless deed:
For, by the Queen of Night, whom I revere
Above all, and for fellow-worker chose,
Hecate, dweller by mine hearth's dark shrine,
Not one shall vex my soul, and rue it not.
Bitter and woeful bridal will I give them,
Bitter troth-plight and banishing of me.
Up then!—spare nought of all thy sorcery-lore,
Medea, of thy plotting and contriving;
On to the dread deed! Now is need of daring.
Look on thy wrongs: thou must not make derision
For sons of Sisyphus, for Jason's bride,—
Thou, sprung from royal father, from the Sun!
Thou know'st means. Yea, our woman-nature 'tis—
Say they—to be most helpless for all good,
But fashioners most cunning of all ill.

Strophe 1

Chorus.

Upward aback to their fountains the sacred rivers are stealing;
Justice is turned to injustice, the order of old to confusion:
The thoughts of the hearts of men are treachery wholly, and, reeling
From its ancient foundations, the faith of the Gods is become a delusion.
Changes—and changes!—the voice of the people shall crown me with honour:
My life shall be sunlit with glory; for woman the old-time story
Is ended, the slanders hoary no more shall as chains be upon her.

Antistrophe 1

And the strains of the singers of old generations for shame shall falter,
Which sang evermore of the treason of woman, her faithlessness ever.
Alas, that our lips are not touched with the fire of song from the altar
Of Phoebus, the Harper-king, of the inspiration-giver!
Else had I lifted my voice in challenge of song high-ringing
Unto men: for the roll of the ages shall find for the poet-sages
Proud woman-themes for their pages, heroines worthy their singing.

Strophe 2

But thou from the ancient home didst sail over leagues of foam,
On-sped by a frenzied heart, and the sea-gates sawest dispart,
The Twin Rocks. Now, in the land
Of the stranger, thy doom is to waken
To a widowed couch, and forsaken
Of thy lord, and woe-overtaken,
To be cast forth shamed and banned.

Antistrophe 2

Disannulled is the spell of the oath: no shame for the broken troth
In Hellas the wide doth remain, but heavenward its flight hath it ta'en.
No home of a father hast thou
For thine haven when trouble-storms lower.
Usurped is thy bridal bower
Of another, in pride of her power,
Ill-starred, overqueening thee now.

(*Enter Jason.*)

Jason.

Not now first, nay, but ofttimes have I marked
What desperate mischief is a froward spirit.
For in this land, this home, when thou might'st stay
Bearing unfractiously thy rulers' pleasure,
Banished thou art for wild and whirling words.
Me they vex not—cease never, an thou wilt,
Clamouring, "Jason is of men most base!"
But, for thy words against thy rulers spoken,
Count it all gain—mere exile punishing thee.
For me—still strove I to appease the wrath
Of kings incensed: fain would I thou shouldst stay.
But thou rein'st not thy folly, speaking still
Evil of dignities; art therefore banished.
Yet, for all this, not wearied of my friends,
With so much forethought come I for thee, lady,
That, banished with thy babes, thou lack not gold,
Nor aught beside. Full many an ill is brought
In exile's train. Yea, though thou hatest me,
Ne'er can I harbour evil thought of thee.

Medea.

Caitiff of caitiffs!—blackest of reproaches
My tongue for thine unmanliness can frame—
Thou com'st to me—thou com'st, most hateful proved
To heaven, to me, to all the race of men!
This is not daring, no, nor courage this,
To wrong thy friends, and blench not from their eyes,
But, of all plagues infecting men, the worst,
Even shamelessness. And yet 'tis well thou cam'st,
For I shall ease the burden of mine heart
Reviling thee, and thou be galled to hear.
And with the first things first will I begin.
I saved thee, as they know, what Greeks soe'er
Entered with thee the self-same Argo's hull,
Thee, sent to quell the flame-outbreathing bulls
With yoke-bands, and to sow the tilth of death.
The dragon, warder of the Fleece of Gold,
That sleepless kept it with his manifold coils,

I slew, and raised deliverance-light for thee.
Myself forsook my father and mine home,
And to Iolcos under Pelion came
With thee, more zealous in thy cause than wise,
And Pelias slew by his own children's hands—
Of all deaths worst,—so cast out all thy fear.
And thus of me, basest of men, entreated,
For a new bride hast thou forsaken me,
Though I had born thee children. Wert thou childless,
Not past forgiving were this marriage-craving.
But faith of oaths hath vanished. I know not
Whether thou deem'st the olden Gods yet rule,
Or that new laws are now ordained for men;
For thine heart speaks thee unto me forsworn.
Out on this right hand, which thou oft wouldst clasp,—
These knees!—how vainly have we been embraced
By a base man, thus frustrate of our hopes!
Come, as a friend will I commune with thee—
Yet what fair dealing should I hope from thee?—
Yet will I: questioned, baser shalt thou show.
Now, whither turn I?—to my father's house,
Which, with my country, I for thee cast off?
To Pelias' hapless daughters?—Graciously
Their father's slayer would they welcome home!
For thus it is: a foe am I become
To mine own house. Whom I should ne'er have harmed,
For grace to thee I made mine enemies.
So then midst Hellas' daughters hast thou made me
Blest in return for all: in thee have I—
O wretched I!—a wondrous spouse and leal,
If from the land cast forth I pass to exile
Forlorn of friends, alone with children lone.
A proud reproach for our new bridegroom this—
In poverty thy babes, thy saviour, wander!
O Zeus, ah wherefore hast thou given to men
Plain signs for gold which is but counterfeit,
But no assay-mark nature-graven shows
On man's form, to discern the base withal?

Chorus.

Awful is wrath, and past all balm of healing,
When they that once loved clash in feud of hate.

Jason.

Needs must I be not ill at speech, meseems,
But, like the careful helmsman of a ship,
With close-reefed canvas run before the gale,
Woman, of thy tempestuous-railing tongue.
I—for thy kindness tower-high thou pilest—
Deem Cypris saviour of my voyaging,
Her, and none other or of Gods or men.
A subtle wit thou hast—what need to force me
To tell the tale how Love, by strong compulsion
Of shafts unerring, made thee save my life?
Yet take I not account too strict thereof;
For, in that thou didst save me, thou didst well.
Howbeit, more hast thou received than given
Of this my safety, as my words shall prove:—
First, then, in Hellas dwell'st thou, in the stead
Of land barbaric, knowest justice, learnest
To live by law without respect of force.
And all the Greeks have heard thy wisdom's fame.
Renown is thine: but if on earth's far bourn
Thou dwelledst yet, thou hadst not lived in story.
Now mine be neither gold mine halls within,
Nor sweeter song be mine than Orpheus sang,
If my fair fortune be to fame unknown.
Thus far of my great labours have I spoken,—
Since thou flung'st down this challenge to dispute:—
But, for thy railings on my royal marriage,
Herein will I show, first, that wise I was;
Then, temperate; third, to thee the best of friends
And to my children—nay, but hear me out.
When I came hither from Iolcos-land
With many a desperate fortune in my train,
What happier treasure-trove could I have found
Than to wed—I, an exile—with a princess?
Not—where it galls thee—loathing couch of thine,
And for a new bride smitten with desire,
Nor eager I to multiply mine offspring;—
Suffice these born to me: no fault in them:—
But that we might with honour live—grave import,—
And be not straitened,—for I know full well
How all friends from the poor man stand aloof,—
And I might nurture as beseems mine house

Our sons, and to these born of thee beget
Brethren, and, knitting in one family all,
Live happy days. Thou, what wouldst thou of children?
But me it profits, through sons to be born
To help the living. Have I planned so ill?
Not thou wouldst say it, but the lost couch galls thee.
But ye—ye women—so unreasoning are
That, wedlock-rights unmarred, ye count all well;
But to the couch if aught untoward hap,
With the best, fairest lot are ye at feud
Most bitter. Would that mortals otherwise
Could get them babes, that womankind were not,
And so no curse had lighted upon men.

Chorus.

Words, Jason, words, tricked out full cunningly:
Yet to me—though I speak not to thy mind—
Unjust thou seem'st, betraying thus thy wife.

Medea.

Of many things I think not as think many.
For in my sight the villain subtle-tongued
Getteth himself for gain exceeding loss,
Who, confident his tongue can gloze the wrong,
Becomes a bold knave:—no great wisdom this.
So be not thou, as touching me, fair-seeming
And crafty-tongued: one word shall overthrow thee.
Thou shouldest, if not base, have wed this bride
With my consent, not hid it from thy friends.

Jason.

Ay, nobly hadst thou helped in this my purpose,
Had I a marriage named, who even now
Canst not refrain thy heart's exceeding wrath!

Medea.

Not this thine hindrance, but the alien wife
No crown of honour was as eld drew on.

Jason.

Now know this well—not for the woman's sake
I wed the royal bride whom I have won,
But, as I said, of my desire to save
Thee, and beget seed royal, to my sons
Brethren, and for mine house a tower of strength.

Medea.

No prosperous life 'neath sorrow's cloud for me,
Nor weal, with thorns of conscience in mine heart!

Jason.

Know'st how to change thy prayer, and show the wiser?
May thy good never seem to thee thy sorrow;
Nor in fair fortune deem thy lot misfortune.

Medea.

O yea, insult!—Thou hast a refuge, thou;
But desolate I am banished from this land.

Jason.

Thyself hast chosen this: none other blame.

Medea.

I?—sooth, by wedding and betraying thee!

Jason.

By cursing princes with an impious curse.

Medea.

Even so,—and thus am cursing now *thine* house?

Jason.

With thee no more I wrangle touching this.
But if, or for the children or thyself,
For help in exile thou wilt take my gold,
Speak: ready am I to give with hand ungrudging,
And send guest-tokens which shall find thee friends.
If this thou wilt not, foolish shalt thou be:
Refrain wrath, and advantaged shalt thou be.

Medea.

Thy friends!—nothing will I of friends of thine.
No whit will I receive, nor offer thou.
No profit is there in a villain's gifts.

Jason.

In any wise I call the Gods to witness
That all help would I give thee and thy sons;
But thy good likes thee not: thy stubborn pride
Spurns friends: the more thy grief shall therefore be.

Medea.

Away!—impatience for the bride new-trapped
Consumes thee while thou loiterest at the doors!
Wed: for perchance—and God shall speed the word—
Thine shall be bridal thou wouldst fain renounce.

(*Exit Jason.*)

Strophe 1

Chorus.

Love bringeth nor glory nor honour to men when it cometh restraining
Not its unscanted excess: but if Cypris, in measure raining
Her joy, cometh down, there is none other Goddess so winsome as she.
Not upon me, O Queen, do thou aim from thy bow all-golden
The arrow desire-envenomed that none may avoid—not on me!

Antistrophe 1

But let Temperance shield me, the fairest of gifts of the Gods ever-living:
Nor ever with passion of jarring contention, nor feuds unforgiving,
In her terrors may Love's Queen visit me, smiting with maddened unrest
For a couch mismated my soul: but the peace of the bride-bed be holden
In honour of her, and her keen eyes choose for us bonds that be best.

Strophe 2

O fatherland, O mine home,
Not mine be the exile's doom!
Into poverty's pathways hard to be trod may my feet not be guided!
Most piteous anguish were this.
By death—O by death ere then may the conflict of life be decided,
Ended be life's little day! To be thus from the homeland divided—
No pang more bitter there is.

Antistrophe 2

We have seen, and it needeth nought
That of others herein we be taught:
For thee not a city, for thee not a friend hath compassionated
When affliction most awful is thine.
But he, who regardeth not friends, accursed may he perish, and hated,
Who opes not his heart with sincerity's key to the hapless-fated—
Never such shall be friend of mine!

(*Enter Aegeus.*)

Aegeus.
Medea, hail!—for fairer greeting-word
None knoweth to accost his friends withal.

Medea.
All hail thou also, wise Pandion's son,
Aegeus. Whence art thou journeying through this land?

Aegeus.
Leaving the ancient oracle of Phoebus.

Medea.
Why didst thou fare to earth's prophetic navel?

Aegeus.
To ask how seed of children might be mine.

Medea.
'Fore Heaven!—aye childless is thy life till now?

Aegeus.
Childless I am, by chance of some God's will.

Medea.
This, with a wife, or knowing not the couch?

Aegeus.
Nay, not unyoked to wedlock's bed am I.

Medea.
Now what to thee spake Phoebus touching issue?

Aegeus.
Deep words of wisdom not for man to interpret.

Medea.
Without sin might I know the God's reply?

Aegeus.
O yea—good sooth, it needs the wise heart most.

Medea.
What said he? Say, if sin be not to hear.

Aegeus.
The wine-skin's prominent foot I should not loose.

Medea.
Till thou shouldst do what thing, or reach what land?

Aegeus.
Till to the hearth ancestral back I came.

Medea.
And thou, what wouldst thou sailing to this shore?

Aegeus.
There is one Pittheus, king of Troezen he,–

Medea.
A man most pious, Pelops' son, they say.

Aegeus.
To him the God's response I fain would tell.

Medea.
Yea–a wise man, and having skill herein.

Aegeus.
Yea, and my best-belovèd spear-ally.

Medea.
Now prosper thou, and win thine heart's desire.

Aegeus.
Why droops thine eye?–why this wan-wasted hue?

Medea.
Aegeus, of all men basest is mine husband.

Aegeus.
What say'st thou? Clearly tell me thine heart's pain.

Medea.
He wrongs me–Jason, nothing wronged of me.

Aegeus.
What hath he done? More plainly tell it out.

Medea.
Another wife he takes, his household's mistress.

Aegeus.
Ha! hath he dared in truth this basest deed?

Medea.
Yea: I am now dishonoured, once beloved.

Aegeus.
Another love was this?–or hate of thee?

Medea.
Love?–yea, of the highest:–traitor he to love!

Aegeus.

Away with him, if he be base as this!

Medea.

His love was for affinity with princes.

Aegeus.

Who giveth him his daughter? End the tale.

Medea.

Creon, who ruleth this Corinthian land.

Aegeus.

Sooth, lady, reason was that thou shouldst grieve.

Medea.

'Tis death to me! Yea, also am I banished.

Aegeus.

Of whom? A new ill this thou namest is.

Medea.

Creon from Corinth driveth me an exile.

Aegeus.

Doth Jason suffer this?—I praise it not.

Medea.

In pretence, no: but to stand firm—not he!
But I beseech thee, touching this thy beard,
Clasping thy knees, and so become thy suppliant;—
Pity, O pity me the evil-starred,
And see me not cast forth to homelessness:
Receive to a hearth-place in thy land and homes.
So by heaven's blessing fruitful be thy love
In children, and in death thyself be blest.
Thou know'st not what good fortune thou hast found:
For I will end thy childlessness, will cause
Thy seed to grow to sons; such drugs I know.

Aegeus.

For many causes am I minded, lady,
This grace to grant thee: for the Gods' sake first;
Then, for the seed of children thou dost promise;
For herein wholly extinct is Aegeus' name.
But thus it is—if to my land thou come,
I thy defence essay, in bounds of justice.
Howbeit of this do I forewarn thee, lady,
From this land will I not consent to lead thee.
But, if thou reachest of thyself mine homes,
Safe shalt thou bide: to no man will I yield thee.
But from this land thou must thyself escape;
For blameless will I be to allies too.

Medea.

So be it. Yet, were oath-pledge given for this
To me, then had I all I would of thee.

Aegeus.

Ha, dost not trust me?—Or at what dost stumble?

Medea.

I trust thee: but my foes are Pelias' house
And Creon. Oath-bound, thou couldst never yield me
To these, when they would drag me from the land.
Hadst thou but promised, to the Gods unpledged,
Thou mightest turn their friend, might'st lightly yield
To herald-summons. Strengthless is my cause:
Wealth is on their side, and a princely house.

Aegeus.

Foresight exceeding, lady, in thy words!
Yet, if this be thy will, I draw not back;
Since for myself is this the safest course,
To have a plea to show unto thy foes;
And surer is thy part. The Oath-gods name.

Medea.

Swear by Earth's plain, and by my father's father
The Sun, and join the Gods' whole race thereto.

Aegeus.

That I will do or not do—what? Say on.

Medea.

That from thy land thyself wilt never cast me,
Nor, if a foe of mine would hale me thence,
Wilt, while thou liv'st, consenting yield me up.

Aegeus.

By Earth, the Sun's pure majesty, and all
The Gods, I swear to abide by this thou hast said.

Medea.

Enough. For broken troth what penalty?

Aegeus.

Whatso befalleth God-despising men.

Medea.

Pass on thy way rejoicing: all is well.
I too will come with all speed to thy burg,
When mine intent is wrought, my wish attained.

(*Exit Aegeus.*)

Chorus.

Now the Scion of Maia, the Wayfarer's King,
Bring thee safe to thine home, and the dream of thine heart,
The sweet visions that wing thy feet, may'st thou bring
To accomplishment, Aegeus, for now this thing
Hath taught me how noble thou art.

Medea.

Zeus, Justice child of Zeus, and Light of the Sun,
Over my foes triumphant now, my friends,
Shall we become: our feet are on the path.
Now is there hope of vengeance on my foes.
For this man, there where lay my chiefest weakness,
Hath for my plots a haven in storm appeared.
To him my bark's stern-hawser make I fast,
To Pallas' burg and fortress when I go.
And all my plots to thee now will I tell;
Nor look I that my words should pleasure thee:—
One of mine household will I send to Jason,
And will entreat him to my sight to come;
And soft words, when he cometh, will I speak,
Saying, "Thy will is mine," and, "It is well."
How that his royal marriage, my betrayal,
Is our advantage, and right well devised.
I will petition that my sons may stay—
Not for that I would leave on hostile soil
Children of mine for foes to trample on,
But the king's daughter so by guile to slay.
For I will send them bearing gifts in hand
Unto the bride, that they may not be banished,
A robe fine-spun, a golden diadem.
If she receive and don mine ornaments,
Die shall she wretchedly, and all who touch her,
With drugs so dread will I anoint my gifts.
Howbeit here I pass this story by,
And wail the deed that yet for me remains
To bring to pass; for I will slay my children,
Yea, mine: no man shall pluck them from mine hand.
Then, having brought all Jason's house to wrack,
I leave the land, fleeing my dear babes' blood,
And having dared a deed most impious.
For unendurable are mocks of foes.

Let all go: what is life to me? Nor country
Nor home have I, nor refuge from mine ills.
Then erred I, in the day when I forsook
My father's halls, by yon Greek's words beguiled,
Who with God's help shall render me requital.
For never living shall he see hereafter
The sons I bare him, nor shall he beget
Of his new bride a son, for doomed is she,
Wretch, to die wretchedly by drugs of mine.
Let none account me impotent, nor weak,
Nor meek of spirit!—Nay, in other sort,
Grim to my foes, and kindly to my friends,
For of such is the life most glorious.

Chorus.

Since thou hast made me partner of this tale,—
Wishing to help thee, championing withal
The laws of men, I say, do thou not this.

Medea.

It cannot be but so: yet reason is
That thou say this, who art not wronged as I.

Chorus.

Woman, wilt have the heart to slay thy sons?

Medea.

Yea: so mine husband's heart shall most be wrung.

Chorus.

But thou of wives most wretched shouldst become.

Medea.

So be it: wasted are all hindering words.
But ho! (*to the Nurse*) go thou and Jason bring to me—
Thou whom I use for every deed of trust.
And look thou tell none aught of mine intent,
If thine is loyal service, thou a woman.

(*Exit Nurse.*)

Strophe 1

Chorus.

O happy the race in the ages olden
  Of Erechtheus, the seed of the blest Gods' line,
In a land unravaged, peace-enfolden,
  Aye quaffing of Wisdom's glorious wine,
Ever through air clear-shining brightly

As on wings uplifted pacing lightly,
Where they tell how Harmonia of tresses golden
  Bare the Pierid Muses, the stainless Nine.

Antistrophe 1

And the streams of Cephisus the lovely-flowing
  They tell how the Lady of Cyprus drew,
And in Zephyr-wafts of the winds sweet-blowing
  Breathed far over the land their dew.
And she sendeth her Loves which, throned in glory
By Wisdom, fashion all virtue's story,
Over her tresses throwing, throwing,
  Roses in odorous wreaths aye new.

Strophe 2

How then should the hallowed city,
  The city of sacred waters,
    Which shields with her guardian hand
    All friends that would fare through her land,
    Receive a murderess banned,
Who had slaughtered her babes without pity,
  A pollution amidst of her daughters?

In thine heart's thoughts set it before thee—
  To murder the fruit of thy womb!
    O think what it meaneth to slay
    Thy sons—what a deed this day
    Thou wouldst do!—By thy knees we pray,
By heaven and earth we implore thee,
  Deal not to thy babes such a doom!

Antistrophe 2

O whence, and O whence wilt thou gain thee
  Such desperate hardihood
    That for spirit so fiendish shall serve,
    That shall strengthen thine heart, that shall nerve
    Thine hand, that it shall not swerve
From the ruthless deed that shall stain thee
  With horror of children's blood?

O how, when thine eyes thou art turning
On thy little ones, wilt thou refrain
The motherhood in thee, to feel
No upwelling of tears?—Canst thou steel
Thy breast when thy children kneel,
To crimson thine hand, with unyearning
Heart for thy darlings slain?

(*Enter Jason.*)

Jason.

Summoned I come: for, though thou be my foe,
This grace thou shalt not miss; but I will hear
What new thing, lady, thou dost wish of me.

Medea.

Jason, I ask thee to forgive the words
Late-spoken, and to bear with that my mood:
Well mayst thou, for remembrance of old loves.
Now have I called myself to account, and railed
Upon myself—"Wretch, wherefore am I mad?
And wherefore rage against good counsellors,
And am at feud with rulers of the land,
And with my lord, who works my veriest good,
Wedding a royal house, to raise up brethren
Unto my sons? Shall I not cease from wrath?
What aileth me, when the Gods proffer boons?
Have I not children? Know I not that we
Are exiles from our own land, lacking friends?"
Thus musing, was I ware that I had nursed
Folly exceeding, anger without cause.
Now then I praise thee; wise thou seem'st to me
In gaining us this kinship, senseless I,
Who in these counsels should have been thine ally,
Have furthered all, have decked the bridal couch,
And joyed to minister unto the bride.
But we are—women: needs not harsher word.
Yet evil shouldst thou not for evil render,
Nor pit against my folly folly of thine.
I yield, confessing mine unwisdom then,
But unto better counsels now am come.
Children, my children, hither: leave the house;

(*Enter Children and their Attendant.*)

Come forth, salute your father, and with me
Bid him farewell: be reconciled to friends
Ye, with your mother, from the hate o'erpast.
Truce is between us, rancour hath given place.
Clasp ye his right hand.—Woe for ambushed ills!
I am haunted by the shadow of hidden things!
Ah children, will ye thus, through many a year
Living, still reach him loving arms? Ah me,
How swift to weep am I, how full of fear!
Feuds with your father ended—ah, so late!—
Have filled with tears these soft-relenting eyes.

Chorus.

And from mine eyes start tears of pale dismay.
Ah may no evil worse than this befall!

Jason.

Lady, I praise this mood, yet blame not that:
'Tis nothing strange that womankind should rage
When the spouse trafficketh in alien marriage.
But now to better thoughts thine heart hath turned,
And thou, though late, upon the victor side
Hast voted: a wise woman's deed is this.
And for you, children, not unheedfully
Your sire hath ta'en much forethought, so help heaven.
For ye, I ween, in this Corinthian land
Shall with your brethren stand the foremost yet.
Grow ye in strength: the rest shall by your sire,
And whatso God is gracious, be wrought out.
You may I see to goodly stature grown,
In manhood's prime, triumphant o'er my foes.
Thou, why bedew'st thou with wan tears thine eyes,
Turning aback from them thy pallid cheek,
And dost not hear with gladness this my speech?

Medea.

'Tis nought: but o'er these children broods mine heart.

Jason.

Fear not: all will I order well for them.

Medea.

This will I:—'Tis not I mistrust thy words;
But woman is but woman—born for tears.

Jason.

Why, hapless one, dost make moan over these?

Medea.

I bare them. When thou prayedst life for them,
Pity stole o'er me, whispering, "Shall this be?"
But that for which thou cam'st to speech of me
In part is said; to speak the rest is mine:—
Since the king pleaseth forth the land to send me,
For me too this is best,—I know it well,—
That I bide not, a stumblingblock to thee
And the land's lords, whose house's foe I seem,
So fare I forth to exile from this land.
But, that my sons by thine hand may be reared,
Entreat thou Creon that they be not banished.

Jason.

Prevail I may not, yet must I essay.

Medea.

Nay then, thy bride bid thou to pray her sire
That thy sons be not banished from this land.

Jason.

Yea surely; and, I trow, her shall I win,
If of her sister women she is one.

Medea.

I too will bear a part in thine endeavour;
For I will send her gifts unmatched for beauty
Of all that men see now, I know, by far,
A robe fine-spun, a golden diadem;
Our sons to bear them. Now must an attendant
With all speed hither bring the ornaments.
Blessings shall hers be, not one, but untold,
Who winneth thee for lord, a peerless spouse,
Who owneth ornaments which once the Sun,
My father's father, gave unto his offspring!
Take in your hands, my sons, these bridal gifts,
And to the happy princess-bride bear ye
And give: with gifts shall she be satisfied.

Jason.

But, fond one, why make void thine hands of these?
Deem'st thou a royal house hath lack of robes,
Or gold, deem'st thou? Keep these and give them not.
For, if my wife esteems me aught, my wish
Will she prefer to treasure, well I wot.

Medea.

Nay, speak not so: gifts sway the Gods, they say.
Gold weigheth more with men than words untold.
Hers fortune is; God favoureth now her cause;
Young is her power. Life would I give for ransom
Of my sons' banishment, not gold alone.
Now, children, enter ye the halls of wealth.
Unto your sire's new wife, my lady-queen,
Make supplication, pray ye be not exiled,
Giving mine ornaments. Most importeth this,
That she into her hands receive my gifts.
Haste ye, and to your mother bring glad tidings
Of good success in that she longs to win.

(*Exeunt Jason and the Children.*)

Strophe 1

Chorus.

Now for the life of the children mine hope hath been turned to despairing.
No hope any more! On the slaughterward path even now are they faring!
The bride shall receive it, the diadem-garland that beareth enfolden
Doom for the hapless mid glittering sheen:
And to set the adorning of Hades about her tresses golden
She shall take it her hands between.

Antistrophe 1

For its glamour of beauty, its splendour unearthly, shall swiftly persuade her
To bedeck her with robe and with gold-wrought crown: she shall soon have arrayed her
In attire as a bride in the presence of phantoms from Hades uprisen;
In such dread gin shall her feet be ta'en:
In the weird of death shall the hapless be whelmed, and from Doom's dark prison
Shall she steal forth never again.

Strophe 2

And thou, wretch, bridegroom accurst, who art fain of a princely alliance,
Blasting thou bringest—unknowing, unthinking!—
Of life on thy sons, and thy bride shall to foul death plight her affiance.
How far from thy fortune of old art thou sinking!

Antistrophe 2

And amidst my lamentings I mourn for thine anguish, O hapless mother
Of children, who makest thee ready to slaughter
Thy babes, to avenge thee on him who would lawlessly wed with another,
Would forsake thee to dwell with a prince's daughter.

(*Enter Attendant, with the Children.*)

Attendant.

Mistress, remission for thy sons of exile!
Thy gift the princess-bride with joy received
In hand; and there is peace unto thy sons.

Medea.

Alas!

Attendant.

Why dost thou stand confounded mid good hap?
Now wherefore turnest thou thy face away,
And dost not hear with gladness this my speech?

Medea.

Woe's me.

Attendant.

This cry is to the tidings not attuned.

Medea.

Woe yet again!

Attendant.

Can I have brought ill hap
Unwitting—erred in deeming these glad tidings?

Medea.

As they are, are thy tidings: thee I blame not.

Attendant.

Why down-drooped is thine eye? Why flow thy tears?

Medea.

Needs must they, ancient; for these things the Gods
And I withal—O fool!—have ill contrived.

Attendant.

Fear not: thy children yet shall bring thee home.

Medea.

Others ere then shall wretched I send home.

Attendant.

Not thou alone art severed from thy sons.
Submissively must mortals bear mischance.

Medea.

This will I: but within the house go thou,
And for my children's daily needs prepare.

(*Exit Attendant.*)

O children, children, yours a city is,
And yours a home, where, leaving wretched me,
Dwell shall ye, of your mother aye bereft.
I shall go exiled to another land,
Ere I have joyed in you, have seen your bliss,
Ere I have decked for you the couch, the bride,
The bridal bower, and held the torch on high.
O me accurst in this my ruthless mood!
For nought, for nought, my babes, I nurtured you,
And all for nought I laboured, travail-worn,
Bearing sharp anguish in your hour of birth.
Ah for the hopes—unhappy!—all mine hopes
Of ministering hands about mine age,
Of dying folded round with loving arms,
All men's desire! But now—'tis past—'tis past,
That sweet imagining! Forlorn of you
A bitter life and woeful shall I waste.
Your mother never more with loving eyes
Shall ye behold, passed to another life.
Woe! woe! why gaze your eyes on me, my darlings?
Why smile to me the latest smile of all ?
Alas! what shall I do?—Mine heart is failing
As I behold my children's laughing eyes!
Women, I cannot! farewell, purposes
O'erpast! I take my children from the land.

What need to wring the father's heart with ills
Of these, to gain myself ills twice so many?
Not I, not I!—Ye purposes, farewell!
Yet—yet—what ails me? Would I earn derision,
Letting my foes slip from mine hand unpunished?
I must dare this. Out on my coward mood
That from mine heart let loose relenting words!
Children, pass ye within.

(*Exeunt Children.*)

Now, whoso may not
Sinless be present at my sacrifice,
On his head be it: mine hand faltereth not.
Oh! Oh!
O heart, mine heart, do not—do not this deed!
Let them be, wretched heart, spare thou thy babes!
There dwelling with me shall they gladden thee.—
No!—by the nether fiends that dwell with Hades,
Never shall this betide, that I will leave
My children for my foes to trample on.
They needs must die. And, since it needs must be,
Even I will slay them, I, who gave them life.
All this is utter doom:—she shall not 'scape!
Yea, on her head the wreath is; in my robes
The princess-bride is perishing—I know it.
But—for I fare on journey most unhappy,
And shall speed these on yet unhappier—
I would speak to my sons.

(*Re-enter the Children.*)

Give, O my babes,
Give to your mother the right hand to kiss.
O dearest hand, O lips most dear to me,
O form and noble feature of my children,
Blessing be on you—*there*!—for all things here
Your sire hath reft. O sweet, O sweet embrace!
O children's roseleaf skin, O balmy breath!
Away, away! Strength faileth me to gaze
On you, but I am overcome of evil.

Now, now, I learn what horrors I intend:
But passion overmastereth sober thought:
And this is cause of direst ills to men.

(*Exeunt Medea and Children.*)

Chorus.

Full oft ere this my soul hath scaled
  Lone heights of thought, empyrean steeps,
  Or plunged far down the darkling deeps,
Where woman's feebler heart hath failed.

Yet wherefore failed? Should woman find
  No inspiration thrill her breast,
  Nor welcome ever that sweet guest
Of Song, that uttereth Wisdom's mind?

Alas! not all! Few, few are they,—
  Perchance amid a thousand one
  Thou shouldest find,—for whom the sun
Of poesy makes an inner day.

Now this I say—calm bliss, that ne'er
  Knew love's wild fever of the blood,
  The pains, the joys, of motherhood,
Passeth all parents' joy-blent care.

The childless, they that never prove
  If sunshine comes, or cloud, to men
  With babes, far lie beyond their ken
The toils, the griefs, of parent-love.

But they whose halls with laughter sweet
  Of children ring—I mark them aye
  Care-fretted, travailing alway
To win their loved ones nurture meet.

One toils with love more strong than death:
  Yet—yet—who knoweth whether he
  A wise man or a fool shall be
To whom he shall his wealth bequeath?

But last, but worst, remains to tell:
  For though ye get you wealth enow,
  And though your sons to manhood grow,
Fair sons and good:—if Death the fell,

To Hades vanishing, bears down
  Your children's lives, what profit is
  That Heaven hath laid, with all else, this
Upon mankind, this sorrow's crown?

(*Re-enter Medea.*)

Medea.

Friends, long have I, abiding fortune's hap,
Expected what from yonder shall befall.
And lo, a man I see of Jason's train
Hitherward coming, and my eager heart
Foretelleth him the herald of new ills.

(*Enter Messenger.*)

Messenger.

O thou who hast wrought an awful deed and lawless,
Flee, O Medea, flee, nor once leave thou
The sea-wain, or the car that scours the plain.

Medea.

Now what hath happed that calleth for such flight?

Messenger.

Dead is the princess even now, and dead
Creon her father, by thy poison-drugs.

Medea.

A glorious tale thou tellest: thou henceforth
Art of my benefactors and my friends.

Messenger.

What say'st?—Of sound mind art thou, and not mad,
Who, hearing of the havoc of the hearth
Of kings, art glad, and hast no fear for this?

Medea.

O yea; I too with words of controversy
Could answer thee:—yet be not hasty, friend,
But tell how died they: thou shouldst gladden me
Doubly, if these most horribly have perished.

Messenger.

When, with their father, came thy children twain,
And passed into the halls for marriage decked,
Glad were we thralls who sorrowed for thy woes.
And straightway buzzed from ear to ear the tale
Of truce to old feuds 'twixt thy lord and thee.
The hand one kisseth, one the golden head
Of those thy sons: myself by joy on-drawn
Followed thy children to the women's bowers.
Now she which had our worship in thy stead,
Ere she beheld thy chariot-yoke of sons,
Aye upon Jason turned her yearning gaze.
But then her veil before her eyes she cast,
And swept aback the scorn of her white neck,
Loathing thy sons' approach: but now thy lord,
To turn the maiden's wrath and spite aside,
Thus spake: "Nay, be not hostile to thy friends:
Cease from thine anger, turn thine head again,
Accounting friends whomso thy spouse accounts.
Their gifts receive, and plead thou with thy sire
To pardon these their exile:—for my sake."
She, when she saw the attire, could not refrain,
But yielded her lord all. And ere their father
Far from her bower with those thy sons had gone,
She took the rich-wrought robes and clad herself,
Circling her ringlets with the golden crown,
And by a shining mirror ranged her tresses,
Smiling at her own phantom image there.
Then, rising from her seat, she paced adown
The halls with mincing tread of ivory feet,
Exulting in the gifts, and oftentimes
Sweeping her glance from neck to ankle-hem.
But then was there a fearful sight to see.
Suddenly changed her colour: reeling back
With trembling limbs she goes; and scarce in time
Drops on the couch to fall not on the ground.
Then a grey handmaid, deeming peradventure
That frenzy was of Pan or some God sent,
Raised the prayer-cry, before she saw the foam
White-frothing from her lips, or marked how rolled
Her eyeballs, and her face's bloodless hue.
Then a scream, unaccordant, long and loud,

She shrilled forth. Straight to her father's chambers one
Darted, and one unto her new-made spouse,
To tell the bride's mischance: and all the roof
Echoed with multitudinous-hurrying feet.
And a swift athlete's straining limbs had won
By this the goal of the six-plethra course:
Then she from trance all speechless of closed eyes
Awoke—ah wretch!—with horrible-shrilling shriek:
For like two charging hosts her agony came:—
The golden coil about her head that lay
'Gan spurt a marvellous stream of ravening fire;
While the fine robes, the gift thy children brought,
Devoured the white flesh of the unhappy one.
Upstarting from her seat she flees, all flame,
Shaking her hair, her head, this way and that,
To cast from her the crown; but firmly fixed
The gold held fast its clasp: the fire, whene'er
She shook her locks, with doubled fury blazed.
Then misery-vanquished falls she on the floor,
Past recognising, save for a father, marred.
No more was seen her eyes' imperial calm,
No more her comely features; but the gore
Dripped from her head's crown flecked with blended fire.
The flesh-flakes from her bones, like the pine's tears,
'Neath that mysterious drug's devourings melted,—
Dread sight!—and came on all folk fear to touch
The corpse: her hideous fate had we for warning.
But, ignorant of all, her wretched sire,
Suddenly entering, falls upon her corpse,
And straightway wailed and clasped the body round,
And kissed it, crying, "O my hapless child,
What God thus horribly hath thee destroyed?
Who maketh this old sepulchre bereft
Of thee? Ah me, would I might die with thee!"
But, when from wailing and from moans he ceased,
Fain would he have upraised his aged frame,
Yet clave, as ivy clings to laurel boughs,
To those fine robes: then was a ghastly wrestling:
For, while he laboured to upraise his knee,
She strained against him: if by force he haled,
Then from the bones he tare his agèd flesh.

At last refrained he, and gave up the ghost,
Ill-starred, who could no more withstand his bane.
There lie the corpses, child by agèd sire
Clasped;—such affliction tears, not words, must mourn.
And of thy part no word be said by me:—
Thyself from punishment wilt find escape.
But man's lot now, as oft, I count a shadow,
Nor fear to say that such as seem to be
Wise among men and cunning in speech-lore,
Even these are chargeable with deepest folly;
For among mortals happy man is none.
In fortune's flood-tide might a man become
More prosperous than his neighbour: happy?—no!

(*Exit Messenger.*)

Chorus.

Meseems the God with many an ill this day
Will compass Jason,—yea, and rightfully.
But O the pity of thy calamity,
Daughter of Creon, who to Hades' halls
Hast passed, because with thee would Jason wed!

Medea.

Friends, my resolve is taken, with all speed
To slay my children, and to flee this land,
And not to linger and to yield my sons
To death by other hands more merciless.
They needs must die: and, since it needs must be,
Even I will give them death, who gave them life.
Up, gird thee for the fray, mine heart! Why loiter
To do the dread ill deeds that must be done?
Come, wretched hand of mine, grasp thou the sword;
Grasp it;—move toward life's bitter starting-post,
And turn not craven: think not on thy babes,
How dear they are, how thou didst bear them: nay,
For this short day do thou forget thy sons,
Thereafter mourn them. For, although thou slay,
Yet dear they are, and I a wretched woman.

(*Exit Medea.*)

Strophe

Chorus.

O Earth, O all-revealing splendour
Of the Sun, look down on a woman accurst,
Or ever she slake the murder-thirst
Of a mother whose hands would smite the tender
Fruit of her womb.
Look down, for she sprang of thy lineage golden,
And by terror of men is the Gods' seed holden
And the shadow of doom.
But thou, O heaven-begotten glory,
Restrain her, refrain her: the wretched, the gory
Erinnys by demons dogged, we implore thee,
Cast forth of the home!

Antistrophe

For nought was the childbirth-travail wasted;
For nought didst thou bear them, the near and the dear,
O thou who hast fled through the Pass of Fear,
From the dark-blue Clashing Crags who hast hasted
Speeding thy flight!
Alas for her!—wherefore hath grim wrath stirred her
Through depths of her soul, that ruthless murder
Her wrongs must requite?
For stern upon mortals the vengeance falleth
For kin's blood spilt; from the earth it calleth,
A voice from the Gods, and the slayers appalleth
On whose homes it shall light.

(*Children's cries within.*)

First Child.

What shall I do?—How flee my mother's hands?

Second Child.

I know not, dearest brother. Death is here!

Chorus.

Ah the cry!—dost thou hear it?—the children's cry!
Wretch!—woman of cursèd destiny!
Shall I enter?—My heart crieth, "Rescue the children from murder drawn nigh!"

First Child.

Yea, for the Gods' sake, help! Sore is our need—

Second Child.

For now we are hemmed in by the sword's death-toils!

Chorus.

Wretch! of what rock is thy breast?—of what steel is the heart of thee moulded,
That the babes thou hast born, with the selfsame hands that with love have enfolded
These, thou hast set thee to slay?
Of one have I heard that laid hands on her loved ones of old, one only,
Even Ino distraught of the Gods, when Zeus' bride drave her, lonely
And lost, from her home to stray:
And she fell—ah wretch!—on the brink as she stood
Of the sea-scaur: guilt of her children's blood
Dragged downwards her feet to the salt sea-flood,
And she died with her children twain.
What ghastlier horror remains to be wrought?
O bride-bed of women, with anguish fraught,
What scathe upon mortals ere now hast thou brought,
What manifold bane!

(*Enter Jason.*)

Jason.

Women, which stand anear unto this roof—
Is she within the halls, she who hath wrought
Dread deeds, Medea, or in flight passed thence?
For either must she hide her 'neath the earth,
Or lift on wings her frame to heaven's far depths,
Or taste the vengeance of a royal house.
How, trusts she, having murdered the land's lords,
Scatheless herself from these halls forth to flee?
Yet not for her care I, but for my sons.
Whom she hath wronged shall recompense her wrong:
But I to save my children's life am come,
Lest to my grief the kinsmen of the dead
Avenge on them their mother's impious murder.

Chorus.

Wretch, thou know'st not what depth of woe thou hast reached,
Jason, or thou hadst uttered not such words.

Jason.

What now?—and is she fain to slay me too?

Chorus.

Thy sons are dead, slain by the mother's hand.

Jason.

Ah me!—what say'st thou?—thou hast killed me, woman!

Chorus.

Thy children are no more: so think of them.

Jason.

How?—slew them?—Where?—within, without, the halls?

Chorus.

Open, and thou shalt see thy children's corpses.

Jason.

Shoot back the bolts with all speed, serving-men!
Unbar, that I may see this twofold woe,—
The dead, and her, with slaughter to requite her.

(*Medea appears above, with the Children's corpses, in a chariot drawn by dragons.*)

Medea.

Why shakest thou these doors and wouldst unbar,
Seeking thy dead and me who wrought the deed?
Cease this essay. If thou wouldst aught of me,
Say what thou wilt: thine hand shall touch me never.
Such chariot hath my father's sire, the Sun,
Given me, a defence from foeman's hand.

Jason.

O thing abhorred! O woman hatefullest
To Gods, to me, to all the race of men,
Thou that couldst thrust the sword into the babes
Thou bar'st, and me hast made a childless ruin!
Thus hast thou wrought, yet look'st thou on the sun
And earth, who hast dared a deed most impious?
Now ruin seize thee!—clear I see, who saw not
Then, when from halls and land barbarian
To a Greek home I bare thee, utter bane,
Traitress to sire and land that nurtured thee!
Thy guilt's curse-bolt on me the Gods have launched;
For thine own brother by his hearth thou slewest
Ere thou didst enter fair-prowed Argo's hull.
With such deeds thou begannest. Wedded then
To this man, and the mother of my sons,
For wedlock-right's sake hast thou murdered them.

There is no Grecian woman that had dared
This:—yet I stooped to marry thee, good sooth,
Rather than these, a hateful bride and fell,
A tigress, not a woman, harbouring
A fiercer nature than Tyrrhenian Scylla.
But—for untold revilings would not sting
Thee, in thy nature is such hardihood:—
Avaunt, thou miscreant stained with thy babes' blood!
For me remains to wail my destiny,
Who of my new-wed bride shall have no joy,
And to the sons whom I begat and nurtured
Living I shall not speak—lost, lost to me!

Medea.

I might have lengthened out long controversy
To these thy words, if Father Zeus knew not
How I have dealt with thee and thou with me.
'Twas not for thee to set my couch at nought
And live a life of bliss, bemocking me!
Nor for thy princess, and thy marriage-kinsman,
Creon, unscathed to banish me this land!
Wherefore a tigress call me, an thou wilt,
Or Scylla, haunter of Tyrrhenian shore;
For thine heart have I wrung, as well behoved.

Jason.

Ha, but thou sorrowest too, thou shar'st mine ills!

Medea.

O yea: yet grief is gain, so thou laugh not.

Jason.

O children mine, what miscreant mother had ye!

Medea.

O sons, destroyed by your own father's lust!

Jason.

Sooth, 'twas no hand of mine that murdered them.

Medea.

Nay, but thine insolence and thy new-forged bonds.

Jason.

How, claim the right for wedlock's sake to slay them!

Medea.

A light affliction count'st thou this to woman?

Jason.

So she be wise:—in thy sight nought were good.

Medea.

These live no more: this, this shall cut thine heart!

Jason.

They live—ah me!—avengers on thine head.

Medea.

The Gods know who began this misery.

Jason.

Yea, verily, thy spirit abhorred they know.

Medea.

Abhorred art thou: I loathe thy bitter tongue.

Jason.

And I thine:—yet were mutual riddance easy.

Medea.

How then?—what shall I do?—fain would I this.

Jason.

Yield me my dead to bury and bewail.

Medea.

Never: with this hand will I bury them,
To Mountain Hera's precinct bearing them,
That never foe may do despite to them,
Rifling their tomb. This land of Sisyphus
Will I constrain with solemn festival
And rites to atone for this unhallowed murder.
But I—I go unto Erechtheus' land,
With Aegeus to abide, Pandion's son.
Thou, as is meet, foul wretch, shalt foully die,
By Argo's wreckage smitten on the skull,
Now thou hast seen this bridal's bitter ending.

Jason.

Now the Fury-avenger of children smite thee,
And Justice that looketh on murder requite thee!

Medea.

What God or what spirit will heed thy request,
Caitiff forsworn, who betrayest the guest?

Jason.

Avaunt, foul thing by whose deed thy children have died!

Medea.

Go hence to thine halls, thence lead to the grave thy bride!

Jason.

I go, a father forlorn of the two sons reft from his home!

Medea.

Not yet dost thou truly mourn: abide till thine old age come.

Jason.

O children beloved above all!

Medea.

Of their mother beloved, not of thee.

Jason.

Yet she slew them!

Medea.

That thou mightest fall in the net that thou spreadest for me.

Jason.

Woe's me! I yearn with my lips to press
My sons' dear lips in my wretchedness.

Medea.

Ha, now art thou calling upon them, now wouldst thou kiss,
Who rejectedst them then?

Jason.

For the Gods' sake grant me but this,
The sweet soft flesh of my children to feel!

Medea.

No—wasted in air is all thine appeal.

Jason.

O Zeus, dost thou hear it, how spurned I am?—
What outrage I suffer of yonder abhorred
Child-murderess, yonder tigress-dam?
Yet out of mine helplessness, out of my shame,
I bewail my belovèd, I call to record
High heaven, I bid God witness the word,
That my sons thou hast slain, and withholdest me
That mine hands may not touch them, nor bury their clay!
Would God I had gotten them never, this day
To behold them destroyed of thee!

Chorus.

All dooms be of Zeus in Olympus; 'tis his to reveal them.
Manifold things unhoped-for the Gods to accomplishment bring.
And the things that we looked for, the Gods deign not to fulfil them;
And the paths undiscerned of our eyes, the Gods unseal them.
So fell this marvellous thing.

EURIPIDES

The Trojan Women

Translated by Robert Potter

First produced in 415 B.C., shortly after Euripides' own city had annihilated the island of Melos and as its imperialistic expedition made ready to sail for Sicily. It won second prize.

CHARACTERS IN THE PLAY

Poseidon, God of the Sea

Pallas Athena, a Goddess

Hecuba, wife of Priam the King of Troy, mother of Hector and Paris

Cassandra, daughter of Hecuba, a prophetess fated to be believed by none

Talthybius, Herald of the Greeks

Andromache, wife of the Trojan Prince Hector and mother of Astyanax

Menelaus, King of Sparta

Helen, wife of Menelaus, carried off by the Trojan Prince Paris

Greek Soldiers

Chorus of captive Trojan Women

ARGUMENT

The Greeks—under the command of Agamemnon and Menelaus, sons of Atreus, and other powerful Kings—have taken Troy after a long and renowned siege. The Trojan Women have been captured, including Hecuba, the Queen, who with her endless capacity for suffering symbolizes all the tragedies of mankind. The Women have just been apportioned among the victorious Greek generals; if the captives reveal the other side of glorious conquest, what about the victors, who have sinned against Heaven and for whom Poseidon lies in wait?

SCENE

The Greek camp before Troy (Ilium or Pergamus). Hecuba is asleep on the ground in front of a tent. Poseidon enters.

THE TROJAN WOMEN

Poseidon.

From the vast depths of the Aegean sea,
Where many a maze with graceful-moving feet
Unwinds the choir of Nereids, Poseidon comes.
For from the time when Phoebus and myself
Raised on this land the rampired towers of Troy
With exact skill, my mind hath never lost
Its fondness for this city of the Phrygians,
Which now in ruins by the arms of Greece
Smokes on the ground: for by Athena's art
Epeus of Parnassian Phocis framed
A horse, whose hollow womb was full of arms,
And sent within the walls th' enormous bulk
Big with destruction; hence in after times
It shall be called "The Horse of Spears," the spear
In its dark sides concealed. The sacred groves
Are desolate, the temples of the gods
Flooded with gore, and Priam at the steps
Ascending to the shrine of guardian Zeus
Hath fall'n and died: much gold, and Phrygian spoils
Are to the Grecian vessels borne; the troops
Expect the fav'ring gale to breathe from shore,
That after ten long years, which they have passed
In arms to lay this city low, with joy
They may behold their children and their wives.
But I, by Argive Hera, mighty queen,
O'erpowered, and Pallas, whose united force
Hath crushed the Phrygians, quit the once famed towers
Of Ilium, and my altars: for when once
Wide through a city desolation spreads,
The hallowed rites, the worship of the gods
Must be neglected. Now with loud laments
Of captive dames to their new lords assigned
Scamander's banks resound: th' Arcadian some,
Some the Thessalian bands, and some the sons
Of Theseus, chiefs of Athens, as decides
The lot, obtain. Beneath this roof are those
Of Troy's unhappy daughters by no lot
Disposed, but to the leaders of the host
Selected; these among, by righteous doom

A captive led, the Spartan Helen.
And Hecuba, if any wish to see
Her and her wretched state, before the gates
Lies stretched, and pours an ample flood of tears;
And she hath ample cause, for at the tomb
Raised to Achilles hath her daughter died,
How piteously! the poor Polyxena;
Priam is fall'n, her sons are fall'n; and her,
Cassandra, whom the royal Phoebus gave
To rove a virgin, and declare the fates,
To secret nuptials Agamemnon leads
Perforce, religion and the gods despised.
But, O my town once flourishing, once crowned
With beauteous-structured battlements, farewell!
Had not Athena sunk thee in the dust,
On thy firm base e'en now thou mightst have stood.

(*Enter Pallas Athena.*)

Athena.

Is it permitted me, all former thoughts
Of variance laid aside, t' address a god
Nearest by lineage to my sire allied,
Of mighty power, and honoured by the gods?

Poseidon.

It is permitted thee: for kindred blood,
Royal Athena, hath a potent charm
To reconcile the alienated mind.

Athena.

Thy gentleness in anger claims my praise.
What I would offer, king, imports us both.

Poseidon.

Hast thou of new aught from the gods to speak,
From Zeus, or other of the heavenly powers?

Athena.

No: for the sake of Troy I to thy power
Am come, to use it in one common cause.

Poseidon.

Dost thou, thy former hostile thoughts appeased,
Pity its ruins blazing in the flames?

Athena.

First speak to this: wilt thou with joint design,
Joint labour, aid in what I wish to do?

Poseidon.

Most willingly: but wish to know thy purpose,
If to the Trojans friendly, or to Greece.

Athena.

The Trojans hated once, would I delight,
To th' Argive host embittering their return.

Poseidon.

Why have thy measures this quick change, in love
Or hate, whiche'er betides, too violent?

Athena.

Me knowst thou not how outraged, and my shrine?

Poseidon.

I know: Cassandra Ajax dragged by force.

Athena.

Nor punished by the Grecians, nor reproved.

Poseidon.

Yet by thy power these Grecians wasted Troy.

Athena.

Therefore with thee I now would work them woe.

Poseidon.

Thy purpose finds me prompt: what wouldst thou do?

Athena.

With rig'rous vengeance sadden their return.

Poseidon.

On land, or when they plough the briny wave?

Athena.

When o'er the deep they steer their course for Greece,
The stormy rain, the fierce-descending hail,
And the dark fury of tempestuous winds
My sire will send: to me, his word is passed,
His fiery thunder will he give, to hurl
Against the Grecians, and with lightning flames
To burn their ships. Do thou, for thine the power,
With foaming billows vast and whirling gulfs
Tempest the vexed Aegean; with their dead
Fill the Euboean bay: that they may learn
Henceforth with reverence to approach my shrines,
And pay due honours to the other gods.

Poseidon.

It shall be so: few words this favour needs.
With tempests will I chafe th' Aegean sea;
The shores of Mycone, the Delian rocks,

Scyrus, and Lemnus, and the rugged brow
Of steep Caphareus shall with numerous dead
Be covered. But to high Olympus go,
The bolts of thunder from thy father's hands
Receive: then wait till they unmoor their fleet.
Unwise is he, whoe'er of mortals storms
Beleaguered towns, and crushed in ruins wastes
The temples of the gods, the hallowed tombs
Where sleep the dead; for he shall perish soon.

(*Exeunt. Hecuba wakes.*)

Hecuba.

Rise, thou unhappy; from the cold ground raise
Thy head, thy neck. This is no longer Troy,
In Troy we rule no longer. Ah the change
Of fortune! Bear the change; sail with the tide.
With fortune sail, nor turn the prow of life
Against the wave, nor struggle with thy fate.—
Oh woe, woe, woe! Why is it not allowed
A wretch like me to moan my country lost,
My children, and my husband! Thou high boast
Of noble ancestry, how art thou shrunk,
How vanished! What shall I in silence hold?
Or what not hold in silence? What bewail?
In what a woful state are these poor limbs
Reclined, how ill on this hard bed now stretched?
Ah me, my head! Ah me, my temples! Ah,
My sides! O how I long to change my place,
To roll, and roll, and shift from side to side,
Proofs of the restless torture of my mind!
E'en here th' unhappy have a Muse, to give
These woes a voice, far other than the notes
To joy and dance attuned. Ye wingèd barks,
Which through the purple seas and sheltered bays
Of Greece, whilst to the inauspicious sound
Of flutes and oaten pipes your oars kept time,
With all your streamers flying, proudly sailed
To sacred Ilium, to the ports of Troy
Bringing the hated wife of Menelaus,
A foul disgrace to Castor, and a stain
Dishonouring Eurotas. She hath slain
Priam, the reverend sire of fifty children,
And in this gulf of misery hath plunged

The wretched Hecuba. My seat is now—
Ah, what a seat!—at Agamemnon's tent;
And I am led, in my old age am led
A captive from my house, of its hoar hairs,
Sad argument of grief, this head despoiled.
But, O ye wretched wives of Trojans once
Valiant in war, ye virgins, and ye brides
Torn from your loves, Troy smokes: let us lament;
And, as the parent bird that o'er her young
Swells her shrill notes, I will begin the strain,
Not such as in my happier days I raised,
Leaning on Priam's sceptre, when my foot
In Phrygian measures, by the Graces taught,
Led to th' immortal gods the festive dance.

(Enter Chorus of captive Trojan Women.)

Strophe 1

Chorus.

Why, Hecuba, these cries, these cries of woe?
Why dost thou raise these loud laments? I hear
The wailings, which thou utterest, o'er these roofs
Resound; and terror strikes each Trojan dame,
That in this tent bemoans her slavery.

Hecuba.

O children, in the vessels of the Greeks
The hand now grasps the oar. O wretched me,
What will they do? Will they with spreading sails
Far from my country bear my hapless age?

Chorus.

I know not; but my mind presages ill.
Alas, alas, distracted with our woes,
Soon we shall hear, "Ye Trojan dames, come forth.
The Grecians are preparing their return."

Hecuba.

Ah, send not now the mad Cassandra to me,
That shame to Greece: her ravings to my woe
Would add fresh woe. O Troy, unhappy Troy,
Thou art no more. Unhappy they who leave thee,
Unhappy are the living and the slain.

Antistrophe 1

Chorus.

Ah me! With trembling foot I leave the tent
Of Agamemnon, from thee, queen, to learn
Whether the sentence of the Greeks be passed
To kill me, wretched me; or in the ships
The sailors are prepared to plough the main.

Hecuba.

Early, my child, my soul with terror struck,
Was I brought hither; from the Grecians now
A herald comes informing me to whom
I am assigned—ah wretched me!—a slave.

Chorus.

Soon will thy lot be cast.

Hecuba.

Ah me! Ah me!

Chorus.

Me, miserable me, what Argive leads,
Or who of Phthia's vales, or of the isles
Encircled by the ocean, far from Troy?

Hecuba.

To whom am I, unhappy, in what land
Assigned a slave, useless, worn out with age,
The wretched form of one that is no more,
A lifeless image on a monument?
To keep their gates will they assign my charge?
Or on their children shall my office be
T' attend, at Troy with royal honours graced?

Strophe 2

Chorus.

Ah, with what plaints thy miseries dost thou scan?
No more these hands in the Idaean looms
The shuttle with alternate cast shall throw:
No more my children's sportive youth I see;
Nor, as in youth, shall I to lighter toils
Be destined, or approach some Grecian's bed:
The night itself and fortune cheerless frowns.
But at Peirene's fount shall be my task,
My wretched task, to draw its sacred streams.
Oh, to that happy country might we come,
O'er which th' illustrious Theseus held his reign!

But never to Therapnae, hated town
Of Helen, seated where Eurotas whirls
His eddying stream; exposed my servile state
To Menelaus, who wasted sacred Troy.

Antistrophe 2

The lovely tract, through which Peneus flows,
Delightful base, from which his awful height
Olympus rears, in wealth, so fame reports,
Abounds, and boasts its blooming fruitfulness.
This, next the honoured and divine domains
Where Theseus reigned, would be most pleasing to me.
Much have I heard of the Aetnaean coast
Sacred to the Fire-god, to Punic shore
That rises opposite, the mighty mother
Of the Sicilian mountains, where the wreath
Blooms ever fresh; and of the neighbouring land,
Sweet habitation in th' Ionian sea,
Irriguous with the beauteous-flowing stream
Of Crathis, which the yellow tresses gilds,
And blessings from its sacred fountains pours
Through a rich land, that boasts a generous race.
But from the Grecian host a herald comes,
Fraught with fresh tidings: hasty is his step.
What brings he? what announces? For in truth
We of the Dorian land e'en now are slaves.

(*Enter Talthybius.*)

Talthybius.

Thou, Hecuba, hast seen Talthybius oft
In Troy, a herald from the Grecian host
In frequent intercourse: but now to thee,
In past time not unknown, I come, and bring
The public mandate, which concerns you all.

Hecuba.

This, this, my friends, ye dames of Troy, long since
This was my fear.

Talthybius.

You are by lot assigned,
If this was what you feared.

Hecuba.

Alas, alas!
To what Thessalian, or what Phthian town,
Or to Cadmaean Thebes? I pray thee tell me.

Talthybius.

Singly to single chiefs are you allotted,
And not together all.

Hecuba.

To whom, to whom
Am I appointed, say. What happy fate
Awaits each Trojan dame?

Talthybius.

I can inform thee:
But singly ask of each, not all at once.

Hecuba.

The poor Cassandra, my unhappy daughter,
Where falls her lot?

Talthybius.

Her, a selected prize,
The royal Agamemnon hath received.

Hecuba.

What! For his Spartan spouse a slave? Ah me!

Talthybius.

No: but in secret to the nuptial bed.

Hecuba.

The virgin of Apollo, whom the god
Radiant with golden locks allowed to live
In her pure vow of maiden chastity!

Talthybius.

With love the raptured virgin smote his heart.

Hecuba.

Cast from thee, O my daughter, cast away
Thy sacred wand, rend off the honoured wreaths,
The splendid ornaments that grace thy brows.

Talthybius.

Is it not great to share a monarch's bed?

Hecuba.

But where is she, whom late you took from me,
Where is my daughter?

Talthybius.

Of Polyxena,
Or of whom else is this inquiry made?

Hecuba.

To whom is she allotted?

Talthybius.

At the tomb
Raised to Achilles it is hers to serve.

Hecuba.

Unhappy me! Have I brought forth a child
Doomed at a tomb to serve? But tell me, friend,
What custom or what rite of Greece is this?

Talthybius.

Pronounce her happy: all with her is well.

Hecuba.

What mean thy words? Views she the sun's bright beams?

Talthybius.

Her doth fate hold from every ill released.

Hecuba.

What of Andromache, the wretched wife
Of helmèd Hector? Tell me what her fate?

Talthybius.

Her without lot Achilles' son receives.

Hecuba.

And I, whose age-enfeebled limbs require
A staff, to whom am I assigned a slave?

Talthybius.

Thee hath Odysseus, king of Ithaca,
By lot obtained: to him thou art a slave.

Hecuba.

Ah, let me beat this head, and rend these cheeks.
O miserable me! I am enslaved
To a detested, an insidious foe,
A creeping viper, who with baleful bite
Impoisons justice; one, whose double tongue
With glozing arguments from side to side
All things perverts, and turns to hostile hate
What was before most friendly. Mourn for me,
Ye Trojan dames, for I am wretched, sunk
To the most abject fortune, woe is me.
Totally sunk by this ill-fated lot.

Chorus.

Thy fortune, venerable queen, I know;
But mine what Argive or what Greek commands?

Talthybius.

Go, ye attendants; with what speed you may
Conduct Cassandra hither; I must give her
To the king's hand. The other captives then,
Each as allotted, lead to their new lords.—
But what is this? Why flames the blazing torch
Within? What mean these Trojan dames? To fire
The inmost tent? that, since the hour draws nigh
When from this land they must perforce be borne
To Argos, they may perish in the flames,
Seeking to die; ill brooks th' excessive love
Of freedom woes like these. Open these doors,
Open, lest what to these may give delight,
And grief to Greece, may to my blame be charged.

Hecuba.

It is not so; they raise no flames; but forth
My frentic child, Cassandra, rushes to us.

(*Enter Cassandra, carrying a torch.*)

Strophe

Cassandra.

Wave the torch, and spread its light;
Thus I bear it blazing bright,
Rev'rence and illume the shrine;
Royal Hymen, it is thine.
See, the happy bridegroom see,
And the happy bride in me:
At Argos I shall mount the nuptial bed,
Royal Hymen, by thee led.
Since thy tears, my mother, flow,
And thy heart is rent with woe,
For my slaughtered father's fate,
And my country's ruined state,
At my spousals I will raise
A fire shall shine, shall flame, shall blaze,
And, royal Hymen, on the bridal night
Give to Hecate the light,
For a virgin's nuptial bands;
Sacred custom this demands.

Antistrophe

Nimbly let your feet advance,
Quiv'ring high in festive dance,
As if Priam's prosperous throne
Bright with royal splendours shone.
The choir is hallowed: with them, Phoebus, move:
In thy sacred laurel grove
Off'rings at thy shrine I lay,
Hymen, 'tis my bridal day.
Lead the dance, my mother, lead,
Quick in varying motions tread,
And, my gliding steps to grace,
Light the mazy measure trace.
To royal Hymen raise, O hallowed train,
Raise the joy-announcing strain;
Hail the bride with songs of joy,
Gorgeous-vested nymphs of Troy;
Hail the bridegroom, to my bed
By the Fates' appointment led.

Chorus.

Wilt thou not, queen, thy raving daughter hold,
That she appear not 'midst the host of Greece
Possessed with this indecent levity?

Hecuba.

O Fire, Fire, thou indeed the nuptial torch
Of mortals bearest, but a baleful flame
Dost thou now wave, and void of each fond hope.
Alas, my daughter, little did I think
That ever thou shouldst wed beneath the spear,
Beneath the arms of Greece! Give me the torch;
Ill it beseems thee frentic thus, with step
Thus wild, to bear its flame: nor to thy mind
Have thy misfortunes brought more sober sense;
But, my poor child, thy state remains the same.
Bear in the torches; and, ye Trojan dames,
For tears exchange her nuptial melody.

Cassandra.

Mother, adorn my head; for I have gained
A conquest: in my nuptials with a king
Rejoice. Come, lead me. If I go too slow,
Push me by force; for this is not Apollo.

Th' illustrious Agamemnon, king of Greece,
Weds me; but in these nuptials he shall find
More woe than Paris when he wedded Helen;
For I will kill him, and lay waste his house;
Thus for my brothers' and my father's death
I will have vengeance: but no words of this:
I will say nothing of the axe, which goes
Into my neck, and that of others too;
Nor of the contest where a mother bleeds
(This shall my nuptials raise); nor of the house
Of Atreus sunk in ruins: I will show
This city than the Grecians far more blest
(I feel th' inspiring god, but will awhile
Bid the prophetic fury cease to swell):
They for one woman, and one fatal bed
Sought Helen, and lost thousands; their wise chief
Himself, to gain what most the soul abhors,
Hath thrown away what most it loves, and given
The sweet domestic pleasures of his children
To win his brother's wife; yet was she borne
Consentingly, not forcibly away.
When to Scamander's banks they came, they died;
Nor from their country, or its high-tow'red towns,
Were they driven forth: those whom the sword destroyed
Their children saw no more, nor were their limbs
By their wives' hands in decent vestments wrapt,
But in a foreign land they lie. At home
Like desolation reigns: their widowed wives
Are dead; their parents, childless, have in vain
Reared offspring in their houses; not a son
Survives to pour libations at their tombs.
Such are the triumphs of this martial host.
Deeds of impurity are better hushed
In silence: never Muse be mine, to chaunt
What raises on the modest cheek a blush.
The Trojans, what is glory's brightest grace,
Died for their country: they, beneath the spear
Who fell, were by their friends borne home, and dead
Found in their native land a sepulchre,
Entombed by those from whom those rites were due.
But such, as fell not in the field, each day
Dwelt with their wives and children; whilst the Greeks

Were strangers to that sweet society.
Mournful the fate of Hector seems to thee:
But weigh it well: he dies, among the brave
Esteemed the bravest; this high fame the Greeks
By their arrival raised; had they not come
The hero's virtues had remained obscure.
Paris espoused the daughter of high Zeus;
Had she not been his bride, he would at home
Have formed some mean alliance, unrenowned.
War then the man, whom prudence rules, will shun:
But if its flames are kindled, no mean crown
He wins who bravely for his country dies:
Not to act bravely is inglorious shame.
Therefore behoves thee, mother, not to wail
Thy country, or my bed; for those to thee
Whose deeds have been most hostile, and to me,
I by my nuptials to the dust will bow.

Chorus.

How sweetly at thy house's ills thou smilest,
Chaunting what haply thou wilt not show true!

Talthybius.

But that Apollo hath with frenzy hurt
Thy sense, unpunished with such taunting speech
Thou shouldst not from this country send the chiefs.
But what commands respect, and is held high
As wise, is nothing better than the mean
Of no repute: for this most potent king
Of all the Grecians, the much honoured son
Of Atreus, is enamoured with his prize,
This frentic raver. I am a poor man,
Yet would I not receive her to my bed.
For thee, since thou hast not thy perfect sense,
All thy reproaches on the Greeks and all
Thy praises of the Trojans, to the winds
I give to scatter them. But to the ships
Attend me, beauteous minion of our chief.
Thou, since Odysseus wills to lead thee with him,
Follow; a virtuous lady shalt thou serve,
As they, who came to Ilium, speak her fame.

Cassandra.

This is a busy slave. What one name suits
All heralds? The abhorrence of mankind,
Ye ministers of tyrants and of states,
And dost thou say that to Odysseus' house
My mother shall be led? Where are the words
Of Phoebus then, which say, by me made known,
Here she shall die? The rest revile I not:
But he, unhappy, knows not what a train
Of suff'rings waits him, so that he shall deem
Mine and the Phrygians' ills, with his compared,
Treasures of gold: for after ten long years
To ten long years here wasted, he shall reach
His native land alone; but visit first
The straits, amidst whose gulfs, that now disgorge
And now resorb the floods, Charybdis holds
Her terrible abode; the blood-stained cave
Of the huge Cyclops, mountain savage, gorged
With flesh where life yet quivers; Circe's isle,
Whose charmed cup transforms whoever taste
To swine; tempestuous seas with wrecks o'erspread;
Men in the flow'ry Lotus who delight;
The sacred heifers of the sun, whose flesh
Shall send forth lowings, to Odysseus sound
Of horror: to be brief, to Pluto's realms
Alive shall he descend: and from the waves
Escaped, returning to his country find
A thousand ills. But why repeat the toils
That wait Odysseus? Go, that I with speed
May wed a bridegroom in the shades below.
Thou, who in thought some glorious deed art now
Achieving, leader of the Grecian host,
Wretch, shall be buried wretchedly by night,
Not in the day; and me, a livid corse,
Naked, cast out, the torrent floods shall leave
In their rough channels, nigh my bridegroom's tomb,
A prey to beasts, this priestess of Apollo.
Ye garlands of the gods, most dear to me,
Prophetic ornaments, farewell: the feasts,
In which I once delighted, are to me
No more. Begone! I rend you from me. While
I yet am chaste, I give them to the winds,

To toss, to scatter them, prophetic king!
Where is the leader's bark? How shall my foot
Mount its tall sides? No longer shall thy sails
Wait for the breathing gales; but thou shalt bear me
A Fury, an Erinnys, from this land.
Farewell, my mother! Do not shed a tear.
O my loved country, O my brother, sunk
To the dark realms below, O father soon
Shall you receive me; to your shades I come
Triumphant from the ruin of the house
Of Atreus, by whose sons we thus are fall'n!

(*Exeunt Cassandra and Talthybius.*)

Chorus.

Ye, who attend the aged Hecuba,
Behold you not the queen, how to the ground
Speechless she sinks? Shall not your hands with care
Support her? Wretches, will you let her age
Lie on the earth? Haste, raise her, upright raise her.

Hecuba.

Forbear, ye virgins; what was pleasing once
Pleases no more: here let me lie thus fall'n,
A fall that suits what I have suffered, what
I suffer, and shall suffer. O ye gods,
Unkind associates I indeed invoke,
Yet when affliction rends the anguished heart,
We with becoming grace invoke the gods
First it is pleasing to me to recount
My happier fortunes: thus my woes shall raise
A stronger pity. Royal was my birth,
And marriage joined me to a royal house;
There I was mother of illustrious sons,
Sons with superior excellence adorned
Above the Phrygians; such no Trojan dame,
No Grecian, no Barbarian e'er could boast;
These I saw fall'n beneath the Grecian spear,
And laid my severed tresses on their tomb.
For Priam too, their father, flowed my tears;
His fate I heard not from report, but saw it,
These eyes beheld him murdered at the altar
Of guardian Zeus; my vanquished city stormed;
My daughters, whom I nurtured high in hope
Of choosing honourable nuptials for them,

For others nurtured from my hands are rent;
There is no hope that me they e'er shall see,
And I shall never see them more. Th' extreme,
The height of my afflicting ills is this:
I to some house shall go a hoary slave,
To some base task, most irksome to my age,
Assigned; or at their doors to keep the keys
A portress shall I wait, the mother once
Of Hector, or to labour at the mill;
For royal couches, on the ground to make
My rugged bed; and o'er these worn-out limbs
The tattered remnant of a worn-out robe,
Unseemly to my happier state, to throw.
Ah, for one woman's nuptial bed, what woes
Are mine, and will be mine! Alas, my child,
My poor Cassandra, madd'ning with the gods,
By what misfortunes is thy purity
Defiled? And where art thou, Polyxena,
O thou unhappy! Thus of all my sons
And all my daughters, many though they were,
Not one is left to soothe my miseries.
Why do you raise me, virgins? With what hope
Lead you this foot, which once with stately port
In Troy advanced, but now a slave, to seek
A bed of leaves strewn on the ground, a stone
My pillow, there to lie, to perish there
Wasted with tears? Then deem not of the great
Now flourishing as happy, ere they die.

Strophe

Chorus.

For Troy, O Muse, attune thy woe,
And steep in tears the solemn-breathing song;
To such a theme such notes belong:
For Troy unwonted measures now shall flow,
Shall tell my sorrows, how beneath
The guileful fabric, big with death,
I fell a captive to the Argive spear:
When from th' enormous beast, that hides
A host within its caverned sides,
With golden trappings hung around,
Rolled to the gates with thund'ring sound,
Issuing in arms the chiefs of Greece appear.

But from the rock of Ilium high
With shouts the blinded Phrygians cry,
"Go, from your toils released, ye sons of Troy.
This hallowed fabric draw with joy:
To Zeus-born Pallas place the pledge divine
In favoured Ilium's rampired shrine."
The young, the old promiscuous throng,
And roll with songs of joy the fraudful pest along.

Antistrophe

From every street with eager pace,
The pines of Ida flaming in their hands,
Rush to the gates the Trojan bands,
To Pallas in her favoured tower to place
The fabric formed with Argive wiles,
The pest which Phrygia's state beguiles,
The heaven-framed present of the unyoked steed:
With twisted cables thrown around
They drag it o'er the fatal ground,
Like a new bark in gallant state,
To Pallas in her rocky seat.
To toil and joy the shades of night succeed:
The Libyan pipe swells clear and high,
Attuned to Phrygian melody;
To the light notes in many an airy round
The frolic virgins nimbly bound,
And joyful as they dance their voices raise,
Sweet warbling spritely-fancied lays.
In every house the blazing fires
Sink at the hour of rest, and their swart light expires.

Epode

Then too my vaulted roofs around
The voice of joy was heard to sound;
We to Artemis raised the strain,
Chaste huntress-queen that leads the mountain train.
Sudden a wild tumultuous roar
With shudd'ring horror strikes our souls:
Loud and more loud the city o'er
To Pergamus it deep'ning rolls;
My dear, dear infants round their mother prest,
And grasped with trembling hands my vest.

Now, by Athena's guardian care,
Rushed from its ambush the imprisoned war:
Round the polluted altars slain
In blood are rolled the sons of Troy:
O'er the rich rooms, once scenes of joy,
Horror and desolation reign,
And bear to Greece, her victor sons t' adorn,
The crown from weeping Phrygia borne.

(*Enter Andromache in a chariot, carrying a child.*)

See, royal lady, on this foreign car
Andromache is borne; and at her breast,
Which trembles to the motion of the wheels,
Astyanax, the son of Hector, laid.

Hecuba.

Whither, unhappy woman, art thou borne,
Placed in that car beside the brazen arms
Of Hector, and the spoils by the strong spear
Rent from the Phrygians? Distant far from Troy
In Phthia these the proud son of Achilles
Shall hang, to crown the temples of the gods.

Strophe 1

Andromache.

My Grecian lords force me away.

Hecuba.

Ah me!

Andromache.

Why dost thou heave my sighs?

Hecuba.

Ah wretched me!

Andromache.

That for my sorrows—

Hecuba.

Seest thou this, O Zeus!

Andromache.

And my distresses rise.

Hecuba.

Alas, my children!

Andromache.

We were thy children once.

Antistrophe 1

Hecuba.

My state is fall'n;
Troy too is fall'n.

Andromache.

Unhappy!

Hecuba.

And my sons,
My noble sons are fall'n.

Andromache.

Alas, alas!

Hecuba.

Alas my ills, the miserable fate . . .

Andromache.

Of ruined Troy.

Hecuba.

Which smokes upon the ground.

Strophe 2

Andromache.

Oh, wouldst thou come, my husband!

Hecuba.

Thou dost call
My son, unhappy, in the realms below!

Andromache.

Thou bulwark of thy wife!

Antistrophe 2

Hecuba.

And thou, whose soul
Swelled high against the Grecians, Priam, once
The aged father of my children, lead,
O lead me to the gloomy realms below!

Strophe 3

Chorus.

These griefs are great.

Hecuba.

And dreadful are the ills
We suffer.

Chorus.

For thy ruined country: woes,
Such is the pleasure of the gods, succeed
To woes. Nor hath thy son escaped from death,
Who for a bed abhorred hath sunk in dust
The towers of Troy, and near the rampired rock
Of Pallas stretched the bodies of the slain,
Welt'ring in blood, by vultures to be torn:
And Troy is bowed beneath the servile yoke.

Antistrophe 3

Hecuba.

My country, my unhappy country, thee
Wasted I weep.

Chorus.

Thou seest its wretched end.

Hecuba.

And thee my house, where oft I was a mother.

Chorus.

Unhappy children, wasted is your town,
Your mother desolate.

Hecuba.

What strains are these,
What strains of woe! Tears after tears stream down
In sorrow for my house: the dead forgets
His sorrows, and his tears stream down no more.

Chorus.

How sweet are tears to those who suffer ills?
Sweet are the strains of lamentation, sweet
The mournful Muse that tunes her notes to woe.

Andromache.

Mother of Hector, that brave chief, whose spear
Once pierced the Grecian squadrons, seest thou this?

Hecuba.

I see th' appointment of the gods; the low
How they exalt, and hurl the mighty down.

Andromache.

I, with my child, am led away, the spoil
Of war: th' illustrious progeny of kings,
O fatal change, is sunk to slavery.

Hecuba.

Necessity is rig'rous: from me late
Cassandra went, torn from my arms by force.

Andromache.

Alas! Another Ajax then, it seems,
Thy daughter finds: but thou hast other ills.

Hecuba.

Unmeasured and unnumbered are my ills:
Afflictions with afflictions still contend.

Andromache.

Polyxena, thy daughter is no more:
Devoted to Achilles, on his tomb
An off'ring to the lifeless dead she fell.

Hecuba.

Ah wretched me! This was the dread event
Talthybius hinted to me in dark terms.

Andromache.

I saw her, and descending from this car
Wrapt the vests round her, and bewailed her dead.

Hecuba.

Alas, my daughter, what unhallowed rites!
Alas, alas! unseemly hast thou perished.

Andromache.

She perished, as she perished: but her fate
In death is happier far than mine who live.

Hecuba.

'Tis not one thing, my child, to live or die:
The living hopes await, the dead are nothing.

Andromache.

Hear, that with pleasure I may touch thy soul
Not to be born, I argue, and to die,
Are equal: but to die is better far
Than to live wretched; for he knows not grief
Who hath no sense of misery: but to fall
From fortune's blessed height, to the low state
Of abject wretchedness, distracts the soul
With the keen sense of former happiness.
Like as the light of life she ne'er had seen,
Polyxena is dead, and of her ills
Knows nothing: I, who aimed at glorious rank,

And reached my aim, from fortune widely erred:
All that to prudent matrons gives a grace,
In Hector's house was ever my employ.
First, for in this to women blame is due,
Charged or not charged, to such as rove abroad,
I checked this wand'ring humour, and remained
At home, within my house; nor gay discourse
Of females there admitted, but intent
On ordering what was useful, deemed myself
Well occupied. With silence of the tongue
And cheerfulness of look I entertained
My husband: where my province to command
I knew, and where to yield obedience to him.
The fame of this was bruited through the host
Of Greece, and wrought my ruin; for the son
Of fierce Achilles, soon as I was made
A captive, wished to take me as his wife,
Doomed in the house of those, whose slaught'ring hands
I rue, to be a slave. From my fond heart
Could I rend Hector, and expand my breast
To this new husband, faithless to the dead
Should I appear: if I disdain his love,
I shall excite the malice of my lords.
Short time, they say, to a new lord disarms
A woman's hate: but her my soul abhors,
Who for new nuptials slights her former husband,
And loves another: e'en the social steed,
Divided from its fellow, draws the yoke
Reluctant; yet the beast, by nature formed
Less excellent, nor speech nor reason knows.
O my loved Hector, I was blest in thee,
Thou wast the lord of all my wishes, great
In understanding, noble birth, and wealth,
And valour: from my father's house thou first
Ledd'st me a virgin to the bridal bed:
Now thou art perished, and I mount the bark
For Greece, a captive to the servile yoke.
Hath not the death then of Polyxena,
Whom thou bewailest, lighter ills than mine!
For not to me e'en Hope, which still is left
To all of mortal race, remains; no thought
That better fortune e'er will visit me
With pleasing expectation cheats my mind.

Chorus.

Alike our suff'rings; and thou teachest me,
Thine own ills wailing, my unhappy state.

Hecuba.

I never entered bark; my knowledge springs
From what in picture I have seen, or heard
From others. When a storm, whose moderate force
May be sustained, the curling billows swells,
With prompt alacrity the sailors toil
To guide the vessel safe; one at the helm
His station takes, one tends the sails, one plies
The pump: but if the wild tempestuous sea
Mocks their vain efforts, they to fortune yield,
And leave her to the rolling of the waves.
So fares it now with me: with various ills
Encompassed I am silent, give them way,
And check my vain complaints; for from the gods
This cruel storm o'erpowers me. But do thou,
O my loved child, on Hector's fate no more
Fix thy sad thoughts; not all thy streaming tears
Will save him: honour then thy present lord,
And with thy gentle manners win his soul;
This doing, thou shalt cheer thy friends, and train
This child, my Hector's son, to manhood, strong
To succour Troy; that sons from him may spring,
Who shall again the towers of Ilium raise,
And once more to its state restore the town.
But trouble yet perchance from trouble springs;
This Grecian officer I see again
Advancing to us, bearing new commands.

(*Enter Talthybius.*)

Talthybius.

Thou wife of Hector, of the Phrygian once
The bravest, do not hate me: for my tongue
Unwillingly will utter what the Greeks
Decree and the Pelopidae command.

Andromache.

Why with this tragic proem dost thou greet me?

Talthybius.

It is decreed thy son—how shall I speak it!

Andromache.

What? that he have not the same lord with me?

Talthybius.

None of the Grecians e'er shall be his lord.

Andromache.

To leave him here, a relic of the Trojans?

Talthybius.

I cannot utter, but with pain, thy ills.

Andromache.

I praise thy modest awe, speak thou but good.

Talthybius.

This great ill thou must know: they slay thy son.

Andromache.

This than my marriage is a greater ill.

Talthybius.

Odysseus 'midst th' assembled Greeks prevails.

Andromache.

Ah, these are ills too grievous to be borne.

Talthybius.

Not to bring up a valiant warrior's son.

Andromache.

Thus for his own sons may his voice prevail!

Talthybius.

But that they cast him from the towers of Troy.
In this sad trial be thy prudence shown:
Withhold him not, with noble fortitude
Support thy griefs: nor think that thou hast power,
Where all thou canst is nothing. Thou canst find
No succour: it behoves thee weigh this well.
Low lies thy city, low thy husband lies,
Thou art a captive: we have force enough
Against one woman. Wish not then to strive;
Let no indecent, no despiteful deed
Dishonour thee. Nor would I have thee vent
Thy curses on the Greeks; for shouldst thou speak
What shall disgust the troops, thy son perchance
May lie unpitied, and denied the rites
Of sepulture: but if thou bear thine ills

In silence and with fortitude, his corse
Will not be left unburied, and thyself
Wilt from the Grecians find more courtesy.

Andromache.

O, my dear child, my fondly cherished son,
Thou by the foes shalt die, ah me! and leave
Thy wretched mother. Yes, thy father's worth
Shall kill thee, which to others is a shield
Yielding protection. In an evil hour
For thee thy father's virtues are renowned.
O my unhappy bed, and nuptial rites,
Which led me to the house of Hector, there
Not to be mother of a son to fall
A victim by the Grecians, but to reign
Lord of the fruitful Asia! Dost thou weep,
My son? Hast thou a sense of thy ill fate?
Why dost thou clasp me with thy hands, why hold
My robes, and shelter thee beneath my wings
Like a young bird? No more my Hector comes
Returning from the tomb, he grasps no more
His glitt'ring spear, bringing protection to thee;
No more thy father's kindred, or the force
Of the brave Phrygians: but from Ilium's height,
By merciless hands hurled headlong, shalt thou fall,
And crushed breathe out thy life. O soft embrace,
And to thy mother dear! O fragrant breath!
In vain I swathed thy infant limbs, in vain
I gave thee nurture at this breast, and toiled
Wasted with care. If ever, now embrace,
Now clasp thy mother, throw thine arms around
My neck, and join thy cheek, thy lips to mine.
Why, O ye Grecians, studying barb'rous ills,
Why will you kill my son? He hath not wronged you.
Daughter of Tyndarus, but not of Zeus,
From many fathers must I deem thee sprung,
From Vengeance first, then Hate, from Slaughter, Death,
And all the ills earth breeds: for ne'er from Zeus
Durst I pronounce thy birth. Thou fatal pest
To many Phrygians, and to many Greeks,
Perdition seize thee! By thy beauteous eyes
Thou vilely hast destroyed the realms of Troy.
Here, take him, bear him, hurl him from the height,

If ye must hurl him, feast upon his flesh:
For from the gods hath ruin fall'n on us:
We have no power to save my child from death.
Cover this wretched body, wrap it close,
Cast it into your galley; for I come
To glorious nuptials, having lost my son.

Chorus.

Unhappy Troy, what numbers hast thou lost,
Through one vile woman, and her hateful bed!

Talthybius.

Forbear, O child, forbear thy fond embrace
Of thy afflicted mother. Go, ascend
The summit of those towers, thy father's once,
There leave thy life, for so hath Greece decreed
Take him: fit herald of this deed is he,
Who knows no touch of pity or of shame,
But rather to your mandate gives assent.

Hecuba.

O child, O son of my unhappy son,
We of thy life, beyond our thoughts, are reft,
I, and thy mother! What can I, poor boy,
What can I do for thee, but smite this head,
And beat this breast? That we can give thee that
Is in our power. Ah me, what griefs for Troy
I suffer, what for thee! Is there an ill
We have not? What is wanting to the woes,
Which all the dreadful band of Ruin brings?

(*Exeunt Andromache and Talthybius with Astyanax.*)

Strophe 1

Chorus.

Thou lord of Salamis, where love
The honey-gath'ring bees to rove,
Thou, who didst hold thy island-seat
Around whose rocks the billows beat,
Whose hallowed mounds first boast to show
Ranged down their sloping sides the olive bough,
Of blue-eyed Pallas heavenly crown,
And glory of her polished town:
Thou with Alcmena's son, whose hand
Grasped the strong bow, heldst high command.

Thy soul, like his, to glorious action bold,
  To Troy, O Telamon, to Troy,
  Our rampired city to destroy,
Thou camst, from Greece thou camst in times of old.

Antistrophe 1

When, raging for the steeds denied,
  Of Greece he led the blooming pride;
  Where Simois pours his beauteous flood
  The hero's barks at anchor stood;
  Dauntless he leaped upon the strand,
His bow and arrows grasping in his hand:
  Laomedon with wild affright
Marked how they winged their slaught'ring flight.
  Though Phoebus squared each polished stone,
  The high-raised rampires are o'erthrown;
Around the ruddy flames devouring rise,
  And Troy a heap of ruin lies:
  Twice raged the spear around her walls,
And twice with thund'ring sound the city falls.

Strophe 2

In vain then at the golden bowls of Love
    Hast thou thy honoured place,
  Thy steps composed with sweetest grace,
  Presenting at the feast divine
  To heaven's high king the sparkling wine;
Vain, Dardan boy, thy glorious charge above;
  For war and wasting flames destroy,
  Sunk to the ground, thy native Troy.
    The sea-washed shores around
    Loud cries and shrieks resound,
As for her young when the poor bird complains,
    And anguish swells her strains:
Their husbands some, and some their sons deplore,
  Their mothers some, with age that bow,
    Lament with pious woe.
  Thy brimmed baths are now no more,
  A silent waste the circus lies,
Once thy loved scene of manly exercise,
  But thou the throne of Zeus beside,
  Blooming in all youth's roseate pride,

Sweetly serene dost woo each grace
To give new beauties to thy face:
Yet Priam's realms lie waste, a desert drear,
Beneath the Grecian spear.

Antistrophe 2

O Love, O Love, that to the seats of Troy,
Thy gently glowing fire
Kindling in heavenly breasts desire,
Didst once direct thy pleasing flight,
To what a splendid, stately height,
Whilst gods her dear alliance sought with joy,
Didst thou exalt her glorious fame?
Now must thou bear another name;
No more the joy-kindling Love,
But reproach of gods above.
This fatal morn, with silver-waving wings
Which light to mortals brings,
Hath seen destruction wide its ravage spread,
Hath seen the towers of Troy laid low
Beneath th' insulting foe:
With offspring yet to bless her bed
Her husband from this land she bore;
The favoured youth yon orient regions o'er
Her four ethereal coursers bear,
Placed by her in the golden car.
Hence to thy country Hope might rise,
Graced with the favour of the skies:
But all the love, which touched the gods with joy,
Shrinks from the aid of Troy.

(*Enter Menelaus with soldiers.*)

Menelaus.

O thou bright-beaming radiance of this sun,
Helen in thee, my wife, these hands shall seize,
After the many toils I have sustained,
I, and the Grecian host. I came to Troy,
Not for a woman, as some lightly think,
But armed with vengeance 'gainst the man who broke
Each hospitable law, and from my house
Bore, as his spoil, my wife. But the just gods
He hath his meed, he and his country fall'n
Beneath the arms of Greece. The Spartan dame,

For not with pleasure can my tongue pronounce
Her name who was my wife, once was, I come
To lead from hence: for in this tent, among
The other captive dames of Troy enrolled,
Is she detained. For they, whose toiling spear
Achieved her, have presented her to me
To kill her, or, if such my will, to Greece
Alive to lead her: but my purpose is
The death of Helen to forbear at Troy,
And bear her in my stout bark o'er the seas
To Greece; and there, in vengeance for my friends
Who beneath Ilium died, to give her death.
But, ye attendants, go into the tent,
Bring her forth, drag her by the hair with blood
Deeply polluted: when the fav'ring winds
Breathe in our sails, to Greece shall she be sent.

(*Exeunt soldiers.*)

Hecuba.

O Zeus, who rulest the rolling of the earth,
And o'er it hast thy throne, whoe'er thou art,
The ruling mind, or the necessity
Of nature, I adore thee. Dark thy ways
And silent are thy steps; to mortal man
Yet thou with justice all things dost ordain.

Menelaus.

Why to the gods dost thou renew thy vows?

Hecuba.

I praise thy resolution, Menelaus,
If thou shalt kill thy wife. But fly her sight:
She captivates the eyes of men, takes towns,
Sets houses all on fire; such blandishments
She hath t' allure the soul; I know her well,
Thou knowst her, and all they that suffer by her.

(*The soldiers return. Enter Helen.*)

Helen.

This is a prelude which may well cause fear;
For by thy servants, Menelaus, by force
I from the tent am dragged. But little wants
T' assure me that I am detested by thee.
Yet I would ask thee, by the states of Greece
And thee touching my life what is decreed.

Menelaus.

Justice hath not pronounced fixed sentence on thee;
But all the host of Greece, whom thou hast wronged,
Give thee to me, and thou by me shalt die.

Helen.

May I have leave 'gainst this to urge my plea,
That, if I die, not justly I shall die?

Menelaus.

Not to hold converse came I, but to kill thee.

Hecuba.

Yet hear her, Menelaus, nor let her die,
Her bland excuse not urged: but to her plea
Let me reply, for of the ills in Troy
Thou nothing knowst; but when I sum them all,
From death no refuge shall be left to her.

Menelaus.

This requires leisure; yet if she would speak,
She is allowed: but let her know thy words
Gain her this leave; no grace to her I grant.

Helen.

Let me or well or ill appear to speak,
Thou no reply wilt haply deign me, deemed (*to Menelaus*)
An enemy: yet to the crime, of which
I know thou wilt accuse me, I will make (*to Hecuba*)
Reply, and to thy charge my pleas oppose,
'Gainst thee my charge. She first, then, to these ills
Gave birth, when she gave Paris birth; and next
The aged Priam ruined Troy and thee,
The infant not destroying, at his birth
Denounced a baleful firebrand. Hear from thence
What followed. 'Twixt the rival goddesses
Paris was judge. From Pallas was his meed
To lead the Phrygian arms, and conquer Greece;
From Hera, if to her his voice adjudged
The prize, to hold o'er Asia and the bounds
Of Europe his wide empire: but, my form
Extolling, Cypris promised to his arms
To give me, if in beauty she surpassed
The other goddesses. Mark now th' event.
The prize is given to Cypris; and so far
My nuptials profit Greece: you are not fall'n
Beneath Barbarians or a tyrant's sway,

Nor to protect your country stand in arms.
I, in what Greece is happy, am undone,
Sold for my beauty, and with cruel taunts
Reviled for what my head deserves a crown.
But thou wilt say that to an obvious charge
I have not yet replied, that from thy house
I fled by stealth. Her son, for ruin born,
Or Paris called or Alexander, came,
And brought no feeble goddess in his train:
Him, thou most worthless, leaving in thy house,
From Sparta didst thou hoist thy sails for Crete.
Well, what ensued of thee I will not ask,
But of myself: what could induce my thought,
My country for a stranger, and my house
Betrayed, to follow him? Thy vengeance rouse
Against the goddess, and be thou than Zeus
More potent; he o'er other gods bears rule,
But is her slave: I then may pardon find.
But hence against me thou mayst urge a charge
Of specious argument: When Paris died,
And low in earth was laid, behoved me then,
Since by no god my nuptials then were wrought,
To leave his house, and to the Grecian ships
To come. On this I earnestly was bent;
Witness, ye guards who kept the gates, and you
Who stationed on the walls held careful watch,
How oft you found me from the battlements
With ropes attempting to slide down by stealth:
But this new husband seizing me by force,
Deiphobus, the Trojans much averse,
Held me his wife. How then can justice doom me
To die? With justice how can I be slain
By thee, my husband, since he wedded me
By force? Thus from my house was I a slave
Sold for the prize of conquest. If thou aim
T' exceed the gods in power, the thought is folly.

Chorus.

Defend thy children and thy country, queen;
Refute her glozing speech. Her words are fair,
Her actions foul. In this much danger lies.

Hecuba.

The goddesses my voice shall first defend,
And show that she unjustly charges blame
On them. For Hera never will I deem,
Or virgin Pallas, to such frenzy sunk,
That Argos to Barbarians she would sell,
Or Pallas to the Phrygians e'er enslave
Her favoured Athens, who in sportive mood
And dainty dalliance to Ida came,
For form contesting. Whence this strong desire
In royal Hera of superior charms?
Was it to win a greater lord than Zeus?
Did Pallas, of her father who had asked
To keep her virgin purity unsoiled,
Flying connubial rites, aim now t' obtain
The nuptials of some god? Forbear to charge
These goddesses with folly, to set off
Thy own misdeeds; no credence with the wise
Wilt thou acquire. But Cypris, thou hast said
(High subject this for laughter), with my son
Came to the house of Menelaus. At rest
In heaven remaining, could she not have brought her,
And e'en Amyclae, had she pleased, to Troy?
My son was with surpassing beauty graced;
And thy fond passion, when he struck thy sight,
Became a Cypris: for each foolish fondness
To mortals is a Cypris, and the soul
Bereaves of reason. When thine eyes beheld him
Glitt'ring in rich barbaric vests and gold,
Thy passions were to madness soon inflamed,
At Argos little hadst thou been with wealth
Acquainted. Quitting Sparta, thou hadst hope
The Phrygian state, flowing with gold, would yield
Thy proud expense supplies; nor could the house
Of Menelaus within its narrow walls
Give thy insulting vanities free scope.
Well, let that pass. My son, thou sayst, by force
Bore thee away. What Spartan of that force
Was sensible? With what cries didst thou call
Castor, thy brother, to thy aid, then strong
In manhood's prime, then living, to the stars
Not then exalted? When thou camest to Troy,

And, following close, the Grecians, raged the spear
In conflict fierce; whene'er his arms obtained
Aught of advantage, Menelaus thy praise
Extolled, to grieve my son in that his love
Met with a potent rival: if success
Favoured the Trojans, he was nothing then.
Thine eyes were fixed on Fortune; this thy care,
To follow her; to Virtue thou wouldst pay
No homage. Yet with ropes didst thou attempt,
Such is thy plea, down from the walls to slide
By stealth, as if detained against thy will:
By whom wast thou surprised in act to fix
The pendent rope or point the sharpened sword?
This would a woman of a gen'rous soul,
Who sorrowed for her husband lost, have done.
Yet much did I admonish thee, and oft,
"Leave, O my daughter, leave us: other wives
My sons shall wed: I to the Grecian ships
Will send thee secretly, that war no more
'Twixt Greece and us may rage." To this thy heart
Was much averse; still in thy husband's house
Thy insolence of grandeur wouldst thou hold,
Imperious still from thy barbaric train
Claim prostrate adoration: there thy pride
Found rich supplies; from thence didst thou come forth
Gorgeously vested, and the same bright sky
View with thy husband, O detested wretch,
When it became thee with thy garments rent,
Humble, and cow'ring, and thy tresses shorn,
To have appeared, and for thy former faults
To veil thy shameless pride with modesty.
But, Menelaus, that thou mayst know what end
My words would have, give Greece a glorious crown
By killing her, and this thy law confirm
To other women, "She who dares betray
Her husband, faithless to his bed, shall die."

Chorus.

Oh, for the honour of thy ancestors,
And of thy house, punish thy wife. From Greece
Take this vile woman, this reproach, away
And show thy gen'rous spirit to thy foes.

Menelaus.

In this thy sentiment accords with mine,
That willingly she left my house, and sought
A foreign bed; and, to set off her plea,
Is Cypris introduced. Go, where with stones
Thou shalt be crushed: and in one hour repay
The Grecians for their tedious toils, by death,
That thou mayst learn ne'er to disgrace me more.

Helen.

Low at thy knees a suppliant I beg thee,
To me impute not what the gods have done
Amiss. Ah, do not kill me; pardon me!

Hecuba.

Thy brave associates in this wasteful war,
Whom she hath slain, I beg thee for their sake,
And for my children's, do not thou betray.

Menelaus.

Forbear, age-honoured lady; for of her
I have no heed. You, who attend me, hence
To the bark bear her: she shall sail for Greece.

Hecuba.

Let her not enter the same bark with thee.

Menelaus.

Why? Is the freight more heavy than before?

Hecuba.

He is no lover, who not always loves.

Menelaus.

That every thought of love may be discharged,
Thy will shall be complied with: the same bark
With me she shall not enter: not amiss
Is thy monition. When she comes to Greece,
For her vile deeds as vilely shall she die,
And teach all other women to be chaste,
No easy lesson: yet her death with fear
Shall strike their folly, be they worse than she.

(*Exeunt Menelaus, Helen and soldiers.*)

Strophe 1

Chorus.

So, to the Grecian arms a prey,
The temple Ilium's height that crowned,
The altar breathing odours round,

O Zeus, dost thou betray
The flames of holy sacrifice,
The clouds of incense wreathing to the skies.
The towers of Pergamus that rose
A sacred rampire 'gainst the foes,
The darksome, ivy-vested woods,
The woods that wave on Ida's brow,
Down whose steep sides the cool translucent floods
In mazy channels flow,
The height, which first the sun's bright ray
Impurples with the orient beams of day.

Antistrophe 1

Ah, banished is each solemn rite;
The sacred choirs with tuneful song,
Echoing thy hollow rocks among,
No more shall charm the night:
No more thy summits shall behold
The forms of gods that breathe in sculptured gold:
On thee the full-orbed moon no more
Shall Phrygia's hallowed sports restore.
O king, in yon ethereal skies
High-throned who holdst thy sov'reign state,
Will in thy soul no gentle pity rise,
For Troy's unhappy fate,
Sunk to the dust her towered head
As wide the raging flames their ravage spread?

Strophe 2

Dear to my soul, my wedded lord,
Fall'n, fall'n beneath the slaught'ring sword,
Nor cleansing bath, nor decent tomb
Was thine, but in the Stygian gloom
Wanders thy melancholy ghost.
But me the bark that ploughs the main,
Winged with her swelling sails, shall bear
To Argos famed for steeds that whirl the car
Where by the lab'ring Cyclops rise
The rampired walls that brave the skies.
My children, now a friendless train,
Wailing with sighs and tears their fate,
Call on their mother in the gate:

Their mother from their eyes the Grecian host
In the black vessel bear away,
And dash with oars the foaming sea;
To sacred Salamis they sweep,
Or where the Isthmus o'er the deep
Stretches its head, and views with pride
An ocean rolling 'gainst each side;
Where Pelops in the rocky strait
Fixed in old times his royal seat.

Antistrophe 2

On the detested bark, the waves
In the wide ocean when she braves
May the loud thunder's deep'ning roar
Fierce its tempestuous fury pour;
And, kindled by Idaean Zeus,
The forked light'ning's bick'ring flame,
In haughty triumph as she rides,
Fall on her deck, and pierce her rifted sides:
For me from Ilium, bathed in tears,
From my loved country far she bears
A slave to some proud Grecian dame.
Reflecting Helen's winning grace
The golden mirror there hath place,
At which the virgins joy their charms t' improve.
Ne'er may she reach the Spartan shore,
Her household gods ne'er visit more,
Through Pitane ne'er proudly pass,
Nor through Athena's gates of brass;
For Greece, through all its wide domains,
With shame her fatal marriage stains;
And gives through scenes of bitterest woe
The streams of Simois to flow.

(*Enter Talthybius with soldiers bearing the corpse of Astyanax.*)

Alas! In quick succession o'er this land
Ills roll on ills. Behold, ye Trojan dames
Oppressed with woes, the dead Astyanax,
Thrown by the ruthless Grecians from the towers.

Talthybius.

One vessel, royal Hecuba, yet waits
To plough the deep, the treasures that remain,
Selected for Achilles' son, to bear
To Phthia's shore: the youthful chief is gone,
Informed of some calamities, which late
Have fall'n on Peleus, that Acastus, son
Of Pelias, hath driven him from his realms:
On this with quicker speed, than if the time
Allowed delay, he sailed, and with him bore
Andromache, who from mine eyes wrung tears
At her departure, for her country such
Her mournful sighs, and such at Hector's tomb
Her invocations: earnest her request
To thee, that her dead child, who from the tower
Fell and expired, thou in the earth wouldst lay,
Thy Hector's son; and this brass-plated shield,
The terror of the Grecians, which his father
Before his breast once raised; that to the house
Of Peleus, nay to the same chamber, where
Andromache, the mother of this child,
Must mount the nuptial bed, she may not bear it,
To sorrow at its sight: but for the chest
Of cedar, for the marble tomb, in this
That thou wouldst bury him; conjuring me
To give him to thy arms, that with what robes
And crowns thy present fortune yields thee means,
Thou her dead son wouldst grace, since she is gone,
And her lord's haste allowed her not to give
Her dear child to the tomb. When thou hast dressed
The body with what ornaments thou mayst,
The earth will we heap on him; then we sail.
With thy best speed what is enjoined thee do:
From one toil I have freed thee; passing o'er
Scamander's stream the body I have bathed,
And washed its wounds: but now I go to sink
Deep in the earth his place of sepulture,
That with more speed, with what thou hast in charge
My toil concurring, we may sail for Greece.

(*Exeunt Talthybius and soldiers; the body is left behind.*)

Hecuba.

Place the orbed shield of Hector on the ground,
A mournful sight, nor pleasing to mine eyes.
Why, O ye Grecians, who in arms excel
More than in gen'rous minds, why have you wrought,
Fearing this child, a slaughter to this hour
Unheard of? Was it lest the time might come
When he might raise fall'n Troy? There was no cause:
E'en when my Hector shone in prosperous arms,
And thousands with him shook the purple spear,
We perished: since the vanquished city sunk
Your prey, and in the war the Phrygian force
Was wasted, such an infant could you fear?
The fear, which reason disavows, I blame.
O thou most dear, how hapless was thy death?
Hadst thou in manhood's prime, the nuptial bed
Possessed, and high, imperial, godlike power,
Died for thy country, happy hadst thou been,
If aught of these be happy; now, my child,
These to thine eyes presented and thy thought,
Thou didst not taste, nor aught of what thy house
Contained enjoy. Ah me, how wretchedly
Thy father's walls, the towers by Phoebus raised,
Have rent the crispèd ringlets from thy head,
Which thy fond mother cherished, nor withheld
The frequent kiss! But now, the bones all crushed,
The slaughter riots, to abstain from words
Of harsher utt'rance. Ah, these hands, whose joints
Once the dear image of thy father's bore,
Now lie with loosened nerves! O thou dear mouth,
Which utteredst many a spritely pleasantry,
How art thou mangled? Where thy promise now
Which once thou madst me, hanging on my robes?
"O mother, didst thou say, these clust'ring locks
Will I for thee cut off, and to thy tomb
With my companions bear them, hailing thee
With dear address." Such honours now to me
Thou dost not pay; but thee, unhappy child,
Dead in thy early bloom, must I inter,
Old, of my country, of my children reft.
Ah me, are all my fond embraces, all
My nursing pains to lull thy infancy

To sleep, thus lost? And on thy tomb what verse,
Thy death declaring, shall the bard inscribe?
"This child the Grecians, for they feared him slew;"
A verse recording the disgrace of Greece.
But of thy father's wealth though reft, his shield
Shall yet be thine, and on its plated brass
Thou shalt be laid in th' earth. O thou, the fence
Of Hector's nervous arm, thou hast, O shield,
Lost thy best guardian! Yet how sweet to trace
The mark of his strong grasp, and on the verge
Of thy high orb the sweat, which from his brows
Amidst his toils oft dropt, when to his face
Close he applied thee! For th' unhappy dead
Bring what of ornament is left us now;
For not to splendour hath the god assigned
Our fortunes; but of what I have to grace thee
Thou shalt receive. Of mortals him I deem
Unwise, who, thinking that his state is blest,
Joys as secure: for Fortune, like a man
Distempered in his senses, this way now,
Now that way leaps, inconstant in her course.
No mortal knows stability of bliss.

Chorus.

See, from the spoils of Troy their ready hands
Have brought thee ornaments t' inwrap the dead.

Hecuba.

Thee, O my child, not victor with the bow
O'er thy compeers, nor on the spritely steed,
Customs held high by Phrygia's manly sons,
Unwearied in the chase, thy father's mother
Decks with these ornaments from treasures once
Thine own; but Helen, by the gods abhorred,
Hath rent them from thee, hath destroyed thy life,
And all thy hapless house in ruins laid.

Chorus.

O thou hast touched, O thou hast touched my heart,
Thou, who wast once my city's mighty king!

Hecuba.

Around thy limbs I wrap these gorgeous vests
Of Phrygian texture, which thou shouldst have worn
To grace thy nuptials with some noble bride
Surpassing all the Asiatic dames.

And thou, with conquests glorious, mother once
Of num'rous trophies, be thou crowned, loved shield
Of Hector: for, not dying, with the dead
Shalt thou be laid: with honours to be graced,
Thee worthier than the arms of my new lord,
The wise and base Odysseus, I esteem.

Chorus.

Ah bitter lamentation! Thee, O child,
Thee shall the Earth receive: thou, mother, raise
The cry that wails the dead.

Hecuba.

My heart is rent.

Chorus.

My heart too for thy dreadful ills is rent.

Hecuba.

Thy wounds with hands medicinal—ah me,
Vain service!—will I bind. Among the dead
All that remains shall be thy father's care.

Chorus.

Strike, strike thy head; loud let thy hands resound.
Ah me!

Hecuba.

Ye females dearest to my soul!

Chorus.

Give utterance, royal lady, to thy griefs.

Hecuba.

The gods intended nothing, but my woes,
And hate to Troy, most ruthless hate. In vain
The victims at their altars then we slew.
Yet from the heights above had not their power
Encompassed us, and low beneath the earth
Sunk us in ruin, by the Muse's voice
We had not been recorded, nor the bards
To latest ages given the lofty verse.
Go, in the tomb lay the unhappy dead;
For, as becomes the shades below, with crowns
He is adorned: but little it imports
The dead, I think, if any shall obtain
Magnificent and costly obsequies:
Vain affectation of the living this.

(*The dead child is carried out.*)

Chorus.

Ah the unhappy mother, in thy life
Who wove her brightest hopes! Though highly blest,
As from illustrious parents thy rich stream
Of blood deriving, dreadful was thy death.
Alas, alas! Whom see I on the heights
Of Ilium, blazing torches in their hands
Waving? Some fresh misfortune threatens Troy.

(*Enter Talthybius and soldiers.*)

Talthybius.

Ye leaders of the bands, who have in charge
To burn the town of Priam, from my voice
Hear your instructions: idle in your hands
No longer hold the flames, but hurl them, spread
The wasting blaze, that, Ilium low in dust
O'erturned, we may with joy return to Greece.
And you (for now to you my speech is turned),
Ye Trojan dames, soon as the chiefs shall give
The trumpet's sounding voice, go to the ships
Of Greece, that from this country you may sail.
And thou, unhappy lady worn with age,
Follow: for from Odysseus these are come,
To whom thy fortune sends thee hence a slave.

Hecuba.

O miserable me! This is the last,
This is the extreme bound of all my ills.
I from my country go; my city sinks
In flames. But haste, my aged foot, though weak,
That I may yet salute the wretched town:
O Troy, that once 'mongst the barbaric states
Stoodst high aspiring, thy illustrious name
Soon shalt thou lose, for thee the raging flames
Consume: and from our country us they lead,
Now lead us slaves. Ye gods! But why invoke
The gods? Invoked before they did not hear.
But bear me, let me rush into the flames:
For this would be the greatest glory to me,
With thee my burning country now to die.

Talthybius.

Unhappy, thou art frentic with thine ills.
Lead her, nay force her hence: for to his hand,
Charged by Odysseus, I must give his prize.

Strophe

Hecuba.

Woe, woe, woe, woe, intolerable woe!
O Zeus, O sov'reign lord of Phrygia's realms,
Almighty sire, seest thou our miseries,
Unworthy of the race of Dardanus?

Chorus.

He sees, yet this magnific city, now
No city, is destroyed. Troy is no more.

Hecuba.

O sight of horror! Ilium blazes; high
O'er Pergamus the fiery deluge rolls,
Rolls o'er the city, and its tow'red red walls.

Chorus.

The glories of my country, e'en as smoke
Which on light wings is borne aloft in air,
By war are wasted; all her blazing domes
Are sunk beneath the flames and hostile spear.

Hecuba.

O my dear country, fost'ring land, who gavst
My children nurture!

Chorus.

O unhappy land!

Antistrophe

Hecuba.

Hear, O my children, know your mother's voice!

Chorus.

With mournful voice dost thou address the dead;
And throwing on the ground thy aged limbs
Dig with thy hands the earth. Behold, I bend
My knee with thine, and grov'lling on the ground
Call our unhappy husbands laid beneath.

Hecuba.

Ah, we are borne, are dragged,

Chorus.

O mournful voice!

Hecuba.

Dragged to the house of slavery.

Chorus.

From my country.

Hecuba.

O Priam, Priam, thou indeed art fall'n,
Thou hast no tomb, no friend; but of my woes
Thou knowst not; for black death hath closed thine eyes;
By impious slaughter is the pious fall'n!

Chorus.

Ye temples of the gods, and thou, loved town,
Destruction from the flames and pointed spear
Is on you; low on earth you soon will lie,
Your glories vanished; for the dust, like smoke
On light wings mounting high, will leave my house
An undistinguished ruin; e'en thy name,
My country, shall be lost. In different forms
Destruction comes on all. Troy is no more.

Hecuba.

Heard you that dreadful crash? It was the fall
Of Pergamus. The city rocks—it rocks,
And crushed beneath the rolling ruin sinks.
My limbs, my trembling limbs, hence, bear me hence.

Chorus.

Go to the wretched day of servile life.
Alas, unhappy city! But from hence
Go, to the Grecian ships advance our steps.

PHILOSOPHY

With the rise of democracy, involving as it did the theory of human equality, a demand was created in ancient Greece for a technical education that would fit any man for public life; statesmanship, once based on inborn gifts of speech and political wisdom, had to be democratized. This demand called into being the art of rhetoric whose aim was to equip any man, however humble his talent, for public speaking. But rhetoric concerned itself with nothing beyond the communication of thought and the persuasion to a belief or action; it had to be supplemented by a working knowledge of government and society. Hence arose a class of men who professed to teach not only rhetoric, but all knowledge essential to the statesman. Such instructors in wisdom were termed sophists.

The earliest of this class, and by far the most eminent, was Protagoras of Abdera. Abandoning all hope of discovering the one true essence of the Universe, Protagoras boldly declared that "Man is the measure of all things"—in other words, everything is precisely what it seems to the individual. In two respects this declaration opened a new era. First it directed attention to the mind and its relation to the outside world; and secondly, by shifting the center of attention from the world to man it gave, along with many co-operating forces, a tremendous impetus to the growth of individualism.

Other sophists of the fifth century B.C. borrowed from Protagoras his theory of knowledge and, with varying motive and ability, pursued the same methods. They all laid stress on the distinction between Nature, whose laws are morally binding, and convention—man-made customs and statutes, for which they cherished no reverence. The effect of this principle was to dissolve tradition, including the religion and moral usages of the fathers. In their view the past was an age of ignorance and superstition; the present alone was worthy of consideration. The same principle tended equally to break down the barriers of social class and the boundaries of states. Though solvents of the established political, social, and religious order, the sophists were preparing the way to a world-wide humanism, to more friendly relations among states, to federations and empire.

Sophists without character or earnest purpose, however, pushed to ridiculous extremes the doctrine of Protagoras and asserted that everything is precisely as it appears to every individual. No affirmation can be false, because it is impossible to state that which does not exist. If a thing is true, the opposite is equally true. Thus arose a class of disputants whose sole purpose was to confute their adversaries by quibbling with words, by fallacies of logic, and by sheer effrontery of manner. The effect was to fill the right-minded with disgust at sophistry. It is not surprising, therefore, that as an escape from the hopeless hubbub of skepticism a reaction should arise toward religious and philosophic faith.

A leader of the new movement was the great philosopher, Socrates of Athens (ca. 470-399 B.C.). Socrates' belief in the greatness and wisdom of God was strengthened by the argument of design. The world is made for man, and every part of a human being is admirably adapted to a good purpose. Existing things must, therefore, be the handiwork of a wise artificer, full of love for all things living. As man is superior to animals, the Deity has taken especial thought for him. He is pleased with those things in us which conduce most to our well-being. Socrates drew, too, from experience that the wisest and most enduring of human institutions are the most God-fearing, and that in the individual man the riper his age and judgment, the deeper his religion. It was necessary for Socrates to make his sacrifices correspond with his small means, but he believed that the joy of the Gods is great in proportion to the holiness of the worshiper;

and in the conviction that they well knew his own interest, he used to pray simply, "Give me what is best for me."

In addition to an ample fund of common sense, Socrates had within him humor, imagination, intellectual power, and a love of truth so burning as to become at times ecstatic. With such qualities he fascinated his young companions, and some of them, especially Plato, he awakened to a life of intense mental productivity. With Socrates, true knowledge was not simply the source but the substance of virtue; and he preferably sought that kind of truth which should determine the conduct of men—for example, "what is piety and what impiety? what is the beautiful and what the ugly? what is the noble and what the base? what are meant by just and unjust? what by sobriety and madness? what by courage and cowardice? what is a state and what a statesman? what is a ruler over men and what a ruling character?" and other similar problems.

The Socratic method of research was through conversation with one's fellows. Wherever the crowds were thickest, there Socrates could be found engaged in argument on his favorite subjects. It was easy for him to prove his opponent ignorant of the topic under discussion, as he was the most formidable reasoner of the Periclean Age. Having thus cleared the ground, he proceeded by induction to establish precise definitions of general terms. "There are two things," declared Aristotle, "that one would rightly attribute to Socrates: inductive reasoning and universal definition. In fact these two things are the very foundation of knowledge."

It was thus that, while professing ignorance on all subjects, Socrates built up a body of ethical science which might serve as a guide to himself and others. In assuming man to be the measure of all things, he stood on sophistic ground; but he made a vast advance in pointing to the reason, rather than the senses, as the universal and eternal element in man, the infallible criterion of truth, therefore, in the realm of conduct or nature. As intellectual education, however, might increase a man's power for evil, he was careful first of all to instruct his associates in self-control and to inspire them with a wise spirit in their relations with the gods. Wisdom and Justice we should seek not only because of their use to us, but also because they are pleasing to the gods. His teachings were quite as religious as philosophic.

Throughout his life Socrates gave evidence of loyalty and love for his fellow citizens and his country. Living with rare frugality, he charged no fee for instruction, in the fashion of the sophists, but lavished the wealth of his spirit on rich and poor alike. Many were his exhortations to brothers to love one another, to children to respect and obey their parents, and to citizens to be true to their country. Faithfully he performed his military duties, and as chairman of the Assembly he fearlessly adhered to law against popular clamor for injustice.

Socrates chose as his high duty the task of preparing men to serve the state in war and peace with strong bodies, clear brains, and upright hearts. It is a sad commentary on the spirit of the Athenians, after the collapse of their Empire, that they could be persuaded to condemn him to death, on the ground that he was a corrupting influence on the young and had introduced new deities.

Our chief and best knowledge of Socrates comes from his famous pupil, the great creative philosopher, Plato. Plato was born at Athens in 427 B.C. of aristocratic parents and in early life considered entering politics. But the condemnation of his revered master, Socrates, in 399 B.C., awakened in him a suspicion of democracy. He could do nothing, therefore, but remain in private life and satisfy his political longings with the creation of ideal constitutions, or appeal to a tyrant, such as Dionysius of Syracuse, for the realization of his vision of the perfect state.

Eventually Plato opened in his home a school called the Academy from its proximity to the public garden of that name. There he lectured learnedly on mathematics, astronomy, harmonics, and ethics. He also prepared and published a popular presentation of his views for the laity. These literary works are called Dialogues. They show Plato to have been not a dry reasoner, but a highly imaginative poet. Though prose in form, his language is brilliantly versatile and sparkles with poetic gems. He is gifted, too, with rare dramatic power. The speakers of the Dialogues are living persons, who everywhere retain their psychological identity.

At the basis of Plato's thought lies his doctrine of ideas. Socrates had taught him that the only objects of knowledge are concepts, universal truths established by induction. With Plato the concept becomes an idea, a word derived from the Pythagoreans and signifying form. Ideas are not forms in the geometrical sense, but are colorless, shapeless, intangible realities, which the mind alone can perceive. In distinction from our ideas, which have their being in the mind alone, those of Plato are objective realities, in fact the only things that exist. The objects of sense are real only in so far as they "partake of" these pure realities.

Plato's chief concern was with ethics. The greatest of all ideas, he taught, is God, who created the world and gave to it a soul, through which reason and order and life came into all things. At His command the lesser gods fashioned the body of man, and He Himself prepared the soul, making it of the same substance as the world soul, though less pure. By means of education man advances toward the highest Good, which is neither knowledge nor happiness, but the utmost likeness to God.

An important division of ethics, says Plato, is politics. In his view the state is not the all-in-all of the citizen, as it had been in former time. The calm existence of the philosopher, the solving of the problems of the essential and the eternal, is a nobler being than that of the politician. Only the body of the philosopher lives in the state, while his soul dwells elsewhere, untouched by political ambition. This is true of a community such as Athens, he asserts, which is governed by the ignorant majority and whose greatest statesman, Pericles, utterly failed in the function of improving the character of the citizens. It would be quite otherwise with a state philosophically organized, like that set forth in Plato's *Republic*. As any state is an individual "writ large," the ideal state is constituted like a perfect individual with the baser parts subordinate to the nobler.

The chief value of Plato's writings lies in the powerful impetus they give to the intellectual life of the reader. In brief, it is not the knowledge discovered by Plato, but his belief in spiritual realities, his aspiration to the beautiful, the good, and the true, his conception of the vast heights attainable by man, that place him among the most powerful intellectual and moral forces that operate upon the human race.

Through an active life of eighty-one years Plato's mind continually developed. Accordingly his later works, such as the *Republic* and *Laws*, are chiefly representative of thought in the century following the Periclean Age, but this is not true of all his writings. For example, as a young man Plato was present at Socrates' trial, and presumably wrote his account of it soon afterward. This is the *Apology*, or to translate the Greek more exactly, the *Defense*. It does indeed describe the most famous trial in Greek antiquity, but actually it is a glorification of a great man's whole character. And the *Symposium* also recreates for us scenes and personalities of the Periclean Age. Gilbert Murray has pronounced it Plato's most perfect Dialogue, "absolutely the highest work of prose fiction ever composed, most perfect in power, beauty, imaginative truth, the deepest word yet spoken upon the nature of Love."

Socrates.
British Museum,
London

PLATO

The Apology

Translated by B. Jowett

CHARACTERS

Socrates

Meletus

SCENE

The Court of Justice at Athens in 399 B.C., not long after the fall of the Athenian Empire (404 B.C.) and the restoration of democracy subsequent to the savage rule of the Thirty Tyrants. Socrates, about seventy years of age, has been accused by Meletus, Lycon and Anytus of not believing in the gods of Athens and of introducing new divinities and corrupting the young. These were stock charges against philosophers and sophists, now presented to a panel of 501 war-weary and disillusioned jurors who, like their fellows, were uninformed about the work of intellectuals and therefore suspicious of them.

THE APOLOGY

Socrates.

How you, O Athenians, have been affected by my accusers, I cannot tell; but I know that they almost made me forget who I was—so persuasively did they speak; and yet they have hardly uttered a word of truth. But of the many falsehoods told by them, there was one which quite amazed me;—I mean when they said that you should be upon your guard and not allow yourselves to be deceived by the force of my eloquence. To say this, when they were certain to be detected as soon as I opened my lips and proved myself to be anything but a great speaker, did indeed appear to me most shameless—unless by the force of eloquence they mean the force of truth; for if such is their meaning, I admit that I am eloquent. But in how different a way from theirs! Well, as I was saying, they have scarcely spoken the truth at all; but from me you shall hear the whole truth: not, however, delivered after their manner in a set oration duly ornamented with words and phrases. No, by heaven! but I shall use the words and arguments which occur to me at the moment; for I am confident in the justice of my cause: at my time of life I ought not to be appearing before you, O men of Athens, in the character of a juvenile orator—let no one expect it of me. And I must beg of you to grant me a favour:—If I defend myself in my accustomed manner, and you hear me using the words which I have been in the habit of using in the market place, at the tables of the money-changers, or anywhere else, I would ask you not to be surprised, and not to interrupt me on this account. For I am more than seventy years of age, and appearing now for the first time in a court of law, I am quite a stranger to the language of the place; and therefore I would have you regard me as if I were really a stranger, whom you would excuse if he spoke in his native tongue, and after the fashion of his country:—Am I making an unfair request of you? Never mind the manner, which may or may not be good; but think only of the truth of my words, and give heed to that: let the speaker speak truly and the judge decide justly.

And first, I have to reply to the older charges and to my first accusers, and then I will go on to the later ones. For of old I have had many accusers, who have accused me falsely to you during many years; and I am more afraid of them than of Anytus and his associates, who are dangerous, too, in their own way. But far more dangerous are the others, who began when you were children, and took possession of your minds with their falsehoods, telling of one Socrates, a wise man, who speculated about the heaven above, and searched into the earth beneath, and made the worse appear the better cause. The disseminators of this tale are the accusers whom I dread; for their hearers are apt to fancy that such enquirers do not believe in the existence of the gods. And they are many, and their charges against me are of ancient date, and they were made by them in the days when you were more impressible than you are now—in childhood, or it may have been in youth—and the cause when heard went by default, for there was none to answer. And hardest of all, I do not know and cannot tell the names of my accusers; unless in the chance case of a Comic poet. All who from envy and malice have persuaded you—some of them having first convinced themselves—all this class of men are most difficult to deal with; for I cannot have them up here, and cross-examine them, and therefore I must simply fight with shadows in my own defence, and argue when there is no one who answers. I will ask you then to assume with me, as I was saying, that my opponents are of two kinds; one recent, the other ancient: and I hope that you will see the propriety of my answering the latter first, for these accusations you heard long before the others, and much oftener.

Well, then, I must make my defence, and endeavour to clear away in a short time, a slander which has lasted a long time. May I succeed, if to succeed be for my good and yours, or likely to avail me in my cause! The task is not an easy one; I quite understand the nature of it. And so leaving the event with God, in obedience to the law I will now make my defence.

I will begin at the beginning, and ask what is the accusation which has given rise to the slander of me, and in fact has encouraged Meletus to prefer this charge against me. Well, what do the slanderers say? They shall be my prosecutors, and I will sum up their words in an affidavit: "Socrates is an evil-doer, and a curious person, who searches into things under the earth and in heaven, and he makes the worse appear the better cause; and he teaches the aforesaid doctrines to others." Such is the nature of the accusation: it is just what you have yourselves seen in the comedy of Aristophanes, who has introduced a man whom he calls Socrates, going about and saying that he walks in air, and talking a deal of nonsense concerning matters of which

I do not pretend to know either much or little—not that I mean to speak disparagingly of any one who is a student of natural philosophy. I should be very sorry if Meletus could bring so grave a charge against me. But the simple truth is, O Athenians, that I have nothing to do with physical speculations. Very many of those here present are witnesses to the truth of this, and to them I appeal. Speak, then, you who have heard me, and tell your neighbours whether any of you have ever known me hold forth in few words or in many upon such matters. . . . You hear their answer. And from what they say of this part of the charge you will be able to judge of the truth of the rest.

As little foundation is there for the report that I am a teacher, and take money; this accusation has no more truth in it than the other. Although, if a man were really able to instruct mankind, to receive money for giving instruction would, in my opinion, be an honour to him. There is Gorgias of Leontium, and Prodicus of Ceos, and Hippias of Elis, who go the round of the cities, and are able to persuade the young men to leave their own citizens by whom they might be taught for nothing, and come to them whom they not only pay, but are thankful if they may be allowed to pay them. There is at this time a Parian philosopher residing in Athens, of whom I have heard; and I came to hear of him in this way:—I came across a man who has spent a world of money on the Sophists, Callias, the son of Hipponicus, and knowing that he had sons, I asked him: "Callias," I said, "if your two sons were foals or calves, there would be no difficulty in finding some one to put over them; we should hire a trainer of horses, or a farmer probably, who would improve and perfect them in their own proper virtue and excellence; but as they are human beings, whom are you thinking of placing over them? Is there any one who understands human and political virtue? You must have thought about the matter, for you have sons; is there any one?" "There is," he said. "Who is he?" said I; "and of what country? and what does he charge?" "Evenus the Parian," he replied; "he is the man, and his charge is five minae." Happy is Evenus, I said to myself, if he really has this wisdom, and teaches at such a moderate charge. Had I the same, I should have been very proud and conceited; but the truth is that I have no knowledge of the kind.

I dare say, Athenians, that some one among you will reply, "Yes, Socrates, but what is the origin of these accusations which are brought against you; there must have been something strange which you have been doing? All these rumours and this talk about you would never have arisen if you had been like other men: tell us, then, what is the cause of them, for we should be sorry to judge hastily of you." Now I regard this as a fair challenge, and I will endeavour to explain to you the reason why I am called wise and have such an evil fame. Please to attend then. And although some of you may think that I am joking, I declare that I will tell you the entire truth. Men of Athens, this reputation of mine has come of a certain sort of wisdom which I possess. If you ask me what kind of wisdom, I reply, wisdom such as may perhaps be attained by man, for to that extent I am inclined to believe that I am wise; whereas the persons of whom I was speaking have a superhuman wisdom, which I may fail to describe, because I have it not myself; and he who says that I have, speaks falsely, and is taking away my character. And here, O men of Athens, I must beg you not to interrupt me, even if I seem to say something extravagant. For the word which I will speak is not mine. I will refer you to a witness who is worthy of credit; that witness shall be the God of Delphi—he will tell you about my wisdom, if I have any, and of what sort it is. You must have known Chaerephon; he was early a friend of mine, and also a friend of yours, for he shared in the recent exile of the people, and returned with you. Well, Chaerephon, as you know, was very impetuous in all his doings, and he went to Delphi and boldly asked the oracle to tell him whether—as I was saying, I must beg you not to interrupt—he asked the oracle to tell him whether any one was wiser than I was, and the Pythian prophetess answered, that there was no man wiser. Chaerephon is dead himself; but his brother, who is in court, will confirm the truth of what I am saying.

Why do I mention this? Because I am going to explain to you why I have such an evil name. When I heard the answer, I said to myself, What can the god mean? and what is the interpretation of his riddle? for I know that I have no wisdom, small or great. What then can he mean when he says that I am the wisest of men? And yet he is a god, and cannot lie; that would be against his nature. After long consideration, I thought of a method of trying the question. I reflected that if I could only find a man wiser than myself, then I might go to the god with a refutation in my hand. I should say to him, "Here is a man who is wiser than I am; but you said that I was the wisest." Accordingly I went to one who had the reputation of wisdom, and observed him—his name I need not mention; he was a politician whom I selected for examination—and the result was as follows: When I began to talk with him, I could not help thinking that he was not really wise, although he was thought wise by many, and still wiser by himself; and thereupon I tried to explain to him that he thought himself wise, but was not really wise; and the consequence was that he hated me, and his enmity was shared by several who were present and heard me. So I left him, saying to myself, as I went away: Well, although I do not suppose that either of us knows anything really beautiful and good, I am better off than he is,—for he knows nothing, and thinks that he knows; I neither know nor think that I know. In this latter particular, then, I seem to have slightly the advantage of him. Then I went to another who had still higher pretensions to wisdom, and my conclusion was exactly the same. Whereupon I made another enemy of him, and of many others beside him.

Then I went to one man after another, being not unconscious of the enmity which I provoked, and I lamented and feared this: but necessity was laid upon me,—the word of God, I thought, ought to be considered first. And I said to myself, Go I must to all who appear to know, and find out the meaning of the oracle. And I swear to you, Athenians, by the dog I swear! —for I must tell you the truth—the result of my mission was just this: I found that the men most in repute were all but the most foolish; and that others less esteemed were wiser and better. I will tell you the tale of my wanderings and of the "Herculean" labours, as I may call them, which I endured only to find at last the oracle irrefutable. After the politicians, I went to the poets; tragic, dithyrambic, and all sorts. And there, I said to myself, you will be instantly detected; now you will find out that you are more ignorant than they are. Accordingly, I took them some of the most elaborate passages in their own writings, and asked what was the meaning of them—thinking that they would teach me something. Will you believe me? I am almost ashamed to confess the truth, but I must say that there is hardly a person present who would not have talked better about their poetry than they did themselves. Then I knew that not by wisdom do poets write poetry, but by a sort of genius and inspiration; they are like diviners or soothsayers who also say many fine things, but do not understand the meaning of them. The poets appeared to me to be much in the same case; and I further observed that upon the strength of their poetry they believed themselves to be the wisest of men in other things in which they were not wise. So I departed, conceiving myself to be superior to them for the same reason that I was superior to the politicians.

At last I went to the artisans, for I was conscious that I knew nothing at all, as I may say, and I was sure that they knew many fine things; and here I was not mistaken, for they did know many things of which I was ignorant, and in this they certainly were wiser than I was. But I observed that even the good artisans fell into the same error as the poets;—because they were good workmen they thought that they also knew all sorts of high matters, and this defect in them overshadowed their wisdom; and therefore I asked myself on behalf of the oracle, whether I would like to be as I was, neither having their knowledge nor their ignorance, or like them in both; and I made answer to myself and to the oracle that I was better off as I was.

This inquisition has led to my having many enemies of the worst and most dangerous kind, and has given occasion also to many calumnies. And I am called wise, for my hearers always imagine that I myself possess the wisdom which I find wanting in others: but the truth is, O men of Athens, that God only is wise; and by his answer he intends to show that the wisdom of men is worth little or nothing; he is not speaking of Socrates, he is only using my name by way of illustration, as if he said, He, O men, is the wisest, who, like Socrates, knows that his wisdom is in truth worth nothing. And so I go about the world, obedient to the god, and search and make enquiry into the wisdom of any one, whether citizen or stranger, who appears to be wise; and if he is not wise, then in vindication of the oracle I show him that he is not wise; and my occupation quite absorbs me, and I have no time to give either to any public matter of interest or to any concern of my own, but I am in utter poverty by reason of my devotion to the god.

There is another thing:—young men of the richer classes, who have not much to do, come about me of their own accord; they like to hear the pretenders examined, and they often imitate me, and proceed to examine others; there are plenty of persons, as they quickly discover, who think that they know something, but really know little or nothing; and then those who are examined by them instead of being angry with themselves are angry with me: This confounded Socrates, they say; this villainous misleader of youth!—and then if somebody asks them, Why, what evil does he practise or teach? they do not know, and cannot tell; but in order that they may not appear to be at a loss, they repeat the ready-made charges which are used against all philosophers about teaching things up in the clouds and under the earth, and having no gods, and making the worse appear the better cause; for they do not like to confess that their pretence of knowledge has been detected—which is the truth; and as they are numerous and ambitious and energetic, and are drawn up in battle array and have persuasive tongues, they have filled your ears with their loud and inveterate calumnies. And this is the reason why my three accusers, Meletus and Anytus and Lycon, have set upon me; Meletus, who has a quarrel with me on behalf of the poets; Anytus, on behalf of the craftsmen and politicians; Lycon, on behalf of the rhetoricians: and as I said at the beginning, I cannot expect to get rid of such a mass of calumny all in a moment. And this, O men of Athens, is the truth and the whole truth; I have concealed nothing, I have dissembled nothing. And yet, I know that my plainness of speech makes them hate me, and what is their hatred but a proof that I am speaking the truth? —Hence has arisen the prejudice against me; and this is the reason of it, as you will find out either in this or in any future enquiry.

I have said enough in my defence against the first class of my accusers; I turn to the second class. They are headed by Meletus, that good man and true lover of his country, as he calls himself. Against these, too, I must try to make a defence:—Let their affidavit be read: it contains something of this kind: It says that Socrates is a doer of evil, who corrupts the youth; and who does not believe in the gods of the state, but has other new divinities of his own. Such is the charge; and now let us examine the particular counts. He says that I am a doer of evil, and corrupt the youth; but I say, O men of Athens, that Meletus is a doer of evil, in that he pretends to be in earnest when he is only in jest, and is so eager to bring men to trial from a pretended zeal and interest about matters in which he really never had the smallest interest. And the truth of this I will endeavour to prove to you.

Come hither, Meletus, and let me ask a question of you. You think a great deal about the improvement of youth?

Meletus.

Yes, I do.

Socrates.

Tell the judges, then, who is their improver; for you must know, as you have taken the pains to discover their corrupter, and are citing and accusing me before them. Speak, then, and tell the judges who their improver is.—Observe, Meletus, that you are silent, and have nothing to say. But is not this rather disgraceful, and a very considerable proof of what I was saying, that you have no interest in the matter? Speak up, friend, and tell us who their improver is.

Meletus.

The laws.

Socrates.

But that, my good sir, is not my meaning. I want to know who the person is, who, in the first place, knows the laws.

Meletus.

The judges, Socrates, who are present in court.

Socrates.

What, do you mean to say, Meletus, that they are able to instruct and improve youth?

Meletus.

Certainly they are.

Socrates.

What, all of them, or some only and not others?

Meletus.

All of them.

Socrates.

By the goddess Hera, that is good news! There are plenty of improvers, then. And what do you say of the audience,—do they improve them?

Meletus.

Yes, they do.

Socrates.

And the senators?

Meletus.

Yes, the senators improve them.

Socrates.

But perhaps the members of the assembly corrupt them?—or do they too improve them?

Meletus.

They improve them.

Socrates.

Then every Athenian improves and elevates them; all with the exception of myself; and I alone am their corrupter? Is that what you affirm?

Meletus.

That is what I stoutly affirm.

Socrates.

I am very unfortunate if you are right. But suppose I ask you a question: How about horses? Does one man do them harm and all the world good? Is not the exact opposite the truth? One man is able to do them good, or at least not many;—the trainer of horses, that is to say, does them good, and others who have to do with them rather injure them? Is not that true, Meletus, of horses, or of any other animals? Most assuredly it is; whether you and Anytus say yes or no. Happy indeed would be the condition of youth if they had one corrupter only, and all the rest of the world were their improvers. But you, Meletus, have sufficiently shown that you never had a thought about the young: your carelessness is seen in your not caring about the very things which you bring against me.

And now, Meletus, I will ask you another question—by Zeus I will: Which is better, to live among bad citizens, or among good ones? Answer, friend, I say; the question is one which may be easily answered. Do not the good do their neighbours good, and the bad do them evil?

Meletus.

Certainly.

Socrates.

And is there any one who would rather be injured than benefited by those who live with him? Answer, my good friend, the law requires you to answer—does any one like to be injured?

Meletus.

Certainly not.

Socrates.

And when you accuse me of corrupting and deteriorating the youth, do you allege that I corrupt them intentionally or unintentionally?

Meletus.

Intentionally, I say.

Socrates.

But you have just admitted that the good do their neighbours good, and the evil do them evil. Now, is that a truth which your superior wisdom has recognized thus early in life, and am I, at my age, in such darkness and ignorance as not to know that if a man with whom I have to live is corrupted by me, I am very likely to be harmed by him; and yet I corrupt him, and intentionally, too—so you say, although neither I nor any other human being is ever likely to be convinced by you. But either I do not corrupt them, or I corrupt them unintentionally; and on either view of the case you lie. If my offence is unintentional, the law has no cognizance of unintentional offences: you ought to have taken me privately, and warned and admonished me; for if I had been better advised, I should have left off doing what I only did unintentionally—no doubt I should; but you would have nothing to say to me and refused to teach me. And now you bring me up in this court, which is a place not of instruction, but of punishment.

It will be very clear to you, Athenians, as I was saying, that Meletus has no care at all, great or small, about the matter. But still I should like to know, Meletus, in what I am affirmed to corrupt the young. I suppose you mean, as I infer from your indictment, that I teach them not to acknowledge the gods which the state acknowledges, but some other new divinities or spiritual agencies in their stead. These are the lessons by which I corrupt the youth, as you say.

Meletus.

Yes, that I say emphatically.

Socrates.

Then, by the gods, Meletus, of whom we are speaking, tell me and the court, in somewhat plainer terms, what you mean!

for I do not as yet understand whether you affirm that I teach other men to acknowledge some gods, and therefore that I do believe in gods, and am not an entire atheist—this you do not lay to my charge,—but only you say that they are not the same gods which the city recognizes—the charge is that they are different gods. Or, do you mean that I am an atheist simply, and a teacher of atheism?

Meletus.

I mean the latter—that you are a complete atheist.

Socrates.

What an extraordinary statement! Why do you think so, Meletus? Do you mean that I do not believe in the godhead of the sun or moon, like other men?

Meletus.

I assure you, judges, that he does not: for he says that the sun is stone, and the moon earth.

Socrates.

Friend Meletus, you think that you are accusing Anaxagoras: and you have but a bad opinion of the judges, if you fancy them illiterate to such a degree as not to know that these doctrines are found in the books of Anaxagoras the Clazomenian, which are full of them. And so, forsooth, the youth are said to be taught them by Socrates, when there are not unfrequently exhibitions of them at the theatre (price of admission one drachma at the most); and they might pay their money, and laugh at Socrates if he pretends to father these extraordinary views. And so, Meletus, you really think that I do not believe in any god?

Meletus.

I swear by Zeus that you believe absolutely in none at all.

Socrates.

Nobody will believe you, Meletus, and I am pretty sure that you do not believe yourself. I cannot help thinking, men of Athens, that Meletus is reckless and impudent, and that he has written this indictment in a spirit of mere wantonness and youthful bravado. Has he not compounded a riddle, thinking to try me? He said to himself:—I shall see whether the wise Socrates will discover my facetious contradiction, or whether I shall be able to deceive him and the rest of them. For he certainly does appear to me to contradict himself in the indictment as much as if he said that Socrates is guilty of not believing in the gods, and yet of believing in them—but this is not like a person who is in earnest.

I should like you, O men of Athens, to join me in examining what I conceive to be his inconsistency; and do you, Meletus, answer. And I must remind the audience of my request that they would not make a disturbance if I speak in my accustomed manner:

Did ever man, Meletus, believe in the existence of human things, and not of human beings? . . . I wish, men of Athens, that he would answer, and not be always trying to get up an interruption. Did ever any man believe in horsemanship, and not in horses? or in flute-playing, and not in flute-players? No, my friend; I will answer to you and to the court, as you refuse to answer for yourself. There is no man who ever did. But now please to answer the next question: Can a man believe in spiritual and divine agencies, and not in spirits or demigods?

Meletus.

He cannot.

Socrates.

How lucky I am to have extracted that answer, by the assistance of the court! But then you swear in the indictment that I teach and believe in divine or spiritual agencies (new or old, no matter for that); at any rate, I believe in spiritual agencies, —so you say and swear in the affidavit: and yet if I believe in divine beings, how can I help believing in spirits or demigods; —must I not? To be sure I must; and therefore I may assume that your silence gives consent. Now what are spirits or demigods? are they not either gods or the sons of gods?

Meletus.

Certainly they are.

Socrates.

But this is what I call the facetious riddle invented by you: the demigods or spirits are gods, and you say first that I do not believe in gods, and then again that I do believe in gods; that is, if I believe in demigods. For if the demigods are the illegitimate sons of gods, whether by the nymphs or by any other mothers, of whom they are said to be the sons—what human being will ever believe that there are no gods if they are the sons of gods? You might as well affirm the existence of mules, and deny that of horses and asses. Such nonsense, Meletus, could only have been intended by you to make trial of me. You have put this into the indictment because you had nothing real of which to accuse me. But no one who has a particle of understanding will ever be convinced by you that the same men can believe in divine and superhuman things, and yet not believe that there are gods and demigods and heroes.

I have said enough in answer to the charge of Meletus: any elaborate defence is unnecessary; but I know only too well how many are the enmities which I have incurred, and this is what will be my destruction if I am destroyed;—not Meletus, nor yet Anytus, but the envy and detraction of the world, which has been the death of many good men, and will probably be the death of many more; there is no danger of my being the last of them.

Some one will say: And are you not ashamed, Socrates, of a course of life which is likely to bring you to an untimely end? To him I may fairly answer: There you are mistaken: a man who is good for anything ought not to calculate the chance of living or dying; he ought only to consider whether in doing anything he is doing right or wrong—acting the part of a good man or of a bad. Whereas, upon your view, the heroes who fell at Troy were not good for much, and the son of Thetis above all, who altogether despised danger in comparison with disgrace; and when he was so eager to slay Hector, his goddess mother said to him, that if he avenged his companion Patroclus, and slew Hector, he would die himself—"Fate," she said, in these or the like words, "waits for you next after Hector"; he, receiving this warning, utterly despised danger and death, and instead of fearing them, feared rather to live in dishonour, and not to avenge his friend. "Let me die forthwith," he replies, "and be avenged of my enemy, rather than abide here by the beaked ships, a laughing-stock and a burden of the earth." Had Achilles any thought of death and danger? For wherever a man's place is, whether the place which he has chosen or that in which he has been placed by a commander, there he ought to remain in the hour of danger; he should not think of death or of anything but of disgrace. And this, O men of Athens, is a true saying.

Strange, indeed, would be my conduct, O men of Athens, if I who, when I was ordered by the generals whom you chose to command me at Potidaea and Amphipolis and Delium, remained where they placed me, like any other man, facing death —if now, when, as I conceive and imagine, God orders me to fulfil the philosopher's mission of searching into myself and other men, I were to desert my post through fear of death, or any other fear; that would indeed be strange, and I might justly be arraigned in court for denying the existence of the gods, if I disobeyed the oracle because I was afraid of death, fancying that I was wise when I was not wise. For the fear of death is indeed the pretence of wisdom, and not real wisdom, being a pretence of knowing the unknown; and no one knows whether death, which men in their fear apprehend to be the greatest evil, may not be the greatest good. Is not this ignorance of a disgraceful sort, the ignorance which is the conceit that a man knows what he does not know? And in this respect only I believe myself to differ from men in general, and may perhaps claim to be wiser than they are:—that whereas I know but little of the world below, I do not suppose that I know: but I do know that injustice and disobedience to a better, whether God or man, is evil and dishonourable, and I will never fear or avoid a possible good rather than a certain evil. And therefore if you let me go now, and are not convinced by Anytus, who said that since I had been prosecuted I must be put to death; (or if not that I ought never to have been prosecuted at all); and that if I escape now, your sons will all be utterly ruined by listening to my words—if you say to me, Socrates, this time we will not mind Anytus, and you shall be let off, but upon one condition, that you are not to enquire and speculate in this way any more, and that if you are caught doing so again you shall die;—if this was the condition on which you let me go, I should reply: Men of Athens, I honour and love you; but I shall obey God rather than you, and while I have life and strength I shall never cease from the practice and teaching of philosophy, exhorting any one whom I meet and saying to him after my manner: You, my friend,—a citizen of the great and mighty and wise city of Athens,—are you not ashamed of heaping up the greatest amount of money and honour and reputation, and caring so little about wisdom and truth and the greatest improvement of the soul, which you never regard or heed at all? And if the person with whom I am arguing, says: Yes, but I do care; then I do not leave him or let him go at once; but I proceed to interrogate and examine and cross-examine him, and if I think that he has no virtue in him, but only says that he has, I reproach him with undervaluing the greater, and overvaluing the less. And I shall repeat the same words to every one whom I meet, young and old, citizen and alien, but especially to the citizens, inasmuch as they are my brethren. For know that this is the command of God; and I believe that no greater good has ever happened in the state than my service to the God. For I do nothing but go about persuading you all, old and young alike, not to take thought for your persons or your properties, but first and chiefly to care about the greatest improvement of the soul. I tell you that virtue is not given by money, but that from virtue comes money and every other good of man, public as well as private. This is my teaching, and if this is the doctrine which corrupts the youth, I am a mischievous person. But if any one says that this is not my teaching, he is speaking an untruth. Wherefore, O men of Athens, I say to you, do as Anytus bids or not as Anytus bids, and either acquit me or not; but whichever you do, understand that I shall never alter my ways, not even if I have to die many times.

Men of Athens, do not interrupt, but hear me; there was an understanding between us that you should hear me to the end: I have something more to say, at which you may be inclined to cry out; but I believe that to hear me will be good for you, and therefore I beg that you will not cry out. I would have you know, that if you kill such an one as I am, you will injure yourselves more than you will injure me. Nothing will injure me, not Meletus nor yet Anytus—they cannot, for a bad man is not permitted to injure a better than himself. I do not deny that Anytus may, perhaps, kill him, or drive him into exile, or deprive him of civil rights; and he may imagine, and others may imagine, that he is inflicting a great injury upon him: but there I do not agree. For the evil of doing as he is doing—the evil of unjustly taking away the life of another—is greater far.

And now, Athenians, I am not going to argue for my own sake, as you may think, but for yours, that you may not sin against the God by condemning me, who am his gift to you. For if you kill me you will not easily find a successor to me, who, if I may use such a ludicrous figure of speech, am a sort of gadfly, given to the state by God; and the state is a great and noble steed who is tardy in his motions owing to his very size, and requires to be stirred into life. I am that gadfly which God has attached to the state, and all day long and in all places am always fastening upon you, arousing and persuading and reproaching you. You will not easily find another like me, and therefore I would advise you to spare me. I dare say that you may feel out of temper (like a person who is suddenly awakened from sleep), and you think that you might easily strike me dead as Anytus advises, and then you would sleep on for the remainder of your lives, unless God in his care of you sent you another gadfly. When I say that I am given to you by God, the proof of my mission is this:—if I had been like other men, I should not have neglected all my own concerns or patiently seen the neglect of them during all these years, and have been doing yours, coming to you individually like a father or elder brother, exhorting you to regard virtue; such conduct, I say, would be unlike human nature. If I had gained anything, or if my exhortations had been paid, there would have been some sense in my doing so; but now, as you will perceive, not even the impudence of my accusers dares to say that I have ever exacted or sought pay of any one; of that they have no witness. And I have a sufficient witness to the truth of what I say—my poverty.

Some one may wonder why I go about in private giving advice and busying myself with the concerns of others, but do not venture to come forward in public and advise the state. I will tell you why. You have heard me speak at sundry times and in divers places of an oracle or sign which comes to me, and is the divinity which Meletus ridicules in the indictment. This sign, which is a kind of voice, first began to come to me when I was a child; it always forbids but never commands me to do anything which I am going to do. This is what deters me from being a politician. And rightly, as I think. For I am certain, O men of Athens, that if I had engaged in politics, I should have perished long ago, and done no good either to you or to myself. And do not be offended at my telling you the truth: for the truth is, that no man who goes to war with you or any other multitude, honestly striving against the many lawless and unrighteous deeds which are done in a state, will save his life; he who will fight for the right, if he would live even for a brief space, must have a private station and not a public one.

I can give you convincing evidence of what I say, not words only, but what you value far more—actions. Let me relate to you a passage of my own life which will prove to you that I should never have yielded to injustice from any fear of death, and that "as I should have refused to yield" I must have died at once. I will tell you a tale of the courts, not very interesting perhaps, but nevertheless true. The only office of state which I ever held, O men of Athens, was that of senator: the tribe Antiochis, which is my tribe, had the presidency at the trial of the generals who had not taken up the bodies of the slain after the battle of Arginusae; and you proposed to try them in a body, contrary to law, as you all thought afterwards; but at the time I was the only one of the Prytanes who was opposed to the illegality, and I gave my vote against you; and when the orators threatened to impeach and arrest me, and you called and shouted, I made up my mind that I would run the risk, having law and justice with me, rather than take part in your injustice because I feared imprisonment and death. This happened in the days of the democracy. But when the oligarchy of the Thirty was in power, they sent for me and four others into the rotunda, and bade us bring Leon the Salaminian from Salamis, as they wanted to put him to death. This was a specimen of the sort of commands which they were always giving with the view of implicating as many as possible in their crimes; and then I showed, not in word only but in deed, that, if I may be allowed to use such an expression, I cared not a straw for death, and that my great and only care was lest I should do an unrighteous or unholy thing. For the strong arm of that oppressive power did not frighten me into doing wrong; and when we came out of the rotunda the other four went to Salamis and fetched Leon, but I went quietly home. For which I might have lost my life, had not the power of the Thirty shortly afterwards come to an end. And many will witness to my words.

Now do you really imagine that I could have survived all these years, if I had led a public life, supposing that like a good man I had always maintained the right and had made justice, as I ought, the first thing? No indeed, men of Athens, neither I nor any other man. But I have been always the same in all my actions, public as well as private, and never have I yielded any base compliance to those who are slanderously termed my disciples, or to any other. Not that I have any regular disciples. But if any one likes to come and hear me while I am pursuing my mission, whether he be young or old, he is not excluded. Nor do I converse only with those who pay; but any one, whether he be rich or poor, may ask and answer me and listen to my words; and whether he turns out to be a bad man or a good one, neither result can be justly imputed to me; for I never taught or professed to teach him anything. And if any one says that he has ever learned or heard anything from me in private which all the world has not heard, let me tell you that he is lying.

But I shall be asked, Why do people delight in continually conversing with you? I have told you already, Athenians, the whole truth about this matter: they like to hear the cross-examination of the pretenders to wisdom; there is amusement in it. Now this duty of cross-examining other men has been imposed upon me by God; and has been signified to me by oracles, visions, and in every way in which the will of divine power was ever intimated to any one. This is true, O Athenians; or, if not true, would be soon refuted. If I am or have been corrupting the youth, those of them who are now grown up and have become sensible that I gave them bad advice in the days of their youth should come forward as accusers, and take their revenge; or if they do not like to come themselves, some of their relatives, fathers, brothers, or other kinsmen, should say what evil their families have suffered at my hands. Now is their time. Many of them I see in the court. There is Crito, who is of the same age and of the same deme with myself, and there is Critobulus his son, whom I also see. Then again there is Lysanias of Sphettus, who is the father of Aeschines—he is present; and also there is Antiphon of Cephisus, who is the father of Epigenes; and there are the brothers of several who have associated with me. There is Nicostratus the son of Theosdotides, and the brother of Theodotus (now Theodotus himself is dead, and therefore he, at any rate, will not seek to stop him); and there is Paralus the son of Demodocus, who had a brother Theages; and Adeimantus the son of Ariston, whose brother Plato is present; and Aeantodorus, who is the brother of Apollodorus, whom I also see. I might mention a great many others, some of whom Meletus should have produced as witnesses in the course of his speech; and let him still produce them, if he has forgotten—I will make way for him. And let him say, if he has any testimony of the sort which he can produce. Nay, Athenians, the very opposite is the truth. For all these are ready to witness on behalf of the corrupter, of the injurer of their kindred, as Meletus and Anytus call me; not the corrupted youth only—there might have been a motive for that—but their uncorrupted elder relatives. Why should they too support me with their testimony?

Why, indeed, except for the sake of truth and justice, and because they know that I am speaking the truth, and that Meletus is a liar.

Well, Athenians, this and the like of this is all the defence which I have to offer. Yet a word more. Perhaps there may be some one who is offended at me, when he calls to mind how he himself on a similar, or even a less serious occasion, prayed and entreated the judges with many tears, and how he produced his children in court, which was a moving spectacle, together with a host of relations and friends; whereas I, who am probably in danger of my life, will do none of these things. The contrast may occur to his mind, and he may be set against me, and vote in anger because he is displeased at me on this account. Now if there be such a person among you,—mind, I do not say that there is,—to him I may fairly reply: My friend, I am a man, and like other men, a creature of flesh and blood, and not "of wood or stone," as Homer says; and I have a family, yes, and sons, O Athenians, three in number, one almost a man, and two others who are still young; and yet I will not bring any of them hither in order to petition you for an acquittal. And why not? Not from any self-assertion or want of respect for you. Whether I am or am not afraid of death is another question, of which I will not now speak. But, having regard to public opinion, I feel that such conduct would be discreditable to myself, and to you, and to the whole state. One who has reached my years, and who has a name for wisdom, ought not to demean himself. Whether this opinion of me be deserved or not, at any rate the world has decided that Socrates is in some way superior to other men. And if those among you who are said to be superior in wisdom and courage, and any other virtue, demean themselves in this way, how shameful is their conduct! I have seen men of reputation, when they have been condemned, behaving in the strangest manner: they seemed to fancy that they were going to suffer something dreadful if they died, and that they could be immortal if you only allowed them to live; and I think that such are a dishonour to the state, and that any stranger coming in would have said of them that the most eminent men of Athens, to whom the Athenians themselves give honour and command, are no better than women. And I say that these things ought not to be done by those of us who have a reputation; and if they are done, you ought not to permit them; you ought rather to show that you are far more disposed to condemn the man who gets up a doleful scene and makes the city ridiculous, than him who holds his peace.

But, setting aside the question of public opinion, there seems to be something wrong in asking a favour of a judge, and thus procuring an acquittal, instead of informing and convincing him. For his duty is, not to make a present of justice, but to give judgment; and he has sworn that he will judge according to the laws, and not according to his own good pleasure; and we ought not to encourage you, nor should you allow yourselves to be encouraged, in this habit of perjury—there can be no piety in that. Do not then require me to do what I consider dishonourable and impious and wrong, especially now, when I am being tried for impiety on the indictment of Meletus. For if, O men of Athens, by force of persuasion and entreaty I could overpower your oaths, then I should be teaching you to believe that there are no gods, and in defending should simply convict myself of the charge of not believing in them. But that is not so—far otherwise. For I do believe that there are gods, and in a sense higher than that in which any of my accusers believe in them. And to you and to God I commit my cause, to be determined by you as is best for you and me.

(*Socrates is found guilty by 281 votes to 220.*)

There are many reasons why I am not grieved, O men of Athens, at the vote of condemnation. I expected it, and am only surprised that the votes are so nearly equal; for I had thought that the majority against me would have been far larger; but now, had thirty votes gone over to the other side, I should have been acquitted. And I may say, I think, that I have escaped Meletus. I may say more; for without the assistance of Anytus and Lycon, any one may see that he would not have had a fifth part of the votes, as the law requires, in which case he would have incurred a fine of a thousand drachmae.

And so he proposes death as the penalty. And what shall I propose on my part, O men of Athens? Clearly that which is my due. And what is my due? What return shall be made to the man who has never had the wit to be idle during his whole life; but has been careless of what the many care for—wealth, and family interests, and military offices, and speaking in the assembly, and magistracies, and plots, and parties. Reflecting that I was really too honest a man to be a politician and live, I did not go where I could do no good to you or to myself; but where I could do the greatest good privately to every one of you, thither I went, and sought to persuade every man among you that he must look to himself, and seek virtue and wisdom before he looks to his private interests, and look to the state before he looks to the interests of the state; and that this should be the order which he observes in all his actions. What shall be done to such an one? Doubtless some good thing, O men of Athens, if he has his reward; and the good should be of a kind suitable to him. What would be a reward suitable to a poor man who is your benefactor, and who desires leisure that he may instruct you? There can be no reward so fitting as maintenance in the Prytaneum—the town hall—a reward which he deserves far more than the citizen who has won the prize at Olympia in the horse or chariot race, whether the chariots were drawn by two horses or by many. For I am in want, and he has enough; and he only gives you the appearance of happiness, and I give you the reality. And if I am to estimate the penalty fairly, I should say that maintenance in the Prytaneum is the just return.

Perhaps you think that I am braving you in what I am saying now, as in what I said before about the tears and prayers. But this is not so. I speak rather because I am convinced that I never intentionally wronged any one, although I cannot convince you—the time has been too short; if there were a law at Athens, as there is in other cities, that a capital cause should not be decided in one day, then I believe that I should have convinced you. But I cannot in a moment refute great slanders; and, as I am convinced that I never wronged another, I will assuredly not wrong myself. I will not say of myself that I deserve any evil, or propose any penalty. Why should I? Because I am afraid of the penalty of death which Meletus proposes? When I do not know whether death is a good or an evil, why should I propose a penalty which would certainly be an evil? Shall I say imprisonment? And why should I live in prison, and be the slave of the magistrates of the year—of the Eleven? Or shall the penalty be a fine, and imprisonment until the fine is paid? There is the same objection. I should have to lie in prison, for money I have none, and cannot pay. And if I say exile (and this may possibly be the penalty which you will affix), I must indeed be blinded by the love of life, if I am so irrational as to expect that when you, who are my own citizens, cannot endure my discourses and words, and have found them so grievous and odious that you will have no more of them, others are likely to endure me. No indeed, men of Athens, that is not very likely. And what a life should I lead, at my age, wandering from city to city, ever changing my place of exile, and always being driven out! For I am quite sure that wherever I go, there, as here, the young men will flock to me; and if I drive them away, their elders will drive me out at their request; and if I let them come, their fathers and friends will drive me out for their sakes.

Some one will say: Yes, Socrates, but cannot you hold your tongue, and then you may go into a foreign city, and no one will interfere with you? Now I have great difficulty in making you understand my answer to this. For if I tell you that to do as you say would be a disobedience to the God, and therefore that I cannot hold my tongue, you will not believe that I am serious; and if I say again that daily to discourse about virtue, and of those other things about which you hear me examining myself and others, is the greatest good of man, and that the unexamined life is not worth living, you are still less likely to believe me. Yet I say what is true, although a thing of which it is hard for me to persuade you. Also, I have never been accustomed to think that I deserve to suffer any harm. Had I money I might have estimated the offence at what I was able to pay, and not have been much the worse. But I have none, and therefore I must ask you to proportion the fine to my means. Well, perhaps I could afford a mina, and therefore I propose that penalty: Plato, Crito, Critobulus, and Apollodorus, my friends here, bid me say thirty minae, and they will be the sureties. Let thirty minae be the penalty; for which sum they will be ample security to you.

(*Socrates is condemned to death.*)

Not much time will be gained, O Athenians, in return for the evil name which you will get from the detractors of the city, who will say that you killed Socrates, a wise man; for they will call me wise, even although I am not wise, when they want to reproach you. If you had waited a little while, your desire would have been fulfilled in the course of nature. For I am far advanced in years, as you may perceive, and not far from death.

I am speaking now not to all of you, but only to those who have condemned me to death. And I have another thing to say to them: You think that I was convicted because I had no words of the sort which would have procured my acquittal—I mean, if I had thought fit to leave nothing undone or unsaid. Not so; the deficiency which led to my conviction was not of words—certainly not. But I had not the boldness or impudence or inclination to address you as you would have liked me to do, weeping and wailing and lamenting, and saying and doing many things which you have been accustomed to hear from others, and which, as I maintain, are unworthy of me. I thought at the time that I ought not to do anything common or mean when in danger: nor do I now repent of the style of my defence; I would rather die having spoken after my manner, than speak in your manner and live. For neither in war nor yet at law ought I or any man to use every way of escaping death. Often in battle there can be no doubt that if a man will throw away his arms, and fall on his knees before his pursuers, he may escape death; and in other dangers there are other ways of escaping death, if a man is willing to say and do anything. The difficulty, my friends, is not to avoid death, but to avoid unrighteousness; for that runs faster than death. I am old and move slowly, and the slower runner has overtaken me, and my accusers are keen and quick, and the faster runner, who is unrighteousness, has overtaken them. And now I depart hence condemned by you to suffer the penalty of death,—they too go their ways condemned by the truth to suffer the penalty of villainy and wrong; and I must abide by my award—let them abide by theirs. I suppose that these things may be regarded as fated,—and I think that they are well.

And now, O men who have condemned me, I would fain prophesy to you; for I am about to die, and in the hour of death men are gifted with prophetic power. And I prophesy to you who are my murderers, that immediately after my departure punishment far heavier than you have inflicted on me will surely await you. Me you have killed because you wanted to escape the accuser, and not to give an account of your lives. But that will not be as you suppose: far otherwise. For I say that there will be more accusers of you than there are now; accusers whom hitherto I have restrained: and as they are younger they will be more inconsiderate with you, and you will be more offended at them. If you think that by killing men you can prevent some one from censuring your evil lives, you are mistaken; that is not a way of escape which is either possible or honourable; the easiest and the noblest way is not to be disabling others, but to be improving yourselves. This is the prophecy which I utter before my departure to the judges who have condemned me.

Friends, who would have acquitted me, I would like also to talk with you about the thing which has come to pass, while the magistrates are busy, and before I go to the place at which I must die. Stay then a little, for we may as well talk with one another while there is time. You are my friends, and I should like to show you the meaning of this event which has happened to me. O my judges—for you I may truly call judges—I should like to tell you of a wonderful circumstance. Hitherto the divine faculty of which the internal oracle is the source has constantly been in the habit of opposing me even about trifles, if I was going to make a slip or error in any matter; and now as you see there has come upon me that which may be thought, and is generally believed to be, the last and worst evil. But the oracle made no sign of opposition, either when I was leaving my house in the morning, or when I was on my way to the court, or while I was speaking, at anything which I was going to say; and yet I have often been stopped in the middle of a speech, but now in nothing I either said or did touching the matter in hand has the oracle opposed me. What do I take to be the explanation of this silence? I will tell you. It is an intimation that what has happened to me is a good, and that those of us who think that death is an evil are in error. For the customary sign would surely have opposed me had I been going to evil and not to good.

Let us reflect in another way, and we shall see that there is great reason to hope that death is a good; for one of two things—either death is a state of nothingness and utter unconsciousness, or, as men say, there is a change and migration of the soul from this world to another. Now if you suppose that there is no consciousness, but a sleep like the sleep of him who is undisturbed even by dreams, death will be an unspeakable gain. For if a person were to select the night in which his sleep was undisturbed even by dreams, and were to compare with this the other days and nights of his life, and then were to tell us how many days and nights he had passed in the course of his life better and more pleasantly than this one, I think that any man, I will not say a private man, but even the great king will not find many such days or nights, when compared with the others. Now if death be of such a nature, I say that to die is gain; for eternity is then only a single night. But if death is the journey to another place, and there, as men say, all the dead abide, what good, O my friends and judges, can be greater than this? If indeed when the pilgrim arrives in the world below, he is delivered from the professors of justice in this world, and finds the true judges who are said to give judgment there, Minos and Rhadamanthus and Aeacus and Triptolemus, and other sons of God who were righteous in their own life, that pilgrimage will be worth making. What would not a man give if he might converse with Orpheus and Musaeus and Hesiod and Homer? Nay, if this be true, let me die again and again. I myself, too, shall have a wonderful interest in there meeting and conversing with Palamedes, and Ajax the son of Telamon, and any other ancient hero who has suffered death through an unjust judgment; and there will be no small pleasure, as I think, in comparing my own sufferings with theirs. Above all, I shall then be able to continue my search into true and false knowledge; as in this world, so also in the next; and I shall find out who is wise, and who pretends to be wise, and is not. What would not a man give, O judges, to be able to examine the leader of the great Trojan expedition; or Odysseus or Sisyphus, or numberless others, men and women too! What infinite delight would there be in conversing with them and asking them questions! In another world they do not put a man to death for asking questions: assuredly not. For besides being happier than we are, they will be immortal, if what is said is true.

Wherefore, O judges, be of good cheer about death, and know of a certainty, that no evil can happen to a good man, either in life or after death. He and his are not neglected by the gods; nor has my own approaching end happened by mere chance. But I see clearly that the time had arrived when it was better for me to die and be released from trouble; wherefore the oracle gave no sign. For which reason, also, I am not angry with my condemners, or with my accusers; they have done me no harm, although they did not mean to do me any good; and for this I may gently blame them.

Still I have a favour to ask of them. When my sons are grown up, I would ask you, O my friends, to punish them; and I would have you trouble them, as I have troubled you, if they seem to care about riches, or anything, more than about virtue; or if they pretend to be something when they are really nothing,—then reprove them, as I have reproved you, for not caring about that for which they ought to care, and thinking that they are something when they are really nothing. And if you do this, both I and my sons will have received justice at your hands.

The hour of departure has arrived, and we go our ways—I to die, and you to live. Which is better God only knows.

PLATO

The Symposium

Translated by Percy Bysshe Shelley

CHARACTERS OF THE DIALOGUE

Apollodorus

A Companion of Apollodorus

Aristodemus

Socrates

Agathon

Phaedrus

Pausanias

Eryximachus

Aristophanes

Alcibiades

SCENE

Athens. Some years previously, during a banquet at the house of the tragic poet Agathon (who had just won a prize at the City Dionysia), Socrates and others had spoken in praise of Love. Apollodorus, a friend of Socrates, was not present during the dialogue, but had heard of it from Aristodemus. Apollodorus, having already once narrated the dialogue to Glaucon, now repeats it to a companion.

THE SYMPOSIUM

Apollodorus.

I think that the subject of your inquiries is still fresh in my memory; for yesterday, as I chanced to be returning home from Phaleron, one of my acquaintance, seeing me before him, called out to me from a distance, jokingly, "Apollodorus, you Phalerian, will you not wait a minute?"—I waited for him, and as soon as he overtook me, "I have just been looking for you, Apollodorus," he said, "for I wished to hear what those discussions were on Love, which took place at the party, when Agathon, Socrates, Alcibiades, and some others, met at supper. Some one who heard it from Phoenix, the son of Philip, told me that you could give a full account, but he could relate nothing distinctly himself. Relate to me, then, I entreat you, all the circumstances. I know you are a faithful reporter of the discussions of your friends; but, first tell me, were you present at the party or not?"

"Your informant," I replied, "seems to have given you no very clear idea of what you wish to hear, if he thinks that these discussions took place so lately as that I could have been of the party."—"Indeed, I thought so," replied he.—"For how," said I, "O Glaucon! could I have been present? Do you not know that Agathon has been absent from the city many years? But, since I began to converse with Socrates, and to observe each day all his words and actions, three years are scarcely past. Before this time I wandered about wherever it might chance, thinking that I did something, but being in truth, a most miserable wretch, not less than you are now, who believe that you ought to do anything rather than practise the love of wisdom."—"Do not cavil," interrupted Glaucon, "but tell me, when did this party take place?"

"Whilst we were yet children," I replied, "when Agathon first gained the prize of tragedy, and the day after that on which he and the chorus made sacrifices in celebration of their success." —"A long time ago, it seems. But who told you all the circumstances of the discussion? Did you hear them from Socrates himself?" "No, by Zeus! But the same person from whom Phoenix had his information, one Aristodemus, a Cydathenean,—a little man who always went about without sandals. He was present at this feast, being, I believe, more than any of his contemporaries, a lover and admirer of Socrates. I have questioned

Socrates concerning some of the circumstances of his narration, who confirms all that I have heard from Aristodemus."—"Why, then," said Glaucon, "why not relate them, as we walk, to me? The road to the city is every way convenient, both for those who listen and those who speak."

Thus as we walked I gave him some account of those discussions concerning Love; since, as I said before, I remember them with sufficient accuracy. If I am required to relate them also to you, that shall willingly be done; for, whensoever either I myself talk of philosophy, or listen to others talking of it, in addition to the improvement which I conceive there arises from such conversation, I am delighted beyond measure; but whenever I hear your discussions about moneyed men and great proprietors, I am weighed down with grief, and pity you, who, doing nothing, believe that you are doing something. Perhaps you think that I am a miserable wretch; and, indeed, I believe that you think truly. I do not think, but well know, that you are miserable.

Companion.

You are always the same, Apollodorus—always saying some ill of yourself and others. Indeed, you seem to me to think every one miserable except Socrates, beginning with yourself. I do not know what could have entitled you to the surname of the "Madman," for, I am sure, you are consistent enough, for ever inveighing with bitterness against yourself and all others except Socrates.

Apollodorus.

My dear friend, it is manifest that I am out of my wits from this alone—that I have such opinion as you describe concerning myself and you.

Companion.

It is not worth while, Apollodorus, to dispute now about these things; but do what I entreat you and relate to us what were these discussions.

Apollodorus.

They were such as I will proceed to tell you. But let me attempt to relate them in the order which Aristodemus observed in relating them to me. He said that he met Socrates washed, and, contrary to his usual custom, sandalled, and having inquired whither he went so gaily dressed, Socrates replied, "I am going to sup at Agathon's; yesterday I avoided it, disliking the crowd, which would attend at the prize sacrifices then celebrated; today I promised to be there, and I made myself so gay, because one ought to be beautiful to approach one who is beautiful. But you, Aristodemus, what think you of coming uninvited to supper?"—"I will do," he replied, "as you command."—"Follow, then, that we may, by changing its application, disarm that proverb which says, *To the feasts of the good, the good come uninvited.* Homer, indeed, seems not only to destroy, but to outrage the proverb; for, describing Agamemnon as excellent in battle, and Menelaus but a faint-hearted warrior, he represents Menelaus as coming uninvited to the feast of one better and braver than himself."—Aristodemus hearing this, said, "I also am in some danger, Socrates, not as you say, but according to Homer, of approaching like an unworthy inferior, the banquet of one more wise and excellent than myself. Will you not, then, make some excuse for me? for I shall not confess that I came uninvited, but shall say that I was invited by you."—"As we walk together," said Socrates, "we will consider together what excuse to make—but let us go."

Thus discoursing, they proceeded. But, as they walked, Socrates, engaged in some deep contemplation, slackened his pace, and, observing Aristodemus waiting for him, he desired him to go on before. When Aristodemus arrived at Agathon's house he found the door open, and it occurred somewhat comically, that a slave met him at the vestibule, and conducted him where he found the guests already reclined. As soon as Agathon saw him, "You arrive just in time to sup with us, Aristodemus," he said; "if you have any other purpose in your visit, defer it to a better opportunity. I was looking for you yesterday, to invite you to be of our party; I could not find you anywhere. But how is it that you do not bring Socrates with you?"

But he turning round, and not seeing Socrates behind him, said to Agathon, "I just came hither in his company, being invited by him to sup with you."—"You did well," replied Agathon, "to come; but where is Socrates?"—"He just now came hither behind me; I myself wonder where he can be."—"Go and look, boy," said Agathon, "and bring Socrates in; meanwhile, you, Aristodemus, recline there near Eryximachus." And he bade a slave wash his feet that he might recline. Another slave, meanwhile, brought word that Socrates had retired into a neighbouring vestibule, where he stood, and, in spite of his message, refused to come in.—"What absurdity you talk," cried Agathon, "call him, and do not leave him till he comes."—"Leave him alone, by all means," said Aristodemus, "it is customary with him sometimes to retire in this way and stand wherever it may chance. He will come presently, I do not doubt; do not disturb him."—"Well, be it as you will," said Agathon; "as it is, you boys, bring supper for the rest; put before us what you will, for I resolved that there should be no master of the feast. Consider me, and these, my friends, as guests, whom you have invited to supper, and serve them so that we may commend you."

After this they began supper, but Socrates did not come in. Agathon ordered him to be called, but Aristodemus perpetually forbade it. At last he came in, much about the middle of supper, not having delayed so long as was his custom. Agathon (who happened to be reclining at the end of the table, and alone,) said, as he entered, "Come hither, Socrates, and sit down by me; so that by the mere touch of one so wise as you are, I may enjoy the fruit of your meditations in the vestibule; for, I well know, you would not have departed till you had discovered and secured it."

Socrates having sat down as he was desired, replied, "It would be well, Agathon, if wisdom were of such a nature, as that when we touched each other, it would overflow of its own accord, from him who possesses much to him who possesses little; like the water in two chalices, which will flow through a flock of wool from the fuller into the emptier, until both are equal. If wisdom had this property, I should esteem myself most fortunate in reclining near to you. I should thus soon be filled, I think, with the most beautiful and various wisdom. Mine, indeed, is something obscure, and doubtful, and dreamlike. But yours is radiant, and has been crowned with amplest reward; for, though you are yet so young, it shone forth from you, and became so manifest yesterday, that more than thirty thousand Greeks can bear testimony to its excellence and loveliness."—"You are laughing at me, Socrates," said Agathon, "but you and I will decide this controversy about wisdom by and bye, taking Dionysus for our judge. At present turn to your supper."

After Socrates and the rest had finished supper, and had reclined back on their couches, and the libations had been poured forth, and they had sung hymns to the god, and all other rites which are customary had been performed, they turned to drinking. Then Pausanias made this kind of proposal. "Come, my friends," said he, "in what manner will it be pleasantest for us to drink? I must confess to you that, in reality, I am not very well from the wine we drank last night, and I have need of some intermission. I suspect that most of you are in the same condition, for you were here yesterday. Now, consider how we shall drink most easily and comfortably."

" 'Tis a good proposal, Pausanias," said Aristophanes, "to contrive, in some way or other, to place moderation in our cups. I was one of those who were drenched last night."—Eryximachus, the son of Acumenus, hearing this, said: "I am of your opinion; I only wish to know one thing—whether Agathon is in the humour for hard drinking?"—"Not at all," replied Agathon; "I confess that I am not able to drink much this evening."—"It is an excellent thing for us," replied Eryximachus, "I mean myself, Aristodemus, Phaedrus, and these others, if you who are such invincible drinkers, now refuse to drink. I ought to except Socrates, for he is capable of drinking everything, or nothing; and whatever we shall determine will equally suit him. Since, then, no one present has any desire to drink much wine, I shall perhaps give less offence if I declare the nature of drunkenness. The science of medicine teaches us that drunkenness is very pernicious: nor would I choose to drink immoderately myself, or counsel another to do so, especially if he had been drunk the night before."—"Yes," said Phaedrus, the Myrinusian, interrupting him, "I have been accustomed to confide in you, especially in your directions concerning medicine; and I would now willingly do so, if the rest will do the same." All then agreed that they would drink at this present banquet not for drunkenness, but for pleasure.

"Since, then," said Eryximachus, "it is decided that no one shall be compelled to drink more than he pleases, I think that we may as well send away the flute-player to play to herself; or, if she likes, to the women within. Let us devote the present occasion to conversation between ourselves, and if you wish, I will propose to you what shall be the subject of our discussion." All present desired and entreated that he would explain.—"The exordium of my speech," said Eryximachus, "will be in the style of the Menalippe of Euripides, for the story which I am about to tell belongs not to me, but to Phaedrus. Phaedrus has often indignantly complained to me, saying—'Is it not strange, Eryximachus, that there are innumerable hymns and paeans composed for the other gods, but that not one of the many poets who spring up in the world have ever composed a verse in honour of Love, who is such and so great a god? Nor any one of those accomplished sophists, who, like the famous Prodicus, have celebrated the praise of Heracles and others, have ever celebrated that of Love; but what is more astonishing, I have lately met with the book of some philosopher, in which salt is extolled on account of its utility, and many other things of the same nature are in like manner celebrated with elaborate praise. That so much serious thought is expended on such trifles, and that no man has dared to this day to frame a hymn in honour of Love, who being so great a deity, is thus neglected, may well be sufficient to excite my indignation.'

"There seemed to me some justice in these complaints of Phaedrus; I propose, therefore, at the same time for the sake of giving pleasure to Phaedrus, and that we may on the present occasion do something well and befitting us, that this God should receive from those who are now present the honour which is most due to him. If you agree to my proposal, an excellent discussion might arise on the subject. Every one ought, according to my plan, to praise Love with as much eloquence as he can. Let Phaedrus begin first, both because he reclines the first in order, and because he is the father of the discussion."

"No one will vote against you, Eryximachus," said Socrates, "for how can I oppose your proposal, who am ready to confess that I know nothing on any subject but love? Or how can Agathon, or Pausanias, or even Aristophanes, whose life is one perpetual ministration to Aphrodite and Dionysus? Or how can any other whom I see here? Though we who sit last are scarcely on an equality with you; for if those who speak before us shall have exhausted the subject with their eloquence and reasonings, our discourses will be superfluous. But in the name of Good Fortune, let Phaedrus begin and praise Love." The whole party agreed to what Socrates said, and entreated Phaedrus to begin.

What each then said on this subject, Aristodemus did not entirely recollect, nor do I recollect all that he related to me; but only the speeches of those who said what was most worthy of remembrance. First, then, Phaedrus began thus:—

"Love is a mighty deity, and the object of admiration, both to Gods and men, for many and for various claims; but especially on account of his origin. For that he is to be honoured as one of the most ancient of the gods, this may serve as a testimony, that Love has no parents, nor is there any poet or other person who has ever affirmed that there are such. Hesiod says, that first 'Chaos was produced; then the broad-bosomed Earth, to be a secure foundation for all things; then Love.' He says that after Chaos these two were produced, the Earth and Love. Parmenides, speaking of generation, says:—'But he created Love before any of the gods.' Acusilaus agrees with Hesiod. Love, therefore, is universally acknowledged to be among the oldest of things. And in addition to this, Love is the author of our greatest advantages; for I cannot imagine a greater happiness and advantage to one who is in the flower of youth than an amiable lover, or to a lover, than an amiable object of his love. For neither birth, nor wealth, nor honours, can awaken in the minds of men the principles which should guide those who from their youth aspire to an honourable and excellent life, as Love awakens them. I speak of the fear of shame, which deters them from that which is disgraceful; and the love of glory, which incites to honourable deeds. For it is not possible that a state or private person should accomplish, without these incitements, anything beautiful or great. I assert, then, that should one who loves be discovered in any dishonourable action, or tamely enduring insult through cowardice, he would feel more anguish and shame if observed by the object of his passion, than if he were observed by his father, or his companions, or any other person. In like manner, among warmly attached friends, a man is especially grieved to be discovered by his friend in any dishonourable act. If, then, by any contrivance, a state or army could be composed of friends bound by strong attachment, it is beyond calculation how excellently they would administer their affairs, refraining from anything base, contending with each other for the acquirement of fame, and exhibiting such valour in battle as that, though few in numbers, they might subdue all mankind. For should one friend desert the ranks or cast away his arms in the presence of the other, he would suffer far acuter shame from that one person's regard, than from the regard of all other men. A thousand times would he prefer to die, rather than desert the object of his attachment, and not succour him in danger.

"There is none so worthless whom Love cannot impel, as it were by a divine inspiration, towards virtue, even so that he may through this inspiration become equal to one who might naturally be more excellent; and, in truth, as Homer says: The God breathes vigour into certain heroes—so Love breathes into those who love, the spirit which is produced from himself. Not only men, but even women who love, are those alone who willingly expose themselves to die for others. Alcestis, the daughter of Pelias, affords to the Greeks a remarkable example of this opinion; she alone being willing to die for her husband, and so surpassing his parents in the affection with which love inspired her towards him, as to make them appear, in the comparison with her, strangers to their own child, and related to him merely in name; and so lovely and admirable did this action appear, not only to men, but even to the Gods, that, although they conceded the prerogative of bringing back the spirit from death to few among the many who then performed excellent and honourable deeds, yet, delighted with this action, they redeemed her soul from the infernal regions: so highly do the Gods honour zeal and devotion in love. They sent back indeed Orpheus, the son of Oeagrus, from Hell, with his purpose unfulfilled, and, showing him only the spectre of her for whom he came, refused to render up herself. For Orpheus seemed to them, not as Alcestis, to have dared die for the sake of her whom he loved, and thus to secure to himself a perpetual intercourse with her in the regions to which she had preceded him, but like a cowardly musician, to have contrived to descend alive into Hell; and, indeed, they appointed as a punishment for his cowardice, that he should be put to death by women.

"Far otherwise did they reward Achilles, the son of Thetis, whom they sent to inhabit the islands of the blessed. For Achilles, though informed by his mother that his own death would ensue upon his killing Hector, but that if he refrained from it he might return home and die in old age, yet preferred revenging and honouring his beloved Patroclus; not to die for him merely, but to disdain and reject that life which he had ceased to share. Therefore the Greeks honoured Achilles beyond all other men, because he thus preferred his friend to all things else.

"On this account have the Gods rewarded Achilles more amply than Alcestis; permitting his spirit to inhabit the islands of the blessed. Hence do I assert that Love is the most ancient and venerable of deities, and most powerful to endow mortals with the possession of happiness and virtue, both whilst they live and after they die."

Thus Aristodemus reported the discourse of Phaedrus; and after Phaedrus, he said that some others spoke, whose discourses he did not well remember. When they had ceased, Pausanias began thus:—

"Simply to praise Love, O Phaedrus, seems to me too bounded a scope for our discourse. If Love were one, it would be well. But since Love is not one, I will endeavour to distinguish which is the Love whom it becomes us to praise, and having thus discriminated one from the other, will attempt to render him who is the subject of our discourse the honour due to his divinity. We all know that Aphrodite is never without Love; and if Aphrodite were one, Love would be one; but since there are two goddesses, of necessity also must there be two Loves. For assuredly are there two goddesses; one, the eldest, the daughter of Uranus, born without a mother, whom we call the Uranian; the other younger, the daughter of Zeus and Dione, whom we call the Pandemian;—of necessity must there also be two Loves, the Uranian and Pandemian companions of these goddesses. It is becoming to praise all the Gods, but the attributes which fall to the lot of each may be distinguished and selected. For any particular action whatever in itself is neither good nor evil; what we are now doing—drinking, singing, talking, none of these things are good in themselves, but the mode in which they are done stamps them with its own nature; and that which is done well, is good, and that which is done ill, is evil. Thus, not all love, nor every mode of love is beautiful, or worthy of commendation, but that alone which excites us to love worthily. The Love, therefore, which attends upon Aphrodite Pandemos is, in truth, common to the vulgar, and presides over transient and fortuitous connexions, and is worshipped by the least excellent of mankind. The votaries of this deity seek the body rather than the soul, and the ignorant rather than the wise, disdaining all that is honourable and lovely, and considering how they shall best satisfy their sensual necessities. This Love is derived from the younger goddess, who partakes in her nature both of male and female. But the attendant on the other, the Uranian, whose nature is entirely masculine, is the Love who inspires us with affection, and exempts us from all wantonness and libertinism. Those who are inspired by this divinity seek the affections of those who are endowed by nature with greater excellence and vigour both of body and mind. And it is easy to distinguish those who especially exist under the influence of this power, by their choosing in early youth as the objects of their love those in whom the intellectual faculties have begun to develop. For those who begin to love in this manner seem to me to be preparing to pass their whole life together in a community of good and evil, and not ever lightly deceiving those who love them, to be faithless to their vows. There ought to be a law that none should love the very young; so much serious affection as this deity enkindles should not be doubtfully bestowed; for the body and mind of those so young are yet unformed, and it is difficult to foretell what will be their future tendencies and power. The good voluntarily impose this law upon themselves, and those vulgar lovers ought to be compelled to the same observance, as we deter them with all the power of the laws from the love of free matrons. For these are the persons whose shameful actions embolden those who observe their importunity and intemperance to assert, that it is dishonourable to serve and gratify the objects of our love. But no one who does this gracefully and according to law, can justly be liable to the imputation of blame.

"Not only friendship, but philosophy and the practice of the gymnastic exercises, are represented as dishonourable by the tyrannical governments under which the barbarians live. For I imagine it would little conduce to the benefit of the governors, that the governed should be disciplined to lofty thoughts and to the unity and communion of steadfast friendship, of which admirable effects the tyrants of our own country have also learned that Love is the author. For the love of Harmodius and Aristogeiton, strengthened into a firm friendship, dissolved the tyranny. Wherever, therefore, it is declared dishonourable in any case to serve and benefit friends, that law is a mark of the depravity of the legislator, the avarice and tyranny of the rulers, and the cowardice of those who are ruled. Wherever it is simply declared to be honourable without distinction of cases, such a declaration denotes dulness and want of subtlety of mind in the authors of the regulation. Here the degrees of praise or blame to be attributed by law are far better regulated; but it is yet difficult to determine the cases to which they should refer.

"It is evident, however, for one in whom passion is enkindled, it is more honourable to love openly than secretly; and most honourable to love the most excellent and virtuous, even if they should be less beautiful than others. It is honourable for the lover to exhort and sustain the object of his love in virtuous conduct. It is considered honourable to attain the love of those whom we seek, and the contrary shameful; and to facilitate this attainment, opinion has given to the lover the permission of acquiring favour by the most extraordinary devices, which if a person should practise for any purpose besides this, he would incur the severest reproof of philosophy. For if any one desirous of accumulating money, or ambitious of procuring power, or seeking any other advantage, should, like a lover seeking to acquire the favour of his beloved, employ prayers and entreaties in his necessity, and swear such oaths as lovers swear, and sleep before the threshold, and offer to subject himself to such slavery as no slave even would endure; he would be frustrated of the attainment of what he sought, both by his enemies and friends, these reviling him for his flattery, those sharply admonishing him, and taking to themselves the shame of his servility. But there is a certain grace in a lover who does all these things, so that he alone may do them without dishonour. It is commonly said that the Gods accord pardon to the lover alone if he should break his oath, and that there is no oath by Aphrodite. Thus, as our law declares, both gods and men have given to lovers all possible indulgence.

"The affair, however, I imagine, stands thus: As I have before said, love cannot be considered in itself as either honourable or dishonourable: if it is honourably pursued, it is honourable; if dishonourably, dishonourable: it is dishonourable basely to serve and gratify a worthless person; it is honourable honourably to serve a person of virtue. That Pandemic lover who loves rather the body than the soul is worthless, nor can be constant and consistent, since he has placed his affections on that which has no stability. For as soon as the flower of the form, which was the sole object of his desire, has faded, then he departs and is seen no more; bound by no faith nor shame of his many promises and persuasions. But he who is the lover of virtuous manners is constant during life, since he has placed himself in harmony and desire with that which is consistent with itself.

"These two classes of persons we ought to distinguish with careful examination, so that we may serve and converse with the one and avoid the other; determining, by that inquiry, by what a man is attracted, and for what the object of his love is dear to him. On the same account it is considered as dishonourable to be inspired with love at once, lest time should be wanting to know and approve the character of the object. It is considered dishonourable to be captivated by the allurements of wealth and power, or terrified through injuries to yield up the affections, or not to despise in the comparison with an unconstrained choice all political influence and personal advantage. For no circumstance is there in wealth or power so invariable and consistent, as that no generous friendship can ever spring up from amongst them. We have an opinion with respect to lovers which declares that it shall not be considered servile or disgraceful, though the lover should submit himself to any species of slavery for the sake of his beloved. The same opinion holds with respect to those who undergo any degradation for the sake of virtue. And also it is esteemed among us, that if any one chooses to serve and obey another for the purpose of becoming more wise or more virtuous through the intercourse that might thence arise, such willing slavery is not the slavery of a dishonest flatterer. Through this we should consider in the same light a servitude undertaken for the sake of love as one undertaken for the acquirement of wisdom or any other excellence, if indeed the devotion of a lover to his beloved is to be considered a beautiful thing. For when the lover and the beloved have once arrived at the same point, the province of each being distinguished; the one able to assist in the cultivation of the mind and in the acquirement of every other excellence; the other yet requiring education, and seeking the possession of wisdom; then alone, by the union of these conditions, and in no other case, is it honourable for the beloved to yield up the affections to the lover. In this servitude alone there is no disgrace in being deceived and defeated of the object for which it was undertaken, whereas every other is disgraceful, whether we are deceived or no.

"On the same principle, if any one seeks the friendship of another, believing him to be virtuous, for the sake of becoming better through such intercourse and affection, and is deceived, his friend turning out to be worthless, and far from the possession of virtue; yet it is honourable to have been so deceived. For such a one seems to have submitted to a kind of servitude, because he would endure anything for the sake of becoming more virtuous and wise; a disposition of mind eminently beautiful.

"This is that Love who attends on the Uranian deity, and is Uranian; the author of innumerable benefits both to the state and to individuals, and by the necessity of whose influence those who love are disciplined into the zeal of virtue. All other loves are the attendants on Aphrodite Pandemos. So much, although unpremeditated, is what I have to deliver on the subject of love, O Phaedrus."

Pausanias having ceased (for so the learned teach me to denote the changes of the discourse), Aristodemus said that it came to the turn of Aristophanes to speak; but it happened that, from repletion or some other cause, he had an hiccough which prevented him; so he turned to Eryximachus, the physician, who was reclining close beside him, and said—"Eryximachus, it is but fair that you should cure my hiccough, or speak instead of me until it is over."—"I will do both," said Eryximachus; "I will speak in your turn, and you, when your hiccough has ceased, shall speak in mine. Meanwhile, if you hold your breath some time, it will subside. If not, gargle your throat with water; and if it still continue, take something to stimulate your nostrils, and sneeze; do this once or twice, and even though it should be very violent it will cease."—"Whilst you speak," said Aristophanes, "I will follow your directions."—Eryximachus then began:—

"Since Pausanias, beginning his discourse excellently, placed no fit completion and development to it, I think it necessary to attempt to fill up what he has left unfinished. He has reasoned well in defining love as of a double nature. The science of medicine, to which I have addicted myself, seems to teach me that the love which impels towards those who are beautiful, does not subsist only in the souls of men, but in the bodies also of those of all other living beings which are produced upon earth, and, in a word, in all things which are. So wonderful and mighty is this divinity, and so widely is his influence extended over all divine and human things! For the honour of my profession, I will begin by adducing a proof from medicine. The nature of the body contains within itself this double love. For that which is healthy and that which is diseased in a body differ and are unlike: that which is unlike loves and desires that which is unlike. Love, therefore, is different in a sane and in a diseased body. Pausanias has asserted rightly that it is honourable to gratify those things in the body which are good and healthy, and in this consists the skill of the physician; whilst those which are bad and diseased ought to be treated with no indulgence. The science of medicine, in a word, is a knowledge of the love affairs of the body, as they bear relation to repletion and evacuation; and he is the most skilful physician who can trace those operations of the good and evil love, can make the one change places with the other, and attract love into those parts from which he is absent, or expel him from those which he ought not to occupy. He ought to make those things which are most inimical, friendly, and excite them to mutual love. But those things are most inimical which are most opposite to each other; cold to heat, bitterness to sweetness, dryness to moisture. Our progenitor, Asclepius, as the poets inform us, (and indeed I believe them,) through the skill which he possessed to inspire love and concord in these contending principles, established the science of medicine.

"The gymnastic arts and agriculture, no less than medicine, are exercised under the dominion of this God. Music, as any one may perceive who yields a very slight attention to the subject, originates from the same source; which Heracleitus probably meant, though he could not express his meaning very clearly in words, when he says, 'One though apparently differing, yet so agrees with itself, as the harmony of a lyre and a bow.' It is great absurdity to say that a harmony differs, and can exist between things whilst they are dissimilar; but probably he meant that from sounds which first differed, like the grave and the acute, and which afterwards agreed, harmony was produced according to musical art. For no harmony can arise from the grave and the acute whilst yet they differ. But harmony is symphony: symphony is, as it were, concord. But it is impossible that concord should subsist between things that differ, so long as they differ. Between things which are discordant and dissimilar there is then no harmony. A rhythm is produced from that which is quick, and that which is slow, first being distinguished and opposed to each other, and then made accordant; so does medicine, no less than music, establish a concord between the objects of its art, producing love and agreement between adverse things.

"Music is then the knowledge of that which relates to love in harmony and system. In the very system of harmony and rhythm, it is easy to distinguish love. The double love is not distinguishable in music itself; but it is required to apply it to the service of mankind by system and harmony, which is called poetry, or the composition of melody; or by the correct use of songs and measures already composed, which is called discipline; then one can be distinguished from the other, by the aid of an extremely skilful artist. And the better love ought to be honoured and preserved for the sake of those who are virtuous, and that the nature of the vicious may be changed through the inspiration of its spirit. This is that beautiful Uranian love, the attendant on the Uranian muse: the Pandemian is the attendant of Polyhymnia; to whose influence we should only so far subject ourselves, as to derive pleasure from it without indulging to excess; in the same manner as, according to our art, we are instructed to seek the pleasures of the table, only so far as we can enjoy them without the consequences of disease. In music, therefore, and in medicine, and in all other things, human and divine, this double love ought to be traced and discriminated; for it is in all things.

"Even the constitution of the seasons of the year is penetrated with these contending principles. For so often as heat and cold, dryness and moisture, of which I spoke before, are influenced by the more benignant love, and are harmoniously and temperately intermingled with the seasons, they bring maturity and health to men, and to all the other animals and plants. But when the evil and injurious love assumes the dominion of the seasons of the year, destruction is spread widely abroad. Then pestilence is accustomed to arise, and many other blights and diseases fall upon animals and plants: and hoar frosts, and hails, and mildew on the corn, are produced from that excessive and disorderly love, with which each season of the year is impelled towards the other; the motions of which and the knowledge of the stars, is called astronomy. All sacrifices, and all those things in which divination is concerned (for these things are the links by which is maintained an intercourse and communion between the Gods and men), are nothing else than the science of preservation and right government of Love. For impiety is accustomed to spring up, so soon as any one ceases to serve the more honourable Love, and worship him by the sacrifice of good actions; but submits himself to the influences of the other, in relation to his duties towards his parents, and the Gods, and the living, and the dead. It is the object of divination to distinguish and remedy the effects of these opposite loves; and divination is therefore the author of the friendship of Gods and men, because it affords the knowledge of what in matters of love is lawful or unlawful to men.

"Thus every species of love possesses collectively a various and vast, or rather universal power. But love which incites to the acquirement of its objects according to virtue and wisdom, possesses the most exclusive dominion, and prepares for his worshippers the highest happiness through the mutual intercourse of social kindness which it promotes among them, and through the benevolence which he attracts to them from the Gods, our superiors.

"Probably in thus praising Love, I have unwillingly omitted many things; but it is your business, O Aristophanes, to fill up all that I have left incomplete; or, if you have imagined any other mode of honouring the divinity: for I observe your hiccough is over."

"Yes," said Aristophanes, "but not before I applied the sneezing. I wonder why the harmonious construction of our body should require such noisy operations as sneezing; for it ceased the moment I sneezed."—"Do you not observe what you do, my good Aristophanes?" said Eryximachus; "you are going to speak, and you predispose us to laughter, and compel me to watch for the first ridiculous idea which you may start in your discourse, when you might have spoken in peace."—"Let me unsay what I have said, then," replied Aristophanes, laughing. "Do not watch me, I entreat you; though I am not afraid of saying what is laughable (since that would be all gain, and quite in the accustomed spirit of my muse), but lest I should say what is ridiculous."—"Do you think to throw your dart, and escape with impunity, Aristophanes? Attend, and what you say be careful you maintain; then, perhaps, if it pleases me, I may dismiss you without question."

"Indeed, Eryximachus," proceeded Aristophanes, "I have designed that my discourse should be very different from yours and that of Pausanias. It seems to me that mankind are by no means penetrated with a conception of the power of Love, or they would have built sumptuous temples and altars, and have established magnificent rites of sacrifice in his honour; he deserves worship and homage more than all the other Gods, and he has yet received none. For Love is of all the Gods the most friendly to mortals; and the physician of those wounds, whose cure would be the greatest happiness which could be conferred upon the human race. I will endeavour to unfold to you his true power, and you can relate what I declare to others.

"You ought first to know the nature of man, and the adventures he has gone through; for his nature was anciently far different from that which it is at present. First, then, human beings were formerly not divided into two sexes, male and female; there was also a third, common to both the others, the name of which remains, though the sex itself has disappeared. The androgynous sex, both in appearance and in name, was common both to male and female; its name alone remains, which labours under a reproach.

"At the period to which I refer, the form of every human being was round, the back and the sides being circularly joined, and each had four arms and as many legs; two faces fixed upon a round neck, exactly like each other; one head between the two faces; four ears, and everything else as from such proportions it is easy to conjecture. Man walked upright as now, in whatever direction he pleased; but when he wished to go fast he made use of all his eight limbs, and proceeded in a rapid motion by rolling circularly round,—like tumblers, who, with their legs in the air, tumble round and round. We account for the production of three sexes by supposing that, at the beginning, the male was produced from the sun, the female from the earth; and that sex which participated in both sexes, from the moon, by reason of the androgynous nature of the moon. They were round, and their mode of proceeding was round, from the similarity which must needs subsist between them and their parent.

"They were strong also, and had aspiring thoughts. They it was who levied war against the Gods; and what Homer writes concerning Ephialtes and Otys, that they sought to ascend heaven and dethrone the Gods, in reality relates to this primitive people. Zeus and the other Gods debated what was to be done in this emergency. For neither could they prevail on themselves to destroy them, as they had the giants, with thunder, so that the race should be abolished; for in that case they would be deprived of the honours of the sacrifices which they were in the custom of receiving from them; nor could they permit a continuance of their insolence and impiety. Zeus, with some difficulty having desired silence, at length spoke. 'I think,' said he, 'I have contrived a method by which we may, by rendering the human race more feeble, quell the insolence which they exercise, without proceeding to their utter destruction. I will cut each of them in half; and so they will at once be weaker and more useful on account of their numbers. They shall walk upright on two legs. If they show any more insolence, and will not keep quiet, I will cut them up in half again, so they shall go about hopping on one leg.'

"So saying, he cut human beings in half, as people cut eggs before they salt them, or as I have seen eggs cut with hairs. He ordered Apollo to take each one as he cut him, and turn his face and half his neck towards the operation, so that by contemplating it he might become more cautious and humble; and then, to cure him, Apollo turned the face round, and drawing the skin upon what we now call the belly, like a contracted pouch, and leaving one opening, that which is called the navel, tied it in the middle. He then smoothed many other wrinkles, and moulded the breast with much such an instrument as the leather-cutters use to smooth the skins upon the block. He left only a few wrinkles in the belly, near the navel, to serve as a record of its former adventure. Immediately after this division, as each desired to possess the other half of himself, these divided people threw their arms around and embraced each other, seeking to grow together; and from this resolution to do nothing without the other half, they died of hunger and weakness: when one half died and the other was left alive, that which was thus left sought the other and folded it to its bosom; whether that half were an entire woman (for we now call it a woman) or a man; and thus they perished. But Zeus, pitying them, thought of another contrivance. In this manner is generation now produced, by the union of male and female; so that from the embrace of a man and woman the race is propagated.

"From this period, mutual love has naturally existed between human beings; that reconciler and bond of union of their original nature, which seeks to make two one, and to heal the divided nature of man. Every one of us is thus the half of what may be properly termed a man, and like a pselta cut in two, is the imperfect portion of an entire whole, perpetually necessitated to seek the half belonging to him.

"Such as I have described is ever an affectionate lover and a faithful friend, delighting in that which is in conformity with his own nature. Whenever, therefore, any such as I have described are impetuously struck, through the sentiment of their former union, with love and desire and the want of community, they are unwilling to be divided even for a moment. These are they who devote their whole lives to each other, with a vain and inexpressible longing to obtain from each other something they know not what; for it is not merely the sensual delights of their intercourse for the sake of which they dedicate themselves to each other with such serious affection; but the soul of each manifestly thirsts for, from the other, something which there are no words to describe, and divines that which it seeks, and traces obscurely the footsteps of its obscure desire. If Hephaestus should say to persons thus affected, 'My good people, what is it that you want with one another?' And if, while they were hesitating what to answer, he should proceed to ask, 'Do you not desire the closest union and singleness to exist between you, so that you may never be divided night or day? If so, I will melt you together, and make you grow into one, so that both in life and death ye may be undivided. Consider, is this what you desire? Will it content you if you become that which I propose?' We all know that no one would refuse such an offer, but would at once feel that this was what he had ever sought; and intimately to mix and melt and to be melted together with his beloved, so that one should be made out of two.

"The cause of this desire is, that according to our original nature, we were once entire. The desire and the pursuit of integrity and union is that which we all love. First, as I said, we were entire, but now we have been dwindled through our own weakness, as the Arcadians by the Lacedaemonians. There is reason to fear, if we are guilty of any additional impiety towards the Gods, that we may be cut in two again, and may go about like those figures painted on the columns, divided through the middle of our nostrils, as thin as lispae. On which account every man ought to be exhorted to pay due reverence to the Gods, that we may escape so severe a punishment, and obtain those things which Love, our general and commander, incites us to desire; against whom let none rebel by exciting the hatred of the Gods. For if we continue on good terms with them, we may discover and possess those lost and concealed objects of our love; a good fortune which now befalls to few.

"I assert, then, that the happiness of all, both men and women, consists singly in the fulfilment of their love, and in that possession of its objects by which we are in some degree restored to our ancient nature. If this be the completion of felicity, that must necessarily approach nearest to it, in which we obtain the possession and society of those whose natures most intimately accord with our own. And if we would celebrate any God as the author of this benefit, we should justly celebrate

Love with hymns of joy; who, in our present condition, brings good assistance in our necessity, and affords great hopes, if we persevere in piety towards the Gods, that he will restore us to our original state, and confer on us the complete happiness alone suited to our nature.

"Such, Eryximachus, is my discourse on the subject of Love; different indeed from yours, which I nevertheless entreat you not to turn into ridicule, that we may not interrupt what each has separately to deliver on the subject."

"I will refrain at present," said Eryximachus, "for your discourse delighted me. And if I did not know that Socrates and Agathon were profoundly versed in the science of love affairs, I should fear that they had nothing new to say, after so many and such various imaginations. As it is, I confide in the fertility of their geniuses."—"Your part of the contest, at least, was strenuously fought, Eryximachus," said Socrates, "but if you had been in the situation in which I am, or rather shall be, after the discourse of Agathon, like me, you would then have reason to fear, and be reduced to your wits' end."—"Socrates," said Agathon, "wishes to confuse me with the enchantments of his wit, sufficiently confused already with the expectation I see in the assembly in favour of my discourse."—"I must have lost my memory, Agathon," replied Socrates, "if I imagine that you could be disturbed by a few private persons, after having witnessed your firmness and courage in ascending the rostrum with the actors, and in calmly reciting your compositions in the presence of so great an assembly as that which decreed you the prize of tragedy."—"What then, Socrates," retorted Agathon, "do you think me so full of the theatre as to be ignorant that the judgment of a few wise is more awful than that of a multitude of others, to one who rightly balances the value of their suffrages?"—"I should judge ill indeed, Agathon," answered Socrates, "in thinking you capable of any rude and unrefined conception, for I well know that if you meet with any whom you consider wise, you esteem such alone of more value than all others. But we are far from being entitled to this distinction, for we were also of that assembly, and to be numbered among the rest. But should you meet with any who are really wise, you would be careful to say nothing in their presence which you thought they would not approve—is it not so?"—"Certainly," replied Agathon.—"You would not then exercise the same caution in the presence of the multitude in which they were included?"—"My dear Agathon," said Phaedrus, interrupting him, "if you answer all the questions of Socrates, they will never have an end; he will urge them without conscience so long as he can get any person, especially one who is so beautiful, to dispute with him. I own it delights me to hear Socrates discuss; but at present, I must see that Love is not defrauded of the praise, which it is my province to exact from each of you. Pay the God his due, and then reason between yourselves if you will."

"Your admonition is just, Phaedrus," replied Agathon, "nor need any reasoning I hold with Socrates impede me: we shall find many future opportunities for discussion. I will begin my discourse then; first having defined what ought to be the subject of it. All who have already spoken seem to me not so much to have praised Love, as to have felicitated mankind on the many advantages of which that deity is the cause; what he is, the author of these great benefits, none have yet declared. There is one mode alone of celebration which would comprehend the whole topic, namely, first to declare what are those benefits, and then what he is who is the author of those benefits, which are the subject of our discourse. Love ought first to be praised, and then his gifts declared. I assert, then, that although all the Gods are immortally happy, Love, if I dare trust my voice to express so awful a truth, is the happiest, and most excellent, and the most beautiful. That he is the most beautiful is evident; first, O Phaedrus, from this circumstance, that he is the youngest of the Gods; and, secondly, from his fleetness, and from his repugnance to all that is old; for he escapes with the swiftness of wings from old age; a thing in itself sufficiently swift, since it overtakes us sooner than there is need; and which Love, who delights in the intercourse of the young, hates, and in no manner can be induced to enter into community with. The ancient proverb, which says that like is attracted by like, applies to the attributes of Love. I concede many things to you, O Phaedrus, but this I do not concede, that Love is more ancient than Cronus and Zeus. I assert that he is not only the youngest of the Gods, but invested with everlasting youth. Those ancient deeds among the Gods recorded by Hesiod and Parmenides, if their relations are to be considered as true, were produced not by Love, but by Necessity. For if Love had been then in Heaven, those violent and sanguinary crimes never would have taken place; but there would ever have subsisted that affection and peace, in which the Gods now live, under the influence of Love.

"He is young, therefore, and being young is tender and soft. There were need of some poet like Homer to celebrate the delicacy and tenderness of Love. For Homer says, that the goddess Calamity is delicate, and that her feet are tender. 'Her feet are soft,' he says, 'for she treads not upon the ground, but makes her path upon the heads of men.' He gives as an evidence of her tenderness, that she walks not upon that which is hard, but that which is soft. The same evidence is sufficient to make manifest the tenderness of Love. For Love walks not upon the earth, nor over the heads of men, which are not indeed very soft; but he dwells within, and treads on the softest of existing things, having established his habitation within the souls and inmost nature of Gods and men; not indeed in all souls—for wherever he chances to find a hard and rugged disposition, there he will not inhabit, but only where it is most soft and tender. Of needs must he be the most delicate of all things, who touches lightly with his feet only the softest parts of those things which are the softest of all.

"He is then the youngest and the most delicate of all divinities; and in addition to this, he is, as it were, the most moist and liquid. For if he were otherwise, he could not, as he does, fold himself around everything, and secretly flow out and into every soul. His loveliness, that which Love possesses far beyond all other things, is a manifestation of the liquid and flowing symmetry of his form; for between deformity and Love there is eternal contrast and repugnance. His life is spent among flowers, and this accounts for the immortal fairness of his skin; for the winged Love rests not in his flight on any form, or within any soul the flower of whose loveliness is faded, but there remains most willingly where is the odour and radiance of blossoms, yet unwithered. Concerning the beauty of the God, let this be sufficient, though many things must remain unsaid. Let us next consider the virtue and power of Love.

"What is most admirable in Love is, that he neither inflicts nor endures injury in his relations either with Gods or men. Nor if he suffers any thing does he suffer it through violence, nor doing any thing does he act it with violence, for Love is never even touched with violence. Every one willingly administers every thing to Love; and that which every one voluntarily concedes to another, the laws, which are the kings of the republic, decree that is just for him to possess. In addition to justice, Love participates in the highest temperance; for if temperance is defined to be the being superior to and holding under dominion pleasures and desires; then Love, than whom no pleasure is more powerful, and who is thus more powerful than all persuasions and delights, must be excellently temperate. In power and valour Ares cannot contend with Love: the love of Aphrodite possesses Ares; the possessor is always superior to the possessed, and he who subdues the most powerful must of necessity be the most powerful of all.

"The justice and temperance and valour of the God have been thus declared;—there remains to exhibit his wisdom. And first, that, like Eryximachus, I may honour my own profession, the God is a wise poet; so wise that he can even make a poet one who was not before: for every one, even if before he were ever so undisciplined, becomes a poet as soon as he is touched by Love;—a sufficient proof that Love is a great poet, and well skilled in that science according to the discipline of music. For what any one possesses not, or knows not, that can he neither give nor teach another. And who will deny that the divine poetry, by which all living things are produced upon the earth, is not harmonised by the wisdom of Love? Is it not evident that Love was the author of all the arts of life with which we are acquainted, and that he whose teacher has been Love, becomes eminent and illustrious, whilst he who knows not Love, remains forever unregarded and obscure? Apollo invented medicine, and divination, and archery, under the guidance of desire and Love; so that Apollo was the disciple of Love. Through him the Muses discovered the arts of literature, and Hephaestus that of moulding brass, and Athena the loom, and Zeus the mystery of the dominion which he now exercises over gods and men. So were the Gods taught and disciplined by the love of that which is beautiful; for there is no love towards deformity.

"At the origin of things, as I have before said, many fearful deeds are reported to have been done among the Gods, on account of the dominion of Necessity. But so soon as this deity sprang forth from the desire which forever tends in the universe towards that which is lovely, then all blessings descended upon all living things, human and divine. Love seems to me, O Phaedrus, a divinity the most beautiful and the best of all, and the author to all others of the excellencies with which his own nature is endowed. Nor can I restrain the poetic enthusiasm which takes possession of my discourse, and bids me declare that Love is the divinity who creates peace among men, and calm upon the sea, the windless silence of storms, repose and sleep in sadness. Love divests us of all alienation from each other, and fills our vacant hearts with overflowing sympathy; he gathers us together in such social meetings as we now delight to celebrate, our guardian and our guide in dances, and sacrifices, and feasts. Yes, Love, who showers benignity upon the world, and before whose presence all harsh passions flee and perish; the author of all soft affections; the destroyer of all ungentle thoughts; merciful, mild; the object of the admiration of the wise, and the delight of gods; possessed by the fortunate, and desired by the unhappy, therefore unhappy because they possess him not; the father of grace, and delicacy, and gentleness, and delight, and persuasion, and desire; the cherisher of all that is good, the abolisher of all evil; our most excellent pilot, defence, saviour and guardian in labour and in fear, in desire and in reason; the ornament and governor of all things human and divine; the best, the loveliest; in whose footsteps every one ought to follow, celebrating him excellently in song, and bearing each his part in that divinest harmony which Love sings to all things which live and are, soothing the troubled minds of Gods and men. This, O Phaedrus, is what I have to offer in praise of the divinity; partly composed, indeed, of thoughtless and playful fancies, and partly of such serious ones as I could well command."

No sooner had Agathon ceased, than a loud murmur of applause arose from all present; so becomingly had the fair youth spoken, both in praise of the God, and in extenuation of himself. Then Socrates, addressing Eryximachus, said, "Was not my fear reasonable, son of Acumenus? Did I not divine what has, in fact, happened,—that Agathon's discourse would be so wonderfully beautiful, as to preoccupy all interest in what I should say?"—"You, indeed, divined well so far, O Socrates," said Eryximachus, "that Agathon would speak eloquently, but not that, therefore, you would be reduced to any difficulty."—"How, my good friend, can I or any one else be otherwise than reduced to difficulty, who speak after a discourse so various and so eloquent, and which otherwise had been sufficiently wonderful, if, at the conclusion, the splendour of the sentences, and the choice selection of the expressions, had not struck all the hearers with astonishment; so that I, who well know that

I can never say anything nearly so beautiful as this, would, if there had been any escape, have run away for shame. The story of Gorgias came into my mind, and I was afraid lest in reality I should suffer what Homer describes; and lest Agathon, scanning my discourse with the Gorgonian head of the master of rhetoric, should turn me to stone for speechlessness. I immediately perceived how ridiculously I had engaged myself with you to assume a part in rendering praise to love, and had boasted that I was well skilled in amatory matters, being so ignorant of the manner in which it is becoming to render him honour, as I now perceive myself to be. I, in my simplicity, imagined that the truth ought to be spoken concerning each of the topics of our praise, and that it would be sufficient, choosing those which are the most honourable to the God, to place them in as luminous an arrangement as we could. I had, therefore, great hopes that I should speak satisfactorily, being well aware that I was acquainted with the true foundations of the praise which we have engaged to render. But since, as it appears, our purpose has been, not to render Love his due honour, but to accumulate the most beautiful and the greatest attributes of his divinity, whether they in truth belong to it or not, and that the proposed question is not how Love ought to be praised, but how we should praise him most eloquently, my attempt must of necessity fail. It is on this account, I imagine, that in your discourses you have attributed everything to Love, and have described him to be the author of such and so great effects as, to those who are ignorant of his true nature, may exhibit him as the most beautiful and the best of all things. Not, indeed, to those who know the truth. Such praise has a splendid and imposing effect, but as I am unacquainted with the art of rendering it, my mind, which could not foresee what would be required of me, absolves me from that which my tongue promised. Farewell, then, for such praise I can never render.

"But if you desire, I will speak what I feel to be true; and that I may not expose myself to ridicule, I entreat you to consider that I speak without entering into competition with those who have preceded me. Consider, then, Phaedrus, whether you will exact from me such a discourse, containing the mere truth with respect to Love, and composed of such unpremeditated expressions as may chance to offer themselves to my mind."—Phaedrus and the rest bade him speak in the manner which he judged most befitting.—"Permit me, then, O Phaedrus, to ask Agathon a few questions, so that, confirmed by his agreement with me, I may proceed."—"Willingly," replied Phaedrus, "ask." —Then Socrates thus began:—

"I applaud, dear Agathon, the beginning of your discourse, where you say we ought first to define and declare what Love is, and then his works. This rule I particularly approve. But, come, since you have given us a discourse of such beauty and majesty concerning Love, you are able, I doubt not, to explain this question, whether Love is the love of something or nothing? I do not ask you of what parents Love is; for the inquiry, of whether Love is the love of any father or mother, would be sufficiently ridiculous. But if I were asking you to describe that which a father is, I should ask, not whether a father was the love of any one, but whether a father was the father of any one or not; you would undoubtedly reply, that a father was the father of a son or daughter; would you not?"— "Assuredly."—"You would define a mother in the same manner?"—"Without doubt."—"Yet bear with me, and answer a few more questions, for I would learn from you that which I wish to know. If I should inquire, in addition, is not a brother, through the very nature of his relation, the brother of some one?"—"Certainly." —"Of a brother or sister, is he not?"—"Without question."—"Try to explain to me then the nature of Love; Love is the love of something or nothing?"—"Of something, certainly."

"Observe and remember this concession. Tell me yet farther, whether Love desires that of which it is the Love or not?"—"It desires it, assuredly."—"Whether possessing that which it desires and loves, or not possessing it, does it desire and love?" —"Not possessing it, I should imagine."—"Observe now, whether it does not appear, that, of necessity, desire desires that which it wants and does not possess, and no longer desires that which it no longer wants: this appears to me, Agathon, of necessity to be; how does it appear to you?"—"It appears so to me also." —"Would any one who was already illustrious, desire to be illustrious; would any one already strong, desire to be strong? From what has already been conceded, it follows that he would not. If any one already strong, should desire to be strong; or any one already swift, should desire to be swift; or any one already healthy, should desire to be healthy, it must be concluded that they still desired the advantages of which they already seemed possessed. To destroy the foundation of this error, observe, Agathon, that each of these persons must possess the several advantages in question, at the moment present to our thoughts, whether he will or no. And, now, is it possible that those advantages should be at that time the objects of his desire? For, if any one should say, being in health, 'I desire to be in health'; being rich, 'I desire to be rich, and thus still desire those things which I already possess'; we might say to him, 'You, my friend, possess health, and strength, and riches; you do not desire to possess now, but to continue to possess them in future; for, whether you will or no, they now belong to you. Consider then, whether, when you say that you desire things present to you, and in your own possession, you say anything else than that you desire the advantages to be for the future also in your possession.' What else could he reply?"—"Nothing, indeed."—"Is not Love, then, the love of that which is not within its reach, and which cannot hold in security, for the future, those things of which it obtains a present and transitory possession?"—"Evidently."—"Love, therefore, and everything else that desires anything, desires that which is absent and beyond his reach, that which it has not, that which is not itself, that which it wants; such are the things of which there are desire and love?"—"Assuredly."

"Come," said Socrates, "let us review your concessions. Is Love anything else than the love first of something; and, secondly, of those things of which it has need?"—"Nothing."—"Now, remember of those things you said in your discourse, that Love was the love—if you wish I will remind you. I think you said something of this kind, that all the affairs of the gods were admirably disposed through the love of the things which are beautiful; for, there was no love of things deformed; did you not say so?"—"I confess that I did."—"You said what was most likely to be true, my friend; and if the matter be so, the love of beauty must be one thing, and the love of deformity another."—"Certainly."—"It is conceded, then, that Love loves that which he wants but possesses not?"—"Yes, certainly."—"But Love wants and does not possess beauty?"—"Indeed it must necessarily follow."—"What, then! call you that beautiful which has need of beauty and possesses not?"—"Assuredly no."—"Do you still assert, then, that Love is beautiful, if all that we have said be true?"—"Indeed, Socrates," said Agathon, "I am in danger of being convicted of ignorance, with respect to all that I then spoke."—"You spoke most eloquently, my dear Agathon; but bear with my questions yet a moment. You admit that things which are good are also beautiful?"—"No doubt."—"If Love, then, be in want of beautiful things, and things which are good are beautiful, he must be in want of things which are good?"—"I cannot refute your arguments, Socrates."—"You cannot refute truth, my dear Agathon: to refute Socrates is nothing difficult.

"But I will dismiss these questionings. At present let me endeavour, to the best of my power, to repeat to you, on the basis of the points which have been agreed upon between me and Agathon, a discourse concerning Love, which I formerly heard from the prophetess Diotima, who was profoundly skilled in this and many other doctrines, and who, ten years before the plague, procured to the Athenians, through their sacrifices, a delay of the disease; for it was she who taught me the science of things relating to Love.

"As you well remarked, Agathon, we ought to declare who and what is Love, and then his works. It is easiest to relate them in the same order as the foreign prophetess observed when, questioning me, she related them. For I said to her much the same things that Agathon has just said to me—that Love was a great deity, and that he was beautiful; and she refuted me with the same reasons as I have employed to refute Agathon, compelling me to infer that he was neither beautiful nor good, as I said.—'What then,' I objected, 'O Diotima, is Love ugly and evil?'—'Good words, I entreat you,' said Diotima; 'do you think that every thing which is not beautiful, must of necessity be ugly?'—'Certainly.'—'And everything that is not wise, ignorant? Do you not perceive that there is something between ignorance and wisdom?'—'What is that?'—'To have a right opinion or conjecture. Observe, that this kind of opinion, for which no reason can be rendered, cannot be called knowledge; for how can that be called knowledge, which is without evidence or reason? Nor ignorance, on the other hand; for how can that be called ignorance which arrives at the persuasion of that which it really is? A right opinion is something between understanding and ignorance.'—I confessed that what she alleged was true.—'Do not then say,' she continued, 'that what is not beautiful is of necessity deformed, nor what is not good is of necessity evil; nor, since you have confessed that Love is neither beautiful nor good, infer, therefore, that he is deformed or evil, but rather something intermediate.'

" 'But,' I said, 'love is confessed by all to be a great God.'—'Do you mean, when you say all, all those who know, or those who know not, what they say?'—'All collectively.'—'And how can that be, Socrates?' said she laughing; 'how can he be acknowledged to be a great God, by those who assert that he is not even a God at all ?'—'And who are they?' I said—'You for one, and I for another.'—'How can you say that, Diotima?'—'Easily,' she replied, 'and with truth; for tell me, do you not own that all the Gods are beautiful and happy? or will you presume to maintain that any God is otherwise?'—'By Zeus, not I!'—'Do you not call those alone happy who possess all things that are beautiful and good?'—'Certainly.'—'You have confessed that Love, through his desire for things beautiful and good, possesses not those materials of happiness.'—'Indeed such was my concession.'—'But how can we conceive a God to be without the possession of what is beautiful and good?'—'In no manner, I confess.'—'Observe, then, that you do not consider Love to be a God.'—'What, then,' I said, 'is Love a mortal?'—'By no means.'—'But what, then?'—'Like those things which I have before instanced, he is neither mortal nor immortal, but something intermediate.'—'What is that, O Diotima?'—'A great daemon, Socrates; and everything daemoniacal holds an intermediate place between what is divine and what is mortal.'

"'What is his power and nature?' I inquired.—'He interprets and makes a communication between divine and human things, conveying the prayers and sacrifices of men to the Gods, and communicating the commands and directions concerning the mode of worship most pleasing to them, from Gods to men. He fills up that intermediate space between these two classes of beings, so as to bind together, by his own power, the whole universe of things. Through him subsist all divination, and the science of sacred things as it relates to sacrifices, and expiations, and disenchantments, and prophecy, and magic. The divine nature cannot immediately communicate with what is human, but all that intercourse and converse which is conceded by the Gods to men, both whilst they sleep and when they wake, subsists through the intervention of Love; and he who is wise in the science of this intercourse is supremely happy, and participates in the daemoniacal nature; whilst he who is wise in any other science or art, remains a mere ordinary slave. These daemons are, indeed, many and various, and one of them is Love.'

"'Who are the parents of Love?' I inquired.—'The history of what you ask,' replied Diotima, 'is somewhat long; nevertheless

I will explain it to you. On the birth of Aphrodite the Gods celebrated a great feast, and among them came Plenty, the son of Metis. After supper, Poverty, observing the profusion, came to beg, and stood beside the door. Plenty being drunk with nectar, for wine was not yet invented, went out into Zeus' garden, and fell into a deep sleep. Poverty wishing to have a child by Plenty, on account of her low estate, lay down by him, and from his embraces conceived Love. Love is, therefore, the follower and servant of Aphrodite, because he was conceived at her birth, and because by nature he is a lover of all that is beautiful, and Aphrodite was beautiful. And since Love is the child of Poverty and Plenty, his nature and fortune participate in that of his parents. He is for ever poor, and so far from being delicate and beautiful, as mankind imagine, he is squalid and withered; he flies low along the ground, and is homeless and unsandalled; he sleeps without covering before the doors, and in the unsheltered streets; possessing thus far his mother's nature, that he is ever the companion of want. But, inasmuch as he participates in that of his father, he is for ever scheming to obtain things which are good and beautiful; he is fearless, vehement, and strong; a dreadful hunter, for ever weaving some new contrivance; exceedingly cautious and prudent, and full of resources; he is also, during his whole existence, a philosopher, a powerful enchanter, a wizard, and a subtle sophist. And, as his nature is neither mortal nor immortal, on the same day when he is fortunate and successful, he will at one time flourish, and then die away, and then, according to his father's nature, again revive. All that he acquires perpetually flows away from him, so that Love is never either rich or poor, and holding for ever an intermediate state between ignorance and wisdom. The case stands thus;—no God philosophises or desires to become wise, for he is wise; nor, if there exist any other being who is wise, does he philosophise. Nor do the ignorant philosophise, for they desire not to become wise; for this is the evil of ignorance, that he who has neither intelligence, nor virtue, nor delicacy of sentiment, imagines that he possesses all those things sufficiently. He seeks not, therefore, that possession, of whose want he is not aware.'—'Who, then, O Diotima,' I inquired, 'are philosophers, if they are neither the ignorant nor the wise?'—'It is evident, even to a child, that they are those intermediate persons, among whom is Love. For Wisdom is one of the most beautiful of all things; Love is that which thirsts for the beautiful, so that

Love is of necessity a philosopher, philosophy being an intermediate state between ignorance and wisdom. His parentage accounts for his condition, being the child of a wise and well provided father, and of a mother both ignorant and poor.

" 'Such is the daemoniacal nature, my dear Socrates; nor do I wonder at your error concerning Love, for you thought, as I conjecture from what you say, that Love was not the lover but the beloved, and thence, well concluded that he must be supremely beautiful; for that which is the object of Love must indeed be fair, and delicate, and perfect, and most happy; but Love inherits, as I have declared, a totally opposite nature.'—'Your words have persuasion in them, O stranger,' I said; 'be it as you say. But this Love, what advantages does he afford to men?'—'I will proceed to explain it to you, Socrates. Love being such and so produced as I have described, is, indeed, as you say, the love of things which are beautiful. But if any one should ask us, saying: O Socrates and Diotima, why is Love the love of beautiful things? Or, in plainer words, what does the lover of that which is beautiful, love in the object of his love, and seek from it?'—'He seeks,' I said, interrupting her, 'the property and possession of it.'—'But that,' she replied, 'might still be met with another question, What has he, who possesses that which is beautiful?'—'Indeed, I cannot immediately reply.'—'But, if changing the beautiful for good, any one should inquire,—I ask, O Socrates, what is that which he who loves that which is good, loves in the object of his love?'—'To be in his possession,' I replied.—'And what has he, who has the possession of good?' —'This question is of easier solution, he is happy.'—'Those who are happy, then, are happy through the possession; and it is useless to inquire what he desires, who desires to be happy; the question seems to have a complete reply. But do you think that this wish and this love are common to all men, and that all desire that that which is good should be for ever present to them?'—'Certainly, common to all.'—'Why do we not say then, Socrates, that every one loves? if, indeed, all love perpetually the same thing? But we say that some love, and some do not.'—'Indeed I wonder why it is so.'—'Wonder not,' said Diotima, 'for we select a particular species of love, and apply to it distinctively, the appellation of that which is universal.'

" 'Give me an example of such a select application.'—'Poetry; which is a general name signifying every cause whereby anything proceeds from that which is not, into that which is; so that the exercise of every inventive art is poetry, and all such artists poets. Yet they are not called poets, but distinguished by other names; and one portion or species of poetry, that which has relation to music and rhythm, is divided from all others, and known by the name belonging to all. For this is alone properly called poetry, and those who exercise the art of this species of poetry, poets. So with respect to Love. Love is indeed universally all that earnest desire for the possession of happiness and that which is good; the greatest and the subtlest love, and which inhabits the heart of every living being; but those who seek this object through the acquirement of wealth, or the exercise of the gymnastic arts, or philosophy, are not said to love, nor are called lovers; one species alone is called love, and those alone are said to be lovers, and to love, who seek the attainment of the universal desire through one species of love, which is peculiarly distinguished by the name belonging to the whole. It is asserted by some, that they love, who are seeking the lost half of their divided being. But I assert, that Love is neither the love of half nor of the whole, unless, my friend, it meets with that which is good; since men willingly cut off their own hands and feet, if they think that they are the cause of evil to them. Nor do they cherish and embrace that which may belong to themselves, merely because it is their own; unless, indeed, any one should choose to say, that that which is good is attached to his own nature and is his own, whilst that which is evil is foreign and accidental; but love nothing but that which is good. Does it not appear so to you?'—'Assuredly.'—'Can we then simply affirm that men love that which is good?'—'Without doubt.'—'What, then, must we not add, that, in addition to loving that which is good, they love that it should be present to themselves?'—'Indeed that must be added.'—'And not merely that it should be present, but that it should ever be present?'—'This also must be added.'

" 'Love, then, is collectively the desire in men that good should be for ever present to them.'—'Most true.'—'Since this is the general definition of Love, can you explain in what mode of attaining its object, and in what species of actions, does Love peculiarly consist?'—'If I knew what you ask, O Diotima, I should not have so much wondered at your wisdom, nor have sought you out for the purpose of deriving improvement from your instructions.'—'I will tell you,' she replied: 'Love is the desire of generation in the beautiful, both with relation to the body and the soul.'—'I must be a diviner to comprehend what you say, for, being such as I am, I confess that I do not understand it.' —'But I will explain it more clearly. The bodies and the souls of all human beings are alike pregnant with their future progeny, and when we arrive at a certain age, our nature impels us to bring forth and propagate. This nature is unable to produce in that which is deformed, but it can produce in that which is beautiful. The intercourse of the male and female in generation, a divine work, through pregnancy and production, is, as it were, something immortal in mortality. These things cannot take place in that which is incongruous; for that which is deformed is incongruous, but that which is beautiful is congruous with what is mortal and divine. Beauty is, therefore, the fate, and the goddess to generation. Wherefore, whenever that which is pregnant with the generative principle, approaches that which is beautiful, it becomes transported with delight, and is poured forth in overflowing pleasure, and propagates. But when it approaches that which is deformed it is contracted by sadness, and being repelled and checked, it does not produce, but retains unwillingly that with which it is pregnant. Wherefore, to one pregnant, and, as it were, already bursting with the load of his desire, the impulse towards that which is beautiful is intense, on account of the great pain of retaining that which he has conceived. Love, then, O Socrates, is not as you imagine the love of the beautiful.'—'What, then?'—'Of generation and production in the beautiful.'—'Why then of generation?'—'Generation is something eternal and immortal in mortality. It necessarily, from what has been confessed, follows, that we must desire immortality together with what is good, since Love is the desire that good be for ever present to us. Of necessity Love must also be the desire of immortality.'

"Diotima taught me all this doctrine in the discourse we had together concerning Love; and, in addition, she inquired, 'What do you think, Socrates, is the cause of this love and desire? Do you not perceive how all animals, both those of the earth and of the air, are affected when they desire the propagation of their species, affected even to weakness and disease by the impulse of their love; first, longing to be mixed with each other, and then seeking nourishment for their offspring, so that the feeblest are ready to contend with the strongest in obedience to this law, and to die for the sake of their young, or to waste away with hunger, and do or suffer anything so that they may not want nourishment. It might be said that human beings do these things through reason, but can you explain why other animals are thus affected through love?'—I confessed that I did not know.—'Do you imagine yourself,' said she, 'to be skilful in the science of Love, if you are ignorant of these things?'—'As I said before, O Diotima, I come to you, well knowing how much I am in need of a teacher. But explain to me, I entreat you, the cause of these things, and of the other things relating to Love.' —'If,' said Diotima, 'you believe that Love is of the same nature as we have mutually agreed upon, wonder not that such are its effects. For the mortal nature seeks, so far as it is able, to become deathless and eternal. But it can only accomplish this desire by generation, which for ever leaves another new in place of the old. For, although each human being be severally said to live, and be the same from youth to old age, yet, that which is called the same, never contains within itself the same things, but always is becoming new by the loss and change of that which it possessed before; both the hair and the flesh, and the bones, and the entire body.

" 'And not only does this change take place in the body, but also with respect to the soul. Manners, morals, opinions, desires, pleasures, sorrows, fears; none of these ever remain unchanged in the same persons; but some die away, and others are produced. And, what is yet more strange is, that not only does some knowledge spring up, and another decay, and that we are never the same with respect to our knowledge, but that each several object of our thoughts suffers the same revolution. That which is called meditation, or the exercise of memory, is the science of the escape or departure of memory; for, forgetfulness is the going out of knowledge; and meditation, calling up a new memory in the place of that which has departed, preserves knowledge; so that, though for ever displaced and restored, it seems to be the same. In this manner every thing mortal is preserved: not that it is constant and eternal, like that which is divine; but that in the place of what has grown old and is departed, it leaves another new like that which it was itself. By this contrivance, O Socrates, does what is mortal, the body and all other things, partake of immortality; that which is immortal, is immortal in another manner. Wonder not, then, if every thing by nature cherishes that which was produced from itself, for this earnest Love is a tendency towards eternity.'

"Having heard this discourse, I was astonished, and asked,

'Can these things be true, O wisest Diotima?' And she, like an accomplished sophist, said, 'Know well, O Socrates, that if you only regard that love of glory which inspires men, you will wonder at your own unskilfulness in not having discovered all that I now declare. Observe with how vehement a desire they are affected to become illustrious and to prolong their glory into immortal time, to attain which object, far more ardently than for the sake of their children, all men are ready to engage in many dangers, and expend their fortunes, and submit to any labours and incur any death. Do you believe that Alcestis would have died in the place of Admetus, or Achilles for the revenge of Patroclus, or Codrus for the kingdom of his posterity, if they had not believed that the immortal memory of their actions, which we now cherish, would have remained after their death? Far otherwise; all such deeds are done for the sake of ever-living virtue, and this immortal glory which they have obtained; and inasmuch as any one is of an excellent nature, so much the more is he impelled to attain this reward. For they love what is immortal.

" 'Those whose bodies alone are pregnant with this principle of immortality are attracted by women, seeking through the production of children what they imagine to be happiness and immortality and an enduring remembrance; but they whose souls are far more pregnant than their bodies, conceive and produce that which is more suitable to the soul. What is suitable to the soul? Intelligence, and every other power and excellence of the mind; of which all poets, and all other artists who are creative and inventive, are the authors. The greatest and most admirable wisdom is that which regulates the government of families and states, and which is called moderation and justice. Whosoever, therefore, from his youth feels his soul pregnant with the conception of these excellencies, is divine; and when due time arrives, desires to bring forth; and wandering about, he seeks the beautiful in which he may propagate what he has conceived; for there is no generation in that which is deformed; he embraces those bodies which are beautiful rather than those which are deformed, in obedience to the principle which is within him, which is ever seeking to perpetuate itself. And if he meets, in conjunction with loveliness of form, a beautiful, generous, and gentle soul, he embraces both at once, and immediately undertakes to educate this object of his love, and is inspired with an overflowing persuasion to declare what is virtue, and what he ought to be who would attain to its possession, and what are the duties which it exacts. For, by the intercourse with, and as it were, the very touch of that which is beautiful, he brings forth and produces what he had formerly conceived; and nourishes and educates that which is thus produced together with the object of his love, whose image, whether absent or present, is never divided from his mind. So that those who are thus united are linked by a nobler community and a firmer love, as being the common parents of a lovelier and more endearing progeny than the parents of other children. And every one who considers what posterity Homer and Hesiod, and the other great poets, have left behind them, the sources of their own immortal memory and renown, or what children of his soul Lycurgus has appointed to be the guardians, not only of Lacedaemon, but of all Greece; or what an illustrious progeny of laws Solon has produced, and how many admirable achievements, both among the Greeks and Barbarians, men have left as the pledges of that love which subsisted between them and the beautiful, would choose rather to be the parent of such children than those in a human shape. For divine honours have often been rendered to them on account of such children, but on account of those in human shape, never.

" 'Your own meditation, O Socrates, might perhaps have initiated you in all these things which I have already taught you on the subject of Love. But those perfect and sublime ends to which these are only the means, I know not that you would have been competent to discover. I will declare them, therefore, and will render them as intelligible as possible: do you meanwhile strain all your attention to trace the obscure depth of the subject. He who aspires to love rightly, ought from his earliest youth to seek an intercourse with beautiful forms, and first to make a single form the object of his love, and therein to generate intellectual excellences. He ought, then, to consider that beauty in whatever form it resides is the brother of that beauty which subsists in another form; and if he ought to pursue that which is beautiful in form, it would be absurd to imagine that beauty is not one and the same thing in all forms, and would therefore remit much of his ardent preference towards one, through his perception of the multitude of claims upon his love. In addition, he would consider the beauty which is in souls more excellent than that which is in form. So that one endowed with an admirable soul, even though the flower of the form were withered, would suffice him as the object of his love and care, and the companion with whom he might seek and produce such conclusions as tend to the improvement of youth; so that it might be led to observe the beauty and the conformity which there is in the observation of its duties and the laws, and to esteem little the mere beauty of the outward form. He would then conduct his pupil to science, so that he might look upon the loveliness of wisdom; and that contemplating thus the universal beauty, no longer would he unworthily and meanly enslave himself to the attractions of one form in love, nor one subject of discipline or science, but would turn towards the wide ocean of intellectual beauty, and from the sight of the lovely and majestic forms which it contains, would abundantly bring forth his conceptions in philosophy; until, strengthened and confirmed, he should at length steadily contemplate one science, which is the science of this universal beauty.

"'Attempt, I entreat you, to mark what I say with as keen an observation as you can. He who has been disciplined to this point in Love, by contemplating beautiful objects gradually, and in their order, now arriving at the end of all that concerns Love, on a sudden beholds a beauty wonderful in its nature. This is it, O Socrates, for the sake of which all the former labours were endured. It is eternal, unproduced, indestructible; neither subject to increase nor decay: not, like other things, partly beautiful and partly deformed; not at one time beautiful and at another time not; not beautiful in relation to one thing and deformed in relation to another; not here beautiful and there deformed; not beautiful in the estimation of one person and deformed in that of another; nor can this supreme beauty be figured to the imagination like a beautiful face, or beautiful hands, or any portion of the body, nor like any discourse, nor any science. Nor does it subsist in any other that lives or is, either in earth, or in heaven, or in any other place; but it is eternally uniform and consistent, and monoeidic with itself. All other things are beautiful through a participation of it, with this condition, that although they are subject to production and decay, it never becomes more or less, or endures any change. When any one, ascending from a correct system of Love, begins to contemplate this supreme beauty, he already touches the consummation of his labour. For such as discipline themselves upon this system, or are conducted by another beginning to ascend through these transitory objects which are beautiful, towards that which is beauty itself, proceeding as on steps from the love of one form to that of two, and from that of two, to that of all forms which are beautiful; and from beautiful forms to beautiful habits and institutions, and from institutions to beautiful doctrines; until, from the meditation of many doctrines, they arrive at that which is nothing else than the doctrine of the supreme beauty itself, in the knowledge and contemplation of which at length they repose.

" 'Such a life as this, my dear Socrates,' exclaimed the stranger Prophetess, 'spent in the contemplation of the beautiful, is the life for men to live; which if you chance ever to experience, you will esteem far beyond gold and rich garments, and even those persons whom you and many others now gaze on with astonishment, and are prepared neither to eat nor drink so that you may behold and live for ever with these objects of your love! What then shall we imagine to be the aspect of the supreme beauty itself, simple, pure, uncontaminated with the intermixture of human flesh and colours, and all other idle and unreal shapes attendant on mortality; the divine, the original, the supreme, the monoeidic beautiful itself? What must be the life of him who dwells with and gazes on that which it becomes us all to seek? Think you not that to him alone is accorded the prerogative of bringing forth, not images and shadows of virtue, for he is in contact not with a shadow but with reality; with virtue itself, in the production and nourishment of which he becomes dear to the Gods, and if such a privilege is conceded to any human being, himself immortal.'

"Such, O Phaedrus, and my other friends, was what Diotima said. And being persuaded by her words, I have since occupied myself in attempting to persuade others, that it is not easy to find a better assistant than Love in seeking to communicate immortality to our human natures. Wherefore I exhort every one to honour Love; I hold him in honour, and chiefly exercise myself in amatory matters, and exhort others to do so; and now and ever do I praise the power and excellence of Love, in the best manner that I can. Let this discourse, if it pleases you, Phaedrus, be considered as an encomium of Love; or call it by what other name you will."

The whole assembly praised his discourse, and Aristophanes was on the point of making some remarks on the allusion made by Socrates to him in a part of his discourse, when suddenly they heard a loud knocking at the door of the vestibule, and a clamour as of revellers, attended by a flute-player.—"Go, boys," said Agathon, "and see who is there: if they are any of our friends, call them in; if not, say that we have already done drinking."—A minute afterwards, they heard the voice of Alcibiades in the vestibule excessively drunk and roaring out:— "Where is Agathon? Lead me to Agathon!"—The flute-player, and some of his companions then led him in, and placed him against the door post, crowned with a thick crown of ivy and violets, and having a quantity of fillets on his head.—"My friends," he cried out, "hail! I am excessively drunk already, but I'll drink with you, if you will. If not, we will go away after having crowned Agathon, for which purpose I came. I assure you that I could not come yesterday, but I am now here with these fillets round my temples, that from my own head I may crown his who, with your leave, is the most beautiful and wisest of men. Are you laughing at me because I am drunk? Ay, I know what I say is true, whether you laugh or not. But tell me at once whether I shall come in, or no. Will you drink with me?"

Agathon and the whole party desired him to come in, and recline among them; so he came in, led by his companions. He then unbound his fillets that he might crown Agathon, and though Socrates was just before his eyes, he did not see him, but sat down by Agathon, between Socrates and him, for Socrates moved out of the way to make room for him. When he sat down, he embraced Agathon and crowned him, and Agathon desired the slaves to untie his sandals, that he might make a third, and recline on the same couch. "By all means," said Alcibiades, "but what third companion have we here?" And at the same time turning round and seeing Socrates, he leaped up and cried out:—"O Heracles! what have we here? You, Socrates, lying in ambush for me wherever I go! and meeting me just as you always do, when I least expected to see you! And, now, what are you come here for? Why have you chosen to recline exactly in this place, and not near Aristophanes, or any one else who is, or wishes to be ridiculous, but have contrived to take your place beside the most delightful person of the whole party?"—"Agathon," said Socrates, "see if you cannot defend me. I declare my friendship for this man is a bad business: from the moment that I first began to know him I have never been permitted to converse with, or so much as look upon any one else. If I do, he is so jealous and suspicious that he does the most extravagant things, and hardly refrains from beating me. I entreat you to prevent him from doing anything of that kind at present. Procure a reconciliation: or, if he perseveres in attempting any violence, I entreat you to defend me."—"Indeed," said Alcibiades, "I will not be reconciled to you; I shall find another opportunity to punish you for this. But now," said he, addressing Agathon, "lend me some of those fillets, that I may crown the wonderful head of this fellow, lest I incur the blame, that having crowned you, I neglected to crown him who conquers all men with his discourses, not yesterday alone as you did, but ever."

Saying this he took the fillets, and having bound the head of Socrates, and again having reclined, said: "Come, my friends, you seem to be sober enough. You must not flinch, but drink, for that was your agreement with me before I came in. I choose as president, until you have drunk enough—myself. Come, Agathon, if you have got a great goblet, fetch it out. But no matter, that wine-cooler will do; bring it, boy!" And observing that it held more than eight cups, he first drank it off, and then ordered it to be filled for Socrates, and said:—"Observe, my friends, I cannot invent any scheme against Socrates, for he will drink as much as any one desires him, and not be in the least drunk." Socrates, after the boy had filled up, drank it off; and Eryximachus said:—"Shall we then have no conversation or singing over our cups, but drink down stupidly, just as if we were thirsty?" And Alcibiades said: "Ah, Eryximachus, I did not see you before; hail, you excellent son of a wise and excellent father!"—"Hail to you also," replied Eryximachus, "but what shall we do?"—"Whatever you command, for we ought to submit to your directions; a physician is worth a hundred common men. Command us as you please."—"Listen then," said Eryximachus, "before you came in, each of us had agreed to deliver as eloquent a discourse as he could in praise of Love, beginning at the right hand; all the rest of us have fulfilled our engagement; you have not spoken, and yet have drunk with us: you ought to bear your part in the discussion; and having done so, command what you please to Socrates, who shall have the privilege of doing so to his right-hand neighbour, and so on to the others."—"Indeed, there appears some justice in your proposal, Eryximachus, though it is rather unfair to induce a drunken man to set his discourse in competition with that of those who are sober. And, besides, did Socrates really persuade you that what he just said about me was true, or do you not know that matters are in fact exactly the reverse of his representation? For I seriously believe that, should I praise in his presence, be he god or man, any other beside himself, he would not keep his hands off me. But I assure you, Socrates, I will praise no one beside yourself in your presence."

"Do so, then," said Eryximachus, "praise Socrates if you please."—"What," said Alcibiades, "shall I attack him, and punish him before you all?"—"What have you got into your head now," said Socrates, "are you going to expose me to ridicule, and to misrepresent me? Or what are you going to do?"—"I will only speak the truth; will you permit me on this condition?"—"I not only permit, but exhort you to say all the truth you know," replied Socrates. "I obey you willingly," said Alcibiades, "and if I advance anything untrue, do you, if you please, interrupt me, and convict me of misrepresentation, for I would never willingly speak falsely. And bear with me if I do not relate things in their order, but just as I remember them, for it is not easy for a man in my present condition to enumerate systematically all your singularities.

"I will begin the praise of Socrates by comparing him to a certain statue. Perhaps he will think that this statue is introduced for the sake of ridicule, but I assure you that it is necessary for the illustration of truth. I assert, then, that Socrates is exactly like those Silenuses that sit in the sculptors' shops, and which are carved holding flutes or pipes, but which, when divided in two, are found to contain within the images of the gods. I assert that Socrates is like the satyr Marsyas. That your form and appearance are like these satyrs, I think that even you will not venture to deny; and how like you are to them in all other things, now hear. Are you not scornful and petulant? If you deny this, I will bring witnesses. Are you not a piper, and far more wonderful a one than he? For Marsyas, and whoever now pipes the music that he taught (for the melodies of Olympus are derived from Marsyas who taught them), enchants men through the power of the mouth. For if any musician, be he skilful or not, awakens this music, it alone enables him to retain the minds of men, and from the divinity of its nature makes evident those who are in want of the gods and initiation. You differ only from Marsyas in this circumstance, that you effect without instruments, by mere words, all that he can do. For when we hear Pericles, or any other accomplished orator, deliver a discourse, no one, as it were, cares any thing about it. But when any one hears you, or even your words related by another, though ever so rude and unskilful a speaker, be that person a woman, man or child, we are struck and retained, as it were, by the discourse clinging to our mind.

"If I was not afraid that I am a great deal too drunk, I would confirm to you by an oath the strange effects which I assure you I have suffered from his words, and suffer still; for when I hear him speak, my heart leaps up far more than the hearts of those who celebrate the Corybantic mysteries; my tears are poured out as he talks, a thing I have seen happen to many others beside myself. I have heard Pericles and other excellent orators, and have been pleased with their discourses, but I suffered nothing of this kind; nor was my soul ever on those occasions disturbed and filled with self-reproach, as if it were slavishly laid prostrate. But this Marsyas here has often affected me in the way I describe, until the life which I lead seemed hardly worth living. Do not deny it, Socrates, for I well know that if even now I chose to listen to you, I could not resist, but should again suffer the same effects. For, my friends, he forces me to confess that while I myself am still in want of many things, I neglect my own necessities, and attend to those of the Athenians. I stop my ears, therefore, as from the Sirens, and flee away as fast as possible, that I may not sit down beside him and grow old in listening to his talk. For this man has reduced me to feel the sentiment of shame, which I imagine no one would readily believe was in me; he alone inspires me with remorse and awe. For I feel in his presence my incapacity of refuting what he says, or of refusing to do that which he directs; but when I depart from him, the glory which the multitude confers overwhelms me. I escape, therefore, and hide myself from him, and when I see him I am overwhelmed with humiliation, because I have neglected to do what I have confessed to him ought to be done; and often and often have I wished that he were no longer to be seen among men. But if that were to happen, I well know that I should suffer far greater pain; so that where I can turn, or what I can do with this man, I know not. All this have I and many others suffered from the pipings of this satyr.

"And observe, how like he is to what I said, and what a wonderful power he possesses. Know that there is not one of you who is aware of the real nature of Socrates; but since I have begun, I will make him plain to you. You observe how passionately Socrates affects the intimacy of those who are beautiful, and how ignorant he professes himself to be; appearances in themselves excessively Silenic. This, my friends, is the external form with which, like one of the sculptured Silenuses, he has clothed himself; for if you open him, you will find within admirable temperance and wisdom. For he cares not for mere beauty, but despises more than any one can imagine all external possessions, whether it be beauty or wealth, or glory, or any other thing for which the multitude felicitates the possessor. He esteems these things and us who honour them, as nothing, and lives among men, making all the objects of their admiration the playthings of his irony. But I know not if any one of you have ever seen the divine images which are within, when he has been opened and is serious. I have seen them, and they are so supremely beautiful, so golden, so divine, and wonderful, that everything which Socrates commands surely ought to be obeyed, even like the voice of a God.

"At one time we were fellow soldiers, and had our mess together in the camp before Potidaea. Socrates there overcame not only me, but every one beside, in endurance of toils: when, as often happens in a campaign, we were reduced to few provisions, there were none who could sustain hunger like Socrates; and when we had plenty, he alone seemed to enjoy our military fare. He never drank much willingly, but when he was compelled he conquered all even in that to which he was least accustomed; and what is most astonishing, no person ever saw Socrates drunk either then or at any other time. In the depth of winter (and the winters there are excessively rigid) he sustained calmly incredible hardships; and amongst other things, whilst the frost was intolerably severe, and no one went out of their tents, or if they went out, wrapt themselves up carefully, and put fleeces under their feet, and bound their legs with hairy skins, Socrates went out only with the same cloak on that he usually wore, and walked barefoot upon the ice; more easily, indeed, than those who had sandalled themselves so delicately: so that the soldiers thought that he did it to mock their want of fortitude. It would indeed be worth while to commemorate all that this brave man did and endured in that expedition. In one instance he was seen early in the morning, standing in one place wrapt in meditation; and as he seemed not to be able to unravel the subject of his thoughts, he still continued to stand as inquiring and discussing within himself, and when noon came, the soldiers observed him, and said to one another—'Socrates has been standing there thinking, ever since the morning.' At last some Ionians came to the spot, and having supped, as it was summer, bringing their blankets, they lay down to sleep in the cool; they observed that Socrates continued to stand there the whole night until morning, and that, when the sun rose, he saluted it with a prayer and departed.

"I ought not to omit what Socrates is in battle. For in that battle after which the generals decreed to me the prize of courage, Socrates alone of all men was the saviour of my life, standing by me when I had fallen and was wounded, and preserving both myself and my arms from the hands of the enemy. On that occasion I entreated the generals to decree the prize, as it was most due, to him. And this, O Socrates, you cannot deny, that the generals wishing to conciliate a person of my rank, desired to give me the prize, you were far more earnestly desirous than the generals that this glory should be attributed not to yourself, but me.

"But to see Socrates when our army was defeated and scattered in flight at Delium, was a spectacle worthy to behold. On that occasion I was among the cavalry, and he on foot, heavily armed. After the total rout of our troops, he and Laches retreated together; I came up by chance, and seeing them, bade them be of good cheer, for that I would not leave them. As I was on horseback, and therefore less occupied by a regard of my own situation, I could better observe than at Potidaea the beautiful spectacle exhibited by Socrates on this emergency. How superior was he to Laches in presence of mind and courage! Your representation of him on the stage, O Aristophanes, was not wholly unlike his real self on this occasion, for he walked and darted his regards around with a majestic composure, looking tranquilly both on his friends and enemies; so that it was evident to every one, even from afar, that whoever should venture to attack him would encounter a desperate resistance. He and his companion thus departed in safety; for those who are scattered in flight are pursued and killed, whilst men hesitate to touch those who exhibit such a countenance as that of Socrates even in defeat.

"Many other and most wonderful qualities might well be praised in Socrates; but such as these might singly be attributed to others. But that which is unparalleled in Socrates, is, that he is unlike, and above comparison, with all other men, whether those who have lived in ancient times, or those who exist now. For it may be conjectured, that Brasidas and many others are such as was Achilles. Pericles deserves comparison with Nestor and Antenor; and other excellent persons of various times may, with probability, be drawn into comparison with each other. But to such a singular man as this, both himself and his discourses are so uncommon, no one, should he seek, would find a parallel among the present or the past generations of mankind; unless they should say that he resembled those with whom I lately compared him, for, assuredly, he and his discourses are like nothing but the Silenus and the Satyrs. At first I forgot to make you observe how like his discourses are to those Satyrs when they are opened, for, if any one will listen to the talk of Socrates, it will appear to him at first extremely ridiculous; the phrases and expressions which he employs, fold around his exterior the skin, as it were, of a rude and wanton Satyr. He is always talking about great market-asses, and brass-founders, and leather-cutters, and skin-dressers; and this is his perpetual custom, so that any dull and unobservant person might easily laugh at his discourse. But if any one should see it opened, as it were, and get within the sense of his words, he would then find that they alone of all that enters into the mind of man to utter, had a profound and persuasive meaning, and that they were most divine; and that they presented to the mind innumerable images of every excellence, and that they tended towards objects of the highest moment, or rather towards all that he who seeks the possession of what is supremely beautiful and good need regard as essential to the accomplishment of his ambition.

"These are the things, my friends, for which I praise Socrates."

Alcibiades having said this, the whole party burst into a laugh at his frankness, and Socrates said, "You seem to be sober enough, Alcibiades, else you would not have made such a circuit of words, only to hide the main design for which you made this long speech, and which, as it were carelessly, you just throw in at the last; now, as if you had not said all this for the mere purpose of dividing me and Agathon? You think that I ought to be your friend, and to care for no one else. I have found you out; it is evident enough for what design you invented all this Satyrical and Silenic drama. But, my dear Agathon, do not let his device succeed. I entreat you to permit no one to throw discord between us."—"No doubt," said Agathon, "he sat down between us only that he might divide us; but this shall not assist his scheme, for I will come and sit near you."—"Do so," said Socrates, "come, there is room for you by me."—"Oh, Zeus!" exclaimed Alcibiades, "what I endure from that man! He thinks to subdue every way; but, at least I pray you, let Agathon remain between us."—"Impossible," said Socrates, "you have just praised me; I ought to praise him sitting at my right hand. If Agathon is placed beside you, will he not praise me before I praise him? Now, my dear friend, allow the young man to receive what praise I can give him. I have a great desire to pronounce his encomium."—"Quick, quick, Alcibiades," said Agathon, "I cannot stay here, I must change my place, or Socrates will not praise me."—Agathon then arose to take his place near Socrates.

He had no sooner reclined than there came in a number of revellers—for some one who had gone out had left the door open—and took their places on the vacant couches, and everything became full of confusion; and no order being observed, every one was obliged to drink a great quantity of wine. Eryximachus, and Phaedrus, and some others, said Aristodemus, went home to bed; that, for his part, he went to sleep on his couch, and slept long and soundly—the nights were then long—until the cock crew in the morning. When he awoke he found that some were still fast asleep, and others had gone home, and that Aristophanes, Agathon, and Socrates had alone stood it out, and were still drinking out of a great goblet which they passed round and round. Socrates was disputing between them. The beginning of their discussion Aristodemus said that he did not recollect, because he was half asleep; but it was terminated by Socrates forcing them to confess, that the same person is able to compose both tragedy and comedy, and that the foundations of the tragic and comic arts were essentially the same. They, rather convicted than convinced, went to sleep, first Aristophanes, and then, when day was dawning, Agathon. Socrates, having put them to sleep, went away, Aristodemus following him and coming to the Lyceum he washed himself, and after having spent the day there in his accustomed manner, went home in the evening.

ART

The age-old debate as to the nature and appreciation of quality should have been settled long ago by these words of Plato: "There is no way of putting it into words like other studies, but after much communion and constant intercourse with the thing itself suddenly, like a light kindled from a leaping fire, it is born within the soul and henceforth nourishes itself."* A. E. Housman, the Cambridge poet and scholar, put it a little differently. One day a student asked him how he could tell when a poem was great, and Housman, who also knew his Bible, replied, "When it gives me a pain in the belly." We can only add that the pain is intensified the longer we associate with probable masterpieces. It is the association with greatness and its setting that best helps us to appreciate quality, for it is no more possible to explain genius and its works than it is to assess the factors necessary for the creation of outbursts of intellectual activity.

If we now ask why generations of competent students have agreed to call much of Greek art great, the answer is to be found partly in the fact that the Greeks were an inspired people who loved the best in human experience. The ancient sculptor, moreover, portrayed the generic and the typical rather than the particular and the unique and, in doing so, speaks directly to the beholder with clarity and imagination. This probably explains why great Greek art needs no interpreter.

The early Greek statues, it is true, tend to be stylized because of the artist's lack of technical skill, but with the progress of observation and sculptural technique stylization yields to realism, as it was almost bound to do in the hands of a highly rational

* G. M. A. Richter's translation.

people. It is a realism held in check, however, by a devotion to simplicity and idealization. This is best illustrated by the monuments on the Athenian Acropolis, where the most beautiful buildings of all Greece were located.

The Parthenon, which is the earliest and most important among the surviving buildings, is as much a grand political spectacle as a religious monument, a glorification of both Athens and Athena. It was erected in honor of Athena Parthenos, the serene Maiden who embodied all that is lovely in life, the patron of arts and labors, the protecting deity and symbol of the state. It sums up wonderfully the ideals and ambitions of the Athenians and, let it be said once again, was paid for by the imperial tribute.

The most conspicuous thing about the Parthenon, or any Greek temple, is the surrounding row of columns, in this case eight across the ends and seventeen along the sides. They belong, as does the entablature above them, to the order of architecture known as Doric. The marvelous proportions of the individual parts, the delicate refinements, the curves and deviations from the normal, represent the culmination of a long historical development and were here brought to a peak by the architects Ictinus and Callicrates. Instead of the rigidity and squat-like appearance of early temples, the Parthenon achieves a grand vitality and elasticity.

Except for the timber roof and the doors, the entire structure, including the tiles of the roof, was built of Pentelic marble, a stone containing golden-like veins of iron. The building measures approximately 100 by 230 feet and has two chambers or cellas. The larger cella, facing the east, originally held the famous gold and ivory statue of Athena, the work of the Parthenon's chief sculptor, Pheidias. Though it has long since disappeared, ancient copies and descriptions enable us to create in our imagination some of the overpowering beauty of the original, a veritable symbol of Hellenism and the greatness of Athens. Athena stood erect, wearing the aegis, her left hand grasping a spear and shield, while Victory alighted on her right hand. On either

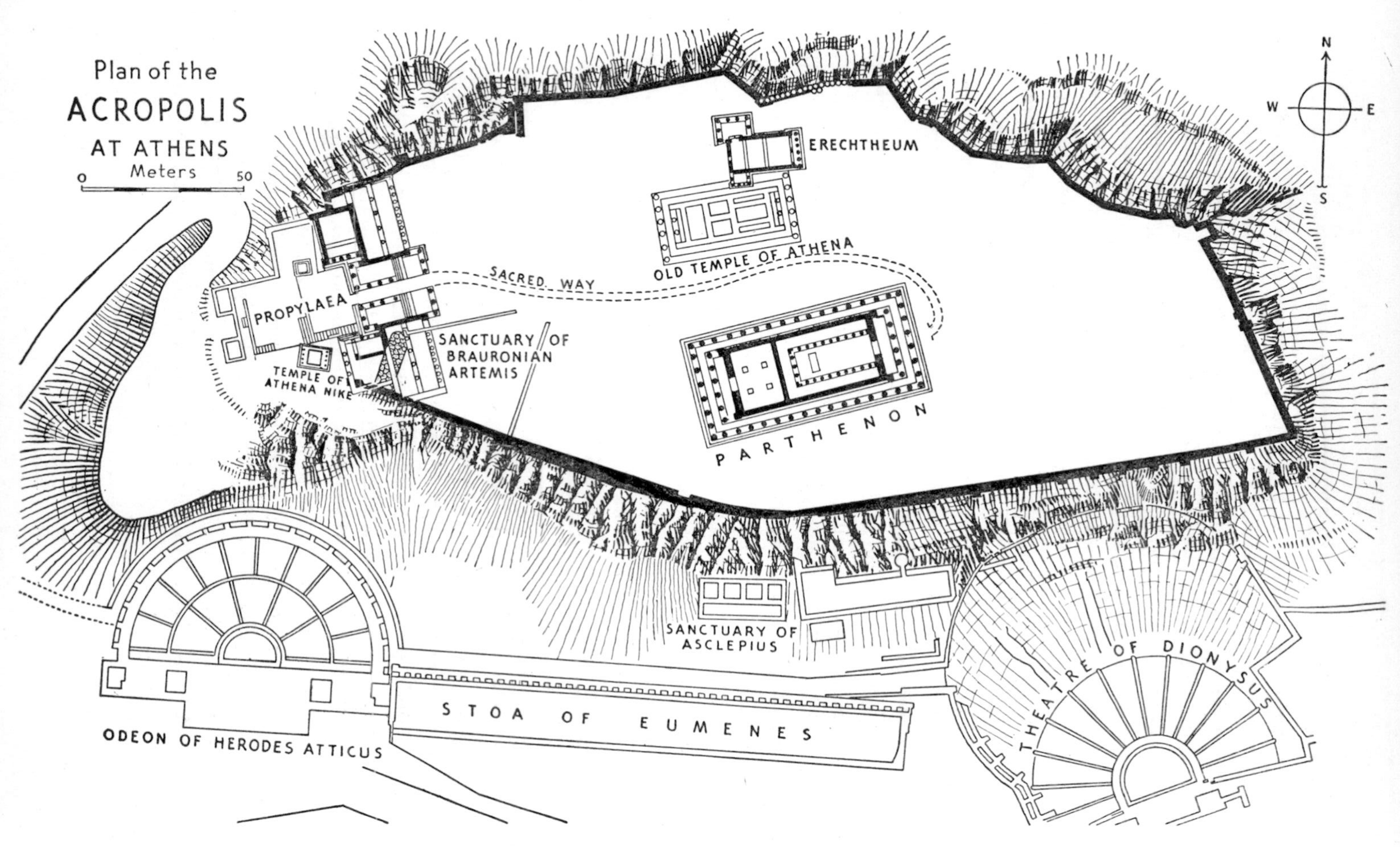
Plan of the
ACROPOLIS
AT ATHENS
Meters
0
50
N
W
E
S
ERECHTHEUM
OLD TEMPLE OF ATHENA
SACRED WAY
PROPYLAEA
SANCTUARY OF
BRAURONIAN
ARTEMIS
TEMPLE OF
ATHENA NIKE
PARTHENON
SANCTUARY OF
ASCLEPIUS
THEATRE OF DIONYSUS
STOA OF EUMENES
ODEON OF HERODES ATTICUS

side of the shield were carved battles of giants and amazons; on her sandals, a struggle between Lapiths and Centaurs, a scene suggesting the triumph of civilization over barbarism.

Sculpture was always the handmaiden of architecture in ancient Greece, and there is no doubt that the grandeur and noble majesty of the Parthenon were greatly enhanced by its numerous sculptures. For example, the carved rectangular blocks (metopes) on the outside of the building form grand compositions, while the continuous frieze along the outside of the cellas represents magnificent drawing as much as it does sculpture in stone. The frieze commemorates the Panathenaic procession, an August festival, when the best blood of Athens, young and old, youths and girls, brought a new robe for the ancient wooden statue of Athena on the Acropolis. We can watch members of the procession gallop along on horseback, full of life and pride. Others bear offerings for the gods, and still others bring animals to the sacrifice. At the eastern end, above the temple's entrance, await the gods of Olympus, giving their blessing the while to this outburst of civic pride and religious feeling.

Perhaps the most wonderful sculptures of the Parthenon are those in the triangular areas, or pediments, at either end. Here we see great gods and idealized men—in the western pediment the momentous struggle between Athena and Poseidon for the honor of being chosen patron god of the state; in the eastern, an event of equal significance for Athens and the world (so the Athenians insisted), the birth of Athena. The center of this group was occupied by the majestic figure of Zeus, nearby gods and goddesses marveling at Athena's wondrous birth, while other gods at a distance, not yet aware of the happy news, sat relaxed in thought. The rising Sun (Helios) with his chariot, and the sinking Moon (Selene), in the corners of the pediment, made the whole affair a matter of world importance.

For many centuries the golden marble of the Parthenon shone in all its splendor on the pink rock of the Acropolis. During the Middle Ages it became a Christian church dedicated to the Virgin Mary. Then in the fifteenth century, with the coming of the Turks, it was turned into a mosque, and in 1687 a Venetian bomb destroyed much of it. Early in the last century Lord Elgin brought many of the sculptures to London, where they now form a part of the famous classical collection in the British Museum; but, for all that, the Parthenon can be really seen only in Athens, and then comes, swiftly, an insight into the imperial greatness of the ancient democracy.

No sooner had the Parthenon been dedicated in 438 B.C. than Pericles inaugurated the construction of a new and finer gateway to the Acropolis. This was known as the Propylaea and was built from the designs of Mnesicles. The outbreak of the Peloponnesian War in 431 B.C. necessitated a curtailment of the original plans, but it did not prevent the Athenians from building a graceful little temple, that of Athena Nike (Victory), at the western bastion of the Acropolis. A marble parapet, showing figures of Victories, was then placed along the edge of the bastion.

By far the most elaborate building on the Acropolis is the Erechtheum, a marvel of grace and delicacy, rich with the honeysuckle and other ornamentation. Like the temple of Athena Nike, it belongs to the Ionic order of architecture, which grew up in Ionia (Asia Minor), whereas the Doric order was native to the Greek mainland. It should not surprise us to find different orders of architecture on the Acropolis, for all ideas were at home in Athens, and even the great Doric Parthenon had Ionic features, such as its continuous frieze. The Erechtheum was begun during a break in the Peloponnesian War known as the Peace of Nicias (421 B.C.), but work on it was soon abandoned and not resumed for a dozen years, when war and suffering made it necessary to find as many jobs as possible for the laborers.

Though it was built of Pentelic marble, the Erechtheum nevertheless had a frieze course of blue limestone, against which were pinned white marble sculptures. The Caryatid Porch on the south side, where stately Maidens support the roof, is the temple's most striking feature; but the porch on the north, with its elaborately carved door, is perhaps even more beautiful.

The minor arts, no less than the major, proclaim the greatness of Periclean Athens; for example, the gems and coins have an exquisite and startling beauty. Unfortunately, we possess nothing of mural and easel pictures, but many vases survive, and these often exhibit some of the finest free-hand drawing in the history of art. Since red figures appear against a black background, the pottery of the day is spoken of as red-figured. Put briefly, the technique was as follows. After the vase had been shaped on the wheel and had been allowed to dry, the surface was polished in preparation for the decoration. The painter then sketched his figure with a dull-pointed instrument on the clay; next he painted with black varnish *around* this outline and thus obtained a red silhouette, for the vase had already been tinted by a transparent wash. The details of muscles and drapery were drawn in relief-lines, and the whole background was painted with a black varnish. The firing in the oven added a lustre to the black glaze.

Red-figured vases combine exuberance with discipline and vigor to create an air of wonderful simplicity. If we wish further to measure the artistic genius of a gifted people, we need only look at the quietly beautiful tombstones, made as they were by sculptors of little contemporary importance. But wherever we turn in Greek art—whether to a stirring statue symbolizing Man or to a lonely temple on a rocky coast or to a tiny gem—we see that it all belongs to that wonderful and larger adventure in culture, embarked upon by a contentious and intellectual race that challenged everything on earth and in heaven. This is the reason, doubtless, why Toynbee could say that "the Hellenic Civilization is perhaps the finest flower of the species that has ever yet come to bloom . . . [it] still outshines every other civilization that has ever come into existence up to the present."

PLATES

1. *The temple of Olympian Zeus and the Acropolis from the southeast*
Photograph by Saul S. Weinberg

2. *The Acropolis from the southwest*
Courtesy of the American School of Classical Studies at Athens

3. *The Areopagus, Acropolis and Mt. Hymettus from the northwest*
Photograph by Alison Frantz

4. *A view of the Parthenon from the west*
Photograph by Saul S. Weinberg

5. *The Parthenon from the west.* 447-432 B.C.
Photograph by Herman Wagner

6. *The Parthenon from the northwest*
Photograph by Alison Frantz

7. The Parthenon. Detail of the west pediment and entablature
Photograph by Alison Frantz

8. *The Parthenon from the east*
Photograph by Herman Wagner

9. *The southeast corner of the Parthenon*
Photograph by Gladys Davidson Weinberg

10. *The northeast corner of the Parthenon*
Detail of the pediment and entablature
Photograph by Alison Frantz

11. *Centaur and Lapith. A metope from the south side of the Parthenon*
British Museum, London

12. *The north colonnade of the Parthenon*
Photograph by Saul S. Weinberg

13. Within the Parthenon, looking west
Photograph by Alison Frantz

14. Dionysus or Ares — formerly known as Theseus — from the east pediment of the Parthenon British Museum, London

15. *Probably Artemis, Dione and Aphrodite—formerly known as the Three Fates—from the east pediment of the Parthenon. British Museum, London*

16. Head of a horse of the moon goddess, Selene, from the east pediment of the Parthenon
British Museum, London

17. So-called Nike (Victory) from the west pediment of the Parthenon
British Museum, London

18. *Cecrops and his daughter. In the west pediment of the Parthenon*

19. *Ilissus from the west pediment of the Parthenon. British Museum, London*

20. Horsemen in the Panathenaic procession. A section of the west frieze of the Parthenon. In situ. Photograph by Alison Frantz

21. *A detail from the west frieze of the Parthenon*
Photograph by Alison Frantz

22. *A detail from the west frieze of the Parthenon*
Photograph by Alison Frantz

23. *A detail from the west frieze of the Parthenon*
Photograph by Alison Frantz

24. *A detail from the west frieze of the Parthenon*

25. *Horsemen in procession. From the north frieze of the Parthenon*

26. Cows being led to the sacrifice
From the north frieze of the Parthenon
Acropolis Museum, Athens

27. Maidens marching in procession
From the east frieze of the Parthenon. The Louvre, Paris
Photograph by Giraudon

28. *The Propylaea from the east.* 437-432 B.C.
Photograph by Alison Frantz

29. *Within the Propylaea*
Photograph by Alison Frantz

30. *Detail of an Ionic capital of the Propylaea*
Photograph by Alison Frantz

31. The Propylaea from the southwest, with the temple of Athena Nike on its bastion. Photograph by Alison Frantz

32. *The temple of Athena Nike from the northwest. About 421* B.C. *Photograph by Alison Frantz*

33. *The temple of Athena Nike from the southeast*
Photograph by Alison Frantz

34. *Nike (Victory) fastening her sandal. About 420* B.C.
From the parapet of the temple of Athena Nike. Acropolis Museum, Athens
Photograph by Alinari

35. *The Erechtheum from the southeast. About 421-406* B.C.
Photograph by Alison Frantz

36. *The Erechtheum from the east, with the Propylaea beyond*
Photograph by Alison Frantz

37. The Erechtheum from the south
Photograph by Alison Frantz

38. The Erechtheum. The Porch of the Maidens from the southeast
Photograph by Alison Frantz

39. *Maidens of the Erechtheum*
Photograph by Alison Frantz

40. *The Erechtheum. Detail of the ornamentation of the south wall and entablature*
Photograph by Alison Frantz

41. The Erechtheum from the southwest
Photograph by Alison Frantz

42. *The Erechtheum. The North Porch from the northeast*
Photograph by Alison Frantz

43. The North Porch of the Erechtheum
Detail of the ornamentation of an anta
Photograph by Alison Frantz

44. *The Erechtheum. Detail of capitals and entablature of the North Porch*
Photograph by Alison Frantz

45. The Erechtheum. Detail of column bases of the North Porch
Photograph by Alison Frantz

46. *The Erechtheum. A detail of the southwest corner*
Photograph by Alison Frantz

47. *Herm of Pericles. Roman copy of the late fifth-century* B.C. *bronze original by Cresilas. British Museum, London*

48. The choregic monument of Thrasyllus on the south slope of the Acropolis, with the stadium and Mt. Hymettus in the distance
Photograph by Saul S. Weinberg

49. The theater of Dionysus on the south slope of the Acropolis
Photograph by Saul S. Weinberg

50. *The temple of Hephaestus, god of metal workers, on the edge of the Athenian market place*
Photograph by Saul S. Weinberg

51. *The temple of Hephaestus, formerly known as the Theseum. About 450* B.C.
Photograph by Alison Frantz

52. *The temple of Poseidon at Sunium on the tip of the Attic peninsula*
Photograph by Saul S. Weinberg

53. *The south colonnade of the temple of Poseidon at Sunium*
Photograph by Alison Frantz

54. *The temple of Poseidon at Sunium. About 425* B.C.
Photograph by Saul S. Weinberg

55. *Grave stele of an athlete, from Sunium*
About 460 B.C. *National Museum, Athens*

58. *Grave stele of Hegeso, from the Athenian cemetery of the Cerameicus. Late fifth century* B.C. *National Museum, Athens*
Photograph by Alinari

59. *A silver coin – tetradrachm – of Athens (enlarged)*
Late fifth century B.C.
Museum of Fine Arts, Boston

62. *Greek and Centaur*
From a red-figured drinking cup (cylix) by an Athenian master
About 460 B.C.
Museum antiker Kleinkunst, Munich

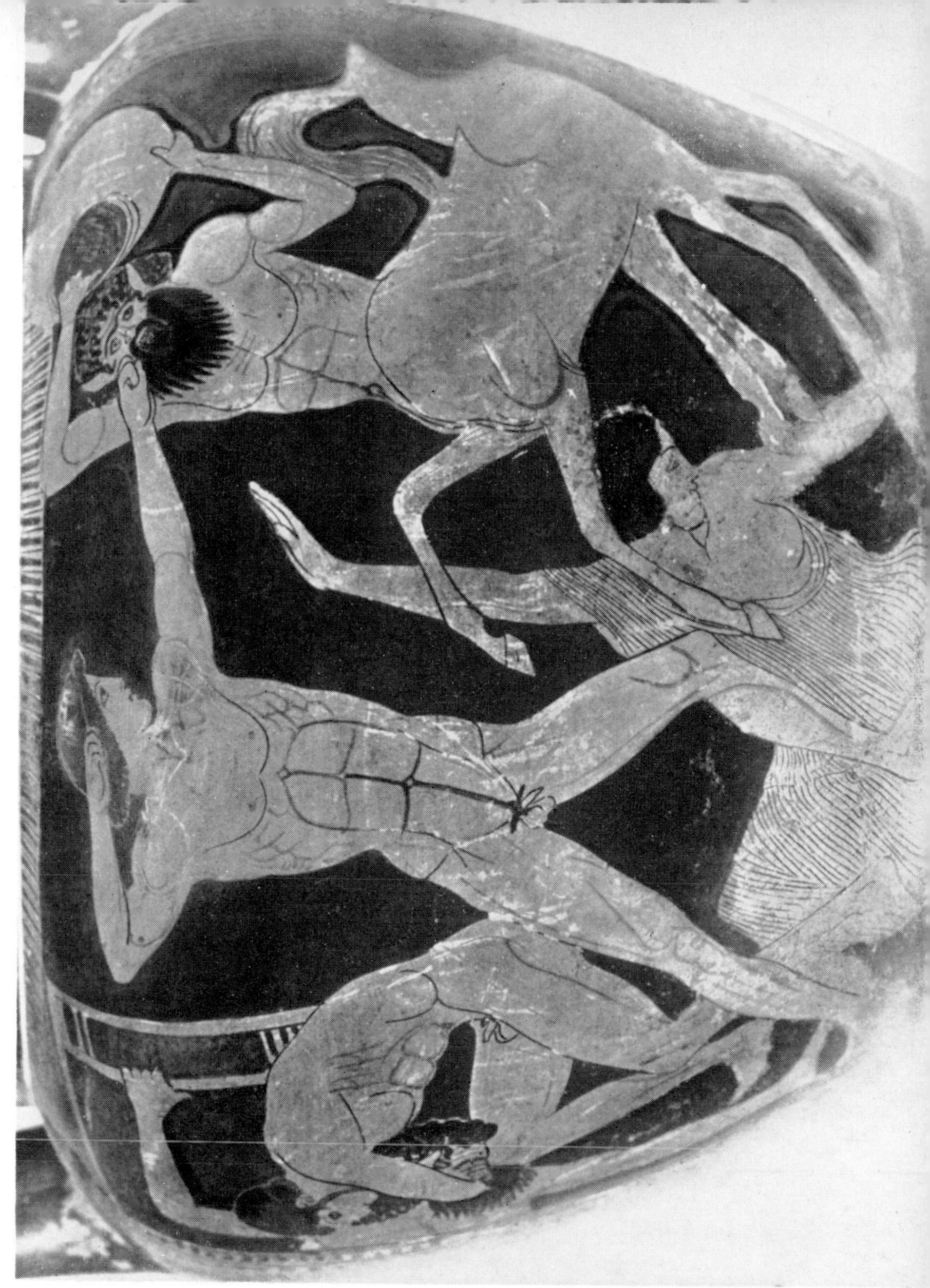

63. *Battle between Greeks and Centaurs, symbol of the triumph of Hellenism over barbarism. From an Athenian red-figured mixing bowl (crater). About 460* B.C. *Museo Archeologico, Florence*

64. Head of an old warrior
From a red-figured mixing bowl
Probably an Athenian work of 455 B.C.
Metropolitan Museum of Art, New York

65. *Orpheus. Fragment of a white-ground drinking cup, probably by the Athenian master Euphronius. About 460* B.C. *National Museum, Athens*

66. Aphrodite on a goose
A white-ground drinking cup, probably by the Athenian master Pistoxenus. About 460 B.C.
British Museum, London

67. A warrior bidding farewell to a woman
From an Athenian white-ground sepulchral oil jar. About 450 B.C.
National Museum, Athens

68. Heron, on an engraved chalcedony (enlarged)
A Greek gem of the late fifth century B.C. *From a cast*
Museum of Fine Arts, Boston

69. *Stags. Greek gems of the late fifth century* B.C.
From casts. Museum of Fine Arts, Boston

70. *Eleutherae, an Athenian fortress in the foothills of Mt. Cithaeron near the border of Boeotia. Photograph by Alison Frantz*

THE PELOPONNESIAN WAR

Speaking at Princeton University in his capacity as Secretary of State, General George C. Marshall remarked, "I doubt seriously whether a man can think with full wisdom and with deep convictions regarding certain of the basic international issues today who has not at least reviewed in his mind the period of the Peloponnesian War and the fall of Athens." It would be enlightening to know the conclusions General Marshall had in mind, but unfortunately he did not say. On the other hand, a review of the evidence makes it difficult to avoid the observation that imperialism leads but to the grave.

There, of course, is the tragedy of ancient Greece. The Athenians had it in their means with wise management to build up a lasting power, the strongest in Hellas, to win wide recognition of their political leadership, and to lift their race to a political destiny worthy of its civilization. All these possibilities they sacrificed. At the very moment when Greek culture had reached its zenith, the Athenians conducted their foreign relations in a way calculated to frighten the land empire southward, known as the Peloponnesian League, and in particular its two leading members, Sparta and Corinth.

The ensuing Peloponnesian War is a familiar story of battles and heroism and suffering and cruelty. It harmed the victors almost as much as the vanquished. Beginning in 431 B.C., it finally ended in 404 B.C. with the overthrow of the Athenian Empire. Never again was Athens a first-rate power, although she remained the cultural leader of the ancient world. In short, the Peloponnesian War closed an epoch in Greek history, and these few words might suffice, were it not for the great historian who lifted the struggle to the plane of a universal conflict of eternal significance. For the essential thing about Thucydides is that he had the genius to reduce the actualities of life to their generic and hence their lasting patterns. Small though his world was, he was able to expose the forces that move political man.

Thucydides (ca. 471-399 B.C.) was an Athenian, the son of Olorus. He resembled other men of the Periclean Age not only in the intensity and power of his thought and style, but also in the fact that he was a man of action, a general in the Peloponnesian War, who could season his writings with practical experience. At the outbreak of the war, foreseeing that it would be memorable, he began to collect material for a history of it. When, not long afterward, he was exiled from Athens—for tardy action, it was claimed—he spent the twenty years of his exile traveling about, visiting the scenes of military operations and ascertaining facts from eye-witnesses on both sides. He carefully examined his evidence and was completely impartial.

Though he loved Athens, Thucydides did not hesitate to criticize her. Like Pericles he loved magnificence and display, and like Pericles he was an imperialist. He believed that it was natural for a state to expand, since the state represented power; and war, he felt, was but an expression of the state's growth. In studying the Peloponnesian War, Thucydides was interested in the causes underlying the political actions of states. With him the forces that make history are the statesmen, who consciously operate to effect a given purpose, secondarily the people in their Assembly, moved by capricious feeling to a wise or a foolish resolution. The ideal republic is one like Athens in the Age of Pericles, in which the best and wisest citizen is able to control the rest, but, he recognized, chance can also affect the course of events.

Thucydides' *History* is a literary masterpiece, influenced somewhat by the dramatists and sophists. The speeches, which occupy a large part of the work, are, so to speak, its soul. Usually they are given in pairs, representing the opposing views of a situation or a question for decision before an Assembly. The language of the speeches is Thucydides'; the ideas, so far as they could be ascertained, are the orators'. Generally, therefore, the speeches embody the historian's understanding of a situation and express most adequately his keen analytical intelligence.

Notwithstanding certain differences between ancient and modern conceptions of history, we may look to Thucydides as a master. In his own personal reserve, in the determination with which he pursues his single aim, rejecting every extraneous matter, in the relentless analysis which lays bare the souls of individuals, of factions, of communities, in the fairness and mental placidity with which he treats of personal enemies and opposing parties, in intellectual depth, keenness, and grasp, we may safely say that he has thus far no equal. A famous sentence in his book —the only boast he ever allowed himself—seems fully justified: "My history is an everlasting possession, not a prize composition which is heard and forgotten."

Of course, no one incident or factor was in itself sufficient for a conflict of interests and ideas that involved the entire Hellenic world. There is no denying the difference in outlook between Sparta and Athens, however. Sparta, or Lacedaemon, was reactionary and narrow-minded, and in her splendid isolation headed a powerful land empire. Athens was democratic and progressive, the intellectual capital of Hellas and the possessor of a far-flung empire. On the other hand, the dualism into which Greece had settled might have lasted, in spite of the growing antipathy between its two leading states.

What, then, was the cause of the Peloponnesian War? Thucydides says, "I will first set forth the grounds of the quarrel that in time to come no man may be at a loss to know what was the origin of this great war. The real though unavowed cause I believe to have been the growth of the Athenian power, which terrified the Lacedaemonians and forced them into war; but the reasons publicly alleged on either side were as follows." Sparta has not fared very well at the bar of history, nor does it deserve to, but the common charge that it was responsible for the Peloponnesian War cannot be made to stick. It was Athens, not Sparta, which represented something new and disturbing in Greek politics. Thucydides himself makes it clear that the ancient naval democracy—guided by the stern hand of Pericles, though opposition among the rich existed—pursued revolutionary policies which so terrified the upholders of the *status quo* that a world conflict became inevitable.

For example, even before the outbreak of hostilities, the Corinthian envoys at Sparta declared: "The Athenians are innovators, equally quick in the conception and in the execution of every new plan; you Spartans, on the other hand, are conservative, careful only to keep what you have." And with remarkable candor the Athenian envoys said: "An empire was offered to us: can you wonder that, acting as human nature always will, we accepted it and refused to give it up again, constrained by three all-powerful motives, ambition, fear, interest. We are not the first who have aspired to rule; the world has ever held that the weaker must be kept down by the stronger. Did justice ever deter anyone from taking by force whatever he could?"

The point about Athenian aggressions in the past was not so much the fact of their success as that they were aimed at many different quarters. Was there a limit to Athenian ambition, or must all states eventually bow before it? The Athenian claim to leadership was generally considered incompatible with the liberties of individual states and with the long-established policy of Sparta. Against this claim the Corinthians charged Athens with the enslavement of her allies and with the design of reducing other Greeks to servitude, and called upon Sparta to take the lead in putting down the tyrant. The Spartans, in spite of their own oligarchical constitution, considered themselves champions of the principle of city sovereignty, and were so regarded by their allies.

Fear of Athens and the universal Greek love of liberty certainly contributed to the Peloponnesian War. Rivalry in trade was another irritant. Thus a variety of ideas and factors so charged the atmosphere of Greece with suspicion and hatred that finally a series of border incidents made it futile to hope for peace any longer. Pericles, now a man of sixty, not only was reconciled to the war, but was convinced that it was better that it should come while he was still in the prime of life and Athens in excellent military condition. Hence he persuaded his countrymen to oppose every concession to the Peloponnesians and their Theban allies.

The strategy of the Peloponnesians was to invade Attica and devastate the fields, hoping that the Athenians would be provoked into making a sally from their walls. But this was just what Athens must not do, because there was insufficient manpower for the city walls, the frontier forts, the navy, and a field army besides. The strategy of Pericles, therefore, was to bring the entire population of the country, with their movable goods, into the city, even though this meant the devastation of the fields. Pericles reasoned that the enemy would not remain long in the country, since most of the Peloponnesians were small farmers, who personally tilled their lands. However much they might ravage the fields, they could accomplish nothing against the strong fortifications of Athens and Piraeus and the Long Walls which connected the capital with its port. The Athenian fleet commanded the sea and would ensure the steady arrival at Athens of food supplies, and at the same time it would attack the Peloponnesian coasts.

In the spring of 431 B.C. the enemy entered Attica, under the able Spartan king, Archidamus, and cut down the orchards and ripe grain. Pericles' cold calculating plan of removing the population into the city subjected Athenian nature to an excessive strain. The people longed to go forth and fight the enemy. Gathering in knots on the streets, they complained bitterly of their plight, and laid the whole blame of the war and their losses upon Pericles. Tragic as was this first year in the struggle between two evenly balanced foes, it was as nothing compared to the years ahead. Two decades later, while the war still had several years to run, we can catch the pathos of it all in the *Lysistrata* of Aristophanes, for, in spite of the buffoonery of the comic poet, we see the ruin of family life at Athens, we see generation after generation of men swept away, leaving the women desolate, robbed of husbands, lovers, and children.

Pericles, however, maintained his policy at home in spite of the grumblings, and sent a fleet to ravage the Peloponnesian coast. Doubtless he was pleased with the results of the first year. At the conclusion of the campaign, the remains of those who had fallen in battle during the summer were solemnly conveyed to the cemetery in the Cerameicus—a beautiful spot outside the walls—and interred amid the lamentations of the populace. An empty bed, covered with a sheet, honored those whose bodies had not been recovered. After the burial Pericles addressed the people in a Funeral Oration which has become one of the most precious documents in the history of civilization. The Funeral Oration is much more than a defense of his own policy or a mere eulogy of Athens. It is a description of the ideal of Pericles in his best moments, and an analysis of the strength of ancient democracy. Perhaps it is well to recall in this connection that Athens was never really checked in the war until it came up against democratic Syracuse. The Funeral Oration lets us see the value of majority rule and free public debate. We sense, too, the tolerance of an ancient democracy which permitted Aristophanes, for example, to produce during the war several plays on the theme of peace. Above all, however, the Funeral Oration makes clear a fundamental trust in human nature and a belief in progress.

"Our constitution is called a democracy [Thucydides* reports Pericles as saying] for the administration is in the hands of the many and not of the few. But while the law secures equal justice to all alike in their private disputes, the claim of excellence is also recognized; and when a citizen is in any way distinguished, he is preferred to the public service, not as a matter of privilege, but as the reward of merit. Neither is poverty a bar, but a man may benefit his country whatever be the obscurity of his condition. There is no exclusiveness in our public life, and in our

* The translations of Thucydides throughout are those of B. Jowett, with slight changes and much abbreviated.

private intercourse we are not suspicious of one another, nor angry with our neighbor if he does what he likes; we do not put on sour looks at him which, though harmless, are not pleasant. While we are thus unconstrained in our private intercourse, a spirit of reverence pervades our public acts; we are prevented from doing wrong by respect for authority and for the laws, having an especial regard to those which are ordained for the protection of the injured as well as to those unwritten laws which bring upon the transgressor of them the reprobation of the general sentiment.

"And we have not forgotten to provide for our weary spirits many relaxations from toil; we have regular games and sacrifices throughout the year; at home the style of our life is refined; and the delight which we daily feel in all these things helps to banish melancholy. Because of the greatness of our city the fruits of the whole earth flow in upon us; so that we enjoy the goods of other countries as freely as of our own.

"We are lovers of the beautiful, yet simple in our tastes, and we cultivate the mind without loss of manliness. Wealth we employ, not for talk and ostentation, but when there is a real use for it. To avow poverty with us is no disgrace; the true disgrace is in doing nothing to avoid it. An Athenian citizen does not neglect the state because he takes care of his own household; and even those of us who are engaged in business have a very fair idea of politics. We alone regard a man who takes no interest in public affairs, not as a harmless, but as a useless character; and if few of us are originators, we are all sound judges of a policy. The great impediment to action is, in our opinion, not discussion, but the want of that knowledge which is gained by discussion preparatory to action. For we have a peculiar power of thinking before we act and of acting too, whereas other men are courageous from ignorance but hesitate upon reflection. And they are surely to be esteemed the bravest spirits who, having the clearest sense both of the pains and pleasures of life, do not on that account shrink from danger. In doing good, again, we are unlike others; we make our friends by conferring, not by receiving favors. To sum up: I say that Athens is the school of Hellas, and that the individual Athenian in his own person seems to have the power of adapting himself to the most varied forms of action with the utmost versatility and grace.

"I have paid the required tribute, in obedience to the law, making use of such fitting words as I had. The tribute of deeds has been paid in part; for the dead have been honorably interred, and it remains only that their children should be maintained at the public charge until they are grown up: this is the solid prize with which, as with a garland, Athens crowns her sons living and dead, after a struggle like theirs. For where the rewards of virtue are greatest, there the noblest citizens are enlisted in the service of the state. And now, when you have duly lamented, every one his own dead, you may depart."

In the second year of the war there was the usual invasion of Attica by the Peloponnesians and the Athenian voyage of desolation along the Peloponnesian coast. In fact, these operations were as a rule repeated during the early period of the war. The season had not far advanced, however, before a terrible plague, beginning in the East, reached Piraeus. Soon it passed up between the Long Walls to Athens.

"As to the plague's probable origin [says Thucydides] or the causes which might or could have produced such a disturbance of nature, every man, whether a physician or not, will give his own opinion. But I shall describe its actual course, and the symptoms by which any one who knows them beforehand may recognize the disorder should it ever reappear. For I was myself attacked, and witnessed the sufferings of others.

"The season was admitted to have been remarkably free from ordinary sickness; and if anybody was already ill of any other disease, it was absorbed in this. Many who were in perfect health, all in a moment, and without any apparent reason, were seized with violent heats in the head and with redness and inflammation of the eyes. Internally the throat and the tongue were quickly suffused with blood, and the breath became unnatural and fetid. There followed sneezing and hoarseness; in a short time the disorder, accompanied by a violent cough, reached the chest; then fastening lower down, it would move the stomach and bring on all the vomits of bile to which physicians have ever given names; and they were very distressing. An ineffectual retching producing violent convulsions attacked most of the sufferers; some as soon as the previous symptoms had abated, others not until long afterwards. The body externally was not so very hot to the touch, nor yet pale; it was of a livid color inclining to red, and breaking out in pustules and ulcers. But the internal fever was intense; the sufferers could not bear to have on them even the finest linen garment; they insisted on being naked, and there was nothing which they longed for more eagerly than to throw themselves into cold water. And many of those who had no one to look after them actually plunged into the cisterns, for they were tormented by unceasing thirst, which was not in the least assuaged whether they drank little or much. They could not sleep; a restlessness which was intolerable never left them.

"While the disease was at its height the body, instead of wasting away, held out amid these sufferings in a marvelous manner, and either they died on the seventh or ninth day, not of weakness, for their strength was not exhausted, but of internal fever, which was the end of most; or, if they survived, then the disease descended into the bowels and there produced violent ulceration; severe diarrhea at the same time set in, and at a later stage caused exhaustion, which finally with few exceptions carried them off. For the disorder which had originally settled in the head passed gradually through the whole body, and, if a person got over the worst, would often seize the extremities and leave its mark, attacking the genitals and the fingers and the toes; and some escaped with the loss of these, some with the loss of their eyes. Some again had no sooner recovered than they were seized with a forgetfulness of all things and knew neither themselves nor their friends.

"The crowding of the people out of the country into the city aggravated the misery; and the newly arrived suffered most. For, having no houses of their own, but inhabiting in the height of summer stifling huts, the mortality among them was dreadful, and they perished in wild disorder. The dead lay as they had died, one upon another, while others hardly alive wallowed in the streets and crawled about every fountain craving for water. The temples in which they lodged were full of the corpses of those who died in them; for the violence of the calamity was such that men, not knowing where to turn, grew reckless of all law, human and divine. The customs which had hitherto been observed at funerals were universally violated, and they buried their dead each one as best he could. Many, having no proper appliances, because the deaths in their household had been so frequent, made no scruple of using the burial place of others. When one man had raised a funeral pile, others would come, and throwing on their dead first, set fire to it; or when some other corpse was already burning, before they could be stopped would throw their own dead upon it and depart.

"There were other and worse forms of lawlessness which the plague introduced at Athens. Men who had hitherto concealed their indulgence in pleasure now grew bolder. For, seeing the sudden change, how the rich died in a moment, and those who had nothing immediately inherited their property, they reflected that life and riches were alike transitory, and they resolved to enjoy themselves while they could, and to think only of pleasure. Who would be willing to sacrifice himself to the law of honor when he knew not whether he would ever live to be held in honor? The pleasure of the moment and any sort of thing which conduced to it took the place both of honor and of expediency. No fear of God or law of man deterred a criminal. Those who saw all perishing alike, thought that the worship or neglect of the gods made no difference. For offenses against human law no punishment was to be feared; no one would live long enough to be called to account. Already a far heavier sentence had been passed and was hanging over a man's head; before that fell, why should he not take a little pleasure?"

Perhaps a third of the population was swept away by the plague, and in 429 B.C. Pericles himself fell a victim to it. Thus died the only man who stood sufficiently high above all individuals and parties to command universal respect. The leadership of the government now passed to men of the industrial class, to demagogues such as Cleon the tanner, who, unable to win the powerful support of the old nobility and of the moderate class, had to resort to lower politics and cater to the baser and more brutal desires and instincts of the populace. The revolution, thus silently effected, was as great as the century-long conflict at Rome which opened the consulship to the plebeians, and in its immediate consequences far more sweeping, for in her war with the Peloponnesus Athens lost through the death of Pericles centralization of leadership and continuity of policy.

The war, with its many expeditions, small defeats, and victories, was a grievous affliction to the Athenians. As the revenues decreased, the expenses greatly increased. Nevertheless, the desire for profit helped keep the war going. Merchants and mechanics expected to suffer little from it, and might hope to extend their business through conquests, while the poor found a livelihood in naval service, or looked to the enlargement of the Empire for increased tribute and a lengthened pay roll. The intellectuals, the landed aristocracy, and most farmers of moderate wealth, however, longed for peace.

In the year after Pericles' death, news reached Athens that her important ally, Mytilene, and most of the other towns on the island of Lesbos had revolted. If this should be allowed to succeed, would Athens' other allies, scattered around the Aegean Sea, follow suit? The Athenians decided to take no chances and, on the fall of Mytilene, voted to put to death all the men and to enslave the women and children. The advocate of this policy of terrorism was Cleon. The next day the Athenians met again to reconsider their cruel sentence. Cleon urged them not to repent: "I still maintain that you should abide by your former decision, and not be misled either by pity, or by the charm of words, or by a too forgiving temper. There are no three things more prejudicial to your power." The arguments against Cleon prevailed, not, however, because of an appeal to pity or kindness or justice, but simply to Athens' self-interest. The punishment of death was limited to the few Mytileneans most guilty, but the lands of the rebels were confiscated and divided among Athenian colonists.

Thucydides' *History* is in part the story of how the most humane of ancient states descended into an abyss of cynicism and cruelty. Athens lost the war, he believes, because, against the advice of Pericles and on the urging of extreme democrats, it pursued a policy of further conquest while the war was still on. Another reason for Athens' fall, he says, was intense party warfare, for many felt that "enslavement to the opposite faction is worse than the dominion of a foreigner." We would also do well to emphasize the terrible effect of the plague upon the Athenians. What happens to a people, when in the midst of war a third of the civilian population is suddenly swept away? Pericles' successors, according to Thucydides, "were more on an equality with one another, and, each one struggling to be first himself, they were ready to sacrifice the whole conduct of affairs to the whims of the people." Cleon, for example, deliberately prolonged the war, "because he fancied that in the days of peace his rogueries would be more transparent and his slanders less credible."

War, says Thucydides, produces violence, and violence political chaos. This he brings out with a vivid psychological insight when, in his description of the revolution that next overwhelmed Corcyra, he analyzes the effect of war on man's character: "Revolution brought upon the cities of Hellas many terrible calamities, such as have been and always will be while human nature remains the same, but which are more or less aggravated and differ in character with every new combination of circumstances. In peace and prosperity both states and individuals are actuated by higher motives, because they do not fall under the dominion of imperious necessities; but war which takes away the comfortable provision of daily life is a hard master, and tends to assimilate men's characters to their conditions.

"When troubles had once begun in the cities, those who followed carried the revolutionary spirit further and further, and determined to outdo the report of all who had preceded them by the ingenuity of their enterprises and the atrocity of their revenges. The meaning of words had no longer the same relation to things, but was changed by them as they thought proper. The lover of violence, moreover, was always trusted, and his opponent suspected. The tie of party was stronger than the tie of blood, because a partisan was more ready to dare without asking why. The seal of good faith was not divine law, but fellowship in crime. Revenge was dearer than self-preservation.

"The cause of all these evils was the love of power, originating in avarice and ambition, and the party spirit which is engendered by them when men are fairly embarked in a contest. For the leaders on either side used specious names, the one party professing to uphold the constitutional equality of the many, the other the wisdom of an aristocracy, while they made the public interests, to which in name they were devoted, in reality their prize. Thus revolution gave birth to every form of wickedness in Hellas. The simplicity which is so large an element in a noble nature was laughed to scorn and disappeared. An attitude of perfidious antagonism everywhere prevailed. Each man was strong only in the conviction that nothing was secure; he must look to his own safety, and could not afford to trust others. Inferior intellects generally succeeded best."

Most fortunately for Greece, the chief obstacles to peace at Athens and Sparta, Cleon and Brasidas, were ultimately killed in a campaign. Both Athenians and Spartans were anxious for peace, and the initiative was taken by an aristocratic Athenian of wealth, Nicias by name (421 B.C.). The Peace of Nicias, as the arrangements came to be called, was to endure for fifty years, and in a general way provided for the exchange of prisoners and captured cities. The Athenian Empire, as Pericles had expected, came through the first decade of war without great difficulty, but the present problem was to keep the peace.

The outstanding feature of Athenian foreign policy in the next years was the dominating influence of Alcibiades, the grandnephew and ward of Pericles. Handsome, brilliant, vain, and daring, this young man had been petted and spoiled by his family and fellow citizens. Saturated in sophistic instruction, he recognized no principle but self-seeking, and deported himself in reckless violation of law and custom. Combining the arts of the demagogue with his own personal fascination, he won the generalship in 420 B.C., and at once began to rehabilitate the war party, in the hope of advancing his own interest.

Under Alcibiades' influence, the Athenians sent an expedition against the little island of Melos. In the famous Melian Dialogue that follows, Thucydides, seemingly without passion, lays bare the soul of a despot nation, his own. By espousing the policy of "Might makes Right," Athens aroused universal hatred and fear and gave to enemies a certain justification for her overthrow.

"The Athenians made an expedition [says Thucydides] against the island of Melos with thirty ships of their own, six Chian, and two Lesbian, 1,200 hoplites and 300 archers besides twenty mounted archers of their own, and about 1,500 hoplites furnished by their allies in the islands. The Melians are colonists of the Lacedaemonians who would not submit to Athens like the other islanders. At first they were neutral and took no part. But when the Athenians tried to coerce them by ravaging their lands, they were driven into open hostilities. The generals, Cleomedes the son of Lycomedes and Tisias the son of Tisimachus, encamped with the Athenian forces on the island. But before they did the country any harm they sent envoys to negotiate with the Melians. Instead of bringing these envoys before the people, the Melians desired them to explain their errand to the magistrates and to the chief men.

"*Athenians:* Well, then, we Athenians will use no fine words; we will not go out of our way to prove at length that we have a right to rule, because we overthrew the Persians; or that we attack you now because we are suffering any injury at your hands. We should not convince you if we did; nor must you expect to convince us by arguing that, although a colony of the Lacedaemonians, you have taken no part in their expeditions, or that you have never done us any wrong. But you and we should say what we really think, and aim only at what is possible, for we both alike know that into the discussion of human affairs the question of justice only enters where the pressure of necessity is equal, and that the powerful exact what they can, and the weak grant what they must.

"*Melians:* Well, then, since you set aside justice and invite us to speak of expediency, in our judgment it is certainly expedient that you should respect a principle which is for the common good; and that to every man when in peril a reasonable claim should be accounted a claim of right, and any plea which he is disposed to urge, even if failing of the point a little, should help his cause. Your interest in this principle is quite as great as ours, inasmuch as you, if you fall, will incur the heaviest vengeance, and will be the most terrible example to mankind.

"*Athenians:* The fall of our empire, if it should fall, is not an event to which we look forward with dismay; for ruling states such as Lacedaemon are not cruel to their vanquished enemies. And we are fighting not so much against the Lacedaemonians, as against our own subjects who may some day rise up and overcome their former masters. But this is a danger which you may leave to us. And we will now endeavor to show that we have come in the interests of our empire, and that we are only seeking the preservation of your city. For we want to make you ours with the least trouble to ourselves, and it is for the interests of us both that you should not be destroyed.

"*Melians:* It may be your interest to be our masters, but how can it be ours to be your slaves?

"*Athenians:* To you the gain will be that by submission you will avert the wrost; and we shall be all the richer for your preservation. We are masters of the sea, and you who are islanders, and insignificant islanders too, must not be allowed to escape us.

"*Melians:* We know only too well how hard the struggle must be against your power, and against fortune, if she does not mean to be impartial. Nevertheless we do not despair of fortune; for we hope to stand as high as you in the favor of heaven, because we are righteous, and you against whom we contend are unrighteous; and we are satisfied that our deficiency in power will be compensated by the aid of our allies the Lacedaemonians.

"*Athenians:* As for the gods, we expect to have quite as much of their favor as you: for we are not doing or claiming anything which goes beyond common opinion about divine or men's desires about human things. For of the gods we believe, and of men we know, that by a law of their nature wherever they can rule they will. This law was not made by us, and we are not the first who have acted upon it; we did but inherit it, and shall bequeath it to all time, and we know that you and all mankind, if you were as strong as we are, would do as we do. So much for the gods; we have told you why we expect to stand as high in their good opinion as you. And then as to the Lacedaemonians—when you imagine that out of very shame they will assist you, we admire the simplicity of your idea, but we do not envy you the folly of it. The Lacedaemonians are exceedingly virtuous among themselves, and according to their national standard of morality. But, in respect of their dealings with others, although many things might be said, a word is enough to describe them, of all men whom we know they are the most notorious for identifying what is pleasant with what is honorable, and what is expedient with what is just. But how inconsistent is such a character with your present blind hope of deliverance!

"*Melians:* That is the very reason we trust them; they will look to their interest, and therefore will not be willing to betray the Melians, who are their own colonists, lest they should be distrusted by their friends in Hellas and play into the hands of their enemies.

"*Athenians:* Help may come from Lacedaemon to you as it has come to others, and should you ever have actual experience of it, then you will know that never once have the Athenians retired from a siege through fear of a foe elsewhere. You told us that the safety of your city would be your first care, but we remark that, in this long discussion, not a word has been uttered by you which would give a reasonable man expectation of deliverance. Your strongest grounds are hopes deferred, and what power you have is not to be compared with that which is already arrayed against you. Unless after we have withdrawn you mean to come, as even now you may, to a wiser conclusion, you are showing a great want of sense. For surely you cannot dream of flying to that false sense of honor which has been the ruin of so many when danger and dishonor were staring them in the face. Many men with their eyes still open to the consequences have found the word 'honor' too much for them, and have suffered a mere name to lure them on, until it has drawn down upon them real and irretrievable calamities; through their own folly they have incurred a worse dishonor than fortune would have inflicted upon them. If you are wise you will not run this risk; you ought to see that there can be no disgrace in yielding to a great city which invites you to become her ally on reasonable terms, keeping your own land, and merely paying tribute; and that you will certainly gain no honor if, having to choose between two alternatives, safety and war, you obstinately prefer the worse. To maintain our rights against equals, to be politic with superiors, and to be moderate towards inferiors is the path of safety. Reflect once more when we have withdrawn, and say to yourselves over and over again that you are deliberating about your one and only country, which may be saved or may be destroyed by a single decision.

"The Athenians left the conference: the Melians, after consulting among themselves, resolved to persevere in their refusal. The Athenian envoys then returned to the army; and the generals, when they found that the Melians would not yield, immediately commenced hostilities. They surrounded the town of Melos with a wall, dividing the work among the several contingents. The place was now closely invested, and there was treachery among the citizens themselves. So the Melians were induced to surrender at discretion. The Athenians thereupon put to death all who were of military age, and made slaves of the women and children. They then colonized the island, sending thither 500 settlers of their own."

The triumphant rise of Alcibiades meant a resumption of the

policy of conquest, and nowhere opened so fair a field as Sicily, with the richest prize of all, Corinth's powerful colony of Syracuse. Nicias strenuously opposed this undertaking, but to no avail.

All the financial reserves of Athens were devoted to the new expedition. The fleet consisted of 134 warships, or triremes, with 130 supply boats. Over 5,000 heavy-armed foot soldiers, or hoplites, 1,300 light-armed troops, and 30 cavalry comprised the army. Counting the crews, at least 27,000 men made up this vast armada. The Athenians placed three generals in charge, Alcibiades, Nicias, and Lamachus, a fighter of the old school. Shortly before the departure the Athenians were horrified one morning to find that the Hermae—stone busts—in front of their doors had been mutilated. The people were seized with terror lest, as a step toward overthrowing the democracy, a band of conspirators had attempted to deprive the city of her divine protectors. In a panic the citizens assembled and voted immunity and rewards to anyone who gave information against the perpetrators. No one came forward, however, for the deed had probably been committed by drunken youths; but it was revealed that certain persons, among them Alcibiades, had once profaned the Eleusinian Mysteries by parodying them at private gatherings in the presence of the uninitiated. Democratic politicians, opposed to Alcibiades, schemed to prosecute him for the sacrilege, and he demanded an immediate trial. But, appreciating his popularity with the soldiers and sailors, they delayed.

Nothing was to be allowed to interfere with the expedition. Various leaders hoped for personal prestige, while the ordinary soldiers saw their chance to escape from humdrum routine and to enrich themselves. "All alike," says Thucydides, "were seized with a passionate desire to sail, the elder among them convinced that they would achieve the conquest of Sicily; the youth were longing to see with their own eyes the marvels of a distant land; the main body of the troops expected to receive present pay, and to conquer a country which would be an inexhaustible mine of pay for the future."

Thucydides paints the picture of the expedition as it was ready to sail in midsummer, 415 B.C.: "Early in the morning of the day appointed for their departure, the Athenians and such of their allies as had already joined them went down to Piraeus and began to man the ships. The entire population of Athens accompanied them, citizens and strangers alike. The citizens came to take farewell, one of an acquaintance, another of a kinsman, another of a son; the crowd as they passed along were full of hope and full of tears; hope of conquering Sicily, tears because they doubted whether they would ever see their friends again, when they thought of the long voyage on which they were sending them. At the moment of parting the danger was nearer; and terrors which had never occurred to them when they were voting the expedition now entered their souls. Nevertheless their spirits revived at the sight of the armament in all its strength and of the abundant provision which they had made.

"No armament so magnificent or so costly had ever been sent out by any single Hellenic power. On the fleet the greatest pains and expense had been lavished by the captains and the state. Men were quite amazed at the boldness of the scheme and the magnificence of the spectacle, which were everywhere spoken of, no less than at the great disproportion of the force when compared with that of the enemy against whom it was intended. Never had a greater expedition been sent to a foreign land; never was there an enterprise in which the hope of future success seemed to be better justified by actual power.

"When the ships were manned and everything required for the voyage had been placed on board, silence was proclaimed by the sound of the trumpet, and all with one voice before setting sail offered up the customary prayers; these were recited, not in each ship, but by a single herald, the whole fleet accompanying him. On every deck both officers and men, mingling wine in bowls, made libations from vessels of gold and silver. The multitude of citizens and other well-wishers who were looking on from the land joined in the prayer. The crews raised the paean, and when the libations were completed, put to sea. After sailing out for some distance in single file, the ships raced with one another as far as Aegina."

After the fleet had departed, the Athenians voted an indictment for sacrilege against Alcibiades and sent a state ship to Sicily to bring him back. On the homeward voyage, however, Alcibiades made his escape to Sparta, where his counsels proved dangerous to his country's welfare. At his suggestion, the Spartans established a regular garrison at Decelea in northern Attica, not far from Athens. As a result, the Athenians were forced to give up their country houses and to withdraw permanently into the city. Thousands of slaves deserted to the enemy; industry and commerce shrank; and the people were soon cramped with want.

Meanwhile in Sicily, the Syracusans received reinforcements under an able Spartan officer, Gylippus. The Athenian commanders, for their part, frittered away several months in petty undertakings, wasting their resources, discouraging their own men, and exciting contempt in the minds of the Sicilian Greeks. Then, during some fighting around Syracuse, Lamachus was killed. This left Nicias, who had opposed the expedition from the beginning, in sole command. He made no headway in the siege of Syracuse and would gladly have abandoned the undertaking, but he dared not face the Athenian Assembly. When, however, the Athenians received his report, which detailed the condition of the armament and asked that it be recalled or reinforced, the Assembly, with extraordinary persistence, voted heavy reinforcements. A small force was sent at once; and the next spring Demosthenes arrived with an armada of 15,000 men.

When Demosthenes arrived at Syracuse, he found the besiegers in a miserable condition. They had lost a naval battle in the harbor, and this failure, together with sickness and privation, sapped their courage. The only hope lay in immediate success. The strenuous offensive of Demosthenes, however, utterly failed, and when he proposed to embark the army and sail away, a total eclipse of the moon caused the superstitious Nicias to urge delay. The Syracusans, taking advantage of this, blocked the mouth of the harbor. Now robbed of the advantage of surprise, nothing remained for the Athenian fleet but to try to force its way into the open sea. The description of the ensuing sea battle, the retreat by land and the annihilation of practically all the 45,000 Athenians and their allies, who had sailed in two glorious fleets against Syracuse with such high hopes, gains in the pages of Thucydides the power of a great tragedy:

"When Gylippus and the other Syracusan generals had, like Nicias, encouraged their troops, perceiving the Athenians to be manning their ships, they presently did the same. Nicias, overwhelmed by the situation, and seeing how great and how near the peril was (for the ships were on the very point of rowing out), feeling too, as men do on the eve of a great struggle, that all which he had done was nothing, and that he had not said half enough, again addressed the captains, and calling each of them by his father's name, and his own name, and the name of his tribe, he entreated those who had made any reputation for themselves not to be false to it, and those whose ancestors were eminent not to tarnish their hereditary fame. He reminded them that they were the inhabitants of the freest country in the world, and how in Athens there was no interference with the daily life of any man. He spoke to them of their wives and children and their fathers' gods, as men will at such a time; for then they do not care whether their commonplace phrases seem to be out of date or not, but loudly reiterate the old appeals, believing that they may be of some service at the awful moment.

"When he thought that he had exhorted them, not enough, but as much as the scanty time allowed, he retired, and led the land forces to the shore, extending the line as far as he could, so that they might be of the greatest use in encouraging the combatants on board ship. Demosthenes, Menander, and Euthydemus, who had gone on board the Athenian fleet to take the command, now quitted their own station, and proceeded straight to the closed mouth of the harbor, intending to force their way to the open sea where a passage was still left.

"The Syracusans and their allies had already put out with nearly the same number of ships as before. A detachment of them guarded the entrance of the harbor; the remainder were disposed all round it in such a manner that they might fall on the Athenians from every side at once, and that their land forces might at the same time be able to co-operate wherever the ships retreated to the shore. Sicanus and Agatharchus commanded the Syracusan fleet, each of them a wing; Pythen and the Corinthians occupied the center. When the Athenians approached the closed mouth of the harbor the violence of their onset overpowered the ships which were stationed there; they then attempted to loosen the fastenings. Whereupon from all sides the Syracusans and their allies came bearing down upon them, and the conflict was no longer confined to the entrance, but extended throughout the harbor. No previous engagement had been so fierce and obstinate. Great was the eagerness with which the rowers on both sides rushed upon their enemies whenever the word of command was given; and keen was the contest between the pilots as they maneuvered one against the other. The marines too were full of anxiety that, when ship struck ship, the service on deck should not fall short of the rest; every one in the place assigned to him was eager to be foremost among his fellows. Many vessels meeting—and never did so many fight in so small a space, for the two fleets together amounted to nearly 200—they were seldom able to strike in the regular manner, because they had no opportunity of first retiring or breaking the line; they generally fouled one another as ship dashed against ship in the hurry of flight or pursuit. All the time that another vessel was bearing down, the men on deck poured showers of javelins and arrows and stones upon the enemy; and when the two closed, the marines fought hand to hand, and endeavored to board. In many places, owing to the want of room, they who had struck another found that they were struck themselves; often two or even more vessels were unavoidably entangled about one, and the pilots had to make plans of attack and defense, not against one adversary only, but against several coming from different sides.

"The crash of so many ships dashing against one another took away the wits of the sailors, and made it impossible to hear the boatswains, whose voices in both fleets rose high, as they gave directions to the rowers, or cheered them on in the excitement of the struggle. On the Athenian side they were shouting to their men that they must force a passage and seize the opportunity now or never of returning in safety to their native land. To the Syracusans and their allies were represented the glory of preventing the escape of their enemies, and of a victory by which every man would exalt the honor of his own city. The commanders too, when they saw any ship backing water without necessity, would call the captain by his name, and ask, of the Athenians, whether they were retreating because they expected to be more at home upon the land of their bitterest foes than upon that sea which had been their own so long; on the Syracusan side, whether, when they knew perfectly well that the Athenians were only eager to find some means of flight, they would themselves fly from the fugitives.

"While the naval engagement hung in the balance the two armies on shore had great trial and conflict of soul. The Sicilian soldier was animated by the hope of increasing the glory which he had already won, while the invader was tormented by the fear that his fortunes might sink lower still. The last chance of the Athenians lay in their ships, and their anxiety was dreadful. The fortune of the battle varied; and it was not possible that the spectators on the shore should all receive the same impression of it. Being quite close and having different points of view, they would some of them see their own ships victorious; their courage would then revive, and they would earnestly call upon the gods not to take from them their hope of deliverance. But others, who saw their ships worsted, cried and shrieked aloud, and were by the sight alone more utterly unnerved than the defeated combatants themselves. Others again, who had fixed their gaze on some part of the struggle which was undecided, were in a state of excitement still more terrible; they kept swaying their bodies to and fro in an agony of hope and fear as the stubborn conflict went on and on; for at every instant they were all but saved or all but lost. And while the strife hung in the balance you might hear in the

Athenian army at once lamentation, shouting, cries of victory or defeat, and all the various sounds which are wrung from a great host in extremity of danger.

"Not less agonizing were the feelings of those on board. At length the Syracusans and their allies, after a protracted struggle, put the Athenians to flight, and triumphantly bearing down upon them, and encouraging one another with loud cries and exhortations, drove them to land. Then that part of the navy which had not been taken in the deep water fell back in confusion to the shore, and the crews rushed out of the ships into the camp. And the land forces, no longer now divided in feeling, but uttering one universal groan of intolerable anguish, ran, some of them to save the ships, others to defend what remained of the wall; but the greater number began to look to themselves and to their own safety. Never had there been a greater panic in an Athenian army than at that moment. They now suffered what they had done to others at Pylos. For at Pylos the Lacedaemonians, when they saw their ships destroyed, knew that their friends who who had crossed over into the island of Sphacteria were lost with them. And so now the Athenians, after the rout of their fleet, knew that they had no hope of saving themselves by land unless events took some extraordinary turn.

"Thus, after a fierce battle and a great destruction of ships and men on both sides, the Syracusans and their allies gained the victory. They gathered up the wrecks and bodies of the dead, and sailing back to the city, erected a trophy. The Athenians, overwhelmed by their misery, never so much as thought of recovering their wrecks or of asking leave to collect their dead. Their intention was to retreat that very night.

"Hermocrates the Syracusan suspected their intention, and dreading what might happen if their vast army, retreating by land and settling somewhere in Sicily, should choose to renew the war, contrived the following plan: when it was growing dark he sent certain of his own acquaintances, accompanied by a few horsemen, to the Athenian camp. They rode up within earshot, and pretending to be friends (there were known to be men in the city who gave information to Nicias of what went on) called to some of the soldiers, and bade them tell him not to withdraw his army during the night, for the Syracusans were guarding the roads; he should make preparation at leisure and retire by day. Having delivered their message they departed, and those who had heard them informed the Athenian generals.

"On receiving this message, which they supposed to be genuine, they remained during the night. And having once given up the intention of starting immediately, they decided to remain during the next day, that the soldiers might, as well as they could, put together their baggage in the most convenient form, and depart, taking with them the bare necessaries of life, but nothing else.

"Meanwhile the Syracusans and Gylippus, going forth before them with their land forces, blocked the roads in the country by which the Athenians were likely to pass, guarded the fords of the rivers and streams, and posted themselves at the best points for receiving and stopping them. Their sailors rowed up to the beach and dragged away the Athenian ships.The Athenians themselves burnt a few of them, as they had intended, but the rest the Syracusans towed away, unmolested and at their leisure, from the places where they had severally run aground, and conveyed them to the city.

"On the third day after the sea fight, when Nicias and Demosthenes thought that their preparations were complete, the army began to move. They were in a dreadful condition; not only was there the great fact that they had lost their whole fleet, and instead of their expected triumph had brought the utmost peril upon Athens as well as upon themselves, but also the sights which presented themselves as they quitted the camp were painful to every eye and mind. The dead were unburied, and when any one saw the body of a friend lying on the ground he was smitten with sorrow and dread, while the sick or wounded who still survived but had to be left were even a greater trial to the living, and more to be pitied than those who were gone. Their prayers and lamentations drove their companions to distraction; they would beg that they might be taken with them, and call by name any friend or relation whom they saw passing; they would hang upon their departing comrades and follow as far as they could, and when their limbs and strength failed them and they dropped behind many were the imprecations and cries which they uttered. So that the whole army was in tears, and such was their despair that they could hardly make up their minds to stir, although they were leaving an enemy's country, having suffered calamities too great for tears already, and dreading miseries yet greater in the unknown future.

"There was also a general feeling of shame and self-reproach, —indeed they seemed, not like an army, but like the fugitive population of a city captured after a siege; and of a great city too. For the whole multitude who were marching together numbered not less than 40,000. Each of them took with him anything he could carry which was likely to be of use. Even the heavy-armed and cavalry, contrary to their practice when under arms, conveyed about their persons their own food, some because they had no attendants, others because they could not trust them; for they had long been deserting, and most of them had gone off all at once. Nor was the food which they carried sufficient; for the supplies of the camp had failed. Their disgrace and the universality of the misery, although there might be some consolation in the very community of suffering, was nevertheless at that moment hard to bear, especially when they remembered from what pomp and splendor they had fallen into their present low estate. Never had an Hellenic army experienced such a reverse. They had come intending to enslave others, and they were going away in fear that they would be themselves enslaved. Instead of the prayers and hymns with which they had put to sea, they were now departing amid appeals to heaven of another sort. They were no longer sailors but landsmen, depending, not upon their fleet, but upon their infantry. Yet in face of the great danger which still threatened them all these things appeared endurable."

The long retreat across land ended in the death of many Athenians and their allies and in the capture of the remainder. Nicias and Demosthenes were put to the sword; the others were thrown into the quarries of Syracuse. "Those who were imprisoned in the quarries [continues Thucydides] were at the beginning of their captivity harshly treated by the Syracusans. There were great numbers of them, and they were crowded in a deep and narrow place. At first the sun by day was still scorching and suffocating, for they had no roof over their heads, while the autumn nights were cold, and the extremes of temperature engendered violent disorders. Being cramped for room they had to do everything on the same spot. The corpses of those who died from their wounds, exposure to the weather, and the like, lay heaped one upon another. The smells were intolerable; and they were at the same time afflicted by hunger and thirst. During eight months they were allowed only about half a pint of water and a pint of food a day. Every kind of misery which could befall man in such a place befell them. This was the condition of all the captives for about ten weeks. At length the Syracusans sold them, with the exception of the Athenians and of any Sicilian or Italian Greeks who had sided with them in the war. The whole number of the public prisoners is not accurately known, but they were not less than 7,000.

"Of all the Hellenic actions which took place in this war, or indeed of all Hellenic actions which are on record, this was the greatest—the most glorious to the victors, the most ruinous to the vanquished; for they were utterly and at all points defeated, and their sufferings were prodigious. Fleet and army perished from the face of the earth; nothing was saved, and of the many who went forth few returned home.

"Thus ended the Sicilian expedition."

This was in September, 413 B.C. The years ahead saw political strife at Athens, general suffering, defeats in battle, and also victories, which so raised the spirits of an indomitable people that they could refuse one offer of peace after another. The Spartans then took the obvious step of sending Lysander, an able general, to the eastern Aegean in order to cut off Athens' food supplies from the Black Sea. The Athenians dispatched against him their last possible fleet manned with their last available crews, 180 ships against the 200 Peloponnesian. The Athenian fleet, stationed on the European side of the Hellespont at the mouth of the Aegospotami River, was taken by surprise while the crews were searching for provisions on shore. The Athenians were massacred. Conon, one of the generals, escaped to Cyprus with eight ships, having sent the state trireme *Paralus* to Piraeus with the sad news. The Athenian Xenophon * has left a memorable description of its arrival and the last days (404 B.C.) of imperial Athens:

"It was night when the *Paralus* reached Athens with her evil tidings, on receipt of which a bitter wail of woe broke forth. From Piraeus, following the line of the Long Walls up to the heart of the city, it swept and swelled, as each man to his neighbor passed on the news. On that night no man slept. There was mourning and sorrow for those that were lost, but the lamentation for the dead was merged in even deeper sorrow for themselves, as they pictured the evils they were about to suffer, the like of which they had themselves inflicted upon the men of Melos, who were colonists of the Lacedaemonians, when they mastered them by siege. Or on the men of Histiaea; on Scione and Torone; on the Aeginetans, and many another Hellenic city. On the following day the public Assembly met, and, after debate, it was resolved to block up all the harbors save one, to put the walls in a state of defense, to post guards at various points, and to make all other necessary preparation for a siege. Such were the concerns of the men of Athens.

"In obedience to a general order of Pausanias, the Spartan king, a levy in force of the Lacedaemonians and all the rest of the Peloponnesus, except the Argives, was set in motion for a campaign. As soon as the several contingents had arrived, the king put himself at their head and marched against Athens, encamping in the Academy, as it is called. Lysander now anchored at Piraeus with 150 ships, and established a strict blockade against all merchant ships entering that harbor.

* Henry G. Dakyns' translation.

"The Athenians, finding themselves besieged by land and sea, did not know what to do. Without ships, without allies, without provisions, the belief gained hold upon them that there was no way of escape. They must now, in their turn, suffer what they had themselves inflicted upon others; not in retaliation, indeed, for ills received, but out of sheer insolence, overriding the citizens of petty states, and for no better reason than these were allies of the very men now at their gates. In this frame of mind they enfranchised those who at any time had lost their civil rights, and schooled themselves to endurance; and, although many were dying of starvation, they refused to negotiate for peace. But when the stock of grain was absolutely insufficient, they sent an embassy to Agis, the other Spartan king, proposing to become allies of the Lacedaemonians on the sole condition of keeping their fortification walls and Piraeus; and to draw up articles of treaty on these terms. Agis bade them betake themselves to Lacedaemon, seeing that he had no authority to act himself. With this answer the ambassadors returned to Athens, and were forthwith sent on to Lacedaemon.

"On reaching Sellasia, a town in Laconian territory, they waited till they got their answer from the ephors, who, having learnt their terms (which were identical with those already proposed to Agis), bade them instantly to be gone, and, if they really desired peace, to come with other proposals, the fruit of happier reflection. Thus the ambassadors returned home, and reported the result of their embassy, whereupon despondency fell upon all. It was a painful reflection that in the end they would be sold into slavery; and meanwhile, pending the return of a second embassy, many must needs fall victims to starvation. The razing of their fortifications was not a solution which any one cared to recommend. Things having reached this pass, Theramenes made a proposal in the public Assembly as follows: If they chose to send him as an ambassador, he would go and find out why the Lacedaemonians were so unyielding about the walls; whether it was they really intended to enslave the city, or merely that they wanted a guarantee of good faith.

"Theramenes and his companions presently reached Sellasia, and being here questioned as to the reason of their visit, replied that they had full powers to treat of peace. After which the ephors ordered them to be summoned to their presence. On their arrival a general assembly was convened, in which the Corinthians and Thebans more particularly, though their views were shared by many other Hellenes also, urged the meeting not to come to terms with the Athenians, but to destroy them. The Lacedaemonians replied that they would never reduce to slavery a city which was itself an integral portion of Hellas, and had performed a great and noble service to Hellas in the Persian emergency. On the contrary, they were willing to offer peace on the terms now specified—namely, 'That the Long Walls and the fortifications of Piraeus should be destroyed; that the Athenian fleet, with the exception of twelve vessels, should be surrendered; that the exiles should be restored; and lastly, that the Athenians should acknowledge the headship of Sparta in peace and war, leaving to her the choice of friends and foes, and following her lead by land and sea.'

"Such were the terms which Theramenes and the rest who acted with him were able to report on their return to Athens. As they entered the city, a vast crowd met them, trembling lest their mission should have proved fruitless. For indeed delay was no longer possible, so long already was the list of victims daily perishing from starvation. On the day following, the ambassadors delivered their report, stating the terms upon which the Lacedaemonians were willing to make peace. Theramenes acted as spokesman, insisting that they ought to obey the Lacedaemonians and pull down the walls. A small minority raised their voice in opposition, but the majority were strongly in favor of the proposition, and the resolution was passed to accept the peace. After that, Lysander sailed into Piraeus, and the exiles were readmitted. And so they fell to leveling the fortifications and walls with much enthusiasm, to the accompaniment of female flute players, deeming that day the beginning of liberty to Greece."

BRIEF CHRONOLOGICAL SUMMARY

OF ANCIENT GREEK HISTORY

All dates are B.C.

Bronze Age Civilization . . . . 3rd and 2nd millennia

The height of this fascinating prehistoric period is best represented by the magnificent palace of Minos at Knossos in Crete (1600); later (1400) the center of the Age shifted to Mycenae on the mainland.

Fall of Troy . . . . *ca.* 1184

The famous War was symptomatic of tribal migrations.

Dorian Invasion . . . . *ca.* 1100

The invasion of rude Dorian Greeks brought the Bronze Age to an end and inaugurated the historical period of Greece.

The Greek Middle Age . . . . *ca.* 1100-750

During these centuries the Greeks settled themselves in their homeland around the Aegean Sea. Time of Homer (*ca.* 800). According to tradition, the first Olympic Games were held in 776.

The Archaic Age . . . . *ca.* 750-479

A wonderfully exuberant civilization now blossoms in the Greek world, stimulated by trade with Egypt and Mesopotamia and by the rise of industry. The Greeks enter on a period of colonization, especially to Sicily and southern Italy. Sparta founds her Peloponnesian league; there are many tyrannies; Athens, under Solon, Peisistratus and Cleisthenes, emerges as a city of first importance and ultimately as a democracy.

Aeschylus . . . . *ca.* 525-456

Expedition of Mardonius 492

The glorious fifth century opens with Persian invasions of Greece.

Battle of Marathon 490

Battles of Thermopylae, Artemisium, Salamis 480

Battles of Plataea and Mycale 479

The victories over Persia by land and sea stirred the Greeks to prodigious efforts.

Athens establishes the Delian league 477

The sacred island of Delos was chosen as the capital of this defensive alliance against Persia.

Pericles becomes leader of the democratic faction at Athens. 461

Further, rapid extension of democracy.

Height of Athenian power on land 456

Treasury of Delian league transferred to Athens 454

Athenian Empire firmly established 448

The Athenian Empire consisted of the former Delian league (a maritime confederacy comprising Greek states along the coast of Asia Minor and the northern Aegean, as well as the islands) and, a later development, an empire on the mainland.

Collapse of the Athenian land empire 446

Athens' strength had not equalled Pericles' calculations, but the maritime empire remained.

The Thirty Years' Peace 445

The troubled affairs between Athens and the Peloponnesians were settled by an agreement which did not run half its course.

The Peloponnesian War 431-404

Athens and her empire join in mortal combat with the Peloponnesian league, led by Sparta and Corinth, and its Theban allies.

Archidamian War 431-421

Athens came successfully through the first phase of the Peloponnesian War, named after the Spartan king, Archidamus.

Death of Pericles 429

Rise of demagogues.

Peace of Nicias 421

Though it brought a welcome halt to hostilities, the Peace was disturbed by the ambitions of Alcibiades and was chiefly honored in the breach.

Athenian expedition to Melos 416

Both Thucydides, in his *History,* and Euripides, in *The Trojan Women,* protested against this outrage.

Athenian expedition to Sicily 415-413

An imperialistic venture that ended in overwhelming disaster.

Battle of Aegospotami 405

For this final battle of the War, Athens dispatched her last possible fleet, manned by the last available crews. Bad generalship cost her the battle, as bad statesmanship had caused her the previous year to turn down offers of peace.

Fall of Athens 404

Never again was Athens a first-rate power, though she remained the cultural center of the ancient world.

The Thirty Tyrants at Athens 404

Democracy was soon re-established.

Construction of temples on the Athenian Acropolis .... 2nd half of 5th cent.

Period of Athenian dramatists, historians, Socrates	2nd half of 5th cent.
Death of Socrates	399
Empires of Sparta and Thebes	1st half of 4th cent.
This was a period of wars, economic depression, confusion, following on Athens' collapse. But it was also a time of great men, such as Praxiteles, Plato and Aristotle.	
Philip II of Macedon	359-336
A new force in Greek history looms on the northern horizon.	
Battle of Chaeronea	338
The city-states of Greece, having failed to solve the problem of federation and autonomy, are defeated by Philip and joined in a league for war against Persia.	
Alexander the Great	336-323
The famous Macedonian conquers the world and introduces new ideas about universalism.	
The Hellenistic Age	323-31
During these three centuries Hellenism spread to the non-Greek world. The large monarchical state (especially the Antigonid in Macedonia, the Seleucid in Asia, and the Ptolemaic in Egypt) supplanted the small city-state. It was a period of great prosperity, centering in Alexandria and other big, new cities. Finally, at the battle of Actium, Rome completed her conquest of the world, and mankind settled down to the Augustan Age and the famous Roman Peace, which lasted more than a quarter of a millennium.	

BRIEF BIBLIOGRAPHY

This list of general English titles will set the reader on the track of a full bibliography.

BEAZLEY, J. D. *Potter and Painter in Ancient Athens*. London, 1945.

BEAZLEY, J. D. and B. ASHMOLE. *Greek Sculpture and Painting*. Cambridge, 1932.

BIEBER, M. *The History of the Greek and Roman Theater*. Princeton, 1939.

BLUCK, R. S. *Plato's Life and Thought*. London, 1949.

BOTSFORD, G. W. and C. A. ROBINSON, JR. *Hellenic History*. 3rd ed. New York, 1950.

BOWRA, C. M. *Sophoclean Tragedy*. New York, 1944.

BURN, A. R. *Pericles and Athens*. New York, 1949.

BURY, J. B. and OTHERS (editors). *Cambridge Ancient History*. 12 vols., 5 vols. of plates. New York, 1923-39.

BUSCHOR, E. *Greek Vase-Painting*. Trans. by G. C. Richards. London, 1921.

CARY, M. and OTHERS (editors). *Oxford Classical Dictionary*. Oxford, 1949.

DINSMOOR, W. B. *The Architecture of Ancient Greece*. London, 1950.

FIELD, G. C. *The Philosophy of Plato*. London, 1949.

FINLEY, J. H., JR. *Thucydides*. Cambridge, Mass., 1942.

FLICKINGER, R. C. *The Greek Theater and Its Drama*. 4th ed. Chicago, 1936.

GODOLPHIN, F. R. B. (editor). *The Greek Historians*. 2 vols. New York, 1942.

GRUBE, G. M. A. *The Drama of Euripides*. London, 1941.

HADAS, M. *A History of Greek Literature*. New York, 1950.

HARSH, P. W. *A Handbook of Classical Drama*. Stanford, 1944.

HEGE, W. and G. RODENWALDT. *The Acropolis*. Oxford, 1930.

HIGHET, G. *The Classical Tradition.* New York, 1949.

JOHNSON, A. C. and OTHERS. *The Greek Political Experience.* Princeton, 1941.

JOWETT, B. *The Dialogues of Plato translated into English.* Introduction by R. Demos. 2 vols. New York, 1937.

KITTO, H. D. F. *Greek Tragedy.* London, 1939.

LAWRENCE, A. W. *Classical Sculpture.* New ed. London, 1944.

MURRAY, G. *Aeschylus, the Creator of Tragedy.* New York, 1940.

OATES, W. J. and C. T. MURPHY (editors). *Greek Literature in Translation.* New York, 1944.

OATES, W. J. and E. O'NEILL, JR. (editors). *The Complete Greek Drama.* 2 vols. New York, 1938.

PFUHL, E. *Masterpieces of Greek Drawing and Painting.* Trans. by J. D. Beazley. New York, 1926.

RICHTER, G. M. A. *Animals in Greek Sculpture.* New York, 1930.

RICHTER, G. M. A. *The Sculpture and Sculptors of the Greeks.* New rev. ed. New Haven, 1950.

ROBERTSON, D. S. *A Handbook of Greek and Roman Architecture.* 2nd ed. Cambridge, 1943.

ROBINSON, C. A., JR. (editor). *An Anthology of Greek Drama.* New York, 1949.

ROBINSON, C. A., JR. *Ancient History.* New York, 1951.

SELTMAN, C. *Masterpieces of Greek Coinage.* London, 1949.

SELTMAN, C. *A Book of Greek Coins.* London, 1952.

TAYLOR, A. E. *Socrates.* New York, 1933.

TOYNBEE, A. J. *A Study of History.* Abridgement by D. C. Somervell. London, 1947.

TOYNBEE, A. J. *Civilization on Trial.* New York, 1948.

WHITMAN, C. H. *Sophocles.* Cambridge, Mass., 1951.

ZIMMERN, A. *The Greek Commonwealth: Politics and Economics in Fifth-Century Athens.* 5th ed. Oxford, 1931.

PLATES

(*These will be found grouped as a unit following page 424.*)

16. Head of a horse of the moon goddess, Selene, from the east pediment of the Parthenon. British Museum, London.
17. So-called Nike (Victory) from the west pediment of the Parthenon. British Museum, London.
18. Cecrops and his daughter. In the west pediment of the Parthenon.
19. Ilissus from the west pediment of the Parthenon. British Museum, London.
20. Horsemen in the Panathenaic procession. A section of the west frieze of the Parthenon. *In situ.* Photograph by Alison Frantz.
21. A detail from the west frieze of the Parthenon. Photograph by Alison Frantz.
22. A detail from the west frieze of the Parthenon. Photograph by Alison Frantz.
23. A detail from the west frieze of the Parthenon. Photograph by Alison Frantz.
24. A detail from the west frieze of the Parthenon.
25. Horsemen in procession. From the north frieze of the Parthenon.
26. Cows being led to the sacrifice. From the north frieze of the Parthenon. Acropolis Museum, Athens.
27. Maidens marching in procession. From the east frieze of the Parthenon. The Louvre, Paris. Photograph by Giraudon.
28. The Propylaea from the east. 437-432 B.C. Photograph by Alison Frantz.
29. Within the Propylaea. Photograph by Alison Frantz.
30. Detail of an Ionic capital of the Propylaea. Photograph by Alison Frantz.
31. The Propylaea from the southwest, with the temple of Athena Nike. Photograph by Alison Frantz.
32. The temple of Athena Nike from the northwest. About 421 B.C. Photograph by Alison Frantz.
33. The temple of Athena Nike from the southeast. Photograph by Alison Frantz.
34. Nike (Victory) fastening her sandal. About 420 B.C. From the parapet of the temple of Athena Nike. Acropolis Museum, Athens. Photograph by Alinari.

35. The Erechtheum from the southeast. About 421-406 B.C. Photograph by Alison Frantz.
36. The Erechtheum from the east. Photograph by Alison Frantz.
37. The Erechtheum from the south. Photograph by Alison Frantz.
38. The Erechtheum. The Porch of the Maidens from the southeast. Photograph by Alison Frantz.
39. Maidens of the Erechtheum. Photograph by Alison Frantz.
40. The Erechtheum. Detail of the ornamentation of the south wall and entablature. Photograph by Alison Frantz.
41. The Erechtheum from the southwest. Photograph by Alison Frantz.
42. The Erechtheum. The North Porch from the northeast. Photograph by Alison Frantz.
43. The North Porch of the Erechtheum. Detail of the ornamentation of an anta. Photograph by Alison Frantz.
44. The Erechtheum. Detail of capitals and entablature of the North Porch. Photograph by Alison Frantz.
45. The Erechtheum. Detail of column bases of the North Porch. Photograph by Alison Frantz.
46. The Erechtheum. A detail of the southwest corner. Photograph by Alison Frantz.
47. Herm of Pericles. Roman copy of the late fifth-century B.C. bronze original by Cresilas. British Museum, London.
48. The choregic monument of Thrasyllus on the south slope of the Acropolis, with the stadium and Mt. Hymettus in the distance. Photograph by Saul S. Weinberg.
49. The theater of Dionysus on the south slope of the Acropolis. Photograph by Saul S. Weinberg.
50. The temple of Hephaestus, god of metal workers, on the edge of the Athenian market place. Photograph by Saul S. Weinberg.
51. The temple of Hephaestus, formerly known as the Theseum. About 450 B.C. Photograph by Alison Frantz.
52. The temple of Poseidon at Sunium on the tip of the Attic peninsula. Photograph by Saul S. Weinberg.
53. The south colonnade of the temple of Poseidon at Sunium. Photograph by Alison Frantz.

54. The temple of Poseidon at Sunium. About 425 B.C. Photograph by Saul S. Weinberg.

55. Grave stele of an athlete, from Sunium. About 460 B.C. National Museum, Athens. Courtesy of Gisela M. A. Richter.

56. The "Mourning Athena." About 455 B.C. Acropolis Museum, Athens.

57. Demeter, Persephone and Triptolemus. About 445 B.C. From Eleusis. National Museum, Athens.

58. Grave stele of Hegeso, from the Athenian cemetery of the Cerameicus. Late fifth century B.C. National Museum, Athens. Photograph by Alinari.

59. A silver coin–tetradrachm–of Athens (enlarged). Late fifth century B.C. Museum of Fine Arts, Boston.

60. Composite cast from various Roman copies of the Discus Thrower by Myron of Athens, about 450 B.C. Photograph by Alinari.

61. Wounded Niobid. Probably an Athenian work of 445 B.C. Museo Nazionale delle Terme, Rome. Photograph by Alinari.

62. Greek and Centaur. From a red-figured drinking cup (cylix) by an Athenian master. About 460 B.C. Museum antiker Kleinkunst, Munich.

63. Battle between Greeks and Centaurs, symbol of the triumph of Hellenism over barbarism. From an Athenian red-figured mixing bowl (crater). About 460 B.C. Museo Archeologico, Florence.

64. Head of an old warrior. From a red-figured mixing bowl. Probably an Athenian work of 455 B.C. Metropolitan Museum of Art, New York.

65. Orpheus. Fragment of a white-ground drinking cup, probably by the Athenian master Euphronius. About 460 B.C. National Museum, Athens.

66. Aphrodite on a goose. A white-ground drinking cup, probably by the Athenian master Pistoxenus. About 460 B.C. British Museum, London.

67. A warrior bidding farewell to a woman. From an Athenian white-ground sepulchral oil jar. About 450 B.C. National Museum, Athens.

68. Heron, on an engraved chalcedony (enlarged). Style of Dexamenus of Chios. Late fifth century B.C. From a cast. Museum of Fine Arts, Boston.

69. Stags. Greek gems of the late fifth century B.C. From casts. Museum of Fine Arts, Boston.

70. Eleutherae, an Athenian fortress in the foothills of Mt. Cithaeron near the border of Boeotia. Photograph by Alison Frantz.